Wartime Schools

Alan R. Sadovnik and Susan F. Semel
General Editors

Vol. 34

PETER LANG
New York • Washington, D.C./Baltimore • Bern
Frankfurt am Main • Berlin • Brussels • Vienna • Oxford

Gerard Giordano

Wartime Schools

How World War II Changed American Education

PETER LANG
New York • Washington, D.C./Baltimore • Bern
Frankfurt am Main • Berlin • Brussels • Vienna • Oxford

Library of Congress Cataloging-in-Publication Data
Giordano, Gerard.
Wartime schools: how World War II
changed American education / Gerard Giordano.
p. cm. — (History of schools and schooling; v. 34)
Includes bibliographical references and index.
1. Education—United States—History—20th century.
2. World War, 1939-1945—Education and the war. I. Title. II. Series.
LA209 .G54   370'.973'09044—dc21   2002151708
ISBN 0-8204-6355-8
ISSN 1089-0678

Bibliographic information published by **Die Deutsche Bibliothek**.
Die Deutsche Bibliothek lists this publication in the "Deutsche
Nationalbibliografie"; detailed bibliographic data is available
on the Internet at http://dnb.ddb.de/.

Cover design by Lisa Barfield

The paper in this book meets the guidelines for permanence and durability
of the Committee on Production Guidelines for Book Longevity
of the Council of Library Resources.

© 2005, 2004 Peter Lang Publishing, Inc., New York
275 Seventh Avenue, 28th Floor, New York, NY 10001
www.peterlangusa.com

All rights reserved.
Reprint or reproduction, even partially, in all forms such as microfilm,
xerography, microfiche, microcard, and offset strictly prohibited.

Printed in the United States of America

For Karen

Contents

List of Illustrations xi

Acknowledgments xvii

Preface xix

Chapter 1 Total War Envelopes Education 1
    Total War   2
        Preparing for Total War before Pearl Harbor   3
        Transition from Total Defense to Total War   5
    Alarmist Educators   7
        Alarmist Rhetoric in the Journals of Professional Educational Organizations   14
        Alarmist Rhetoric from the Government   18
    Extraordinary Wartime Responsibilities for Schools   22
        Stress on Teachers and Administrators   26
        Training Students for Special Wartime Careers   27

Chapter 2 Special Materials and Programs 30
    Distinctive Wartime Resources   30
        Advice to Teachers from Military Personnel   34
        Directories to Wartime Resources   34
        Wartime Resources from Commercial Publishers   36
        Films   43
        Alternative Resources   46
    Distinctive Wartime Programs   49
        Pre-induction   55
        Women   56

Wartime Schools

  African Americans   61
  Persons with Disabilities   63
  Rural Youths   66
  Student Workers   67

Chapter 3   Influencing Educators' Attitudes 69

 Professional Educational Organizations   69
  Organizations Support the War   70
  Organizations Retain Their Self-Interests   72
 Propaganda   74
  American Propaganda   78
  Propaganda through Radio   83
  Propaganda through Cinema   86
 Advertising in Education Journals   90
  Impact of Advertising during World War I   90
  Advertising's Stature Declines between the Wars   94
  Advertising Devices   96

Chapter 4   National Threats from Within 105

 Juvenile Delinquency   105
  Causes of Delinquency   110
  Intervention Programs   113
 Conservatives Lobby for Patriotic Students   116
 Democratic, Patriotic, and Nationalistic Education   120
  Patriotic Education   122
  Nationalistic Education   123
 Seditious Textbooks   125
  Textbooks by Harold Rugg   127
 Liberals Lobby for Peace   130
  Pacifists Are Labeled Antiestablishment   132
  Liberal Ambivalence about War   134
  Liberals Advocate for Democratic Learners   136

Chapter 5   Wartime Curricula 140

 Defining Curriculum   140
 Accelerated Curricula   141
 Vocational Curricula   143
  Changing Attitudes about the Value of Vocational Curricula   145
  Models for Vocational Curricula   147
  Success of Wartime Vocational Programs   148
 Skills-Based Curricula   148
  Mathematics and Science Curricula   152
  Physical Education Curricula   154
 Progressive Curricula   161

English Education Curricula   163
Life Adjustment Curricula   164
Pragmatic Curricula   168

Chapter 6   Educational Patterns Set during World War I 171
Assessing the Significance of World War I   171
Scholastic Nationalism   173
  Benefits of War   174
  Arousing School Support for the War   175
Special Programs   177
  Programs to Develop Patriotism   181
  Pre-induction Training   182
  Programs for Women   187
  Garden Army   191
  Anti-German Initiatives   195
Special Resources   198
Liberal Dissension   202
  Academic Freedom   204
Special Curricula   205
  Vocational Curricula   206

Chapter 7   Dynamics of Wartime Education 211
Postwar Dynamics   211
  Conservatives Define Postwar Issues   215
  Materials That Prepared Educators for Postwar Education   220
Postwar Plight of Progressive Educators   222
  Theories of War and Education   224
  Liberal Theorists   225
Educational Politics during the 1950s   228
  Communism in the Schools   231
  Death of Progressive Education   234

Postscript 238

References 243

Author Index 299

Subject Index 313

Illustrations

Figure 1.1. A World War II Poster Emphasizing Domestic Threats from the Japanese 10

Figure 1.2. A World War II Poster Highlighting the Dangers That Germans Posed to Americans 11

Figure 1.3. A 1942 Illustration about the Dangers American Schools Faced from Enemy Bombs 15

Figure 1.4. A 1940 Illustration Depicting Militarism in the Schools 17

Figure 1.5. A 1943 Advertisement about the Fascist Threat to the United States 18

Figure 1.6. A Flattering 1942 Depiction of Those School Administrators Who Were Initiating Pre-Induction Aviation Training in Their Schools 23

Figure 1.7. A 1943 Depiction of the Extraordinary Wartime Responsibilities That Teachers and Administrators Needed to Inculcate in Students 24

Figure 1.8. This Free Chart from the American Industries Salvage Committee Was Part of a 1942 Campaign to Promote Conservation 25

Figure 2.1. Textbooks from Commercial Publishers Incorporated Government Charts 37

Figure 2.2. A 1943 Advertisement to Support Pre-Induction Vocational Courses 38

xii   Wartime Schools

Figure 2.3. Readers Were Certain to Notice the Introductory Quote in This 1941 Advertisement 39

Figure 2.4. A Prewar Advertisement for Materials to Alert Teachers and Students to Propaganda 40

Figure 2.5. A 1943 Advertisement That Linked Projectors to Wartime Films 44

Figure 2.6. A 1941 Advertisement for a Film Incorporating "Actual War Scenes" 46

Figure 2.7. A 1943 Advertisement for Slides Designed to Help Students Spot Enemy Airplanes 48

Figure 2.8. A Passage That Taught Reading Skills along with Appropriate Attitudes Toward the CCC 51

Figure 2.9. A Page from a CCC Reader That Simultaneously Promoted Career Education and Christianity 52

Figure 2.10. A Cartoon That Accompanied an Article about the High School Victory Corps 54

Figure 2.11. Newspaper Advertisements Indicated Women's Increased Access to Wartime Jobs 58

Figure 2.12. This 1942 Depiction of an African American and White Worker Revealed Changing Racial Attitudes 62

Figure 2.13. Material from an Army Literacy Program for "Academically Retarded Men" 64

Figure 2.14. Material from an Army Mathematics Program for "Academically Retarded Men" 65

Figure 3.1. A 1941 Warning Directed Readers to Look for This Symbol, which Accompanied Propaganda from American Nazi Organizations 80

Figure	3.2.	This 1941 Instance of "Democratic Propaganda" Was Intended to Appeal "To the Highest Emotions and Especially to Reason"	81
Figure	3.3.	A 1918 Advertisement That Appealed to Teachers' Patriotic Convictions	92
Figure	3.4.	An Advertisement Devised in Response to Woodrow Wilson's Acknowledgment of "The Generous Offers of the Advertising Forces of the Nation to Support the Effort of the Government"	93
Figure	3.5.	Wartime Ads for Plentiful Merchandise Still Emphasized Conservation	98
Figure	3.6.	An Attempt to Promote the Sale of Toilets with a Popular Wartime Message	99
Figure	3.7.	When One Corporation's Steel Educational Products Were No Longer Available, It Used This Illustration to Explain the Shortage	100
Figure	3.8.	This World War II Advertisement Promoted High Morale among Librarians and Their Patrons	100
Figure	3.9.	An Effort to Nurture Pride among the Persons Who Manufactured and Purchased School Equipment	101
Figure	3.10.	War Bond Advertisements Were Unqualifiedly Patriotic and Extraordinarily Effective	102
Figure	3.11.	Portion of an Ad That Associated the Brand Name of a School Seating Company with a Critical Wartime Career	103
Figure	4.1.	A 1943 Depiction of "The Law" and "The School" Confronting Wartime Delinquents	108
Figure	4.2.	A 1935 Cartoon Illustrating the Deleterious Activities within American Universities	117
Figure	4.3.	A 1935 Cartoon Highlighting the Influence of Russian Communists on Liberal American Professors	118

Figure 4.4. A 1935 Illustration That Accompanied an American Legion Article about Un-Americanism 119

Figure 4.5. A 1941 Depiction of Textbooks Infested with Un-Americanism 129

Figure 5.1. This Illustration Represented Vocational Education as a Formidable Component of "The First Line of Civilian Defense" 146

Figure 5.2. The Federal Government Published Materials to Help Students Learn about Military Aviation 151

Figure 5.3. A 1943 Political Cartoon That Emphasized the Importance of Active Participation in Competitive Sports 157

Figure 5.4. A World War II Advertisement That Associated Athletic Fabrics with Wartime Defense 158

Figure 5.5. A World War II Advertisement That Linked the Skills of Athletes to Those of Soldiers 159

Figure 5.6. A World War II Advertisement That Associated Sporting Nets with National Defense 160

Figure 6.1. This 1918 Illustration Accompanied a Description of Patriotic Activities for Primary Schools 176

Figure 6.2. A 1918 Illustration Highlighting the Activities of "The Loyal Teacher" 178

Figure 6.3. Uncle Sam Commends Board Members Who Extend School Schedules to Support Wartime Activities 179

Figure 6.4. This 1918 Illustration Linked Home-Front Efforts with the Fighting at the Battle Lines 180

Figure 6.5. These Illustrations Accompanied a 1915 Editorial That Encouraged Parents and Teachers to Prepare School Children for War 184

Figure	6.6.	This 1915 Cartoon Represented Basic Education Skills as a Form of Military Readiness	185
Figure	6.7.	This Photo Was the Frontispiece for a 1917 Book about Women Workers	188
Figure	6.8.	A Government Poster That Lured Students into the Garden Army	192
Figure	6.9.	A 1918 Illustration That Inspired Work in War Gardens	194
Figure	6.10.	This Stamp Was Placed on Those Books Circulated through the War Service Library Program	200
Figure	7.1.	An Allegorical Depiction of the Diabolical and Heavenly Uses of Aircrafts	215
Figure	7.2.	A 1945 Representation of America's Altruistic Rationale for Entering Two World Wars	217
Figure	7.3.	This 1943 Cartoon Warned Liberal Activists That They Would Eventually Have to Confront Returning Veterans	218
Figure	7.4.	This 1943 Ad Predicted That Competitive Sports Would Always Be Needed for Defensive Readiness	219
Figure	7.5.	A 1956 Illustration from a Federal Book about the Dangers Students Faced from Nuclear Weapons	229
Figure	7.6.	This 1956 Illustration from the U.S. Office of Education Indicated Damage from Hydrogen Bombs	230
Figure	7.7.	A 1950s Illustration of Defensive Measures during a Nuclear Strike	231

Acknowledgments

I am grateful to Amanda McAdams and Austin Adamson for their diligence, professionalism, extraordinary creativity, and inexhaustible stamina. Without their support, this project would never have been completed.

Preface

History is past politics, and politics [is] present history.
— SEELEY, 1902

Politically, conservatives revolutionized the schools during World War II. The volume, breadth, intensity, and rapidity of the changes they made were staggering. They affected career counseling, the use of propaganda in classrooms, school discipline, budgeting, teacher employment, administrative responsibilities, scheduling, conservation of natural resources, preparation of workers for the defense industries, extracurricular activities, pre-induction training, building usage, the content of commercial textbooks, educational reporting, government-sponsored learning materials, alternative media, and the advertisements in educational journals. Even though they were intended as expedients, many of these modifications endured for decades.

The reformers themselves were intelligent, zealous, foresightful, organized, and attentive to detail. However, so were most of the other crusaders who had failed in their attempts to change the schools. Those who had not been successful complained about the redoubtable barriers that the educational establishment had thrown before them. The World War II conservatives breached these defenses, assumed command of the schools, and achieved an epic victory. Why did they prevail?

World War I

The scholastic revolution of World War II had begun during the former war. While one portion of that war transpired in the combat theater, another took place at the home front. Prodded by fear, pressured by peers, or inspired by altruism, teachers and school administrators joined in the home-front effort. Not satisfied with their personal involvement, many of them prodded their students into wartime activities. When World War I liberals objected to pupil participation, the conservatives retorted that an unparalleled international menace necessitated unprecedented security measures.

The conservatives used the identical justification to modify curricula. They expanded classes about technology, mathematics, science, physical education, national heritage, progress of the war, and democratic government. They regulated textbooks, foreign language instruction, and the content of social studies courses. They altered school schedules so that students could work part-time in agriculture or the defense industries. They even prepared future soldiers through pre-induction training.

Although they feuded about numerous issues, conservatives and liberals were irreconcilably divided over the progressive curriculum. Whereas the liberals viewed this curriculum as morally and cognitively advantageous, the conservatives saw it as expensive, excessively individualized, difficult to implement, tied inextricably to the humanities, politically biased, and a primary source for many of the problems that had emerged within armed forces training programs. The conservatives advised instructors to eschew progressive practices and rely instead on the more traditional approaches to instruction.

Because they were unable to agree on pedagogical matters, it was inevitable that conservatives and liberals would clash over teachers' rights. World War I liberals demanded unqualified academic freedom so that teachers could speak candidly in their classrooms. Conservatives countered that this would enable disloyal instructors to deliver antigovernment diatribes to impressionable students. By portraying their position as one that was essential to national security, the conservatives won this and most other disputes.

The Depression

Although they had turned much of their attention to domestic problems, citizens of the early 1930s were aware of the changing balance of global power. They debated among themselves about the degree to which international events constituted actual threats to America's security. The conservatives had a hard time maintaining support for educational policies, initiatives, and programs that had been established when the country was in a different political mood. In fact, liberal critics blamed the conservatives for many of the current social, financial, and international problems, as well as the oppressive educational system to which they thought these were linked. They demanded that the conservatives change this system by reducing the scope of structured learning, testing, classroom discipline, and textbooks. The most politically extreme liberals called for a violent revolt to free the schools from the conservatives' dominance.

World War II Conservatives

Just as the liberals had decried self-serving political ambitions, so did the conservatives. However, they reversed this charge, holding the liberals accountable for the nation's recent predicaments. They thought the liberals had been responsible for those individuals who had died when the United States failed to make a timely entrance into the First World War. They judged that the liberals' post–World War I resistance to military preparedness and international leadership had increased the likelihood of domestic subversion, global war, and homeland invasion. They accused them of weakening the nation's democratic spirit by romanticizing socialism, political radicalism, and Communism. They warned that liberal-backed initiatives had enabled Communists to assume control of the labor unions that regulated America's defense production.

To back up their accusations, the conservatives publicized documents in which radical educators had called for the destruction of America's capitalist economy, its class-based society, and its government. They also highlighted the accuracy of the many warnings they had made about the consequences of liberal political actions. For example, their cautions about the danger from organized labor had been validated by irresponsible strikes. The conservatives had forecast that pacifism, nonintervention, voluntary international cooperation, and appeasement would not deter aggression by totalitarian governments. They had predicted that the Communists in the Soviet Union would perpetrate terrible violations of human rights. They had foreseen that national measures limiting military readiness would encourage an attack on the United States. They also had made a positive prediction that turned out to be true. Once the United States entered the war, its citizens became confident about their economy, government, and traditions.

With their reputation restored, the conservatives were able to gather support for their educational programs. They urged attentive teachers to foster altruism, patriotism, knowledge of the war, and national unity. They insisted that unruly, prurient, and criminal youths demonstrate respect and obedience. They also insisted that teachers refrain from liberal political activism in their classrooms.

Assisting, Informing, and Influencing World War II Educators

Although they may have been inspired by eloquent statements about patriotism, teachers had to look elsewhere for the practical information they needed to discharge their wartime responsibilities. They found it in the special reports, pamphlets, posters, journals, books, radio broadcasts, and films that were prepared and distributed by the federal government and the military.

Just as the government and military had advised teachers, so did professional educational organizations. Despite some early reluctance to back American military engagement, these organizations rallied in support after Pearl Harbor. However, they also used their journals as pulpits from which to lobby for their own self-interests. As examples, they aggressively lobbied for new union members, expanded organizational dues, greater school taxes, increased federal aid for education, higher teacher salaries, and greater tolerance for those educators who were expressing unpopular political views. Some businesspersons might have exhibited a comparably conflicted pattern of behavior had not advertisers demonstrated ways in which they could promote national security and their own financial interests at the same time.

Although they were saturated with advice from many sources, most educators turned to their school curricula for guidance about classroom practices. Even though the basic types of curricula had been in place for decades, their public standings shifted dramatically during the war. For example, the popularity of vocational curricula was influenced by their close connection to national security. The popularity of accelerated curricula grew for the identical reason. The status of skills-based curricula benefited when mathematics, science, physical education, and other subjects with which they had been traditionally associated assumed greater wartime prominence. An additional reason that skills-based curricula prospered was the ease with which untrained replacement instructors could implement them.

Unlike the other approaches to instruction, progressive curricula required highly trained personnel. Because a severe teacher shortage reduced the availability of educational specialists, the opportunities for expanding progressive programs were limited. Their expansion was also constrained because they could not readily accommodate the home-front objectives that the public valued.

World War II Liberals

Prewar liberals had insisted that global conflict would end after American educators began to teach tolerance and international cooperation. Although some of them continued to make this case after Pearl Harbor, they had a hard time attracting supporters. Their recruitment problems were compounded because many of their politically moderate colleagues had begun to realign themselves with the conservatives. Even their highly visible leader, President Roosevelt, implemented wartime measures that were incompatible with their philosophy. He restricted free speech, had Japanese Americans relocated to special camps, selectively awarded industrial contracts, used propaganda to manipulate voters, and insisted that the unconditional surrender of enemy nations was the only circumstance under American fighting would cease. Roosevelt's Office of Education ignored liberal advice and championed conservative wartime programs.

The liberals were dismayed and confused by the broad coalition that backed conservative educators. Wishing to attract adherents of their own, they searched for pedagogical adaptations that would allow them to project a more moderate political image. As one example, they demonstrated a closer link to democratic governance by changing the names of their classroom practices. This ideological legerdemain allowed them to espouse the educational goals of the conservatives but not the classroom procedures they recommended for achieving them.

Even after they had repackaged their instructional practices, liberal educators were censured for failing to foster democratic values. They also were indicted for scholastic inefficiency, disregard for student discipline, and a cavalier attitude toward critical wartime subjects. Inescapably tied to the provocative rhetoric of political extremists, they were depicted as Communist sympathizers. As a result, they were unable to gain support from industry, the military, popular educational leaders, moderate liberals, or a public that became increasingly annoyed with their reluctance to embrace home-front defense.

The Post–World War II Era

Which characteristics of conservative educators explained their success during World War II? Two stood out. The first was their pragmatism. Although anxious about the crisis the country was facing, they took advantage of it to advance their political interests. They persuaded an insecure public that the conservative approach could deter international threats to the nation, western democracy, and civilization itself. Although the domestic problems that centered about employment, immigration, race, and crime were hardly new, the conservatives claimed that they were damaging the foundation of the home front. They adroitly couched their educational initiatives as techniques that would reverse this wartime deterioration.

The other key feature of the World War II conservative educators was their ability to persuade a broad national audience. Contemporaries should not have been surprised when the conservatives elicited the backing of industrialists, military leaders, and right-wing congressmen. However, they must have been stunned when they gained the support of Roosevelt and his liberal administrators. Without this sustained, robust, bipartisan backing, the conservatives could not have made changes rapidly and extensively.

Although postwar conservative educators could not retain the unprecedented support that they had gathered during the war, they preserved enough of it to keep many of their programs in place. What was the explanation for their later success? The primary reason was the constancy of the political dynamics influencing education. Still true to their prewar convictions, liberals endorsed the practices that they had been sponsoring for decades. As had been the case during the war, they extracted their greatest allegiance from university academicians. Even though the postwar public agreed with the liberals on scores of domestic matters, it deferred to the conservatives on educational issues. This paradoxical behavior was based on an unshakeable conviction that educational programs were connected just as strongly to national security as they were to domestic prosperity. The conservatives adroitly built on this conviction during periods of international danger. These periods were protracted and recurring, and so were the spans when the conservatives dominated postwar education.

CHAPTER 1

Total War Envelopes Education

> *This is total war—war in which every one of us must take his part whether in the armed forces or in civilian service.*
> —LA SALLE & LARRICK, 1942

Even before entering the war, the United States had been getting ready for two campaigns, one to be fought in the combat arena and the other at the home front. Because schools were an essential component of the home-front campaign, educators were asked to assume extraordinary responsibilities. Some of their new responsibilities, such as promoting sales of war stamps, were straightforward and well defined. Others, such as nurturing patriotism, were more difficult to define. Although political conservatives and liberals viewed wartime roles differently, the conservatives' suggestions were bolstered by the alarmist rhetoric that was so prevalent. The conservatives were also at an advantage because their primary educational goal, which was to deter disaster by preparing students for military service and industrial employment, seemed logical to a broad public audience. The success of the conservatives was discernible in the rapidly and extensively changed responsibilities of teachers and educational administrators.

Total War

The size, impact, and style of the First World War were all unprecedented. In a book about modern warfare, an officer in the French army observed that "the essential characteristic of the present war is that *it is waged by the whole people*, instead of being merely the affair of professional soldiers" (Azan, 1918, p. 2).

Referring to this new genre of conflict as "war of matériel," he directed his readers to think of it as a vast "industrial enterprise" that would dominate a country's "international relations, the industry, the commerce, manufactures, agricultural produce, and wealth" (pp. 6–7). Attempting to clarify the types of changes that modern war entailed, he recommended that American women disregard "the subconscious impulse that urges a certain number of them to cross the water" and instead "stay at home." The officer explained pragmatically that "when millions of young American men have gone to France, these women will be needed in America to take their places" (p. 6).

Hoover and Gibson (1943) later agreed that this beginning-of-the-century war had devolved into a struggle "of civilian effort against civilian effort as well as of armies against armies" (p. 90). Conflict on this grand scale required unity among a nation's constituents, and the World War I leaders realized that they would have to develop the supportive public attitudes that were prerequisite to a cohesive home-front campaign. Following patterns from the past, they did this through speeches, books, and newspaper editorials. However, they also used novel media such as film and radio.

The public contemplated the merits of entering the World War I for a relatively long time, and the federal government used the period to organize systematic propaganda campaigns (Winter & Baggett, 1996). Even the remarks made by educators indicated their satisfaction with the amount of time they had to contemplate America's entry into the war. For example, Seerley (1917) observed that the American teacher "has had the experience of being able for a time to discuss the world situation from the standpoint of free inquiry, to show his neutrality by condemning or commending the parties to the great war" (p. 102). Sisson (1917b) was distressed that Europe displayed "a shocking picture of nations hurried into mortal combat without a single clear cause" (p. 121). In contrast, he believed that the citizens of the United States had enjoyed a "long immunity."

Once the United States did enter the war, educators reassured themselves that they had not been rushed into making their decision. The secretary of the American School Peace League noted that the government had been "loath to join the struggle" and had eventually declared war "only after long and searching deliberation" (Andrews, 1917, p. 9). Dean (1918b) wrote that America's "gradual entrance" gave citizens a "chance of pausing and surveying the situation before acting—advantages which were unfortunately denied England and France" (p. 2). An editorial published in the spring of the previous year indicated that the nation, even though "endangered by every success of Teutonic arms," would still have had "years before any hostile army appeared on our shores" ("America and the War," 1917, p. 5).

Writing several decades later about the circumstances under which the United States had entered World War I, Soule (1942) agreed with the contemporaries of that period that Americans had adequate time to make their decisions. Much later, Gruber (1975) also concurred that the decision to intervene in World War I had been preceded by years of careful deliberation. This prelude provided the opportunity for the public to develop positive attitudes about the righteousness of participating in the war. It also gave it the opportunity to weigh the relative dangers that either entry or isolationism posed. Gruber judged that only after the United States had joined the combatants did a "bandwagon" of war supporters use partisan attacks to change the restrained timbre of this dialogue.

In addition to having the time it needed, the public was able to come to a somewhat dispassionate conclusion because the hostilities in Europe seemed remote from the immediate interests of the United States. After several year of fighting in Europe, Sisson (1917b) reported that "the flames have hardly touched us, and our own home land is wrapt [sic] in profound peace" (p. 120). Dean (1918a) noted that America's "distance from the conflict" was as beneficial as its protracted period of reflection. Although he identified World War I as a global war, Roth (1967) noted that the territories and citizens in some of the participating countries were never directly threatened. Roth concluded that World War I was a global conflict not because the combat had a truly intercontinental scope but because "Europe became an enormous cauldron into which men and resources from Asia, Africa, and America were poured" (p. 105).

In contrast to the deliberative manner in which the United States had entered the First World War, the incidents of World War II truncated the lengthy period of contemplation for which many Americans had hoped. Although World War I had left memories of suffering, destruction, and death, a subsequent and even more perilous war was unavoidable after the Japanese attacked America's territory and armed forces.

Preparing for Total War before Pearl Harbor

Despite the degree to which Americans were surprised by the Pearl Harbor attack, a significant number of them had been demanding a program of *total defense* before it occurred. President Roosevelt helped to elicit these sentiments when he observed that "at no previous time has American security been so seriously threatened from without." As a result, he urged that "our actions and our policy . . . be devoted primarily, almost exclusively, to meeting this foreign peril" (Roosevelt, from a fireside talk delivered on December 30, 1940, quoted by Nevins, 1942, p. 126). As an indication of Roosevelt's personal views about the need to be proactive, he had directed the armed forces to secretly develop a military plan for the invasion of Germany. Referred to as "Rainbow Five," this 1941 proposal was leaked to the press several days before Pearl Harbor (Fleming, 2001).

America's preparation for war was particularly evident in its industrial production, which was quite different from the one that had preceded World War I. In fact, the mistakes that had been made before that earlier war persuaded many individuals that national defense required aggressive preparation. Crowell and Wilson (1921) began their five-volume history of World War I industrial activity by describing the nation's earlier resistance to prewar defensive measures.

> Instead of the attitude of prudence which we might have expected of Washington in those days, we find an official indifference to the future that is not to be explained. The authorities could not righteously plead ignorance of the advancement of the science of warfare. Almost from the outbreak of the war in August, 1914, we had succeeded in placing observers with the various armies in the field. The reports of these observers were filled with data showing the deficiencies of our own military organization for war on the modern scale and the obsolescence of most our materiel. On these reports might have been based a complete rejuvenation of our designs and methods, but what actually happened was the reports were filed away in the archives of the War College to gather the dust of official neglect. (pp. xiv–xv)

Several decades later, the support for prewar defensive programs was significantly stronger. This was to be anticipated from the industrialists who would benefit from the increased military production. However, many educators displayed supportive attitudes. Writing in a politically liberal educational journal, Babcock (1939) judged that those "ostrich-like" teachers who were not preparing students for the "exalted purpose" of combating totalitarianism were demonstrating "intellectual cowardice."

Many examples of similarly histrionic rhetoric from prewar educators were evident. Miller (1940) reported about a popular educational mantra, "education for democracy," that had begun to accompany some of the new programs that were appearing in the schools. He proposed that this slogan be strengthened to read "education to save democracy." That same year, Stone (1940) documented that school boards were under pressure to bolster national defense through high-school military training programs. Writing a month later, Jones (1940) conceded that political groups were being so assertive that many educators were wondering whether they had to modify their school's curriculum in response to "every real or imaginary emergency."

Hartmann (1940) reported that conservative political groups had caused the "enforced dissolution" of the pacifist committees within the Progressive Education Association. He specifically documented the demise of the Committee on Militarism in Education, which had been formed to restrain the "militarization" of the schools. He added that even the politically liberal educators who once had been members of this committee had succumbed to an overwhelming "climate of opinion" and begun to beat "the war drums most loudly." He did not conceal his personal loathing when he predicted that the former liberals were destined to suffer in the "deep, dark pits in Hell."

New York City's Teachers College was the institution of higher education with the most prominent reputation for radical, liberal politics during this period. However, even this bastion of liberalism sponsored a prewar symposium on teacher-centered defense activities ("Schools and the Defense," 1941). The symposium's agenda comprised topics such as promoting nationalism among immigrants, pre-induction curricula, physical fitness, vocational education, and school diet as a critical component of total defense.

Brown (F. J. Brown, 1941) wrote that a presidential declaration of a "limited emergency" in September of 1939 had enabled colleges and universities to develop defensive educational programs that could be transformed readily into wartime training. Writing during that same year, the editors of a monograph (American Council on Education, 1941) agreed that the declaration of the limited national emergency in 1939 had been key to transforming the schools' moderate defensive effort into "an all-out effort." Looking back on prewar activities in the high schools, the government-sponsored *Handbook on Education and the War* (1943) contained a summary observation that "long before Pearl Harbor the secondary school had enlisted in the cause of total defense, and now our school executives and teachers, loyal and generally well-equipped, are anxious to contribute their utmost to the prosecution of total war" (p. 231).

In a publication written immediately after Pearl Harbor, Brown (1942) indicated that the original articles for that issue of the journal in which he was writing had been solicited with *total defense* as their theme. However, the bombing of Pearl Harbor was a "fortunate coincidence" that enabled the articles to be edited with *total war* as their new theme. Kingsley and Petegorsky (1942) employed a remarkably similar prefatory note, reporting that they had written their book about threats to American democracy with a premonition about "the imminence of American entry into the war." As a result of their editorial foresight, they didn't judge that the events at Pearl Harbor had necessitated any "textual changes" in their manuscript.

Transition from Total Defense to Total War

Some educators attempted to build support for the war by characterizing it as an ideological rather than political struggle. Locke (1942) described it as "a planetary civil war" between incompatible political and social principles. Langsdorf (1943) defined it as "a war of mind as well as of guns" (p. 85). Using baroque language, Kotschnig (1943) alerted educators that the current war was "a clash of mutually exclusive worlds of thought and aspiration, as a deliberate attempt on the part of the

Fascist powers to destroy the heritage of Jerusalem, Athens, and Rome, the civilizing ideas and principles of the West, painfully worked out through the centuries" (p. xi). A professor at Harvard was less florid but still in agreement with most of his contemporaries when he warned of an unprecedented "war about ideas" in which the "Japs and the Germans are fighting for a theory of life" (Holmes, 1943, p. 26).

In view of the deepening ideological chasm that separated the United States from potential enemies, the transition from *total defense* to the more aggressive idea of *total war* seemed inevitable to many. This escalation was especially apparent in the rhetoric that American educators used once their enemies were clearly identified. The editors of the politically liberal *Frontiers of Democracy* ("Education and Total War," 1942) joined with the leaders of the National Education Association, the American Federation of Teachers, and the Progressive Education Association when they acknowledged the peril of "the first worldwide total war in history." Carpenter and Capps (1942) insisted that the total war be met with a "total training program" to prepare educators for their new responsibilities. Cottrell (1942) agreed that education had "a clear and crucial role to play in the total war effort" (p. 53). The Connecticut Commissioner of Education postulated that any nation aspiring to survive total war had to prepare for "infinitely more than military combat" (Grace, 1942, p. 156). Rappleye (1942) concurred that "modern warfare must be an all-out effort in which every feature of national life must be geared to its demands" (p. 539). Writing in a U.S. Office of Education manual (*Handbook on Education and the War*, 1943), a general defined total war as battle waged not only on combat fronts but also in factories, homes, and classrooms. Attempting to find a suitable metaphor, Ogburn (1943b) compared the impact of total war on society to the revolutionary influence of the steam engine on industry.

Redefer (1942) believed that total war had helped persons recognize that the efforts in America's classrooms were as important as those at distant battlefronts. The faculty in education at Stanford University began their book about wartime education with the unequivocal adjuration that "the demands of the war must be given priority over all other educational features, no matter how worthy they are under other conditions" (Stanford University School of Education Faculty, 1943, p. v). A District of Columbia superintendent (Reed, 1943) was even more chauvinistic when he urged the substitution of curricula emphasizing "sound nationalism" for those highlighting world amity or international cooperation.

A principal in New York City gave examples of ways in which the wartime committees he had formed in his high school were supporting the total war effort.

> The defense council has jurisdiction over air-raid precautions. A committee on war courses attends to pre-induction and pre-flight curricula. A committee on High School Victory Corps supervises the conversion of the extracurriculum [sic], and enrolls properly qualified pupils. A committee on teachers' courses is the coordinator of in-service

courses given by our teachers for those who wish to qualify for out-of-license teaching and for other purposes (such as first-aid certificate). Numerous other committees, in which pupils play a large part, are devoted to the sale of bonds and stamps, salvage drives, books for those in service, contributions to the Red Cross and to Allied war relief, blood donations, collation of literature on the war, bazaars, and other types of sales drives for numerous war-relief purposes. (Lamm, 1943, p. 451).

The director of the War Savings staff (H. W. Anderson, 1943) advised school board members that victory required efforts by "all human beings," adults as well as youths, those at home as well as those at military fronts. De Boer (1942) implored teachers to "strike at the enemy from our posts in the schools of America" (p. 6). In a pamphlet entitled *The Support of Education in Wartime*, members of the National Education Association (Educational Policies Commission, 1942b) argued that the contributions of teachers and school administrators were "desperately needed." These contributions included organizing youngsters into service clubs, promoting savings, gathering salvage, sponsoring gardening clubs, preparing skilled workers for wartime needs, promoting physical fitness, maintaining student discipline, and developing patriotism.

Although appeals were made to teachers in general and to the educational specialists in critical academic areas, few adjurations were more direct or passionate than those aimed at physical educators. As just one example, La Salle and Larrick (1942) advised physical education teachers that their success in conditioning America's future soldiers would directly influence whether the nation would be victorious.

Alarmist Educators

During World War I, the government had used different media to make American citizens aware of their danger. However, it relied especially on posters, many of which depicted the vulnerability of the United States. One of them had the caption "Save your child from autocracy and poverty—Buy war stamps" (Rawls, 1988, p. 11). Another warned that "If this War is not fought to a finish in Europe, it will be on the soil of the United States" (Rawls, 1988, p. 66). Beneath a picture of books with German emblems on them, a poster contained the message, "Keep these off the U.S.A." (Rawls, 1988, p. 214). One chilling poster showed the Statue of Liberty after it had been decapitated and enflamed by German bombers.

Prior to America's entry into the Second World War, the federal government fanned embers of fear among the public. In an incident that transpired several months before Pearl Harbor, the governor of Utah authorized the formation of a military force to protect that state from "the ravages of foreign enemies within our borders" (Governor Maw, quoted by Foy, 2000, p. C-1). A war that was portrayed as devastating, all engulfing, and inevitable made local defense seem prudent even to the citizens of this rural, landlocked state that shared no international boundaries. Although prewar embers of fear may have glowed, they roared into a blaze once American territory and armed forces had been attacked.

In his book about home-front defense, Bailey (1977) included photographs that revealed the terror of Pearl Harbor. One photo showed a downtown San Francisco building shielded by a mountain of sandbags. Other photos highlighted machine gunners digging nests on California beaches, Indiana industrialists installing smoke screens to hide their factories from enemy bombers, antiaircraft gunners preparing to repel attacks from the roofs of Washington's government buildings, and a workman spreading camouflage over the gold dome of the Massachusetts State House. The April 1942 issue of *Survey Midmonthly* included a full-page photograph of the notice that had been posted outside each of the 70 wartime emergency centers in New York City. The sign indicated that "in case of bombing or other enemy activity COME HERE if you need information, assistance, clothing, temporary shelter, or permanent dwelling—WE WILL BE OPEN DAY & NIGHT."

Published in a popular magazine, a charter developed by the Commission on Children in Wartime (1942) recommended the evacuation of urban children from "danger zones." The Commissioners explained that "these danger zones line our coasts along the Atlantic, the Pacific, and the Gulf—especially where there are military targets, industrial plants, business centers, oil tanks or the like; also, closely built home areas which might be bombed in an effort to break the morale of defense production workers" (p. 109). They thought that city children should receive "war vacations" not only because these would protect them but also because they "would be an admirable test of evacuation methods and an investment for health" (p. 109).

Jersild (1942) was a professor at Teachers College who railed against the alarmist wartime writers who were "making nervous wrecks of children." Preston (1942), a doctoral candidate at Teachers College, also became concerned over the deleterious effects of hysterical rhetoric. Jersild and Preston may have been referring to writers such as Prescott (1942), who had advised elementary school principals in California to search for the wartime "symptoms of deep-seated anxiety." Although a few of Prescott's diagnostic symptoms may have been useful, most were of dubious value. For example, he counseled principals to identify the elementary school students who were experiencing wartime emotional problems on the basis of vomiting, sudden flushing, impudence, daydreaming, truancy, horseplay, joshing, or excessive bragging. Aware that experienced educators might not take his indicators seriously, Presott warned them that "only experience will demonstrate" their actual relevance.

In a book about wartime children, Baruch (1943) used the type of emotional language that was standard during that era. She wrote that Americans were frightened of "possible bombings; of losing our menfolk [sic]; of having our children injured. . . . the altered modes of life confronting us . . . the shifting of ancient values. . . . going without things that have seemed essential, the breaking up of households, the necessity to hunt jobs . . . [and] a million and one [other] elements [that] inhabit the strange new world into which war pitches people without preparation" (pp. 15–16). Many of the adults who became frightened by such warnings transmitted their fears to children. In an article about the wartime anxieties of elementary school children, Eckstein (1942) directed teachers to provide special attention to their young female students, whom he thought tended to be reticent even when they were upset. He advised the teachers to discuss the war openly in order to uncover the emotions that youngsters might be attempting to conceal.

The chilling posters that were produced during World War II were viewed by children as readily as adults. A year after Pearl Harbor, one picture-supplemented article ("War Posters," 1942) demonstrated how poster "artists have been battling within themselves" to communicate wartime anxieties. Zeman (1978) observed that these artists resolved this struggle through "horror posters" or ones that incorporated "soft pornography." These posters explicitly represented threats of enslavement, rape, and murder. For example, one poster, with the title "Deliver Us from Evil," depicted Nazi officers leering at naked female prisoners. Another (Figure 1.1) showed a repulsive Japanese soldier with a pistol in one hand and a nude female captive draped over his shoulder. A particularly appalling one (Figure 1.2) depicted a crying toddler between the corpses of his parents. The father's broken neck had a hangman's noose still attached to it and the mother's ripped dress revealed a fireplace poker that had been plunged into her chest. An ominous, flame-lit face of Hitler hovered surrealistically above this scene.

Frightening images and frenzied rhetoric prompted proportionately excessive responses. Karelsen (1942) reported that bills calling for mandatory military training of high-school boys were introduced into the New York and Pennsylvania legislatures. Osborne (1942), a professor at Teachers College, documented some of the uncalculated effects of alarmist predictions:

> During the air-raid alarms on the East Coast immediately after the declaration of war, a great variety of unfortunate regulations were instituted by school administrators. Children were forced to carry outdoor clothing throughout the school day, air-raid drills were organized in such way as to increase fear and insecurity, and teachers were ordered on all-night patrols of school buildings. Plans for wholesale acceleration of educational programs have been hastily proposed. . . . [and] bills are at present before state legislatures which would release large groups of young people for agricultural work. Men with outstanding names in the field of education are demanding that school programs be centered largely around one or another specific wartime need. . . . State aid has been reduced, class size has been increased, teachers' salaries have been cut, [and] various educational services have been curtailed. (pp. 538–539)

FIGURE 1.1. A World War II Poster Emphasizing Domestic Threats from the Japanese

FIGURE 1.2. A World War II Poster Highlighting the Dangers That Germans Posed to Americans

Osborne did not conceal his personal distaste for the scholastic changes that he chronicled in the preceding passage. Kilpatrick (1942a), a colleague of Osborne's at Teachers College, agreed that the "war excitement threats" to the schools had become "too evident." After he had reported about the many school changes that he thought were excessive, he counseled liberal-minded educators to focus less on the war and more on the alarmist rhetoric that was influencing "what we, all the people, do with the war while we are waging it—what we think and feel and do as we wage it" (Kilpatrick, 1942b, p. 106). Writing 11 months after Pearl Harbor, Cronbach (1942) was also concerned about the effect of alarmist messages on children. After surveying children about the likely impact of the war on America, he found that many were "unduly pessimistic." For example, they grossly overestimated the chances of Allied soldiers being killed in combat or the damage that would result if their cities were bombed.

More than a year after the United States had entered the war, a report ("Protest against War Hysteria," 1943) noted that one congressional representative had proposed to remove the Japanese cherry trees around the Lincoln Memorial. Comparing this proposal to some of those that were being developed for the schools, the author wrote that "now that we are engaged in an all-out war . . . [and] many high schools are vying with one another to see which can be the 'all-outest.'" Towle (1943b) made comparable observations about wartime overreactions that were leading to the suspension of children's "cherished freedoms as individuals." She warned that the mental and emotional damage to students could impair their ability to participate in postwar democracy and peace. Using a Freudian line of reasoning, she cautioned that hysterical adults who overreacted about children's safety were actually exhibiting "a way of justifying the war—a way of easing our feelings of guilt toward those men, many of who were so recently children, who are suffering at the battle front for us" (p. 158). Anna Freud and a colleague (Freud & Burlingham, 1943) cited extensive case studies to demonstrate the emotional harm caused by war. They judged that the most intense psychological damage was connected to children's fear that they would be separated from their parents. Although inevitable even during times of peace, such fear increased radically during war.

Many of the alarmist warnings focused on children. Writing immediately after Pearl Harbor, the Central Committee on Civilian Defense and the Schools (1942) advised civilians to protect school-age children from enemy assaults. However, they thought they could minimize "group anxiety" through a discrete protective plan. Some of the measures within this plan called for dismissing students when air raids were anticipated, teaching children with physical or mental disabilities at home, and regularly clearing all trespassers from school premises. Several months after this advice had been published, Corey (1942) agreed that protecting students from enemy attacks was to be given "absolute and immediate priority." In a book about the impact of World War II on the children of that era, Tuttle (1993b) quoted observations from numerous witnesses about the "fears and nightmares" the war induced. One witness reported that "a whole group of extremely frightened school children were seen running home from school in the middle of the day without hats or coats" because their teacher had heard an ambulance siren and "sent the children scurrying home in the face of her own personal panic" (Joseph Solomon, quoted by Tuttle, 1993b).

A report ("Protecting Children," 1942) published six months after Pearl Harbor listed 14 defensive measures that every school in Wilmington, Delaware, had implemented. Some of these measures involved training of air raid wardens, inventorying of emergency supplies, issuing of student identification tags, specification of neighborhood air raid shelters, mapping of emergency routes from schools to children's homes, and raising awareness about sabotage. An article (J. E. Bond, 1942) about extending wartime readiness beyond the school contained examples of "the safeguarding of . . . homes in case of attack." For example, students could label the gas and water turnoff valves in their homes so that these could be located readily "by anyone" after a bombing raid.

Immediately after Pearl Harbor, the War-time Commission (1942a) had published a checklist for assessing whether schools were developing patriotism and supporting the war. The administrators in charge of nursery and elementary schools were to assure that children were learning about the roles of air raid wardens. The children were also to focus on things of beauty that could "offset the strain of war." Upper-elementary and high-school students were to learn about wartime practices such as filling sandbags, fighting fires, and restricting the damage after incendiary bombings. In another report from the same commission (War-time Commission, 1942d), the members counseled secondary school students to prepare for psychological confrontations with real as well as "incipient" fears.

Many educators used unsettling language when they were advising their colleagues to meet their home-front responsibilities. Hart (1942) warned any reluctant educators that they and their students might soon be looking up the muzzle of a rifle that had "Gestapo fingers on the trigger." Klain (1942) agreed that teachers needed to impress their students that the preservation of freedom was "worthy not only of reverence but of one's very life." Hanna (1942) advised teachers to transform their classrooms into "defense units." Although he acknowledged "a sharp division of opinion among military experts" about the benefits of this transformation, he was convinced that classroom defense units would be needed during the bombing of America's border cities. He added that "equally dangerous to life and limb are the results of possible internal sabotage" (p. 370). Within an educational manual (*Handbook on Education and the War*, 1943), President Roosevelt urged teachers to turn their schools into centers that could "mold men and women who can fight to victory" (p. iii).

Those government officials who strongly supported school-centered defensive measures may have been influenced by a peculiar incident in which Japan launched

6,000 balloons with bombs attached to them (Bailey, 1977; Tuttle, 1993b). After traveling along the jet stream to the coast of the United States, one of these bombs killed a pregnant Sunday-school teacher and five of her students. Worried about public panic, the government persuaded reporters to suppress details of this sensationalistic strike. Nonetheless, those who were aware of it developed greater respect for the government campaigns that urged civilians to take precautions against hostile enemies.

Alarmist Rhetoric in the Journals of Professional Educational Organizations

After Pearl Harbor, alarmist rhetoric could be discerned even within the publications of those professional organizations that earlier had been reluctant to support the war. For example, the NEA's Educational Policy Commission (1942) recommended special wartime school procedures. These seemed justified because Pearl Harbor was a warning of "what the enemy will do." Figure 1.3 is a graphic from another NEA publication. It accompanied a chilling article ("Air Raids and the Schools," 1942) about the danger that bombs presented to the schools. In order to indicate the dimensions and potency of various weapons, the artist placed drawings of bombs next to an adult figure. This artist also depicted a parachute-dropped land mine with a "danger zone" of 2000 feet.

The author of another NEA report (National Education Association, 1943a) acknowledged that no enemy air attacks had occurred on the American mainland. However, this author added that "responsible military leaders expect such attacks and it is to be supposed that the attacks will come at times and places where our preparation is judged by the enemy to be weakest" (p. 52). The writer went on to list 19 precautions that foresightful school personnel should implement in anticipation of an air raid in their vicinity.

Glicksburg (1942a) characterized the war as an "insatiable vortex" that was grasping every aspect of the country. Harding (1943) warned that the elementary school students who were being sucked into this storm needed to learn techniques for withstanding "shock, horror, and emotional reactions." However, most of the adjurations to prepare students for the terrors of war were placed in the journals associated with high-school organizations. The readers of those journals were often instructed to participate in schoolwide programs but then supplement these with individual classroom efforts. In one instance, a reporter ("High-School Science," 1942) pleaded with science teachers to show those students who would remain in school how to contribute to the war. The science teachers were to prepare those who would be leaving school "for the shock of their own actual early participation in the armed forces and noncombatant war activities" (p. 613). Having noted the increasing frequency with which high-school commencement ceremonies revolved around military themes, Ashby (1943b) defended this trend because it prepared graduates

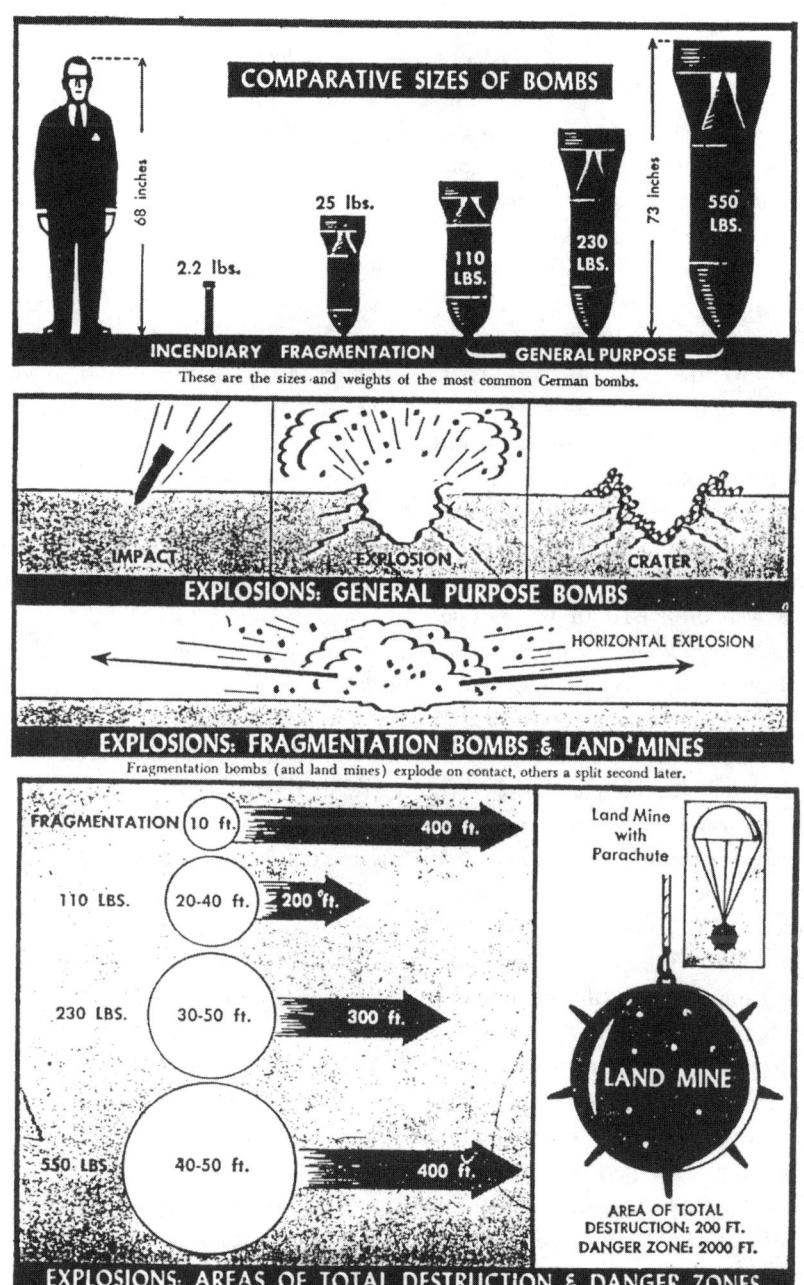

FIGURE 1.3. A 1942 Illustration about the Dangers American Schools Faced from Enemy Bombs (*New York City Board of Education, "Air Raids and the Schools." Journal of the NEA, copyright 1942. Reprinted by permission of the publisher. All rights reserved.*)

for the distress and horror that they would confront after they began their tours of duty with the armed forces. One 1943 issue of the *Bulletin of the National Association of Secondary-School Principals* contained the actual script ("War-Time Graduation Program," 1943) for a commencement program that concluded with an assurance that the graduating seniors would contribute to that "vast number" of students required in the national fight for freedom.

Also writing in the *Bulletin of the National Association of Secondary-School Principals*, a consultant to the national Office of Civilian Defense (Heaton, 1943) warned of the danger that students and school personnel faced from air raids. He contrasted earlier air-raid schedules, in which 270 tons of bombs were dropped on Great Britain during the entire course of World War I, with current bombing schedules, in which thousands of tons of bombs were being dropped on a single city in just several minutes. He adjured school administrators to develop defensive plans that took into account each school's danger, which was to be calculated by its proximity to potential air targets such as tunnels, bridges, factories, and storage sites for inflammable materials. He also urged them to take into account the remote chances for suppressing the neighborhood conflagrations that would ensue if thousands of tons of incendiary devices were dropped during an air raid.

Progressive Education, a liberal journal with editors who initially had opposed entry into the war, began to publish articles that acknowledged the war's distressing emotional effects. A principal on the west coast (Jackson, 1943) recounted that a single school, "by order of the military," had been devastated by the evacuation of 450 Japanese children. A principal on the east coast (Keliher, 1943) noted that his students displayed nervous tics and needed to use the restrooms more frequently. Moreover, this principal thought his school's children were poorly groomed, inadequately fed, unable to concentrate, jittery, and prone to paper chewing. A group of teachers from the Midwest ("Children Like Real Jobs," 1943) documented that the prose, art, and dramatic play of their students incorporated wartime motifs such as weapons, concentration camps, and hostile enemies. One article in *Progressive Education* ("Headlines and Clippings from a Newspaper," 1943) exclusively used junior high newspaper headlines to illustrate the negative emotional impact of the war. Even though these types of articles may have been intended as an indirect rebuke of war supporters, they simultaneously demonstrated the emotional excitement among students and their teachers during this period.

The sense of wartime excitement that was evident in the writing of educators was also discernible in the pictures that accompanied that writing. As examples, some of the illustrations from the widely circulated *American School Board Journal* reflected alarmist messages. Figure 1.4, an editorialized cartoon that appeared on the cover of this journal in September of 1940, depicted the militaristic changes that were being made to protect the schools from anti-American threats.

FIGURE 1.4. A 1940 Illustration Depicting Militarism in the Schools (*Reprinted from American School Board Journal, September 1940.*)

Not restricted to editorialized cartoons, alarmist warnings were embodied in the illustrations that accompanied public service advertisements. For example, the fallen soldier with his face in the dirt, depicted in Figure 1.5, was part of a 1943 advertisement that the Magazine Publishers of America used to promote participation in a citizens' service organization.

Some of the reports that discussed casualties of war created apprehension among teachers. In an article about the need to protect educators from disease, Wetherill

What did *you* do today ... for Freedom?

Today, at the front, he died ... Today, what did *you* do?
Next time you see a list of dead and wounded, ask yourself:
"What have *I* done today for freedom?
What can I do tomorrow that will *save* the lives of
men like this and help them win the war?"

FIGURE 1.5. A 1943 Advertisement about the Fascist Threat to the United States (*Magazine Publishers of America*, "What did you do today ... for Freedom?" *The Nation's Schools*, copyright 1943. Reprinted by permission of the publisher. All rights reserved.)

(1944) warned that all teachers were vulnerable to the respiratory epidemics that were the "subtle by-product" of war. He added that this was especially true for those in urban schools.

Alarmist Rhetoric from the Government

Government officials presented a picture of pending menace within their official journal, *Education for Victory*. In one case, they summarized safety measures ("Air Raid Protection," 1942) that had been implemented by a Pennsylvania school district. Realizing that some might think the chances of Harrisburg being bombed were remote, the officials remonstrated that "it can happen here." Their draconian safety measures included evacuating children to bomb shelters and then removing their eyeglasses, even if an air raid was only anticipated. They also recommended that "large, emotionally stable boys can be organized into a fire watchers squad" and that "their first job would be to see that all children who are crippled are helped" (p. 13). They exhorted school personnel to fingerprint children rather than issue dog tags because "in a school fire a few years ago some pupils were so badly burned by gas that they were identified only by fingerprints." Furthermore, all teachers and custodians were to learn techniques for suppressing the fires that incendiary bombs would start.

Numerous articles ("Relocating Japanese American Students," 1942; "War Relocation Centers: Educational Program," 1942; "War Relocation Centers: Organizing," 1942; "War Relocation Centers: Tule Lake," 1943) highlighted the danger of treason and sabotage from U.S. citizens of Japanese ancestry. One hundred and ten thousand Japanese Americans were detained in camps that the government referred to as "assembly centers." A government publication described the confinement as "one of the largest controlled migrations in history" and an event that was "carried out, in remarkably short time and without serious incident" (War Relocation Authority, 1943a, p. 1).

Myer (1971) judged that this *controlled migration* was carried out for two reasons. He referred to one amorphously as "local pressures." The other factor was fear that Japanese Americans would commit sabotage. Although he was writing decades after the war, Myer judged that the fear of sabotage from this group had been unrealistic. He noted that 70,000 of the 110,000 evacuees "were American citizens, born on the United States soil" and that "the other 40,000, with few exceptions, had lived in the United States from 20 to 40 years, but were ineligible for citizenship under the laws of the United States" (pp. xiii–xiv). Myer added that "in spite of the many rumors to the contrary, not one case of any act of espionage or sabotage by any Japanese American was ever reported."

The government's attitude toward Japanese citizens was revealed when it insisted on their confinement because of "war in the Pacific, including sinking of American ships in American coastal waters, and continuing danger of attacks against Pacific Coast cities and war industries" ("War Relocation Centers: Education Program," 1942, p. 7). Another government publication indicated that "the military situation required the removal of all persons of Japanese ancestry from a broad coastal strip" because an "invasion of the west coast [was] looming as an imminent possibility" ("War Relocation Authority," 1943a, p. 1).

A postwar report (United States Department of the Interior, 1946) contained a passage by Walter Lippmann, the immensely influential newspaper columnist, who had agreed with the government and military that the Japanese Americans on the west coast posed grave dangers. Lippmann had made the following comments in a February 1942 editorial:

> The Pacific coast is in imminent danger of a combined attack from within and from without. This is a sober statement of the situation, in fact a report based not on speculation but on what is known to have taken place and to be taking place in this area of war. It is the fact that the Japanese navy has been reconnoitering the Pacific coast more or less continually and for a considerable period of time, testing and feeling out the American defenses. It is the fact that communication takes place between the enemy at sea and enemy agents on land. These are facts which we shall ignore or minimize at our peril. It is also the fact that since the outbreak of the Japanese war there has been no important sabotage on the Pacific coast. From what we know about Hawaii and about the fifth-column in Europe, this is not, as some have liked to think, a sign that there is nothing to be feared. It is a sign that the blow is well organized and that it is held back until it can be struck with maximum effect. I am sure I understand fully and appreciate thoroughly the unwillingness of Washington to adopt a policy of mass evacuation and internment of all those who are technically enemy aliens. But I submit that Washington is not defining the problem on the Pacific coast correctly. The Pacific coast is officially a combat zone; some part of it may at any moment be a battlefield. Nobody's constitutional rights include the right to reside and do business on a battlefield. And nobody ought to be on a battlefield who has no good reason for being there. (Lippmann, quoted by United States Department of the Interior, 1946, pp. 12–13)

The preceding passage was reproduced in a government-published book (United States Department of the Interior, 1946) that chronicled the activities of the War Relocation Authority (WRA). The authors of this publication indicated that the government originally intended to select administrators for the WRA who did not have "marked antipathies against all persons of Japanese descent." Hiring practices were also to have been designed to avoid "those who indulged themselves in excessive emotionalism about the plight of the evacuated people" (p. 1). The authors conceded that the WRA, because it had experienced an "extreme shortage of qualified personnel," had not been "uniformly successful" in achieving its hiring goals. The authors added defensively that, even with its recruitment problems, the WRA still did attract "sincere, hard-working, public-spirited, job-devoted, and frequently imaginative kind of personnel."

In an earlier government publication that addressed the rationale for relocating Japanese Americans, WRA officers (War Relocation Authority, 1942) had described the circumstance under which the evacuation, which had been designed initially as voluntary, became mandatory.

> At first the Army urged these [Japanese] people to leave voluntarily and resettle on their own initiative in the interior States. During the month of March, several thousands did leave, but their arrival inland in such large numbers in such a short period of time aroused so much protest that the great majority remained behind in the prohibited and restricted zones. Because of this situation, the Army decided on March 27

that all voluntary evacuation should be carried forward thereafter in accordance with an orderly and systematic plan. (p. 1)

Faulkner (1943) faulted the government for the conditions in a California internment camp that led to a riot. He also criticized the government's censors, who had tried to prevent him from reporting about it. Government officials (War Relocation Authority, 1942) did acknowledge that the "assembly centers" prescribed the "arrangements for housing, eating, and general living" and that they restricted "freedom of movement, [and the] right to engage in private enterprise" ("War Relocation Authority," 1942). Nonetheless, the officials hoped that the American public would accept the centers as military expedients. Additionally, they romanticized the stark and oppressive camps as places where prisoners were "guaranteed security and protection, a common measure of food, shelter, clothing, medical attention, and schooling, and opportunity to work for a small fixed wage" ("War Relocation Centers: Education Program," 1942, p. 7). From an equally Panglossian vantage, McWilliams (1942) wrote that the evacuation centers should not to be equated with concentration camps because "people move freely about the camp during the day; they enjoy their own social life; a measure of self-government has been provided, and the utmost good feeling prevails between the camp residents and the management" (p. 361).

An earlier report ("Relocating Japanese American Students," 1942) had indicated that some of the arrested Japanese citizens would be permitted to attend universities, provided that these were not near the west coast. One of the factors that would determine eligibility to attend these distant colleges was evidence of prior "successful Caucasian contacts." A quote from an education official at one of these camps emphasized the need for the detained Japanese Americans to redirect their attention from "the discouragement of the present" and instead "prepare themselves to take their place in the building of a better civilization after the war" ("War Relocation Centers: Tule Lake" 1943, p. 25).

With *A Guidebook for the Residents of Relocation Centers* (War Relocation Authority, 1943b), the government authors included a section on religion. They wrote that "like all other residents of the United States, evacuees at relocation centers are free to worship as they please and to conduct any type of religious service of a non political nature" (p. 12). Nonetheless, the critical shortage of building materials had forced the government to renege on its promise to provide churches. They added that ministers, priests, or any persons involved in religion should not expect any wages for discharging their religious responsibilities. The authors of the guidebook thought the incarcerated religious leaders should still be appreciative because they could "carry on their religious activities and may hold other WRA jobs at regular rates of compensation" (p. 12).

In addition to evacuating Japanese Americans from the west coast, the federal government planned the evacuation of children and "other priority groups" from those areas that were likely to be attacked along the east coast ("Protection of Children," 1942). The federally appointed Joint Committee on Evacuation published bulletins that summarized these evacuation plans. A subsequent report in *Education for Victory* indicated that the evacuation officers who had made the plans remained personally hopeful that "such plans will never need to be put into operation" ("Evacuation Plans," 1942, p. 3).

Extraordinary Wartime Responsibilities for Schools

Nine months after the United States had entered the war, the editors of a major educational journal assured their readers that "public appreciation of the schools is at a high level because of the many services they have rendered during the past year to the war effort" ("Education for Free Men," 1942, p. 185). Also writing less than a year after Pearl Harbor, Dykstra (1942) concluded that "never before have the schools been called upon for service to the armed forces or to our industrial plants in such wholesale fashion, and never before have they met any challenge more quickly or more willingly" (p. 130). Schottland (1942) concurred that the schools were meeting the "numerous demands" for unprecedented services that had been given to them.

Recognizing that many requests for novel services were being made to the schools, the NEA's Educational Policies Commission (1942a) responded that these were to "be given absolute and immediate priority in time, attention, personnel, and funds over any and all other activities." The members of this commission listed some of these requests.

> [The special requests directed at educators have included] training workers for war industries and services, producing goods and services needed for the war, conserving materials by prudent consumption and salvage, helping to raise funds to finance the war, increasing effective man-power by correcting educational deficiencies, promoting health and physical efficiency, protecting school children and property against attack, protecting the ideals of a democracy against war hazards, teaching the issues, aims, and progress of the war and the peace, sustaining the morale of children and adults, [and] maintaining intelligent loyalty to American democracy. (p. 4)

Another early wartime report ("Noncurriculum War Tasks," 1942) noted that the novel responsibilities that had been assigned to schools included entertaining servicemen, disseminating war news, and arranging social services. The schools also developed plans for providing aid in the event of a domestic emergency. The degree to which the schools became invested in some of these efforts was indicated in a postwar

FIGURE 1.6. A Flattering 1942 Depiction of Those School Administrators Who Were Initiating Pre-Induction Aviation Training in Their Schools (*Reprinted from American School Board Journal, December 1942.*)

report from the National Education Association ("Education's Part," 1946). It applauded school personnel for registering millions of men for the armed services, providing more than 70,000 teachers to serve as soldiers, distributing 415,000,000 ration books, and assisting the Junior Red Cross in producing more than 35,000,000 items for the armed forces. School personnel were responsible for $2,000,000,000 in war bond and war stamp sales. Because the schools had been promoting such

FIGURE 1.7. A 1943 Depiction of the Extraordinary Wartime Responsibilities That Teachers and Administrators Needed to Inculcate in Students (*Reprinted from American School Board Journal, April 1943.*)

massive purchases of stamps and bonds, the Secretary of the Treasury (Morgenthau, 1944) wrote teachers and school administrators an open letter of gratitude. He indicated that they had provided invaluable assistance to the direct financing of the war. However, they had also helped indirectly by promoting wartime savings, civic responsibility, thriftiness, and an understanding of wartime economics.

FIGURE 1.8. This Free Chart from the American Industries Salvage Committee Was Part of a 1942 Campaign to Promote Conservation (*American Industries Salvage Committee*, "To Help You Help America." *Journal of the NEA*. Reprinted by permission of the publisher. All rights reserved.)

Illustrations in professional journals emphasized the obligations of school personnel to engage in extraordinary wartime activities. For example, Figure 1.6, which appeared in the December 1942 issue of the *American School Board Journal*, positively depicted school administrators who initiated pre-induction aviation training in their schools. Figure 1.7, which appeared in the same journal a year later, emphasized the extraordinary wartime responsibilities that teachers and administrators needed to inculcate in students. Figure 1.8 was part of a 1942 campaign to promote salvage activities. The accompanying text indicated that a copy of this chart had been sent to every teacher in the United States.

Stress on Teachers and Administrators

A report about unusual wartime responsibilities contained observations that "the teacher, already occupied with new activities outside of school, finds also within his school new responsibilities that overwhelm him" and that "these new responsibilities include not only 'extras' but also radical curricular changes in addition to more 'integration' of war time materials" (Melchior, 1942, p. 102). Because teachers were pressured to assume so many demanding responsibilities, Childs (1942b) complained that school boards "seem to think that the teachers of the nation . . . are to be ordered into any kind of community defense work which the member of the school board outline" (p. 166). Gans (1941) judged that teachers were justifiably exasperated because they had not been consulted about the extraordinary wartime responsibilities delegated to them.

Joyal (1942) made a comparable protest on behalf of school administrators, who were expected to "maintain a regular school program of public education and, in addition, to register men for the draft, ration sugar, gather old paper and scrap iron, and operate new classes for war-workers in the community" (p. 208). Appy (1942) went into more detail.

> [School administrators] organized pre-employment classes in marine pipefitting, in supply personnel training, in aircraft electricity, and hundreds of other activities. They opened schools to Red Cross training, to P.T.A. canteens; they found trucks and adult chaperons for pupil-volunteer aids to berry and fruit growers. They sandbagged schools, planned air-raid shelters, and even made tentative evacuation plans for Bomb Area Number 1. They warned, comforted, and advised parents through bulletins to the homes, answered the universities' and government's questionnaires concerning war-need resources. They handled the multitudinous details involved in the school's share of the Japanese-American relocation. They planned with teachers for the immediate disposal of the tidal wave of transient children that engulfed the Coast schools. (p. 26)

A cartoon that appeared in the December 1942 issue of the *Journal of Education* highlighted the complex responsibilities that schools were assuming. It depicted a young boy in a school hallway that was cluttered with directional signs for wartime boards and agencies. The confused boy was asking an equally befuddled police officer how to find his classroom.

Worried that the effective school administrator might become a "war casualty," McSwain (1943a) recommended that administrators prioritize their multiple and complex tasks. However, Anderson (W. A. Anderson, 1943) indicated that this type of reordering might not be possible because of "a trend toward assigning principals two or more schools." He added that even the superintendents were being "snowed under" by their many wartime responsibilities. Melby (1943) noted that not only were administrators shouldering an unprecedented number of day-to-day tasks, but they were also developing "a new concept and practice of education" that embraced novel content and unprecedented types of learning.

Training Students for Special Wartime Careers

Because the armed services required so many individuals with technical training, teachers were adjured to synchronize their instruction to military needs. After estimating that the United States needed 5,000,000 additional, qualified persons just to complete its prewar defense contracts, Livingston (1941) concluded that they simply were unavailable. Reviewing the prewar shortage of personnel in one New Jersey industrial area, Mason (1940) reported that all local workers had been hired and that the country had been "combed" for additional skilled employees. During the first year of American involvement in the war, Sylvester (1942) noted that the national defense goals assumed a supply of workers that could produce 60,000 airplanes, 45,000 tanks, and 20,000 antiaircraft guns.

Forbes (1942) lectured high-school administrators that World War I had failed to teach them critical lessons about industrial preparedness. As a consequence, the pre–World War II vocational programs had been unable to meet the country's employment targets. He specifically noted that the prewar schools had been graduating a surplus of students in unnecessary fields while ignoring the personnel shortages in the important areas. However, he did observe approvingly that school administrators did begin to coordinate with military and industrial leaders during the national defense initiatives of 1941. As one instance of this coordination, they responded to the federal government's requests for intensive, clerical training programs ("Wartime Business," 1944). High school administrators also responded to calls for wartime nurses through the Cadet Nurse Corps Program ("Presenting the Cadet Nurse Corps," 1943). This prevocational program motivated students toward careers in nursing and managed their high-school coursework in ways that would expedite their subsequent training. The federal government thought highly enough of the Cadet Nurse Corps to supply it with printed and recorded educational materials.

Keller and Pyle (1942) quoted remarks from the First World War to demonstrate that the current need for army engineers had been a problem for decades. They adjured the schools to cooperate with the armed services, industry, and labor unions to train engineers for the defense industries and the army. From a similar point of view, Chalmers (1943) chided prewar American schools for resisting technical programs. He thought that this had been the case even after comparable programs had been implemented in Japanese and German schools. Believing that Americans might never have acknowledged their technical education responsibilities were it not for the war, Chalmers responded emotionally that everyone should "thank heaven for this."

A 1943 reporter ("Survival in Combat") observed that 50 percent of those Army jobs that required special training duplicated civilian careers. As a result, civilians with special expertise were able to readily fill critical positions in the armed forces. Nonetheless, the schools needed to expand their vocational programs to train individuals for the many positions that had been vacated by civilians or that were still available in the armed services. With regard to the military's needs, Fitzpatrick (1942) notified career counselors that the Army was seeking inductees who had been trained in the high schools as automotive mechanics, dental technicians, diesel-engine mechanics, electrical engineers, electricians, instrument technicians, locksmiths, machinists, physicists, radio operators, radio technicians, surveyors, telegraph operators, and telephone technicians. Aware that many more graduates were required than the vocational programs could supply, Fitzpatrick requested that high-school career counselors identify those individuals who had not received vocational training but who could be successful when they later attended one of the Army's specialized schools. Anderson (R. N. Anderson, 1943) agreed that the most important "added wartime duty" of the counselors was to "help the student to envisage his part in the war effort and at the same time encourage him to give some thought and planning to lifetime objectives" (pp. 320–321).

Cassidy (1941) had made a long list of traditionally male jobs that women had begun to fill. Her list included employment in aeronautics, drafting, radio repair, electronics, mechanical maintenance, factory production, photography, and health care. A report ("Enrollment of Women," 1942) about federally funded engineering, science, and management training programs indicated that the number of women enrolled in these programs increased from less than 800 in June of 1941 to almost 120,000 by the end of that year. Another report ("Women in Boys School," 1942) indicated that an all-male Boys Trade School in Massachusetts had changed its admission policies so that it could prepare female students for wartime jobs.

The federal government (United States Office of Education, 1942h) published multiple printings of a booklet about "programs authorized by Congress to train persons for work in defense industries, Governmental agencies, and the armed services." This guide listed six industries for which the supply of workers was especially dire: aircraft, ammunition, foundry, machine tools, ordnance, and shipbuilding. Among the 20 careers for which government-subsidized programs were available, the first five that the guide identified were aircraft assembler, boatbuilder, coremaker, electrical equipment assembler, and electrician. The guide contained detailed information about educational stipends, training programs, and the criteria for admission to the training programs. It also identified the purpose, length, location, and method of application for each training program. It even specified the wages that workers were likely to receive. For example, engineers were to expect annual salaries of $3,000 while nurses were to anticipate $1,300.

Believing that young men should be prepared to "work or fight," Fitzpatrick (1943) provided high-school career counselors with information about "nonessential" jobs. Students who aspired to these positions were to be advised that they would be ineligible for military deferments. The list included interior designers, florists, antique dealers, jewelers, automobile salespersons, masseuses, artists, bartenders, bathhouse attendants, beauticians, bellboys, shoe shiners, dance instructors, fortune-tellers, hairdressers, lavatory attendants, gardeners, and nightclub managers. In a prewar article, Kyker (1941) noted that business education had not been included among those training programs that were eligible for federal support. However, he identified ways of getting around this restriction, such as offering business training to members of the armed services or the National Youth Administration.

Schools responded to the demands from industry and the armed services in several ways. Some developed special career programs that were carefully geared to the extraordinary wartime employment market. For example, the *Handbook on Education and the War* (1943) advised school administrators to develop "intensive vocational courses" that embodied specific military and industrial occupations. The U.S. Army ("Survival in Combat," 1943) indicated that such preparation, even though it could be appropriate for vocational schools, was not suited for most high-school programs. Therefore, it recommended that high-school teachers develop "orientation courses" about army life. These general courses could be supplemented effectively with health, hygiene, physical education, English, and mathematics. Gregg (1943) endorsed this type of "preliminary training" and recommended that teachers combine it with their traditional academic coursework in science, mathematics, industrial arts, and drafting.

CHAPTER 2

Special Materials and Programs

The demands of the war must be given priority over all other educational features.
—STANFORD UNIVERSITY SCHOOL OF EDUCATION FACULTY, 1943

Before the United States entered World War II, the government had begun to advise teachers about their wartime responsibilities. At the same time, it supplied them with materials for discharging their new responsibilities. Although most of the materials were printed, some did rely on innovative media such as radio and cinema. The leaders of professional educational organizations helped the government develop and distribute wartime educational materials. Spurred by patriotism as well as good business sense, scholastic publishers joined in this effort. The three groups also supported special wartime programs. The most popular of these programs were modeled after the military services or the defense industries into which they were designed to lure young men and women.

Distinctive Wartime Resources

Writing during the First World War, Badley (1917) had observed disdainfully that "education is, by common consent, the dullest of subjects to write or read of" (p. v). Since he used this remark to introduce an entire volume about educational issues, he immediately followed with the comment that "there are times, however—and the present is pre-eminently one—when educational changes are admittedly imperative, and the direction that they take is of such vital importance to the nation and the future that the fullest discussion of the subject is necessary."

Special Materials and Programs

As had been the case with educators during the previous conflict, World War II teachers were advised of their extraordinary wartime responsibilities and then directed toward specialized educational materials for help. In the introduction to a bibliography about World War II, Simon and Smith (1992) observed that, even during the early period between 1938 and 1942, wartime writers had produced an "enormous" amount of material. For example, within *No Other Road to Freedom* (Stowe 1941), the publisher identified eight additional volumes that were part of its series of "books for wartime." Williams (1941) wrote *Ways of Dictatorship*, a book in which he underscored the threat to the United States from Fascists. That numerous other prewar books had this same aim was evident from titles such as *Why Europe Fights* (Millis, 1940), *Shall Not Perish from the Earth* (Perry, 1940), *Suicide of a Democracy* (Pol, 1940), *The Strategy of Terror* (Taylor, 1940), *United We Stand!* (Baldwin, 1941), *Looking for Trouble* (Cowles, 1941), *What "Mein Kampf" Means to America* (Hackett, 1941), *Under the Iron Heel* (Moen, 1941), *Arrest and Exile* (Mowrer, 1941), *You Can't Do Business with Hitler* (D. Miller, 1941), *Berlin Diary* (Shirer, 1941), *Fisherman at War* (Walmsley, 1941), *Our War and Our Peace* (Warburg, 1941), and *Democracy's Battle* (Williams, 1941).

Ziemer (1941) did not conceal his personal attitudes toward the Nazi educational system when he selected his novel's title, *Education for Death: The Making of the Nazi*. In the initial chapter, he recounted an incident in which "a squad of Nazi youngsters in their finest Party toggery of black shoes, heavy-black stockings, short black pants, and brown shirts decorated with swastikas" had thrown rocks at Jewish students outside an American school in Berlin. A teacher restrained the students from retaliating because "the Nazi boys were in full uniform" and "the least move on our part would bring the Gestapo about our ears." Later in the book, Ziemer translated the lyrics of a song popular with Nazi youths.

> Adolph Hitler is our savior, our hero.
> He is the noblest being in the whole wide world.
> For Hitler we live,
> For Hitler we die.
> Our Hitler is our Lord
> Who rules a brave new world. (p. 120)

Many prewar publications with wartime themes were intended specifically for educators. During the April before Pearl Harbor, Newlon (1941) had noted that materials about patriotism and democracy were flooding the educational fields. In addition to major speeches presented at "every teachers' meeting or conference," the educational deluge comprised "pronouncements, committee reports, books, units of work, and more pretentious and systematic syllabi" (p. 208). Newlon worried about the amount of these prewar materials as well as their origin, which he thought was with political activists who had confused "super-patriotism" with democracy.

The United States Office of Education was a major supplier of prewar educational materials. Federal bureaucrats (United States Office of Education, 1938b) wrote that their primary mission was to promote education through conferences, committees, public addresses, advisory services, professional organizations, library resources, and special materials. During the 1930s, the national Office of Education had sponsored public forums to distribute information about broad topics such as democracy, capitalism, and the American way of life. It also convened sessions on more precise topics, such as the progress of the war in Europe. In a report (United States Office of Education, 1938a) about the success of these forums, federal educational personnel did admit that their speakers had been criticized for their excessively politicized views.

During the years before the American entry into the war, the Office of Education had published a newsletter with the militaristic title *March of Education*. The newsletter was intended to be "a rapid medium for exchange of vital information." In a 1940 issue (United States Office of Education, 1940), the Commissioner of Education explained that this newsletter, which had commenced publication five years earlier, would be transformed to respond to the current "defense emergency." The Commissioner later described a special series of elementary school pamphlets that had also been initiated before the war to "give to teachers a wealth of suggestions for classroom application" (United States Office of Education, 1942i, p. v).

Although the educational publications from the government may have been voluminous before the war, they increased conspicuously after Pearl Harbor. In a preface to a report by the Harvard Committee on Education and Democracy, Harvard's president (Conant, 1945) observed that a "downpour" of educational materials had followed America's declaration of war. The National Council of Teachers of English was one of the groups that contributed to this early torrent. Its ambitious members met less than a month after Pearl Harbor to develop materials to delineate the responsibilities of wartime English teachers ("Role of the English Teacher," 1942). An advertisement for the annual convention of the American Association of School Administrators appeared in the January 1943 issue of the *Journal of the National Education Association*. This organization's leaders wrote that they would "stimulate the war effort in the schools" by arranging an elaborate exhibit of wartime materials and activities at its convention. The several hundred commercial publishers who would participate in this exhibit were featured in the ad.

The United States Commissioner of Education wrote that his office had relinquished many of its typical responsibilities in order to "bend its efforts to service directly related to the national emergency" (Studebaker, 1942b, p. 321). One of these new responsibilities was providing information to schools about "special educational problems born of the wartime situation." Only several months after Pearl Harbor, the Office of Education (United States Office of Education, 1942a) published a booklet designed to help teachers "air-condition" children in elementary and high schools. In the foreword to this pamphlet, Studebaker wrote that the clouds in Hitler's sky "will never have silver linings" and that "they will be filled, one of these days, with vast fleets of 'fantastic' planes, flown by fearless flyers who got their vision of democracy, their purpose to defend it to the death, and the basic abilities as airmen in the classrooms of American schools" (p. 1). This government publication concluded with a four-page bibliography of additional educational materials about aviation.

Other books intended to predispose students toward military air service emphasized preflight aeronautics (United States Office of Education, 1942f) and "preaviation-cadet training" (United States Office of Education, 1942e). Both of these publications were part of a series of leaflets designed to help school personnel understand their war responsibilities and educational programs to which they were synchronized. Some of the other Office of Education leaflets published soon after Pearl Harbor centered on conservation (United States Office of Education, 1942g; United States Treasury Department—War Savings Staff, 1942) and postwar planning (United States Office of Education, 1942c; 1942d).

In addition to its early wartime leaflets, the Office of Education published a series of bimonthly pamphlets. The theme of these 1942 pamphlets was education and national defense. The first issue (United States Office of Education, 1942b), which was prepared during the month before Pearl Harbor, included a letter in which the United States Commissioner of Education declared that "America must be strong—strong enough to meet any attacks against her way of life by armed aggressors." Subsequent publications in the 1942 series elaborated upon special wartime programs, sources of information for national defense, the interface between schools and community organizations, the wartime roles of libraries, teaching about democracy, teaching about multiculturalism, and teaching about internationalism.

The Children's Bureau published a 1942 set of 12 photograph-filled pamphlets entitled the "Defense of Children Series." These pamphlets were synchronized to a weekly series of government-sponsored radio programs. Each title began with the same phrase. For example, the first two publications were *Children Bear the Promise of a Better World—What Are We Doing to Defend Them?* (United States Department of Labor, 1942b) and *Children Bear the Promise of a Better World—Are We Safeguarding Those Whose Mothers Work?* (United States Department of Labor, 1942a). Other issues from this series concerned diets, health, home life, and democracy.

Because many of the government materials were intended for the widest possible distribution, they were either given away or handed out for minimal costs. As an example of another strategy for increasing distribution, one handbook about school conservation (War Production Board, 1943) contained a notice that "when you have finished reading [this wartime publication], please pass it on to a neighbor or a friend." The same handbook contained another notice that "the materials in this pamphlet may be reproduced without permission."

Advice to Teachers from Military Personnel

Advice to teachers from military personnel constituted another peculiar type of wartime material. Sometimes this advice was featured at professional meetings. For example, Walters (1942) reported about a wartime education conference that spotlighted prominent military officers. When armed forces personnel were unavailable, educators used quotations and bylines from them to bolster their own credibility. On the first page of a survey about aviation education in the schools, Ashby (1943a) made sure to quote a remark about education from the Commanding General of the Army's air force. A year earlier, Cushman (1942) had acknowledged that he had "drawn heavily" from the statements of military leaders while writing an article about the wartime roles of teachers.

In addition to appearing at conferences and providing advice for educators, military personnel began to publish their own thoughts about wartime instruction. The *Handbook on Education and the War* (1943) contained officer-written chapters about the army's personnel needs and the technical training programs that could reduce those needs. In an article from the *Journal of the National Education Association*, the Commanding General of the Army Service Forces (Somervell, 1943) asserted that the Army was interconnected with the educational establishment. Adopting a similar vantage, Colonel Spaulding (1943) argued that military training was actually a type of education that needed to complement the academic experiences in the elementary and secondary schools. Although Sergeant O'Brien (1943) employed the same argument, his editors paired his article with an ideological counterpoint from Staff Sergeant Van Fossen (1943).

Two years later, Lieutenant General Lear (1945), Commander of the Army Ground Forces in the United States, still maintained that the schools and the Army, which had been connected during the war, should remain so afterward. He argued that soldiers required two domains of knowledge, one focused on fighting and the other on patriotism. Although he did not think the armed forces required any assistance with combat training, he believed they had to rely on the schools to foster patriotic values.

Directories to Wartime Resources

Because the jungle of special wartime educational resources was so dense, educators needed maps to lead them through it. These maps, which became available in the form of directories and bibliographies, were found in magazines such as *Education for Victory*. The United States Commissioner of Education (Studebaker, 1942a) explained that this biweekly government magazine had replaced *School Life*, the periodical that the Office of Education had published since 1918. He indicated that the newer magazine was being sent gratis to 60,000 schools as well as to libraries and educational institutions. The initial issue was filled with articles about patriotic radio programs, wartime films, ways that libraries could support the war, sources of wartime educational materials available on loan, constructing models of military airplanes, contributions to the war that could be made by persons with physical disabilities, and school conservation. Additionally, this and subsequent issues contained directories of wartime educational materials. For example, one of the later issues contained a 20-page bibliography ("Victory Corps, 1943–44," 1943) of books, recordings, and films on topics such as wartime careers, citizenship, physical fitness, community service, training for the armed services, training for industry, and preparation for agriculture.

Education for Victory was not the only government resource to help educators tramp through the voluminous professional materials. The Treasury Department (United States Treasury Department, 1943) published a list of the government agencies that had produced school assembly scripts about wartime savings programs, a list of the government units that provided media for school assemblies, and a directory of the nongovernment agencies that supplied materials for school assemblies.

Another federal agency, the Office of War Information, published leaflets to help teachers conduct discussions of wartime issues. The topics included military conscription (United States Office of War Information, 1943b), childcare programs for working mothers (United States Office of War Information, 1943a), and the need to fight for peace (United States Office of War Information, 1943c). Each of these leaflets was distinctive because it ended with a list of sources for additional printed information or films.

The National Association of Secondary School Principals published lists of teaching materials for the sciences, humanities, vocational fields, and cross-disciplinary areas (Heimers, 1943). Additionally, this organization published highly specialized bibliographies, such as a guide to books about the Far East (American Council Institute of Pacific Relations, 1942) and a war bibliography designed especially for principals ("Selected War-Time Bibliography," 1943). The bibliography for principals contained sections on curriculum, social studies, preflight training, pre-induction training, youth manpower programs, and wartime careers. A librarian at the United States Office of Education (McCabe, 1943) published a bibliography that she divided into three categories: general education materials, public-school materials, and postsecondary-school materials. In addition to assembling bibliographies, the Office of Education designated information centers to distribute wartime teaching materials. Heimers (1943) indicated that New

Jersey alone had three of these centers, all located at colleges or universities with teacher education programs.

Before America had entered the war, the president of the American Library Association (C. H. Brown, 1941) explained that his organization had begun to publish a circular entitled *Libraries and National Defense*. Each installment identified materials appropriate to wartime defense. The first issue, which was published the month before Pearl Harbor, organized materials under headings such as *civilian protection*, *vocational books*, *engineering books*, *citizenship education*, and *defense of children*.

After Pearl Harbor, bibliographies of special scholastic materials became more abundant. Although Towsend (1944) was addressing wartime textbooks and pamphlets, she also advised teachers about materials that could prepare future generations for peace. Because the materials on this very precise topic were extensive, she was "of necessity highly selective" and "endeavored to list only the most important, usable resources." She also identified magazines that teachers could consult for additional bibliographies and directories.

The *Wartime Handbook for Education* (National Education Association, 1943c) noted the availability of thousands of special wartime materials, including films and radio programs. Like other bibliographers, the authors of this handbook explained that they were unable to list all of the available materials. As a compromise, they identified the agencies that distributed the materials rather than the materials themselves. These materials included films, exhibits, maps, posters, and radio programs.

Some professional educational books contained extensive bibliographies as well as advice for incorporating the listed materials into effective programs. For example, Myer (1942) counseled teachers about wartime teaching, gave them an actual wartime curriculum, and provided a 100-page list of films, printed materials, and radio programs to incorporate within that curriculum. At the end of a book with the attention-getting title, *Our Children Face War*, Wolf (1942) included lists of materials for both students and teachers. Within another early wartime book, Ware (1942) identified materials that were related to consumer issues and that were available from local agencies, state agencies, the federal government, or commercial organizations.

Wartime Resources from Commercial Publishers

Commercial publishers created some educational materials specifically for the wartime courses in the schools. The Allyn and Bacon Company placed an advertisement for these types of materials in the March 1945 issue of the *Clearing House*. This advertisement for "new textbooks and workbooks for the war emergency" featured materials in geography, American history, civics, home economics, science, mathematics, and communication. The publishers entitled the advertisement "Textbooks Are

Weapons!" and emphasized that their books would "educate young pupils to understand and prepare for the war efforts." They added caveats that "spirit is the chief essential to success" and that "the people whose morale is best always win."

The Silver Burdett Publishing Company produced a book (Brown, Stewart, & Myer, 1942) with the title *America in a World at War*. Intended for a special course, the textbook contained chapters such as "Revolt against Civilization," "Changing Strategy of Modern Warfare," and "Organization and Activities of Our Army." This book was filled with government-supplied photographs of servicemen in combat. It also included government-furnished charts, such as that in Figure 2.1.

Macmillan published the Air-Age Educational Series, which was one of the most ambitious collections of wartime materials. Next to the title page of an early book from this series (Bartlett, 1942), the publisher listed 16 additional volumes that were already available. The other books included texts on aeronautics, air-age geography, air-age science, air-age social studies, air-age industrial arts, the biology of flight, and mathematics for aviators. Convinced that the aeronautical revolution extended to civilians as well as soldiers, the author of *Social Studies for the Air Age* assured teachers that they would "contribute directly to the paramount task of winning the war by helping to train the young men who will give air supremacy to the United Nations" (Bartlett, 1942, p. v). As one more example of the distinctive content within this series, one of the books (Cohen, 1942) used passages from aviators to chronicle the history of flight.

OUR PRODUCTION GOAL
(PRESIDENT ROOSEVELT'S SPEECH, JAN. 6, 1942)

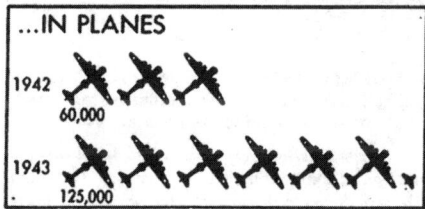

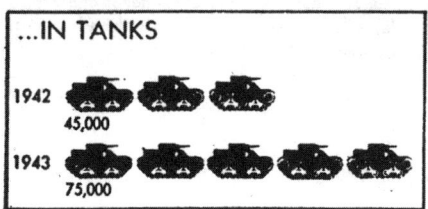

FIGURE 2.1. Textbooks from Commercial Publishers Incorporated Government Charts (*"America in a World at War,"* Brown, William B., Stewart, Maxwell S., & Myer, Walter E., copyright 1942. Reprinted by permission of Pearson Education, Inc.)

38 Wartime Schools

Not all school publishers followed the same course in their wartime marketing campaigns. This is evident in Figure 2.2, which was part of a 1943 advertisement for pre-induction vocational courses. Included within this advertisement were promotions for additional textbooks in subjects such as machinery, electricity, arithmetic, and geography. Figure 2.3 contains a 1941 advertisement from this same publishing company. However, this earlier promotion featured textbooks that had been designed for standard courses in reading, history, music, and other academic areas. Although the 1941 advertisement was accompanied by an illustration that was not at all militaristic, readers were certain to notice the introductory quote, in which a superintendent equated textbooks for students with guns for soldiers. Figure 2.4 was part of a 1939 advertisement for bulletins that were designed to help teachers and students recognize war propaganda.

Some commercial educational magazines contained actual lessons and materials that teachers could use in their classrooms. *Instructor* featured materials that simultaneously reinforced wartime issues and traditional academic skills. The January

PRE-INDUCTION COURSES

SIEMENS
Aeronautics Workbook

A complete, well-organized series of problems and exercises which enable the student to "learn by doing." Follows, unit by unit, the basic Pre-Flight Course as given in U. S. Off. of Educ. Leaflet 63. Covers aerodynamics, meteorology, structure and parts, engines and propellers, and navigation. Has page references to the leading texts.

Each copy contains a large chart with all geographical features for working air-navigation problems in color. $1.00; chart separately, 40 cents.

BASIC BOOKS FOR WARTIME

FIRST OF ALL—to help win the war... NEXT—to instill a knowledge of the fundamentals upon which to build for the future...

For over seventy-five years Ginn and Company has served education—publishing millions of textbooks which have found their way into the schools of every land. Today, in wartime, we meet the needs of changing curricula by helping schools to maintain the educational standards which will make victory secure.

FIGURE 2.2. A 1943 Advertisement to Support Pre-Induction Vocational Courses ("*Basic Books for Wartime*," copyright 1943. Reprinted by permission of Pearson, Education, Inc.)

FIGURE 2.3. Readers Were Certain to Notice the Introductory Quote in This 1941 Advertisement ("Fresh, First-class Equipment for America's Army of Learners," copyright 1941. Reprinted by permission of Pearson Education, Inc.)

FIGURE 2.4. A Prewar Advertisement for Materials to Alert Teachers and Students to Propaganda

1943 issue initiated a column entitled "Facts for Future Flyers." That same issue contained a set of "seatwork" assignments (J. B. Beck, 1943) centering about war stamps. In one of these assignments, students were directed to designate whether the following statements were true or false:

> We can buy War Stamps at school.
> We buy as many Stamps as we can.
> There are some one-cent War Stamps.
> Ten-cent War Stamps are brown.
> It is patriotic to buy War Stamps
> We put War Stamps on letters. (p. 9)

Another article (Noel, 1943) that was published in the same magazine gave detailed instructions about classroom activities with scrap materials. In an issue of *Instructor* with the subtitle "Many Ideas for Wartime Teaching," Sprunk (1943) gave examples of "seatwork" to help young students learn about patriotism.

Grade Teacher was a commercially published journal intended for elementary school teachers. During World War II, the editors inundated their readers with practical materials to instill positive wartime values. For example, the first issues of 1942 included three plays, one about patriotism (Goebel, 1942), one about war stamps (Josephine, 1942), and a third in which Mother Goose characters explained America's defensive strategy (Dally, 1942). The magazine described extracurricular activities to promote conservation, defense, citizenship, and other types of home-front support. It was so practical that it printed classroom decorations and worksheets that teachers could cut out and use. It also included lessons about wartime poems, simulations, cartoons, posters, artwork, and gardens.

Baker's Plays, a publisher of dramas, issued the "patriotic pageant drama" (Field, 1942). This school pageant employed "music and drama, song and story" to promote "America's ideals of life, liberty and the pursuit of happiness," to portray "the tragedy of the loss of our blood-won heritage," and to awaken "a more understanding love and zeal for 'this freedom of ours'" (p. 7). The prelude from this drama contained the following passage:

Narrator: Do you know where this freedom came from?
Chorus: It came from the heart and soul of mankind—from the toil and sweat and tears of mankind.
Narrator: Yes, freedom came to America . . .
Chorus: Through the life and death of thousands
Male Voice: On many battlefields,
Female Voices: In a multitude of towns and cities,
Chorus: In countless homes.

Male Voices: Where men loved God more than gold,
Female Voices: And justice to brother man more than self,
Chorus: That America might be free.
Students: Wait a moment! Let us show you.
Narrator: Who are you?
Students: The youth of America.
Narrator: Tell me. What have you learned in school? (pp. 12–13)

Although many publishers produced books to inform young readers about military training, some of them tried to encourage enlistment. For example, Flint (1943), who had edited the diary entries of two females in the Army, assembled these passages into a single volume with the subtitle *The Autobiography of a WAC*. Gollomb and Taylor (1943) wrote a book with the self-explanatory title *Young Heroes of the War*. A reserve officer (Childs, 1943) wrote a fictionalized account of a Navy gun crew that delivered ordinance to Europe. The book's final paragraph noted that the men "had a deep feeling of satisfaction because they had helped bring the bombs safely across the ocean" and because "they were doing their part to keep the great life line of food and ammunition going to the front" (pp. 110–111).

Writing with unconcealed adulation, Ayling (1943) began a book with the observation that "there is a dash and glamour about a marine. . . . [who] talks a language of his own, sees life with a slant different from men of other corps, and molds his entire life to the tradition of his corps" (p. 1). Although most of the text and photographs depicted heroic achievements, one chapter carefully outlined the types of training available to marines. For example, special military schools trained antiaircraft directors, amphibious tractor operators, and armored cavalry personnel. Ending the book with a passage that was as inspiring as that with which he had begun, Ayling wrote that this branch of the armed services was suited to "men who want to serve their country in a corps with the finest fighting reputation in the world, to acquire an excellent education, and to see the world at the same time" (p. 194).

Another volume about the Marines consisted of stirring passages as well as annotated photographs. One of the pictures showed an officer hugging two Doberman pinschers. The caption noted that this officer had used these "devil dogs" on Guadalcanal, "where he outwitted sullen Japanese prisoners by making them work for their own counterfeit money" (Boswell, 1943, p. 195). Crump (1944) also included a photograph of a Doberman pinscher in his book about the Marines. His picture, in which the dog was accompanied by an armed Marine, was entitled "Two kinds of Devil Dogs—Neither one flinches in the face of enemy fire" (caption from photo facing p. 102).

Cook (1944) provided a set of flattering descriptions of heroic American generals. One of the front pages from this collection displayed an eagle with a book in its talons and a windswept banner in its beak. The banner read: BOOKS ARE THE

WEAPONS IN THE WAR OF IDEAS. The titles of the chapters in this book revealed its tone and content. For example, Cook entitled the chapter on Clark "I'm Sticking to My Guns," the one on Patton "Fabulous but Efficient," that on Halsey "Tough, Tattooed and Scrappy," and the one on MacArthur "Deeds of Valor."

Also aiming his book at an audience of adolescents, Mann (1944) wrote about Jimmy Doolittle, the heralded World War II pilot. He devoted one of the chapters to Doolittle's high-school years, emphasizing the ways in which he benefited from wrestling, boxing, and the "manual arts." The tone of Mann's book was evident in its dedication, which saluted "those who proudly rise with silver wings to keep bright the golden rays of freedom; and to their comrades who have paid the supreme sacrifice in war-torn skies that that same freedom shall not perish" (p. 5).

Addressing young readers in elementary school, Elting and Weaver (1943) entitled their book *Soldiers, Sailors, Fliers and Marines*. They described the training, uniforms, insignia, equipment, and weapons employed in the armed services. The authors depicted military service in the most positive terms. For example, a drawing of soldiers frolicking in water was accompanied by the caption, "The officers usually try to find a camping place where there is a stream or a lake so that the soldiers can take a bath."

Films

Although print may have been a critical medium for conveying information about the war, it was not the only one. A report indicated that the trainers in the armed forces had been relying on "maps, globes, charts, graphs, models, mounted pictures, slides, slidefilms, sound and silent motion pictures, radio programs, and recordings" (National Council for the Social Studies, 1944, p. 32). A report from the Board of Education of the City of New York (1942) advised elementary school teachers to use films and other alternative media, even though these "as useful instructional materials are only in the pioneer stages." The authors explained that the use of experimental media was justified because "war needs demand their rapid and significant development" (p. 36).

After the war, the Committee on Military Training Aids and Instructional Materials (1945) suggested that the elements of Army training programs be extended to public education. The members of this U.S. Office of Education committee indicated that the military had been able to train a force of more than 12,000,000 soldiers in a short period because it had relied on testing, skills-based forms of instruction, and "the utilization of the tools and procedures of experiential learning to the utmost degree, as especially exemplified in the widespread use of training aids including audio-visual aids" (p. x). Acknowledging that the primary audiovisual aids on which the Army had depended were films, the authors staidly concluded that "more people have been subjected to training films as a regular instructional tool than ever before in the history of this country." They added that "the Armed Forces during the past 4 years have produced more than six-fold as great a number of motion pictures and filmstrips as had ever been produced before for strictly educational purposes" (p. 21).

Films had also been used effectively during World War I. These early films had included major motion pictures as well as weekly reviews of the war's progress (Rawls, 1988; Winter & Baggett, 1996; Committee on Public Information, 1972). The government itself had developed more than 60 motion pictures. Even though the government had employed films during World War I, its World War II cinema campaigns had an immensely wider scope. Additionally, some of the World War II films were aimed specifically at students. A very practical reason for this change was the fact the 1940s schools owned half of the nation's 20,000 sixteen-millimeter sound projectors ("Distribution of War Films," 1943). One reporter ("War Films," 1942)

FIGURE 2.5. A 1943 Advertisement That Linked Projectors to Wartime Films (*Reprinted from American School Board Journal, June 1943.*)

noted that the government's production of school films became such a priority that the Office of War Information devoted a special division to it. The films from this division presented information about domestic topics such as farming and recycling as well as military topics such as the construction and use of weapons.

Materials from the National Education Association provide additional evidence of the extensive use of films in the schools. For example, a set of teaching units about democratic government advised teachers to "introduce the unit by showing one or more films picturing the problems and achievements of democracy" (National Education Association, 1942, p. 53). To locate suitable films, teachers were to consult the *List of U.S. War Films* that had been compiled by the Office of War Information. They could also refer to the list of 156 films compiled by the NEA itself.

Three years later, the National Education Association (1944b) confirmed that the war had spurred "a tremendous increase" in educational films. Instead of continuing to precisely identify the multiple films that had become available, it compiled a 24-page bibliography of the agencies and organizations from which educational films could be procured. Because this mimeographed list was "in no way exhaustive," the organization also identified other bibliographies that documented the sources for films. This annotated list was partitioned into 16 categories, the first three of which were general, federal, and state sources. A year later, Cook and Rahbek-Smith (1945) published a guide to 4,340 educational films, the majority of which were accompanied by annotations. One of these described the *Siege of Leningrad*, a 62-minute, Soviet film.

> Shows how men and women, young and old in all walks of life created a fortress of freedom the Axis could not take. Shows the famous guerrilla brigades in action; the lifeline road built across the ice of Lake Ladoga; the arms factories going full blast despite enemy raids; the powerful defense lines. (p. 440)

Figure 2.5 is taken from a 1943 advertisement that marketed projectors as opportunities for showing wartime films. Figure 2.6, which is another advertisement, highlighted one of these wartime films.

Alternative Resources

Other than printed matter, films were the most popular educational material. However, quite a few alternatives to the two dominant types of materials were available. Kent (1943) wrote that the War Department had developed a series of audio aids and visual materials that were "unparalleled in the history of such activity" (p. 79). As another example of alternative materials, the World Book Company had begun to sell phonograph records in 1940 under the title *The Sound of History*. The first

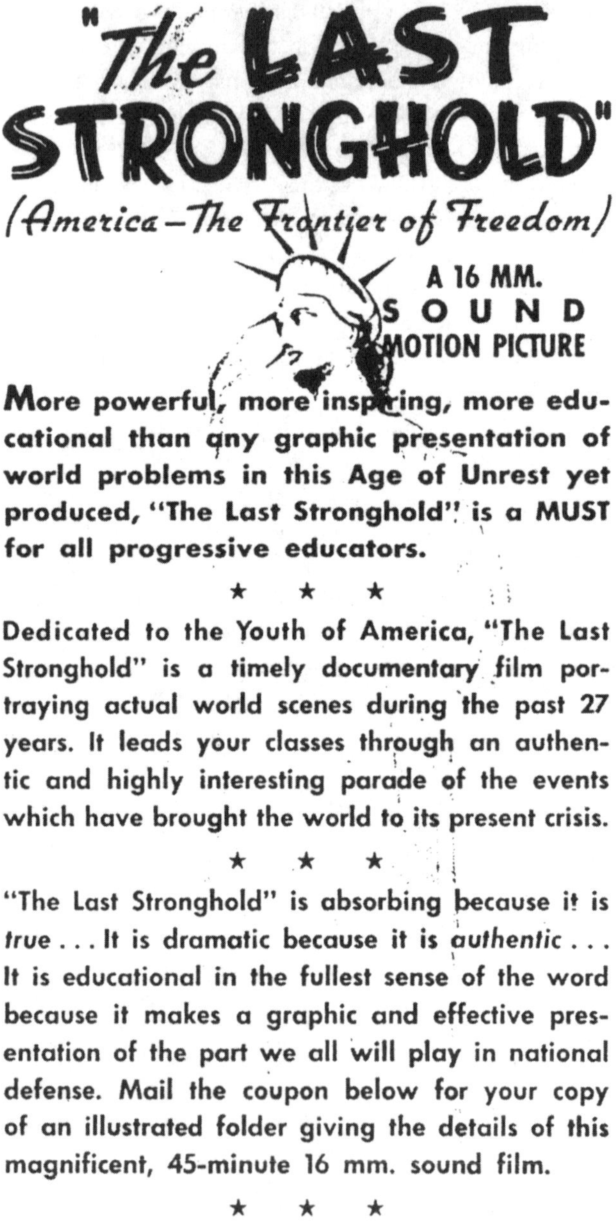

"The LAST STRONGHOLD"

(America — The Frontier of Freedom)

A 16 MM. SOUND MOTION PICTURE

More powerful, more inspiring, more educational than any graphic presentation of world problems in this Age of Unrest yet produced, "The Last Stronghold" is a MUST for all progressive educators.

★ ★ ★

Dedicated to the Youth of America, "The Last Stronghold" is a timely documentary film portraying actual world scenes during the past 27 years. It leads your classes through an authentic and highly interesting parade of the events which have brought the world to its present crisis.

★ ★ ★

"The Last Stronghold" is absorbing because it is *true*... It is dramatic because it is *authentic*... It is educational in the fullest sense of the word because it makes a graphic and effective presentation of the part we all will play in national defense. Mail the coupon below for your copy of an illustrated folder giving the details of this magnificent, 45-minute 16 mm. sound film.

★ ★ ★

FIGURE 2.6 A 1941 Advertisement for a Film Incorporating "Actual War Scenes"

installment, which was subtitled *Then Came War*, used the voices of Hitler, Chamberlain, and other world leaders to create a "new teaching instrument."

Radio provided one more type of educational material. Marshall (1941) wrote in a popular educational journal that "the present war has proved to us that people can be bombed from the air with words just as effectively as with high explosives, and subsequently more and more radio programs have been devoted to our national defense" (p. 70). Issues of the *Journal of the National Education Association* during that same year featured advertisements about the *Cavalcade of America*, "a show which makes the listener proud of American ideals." These advertisements highlighted live radio broadcasts while also reminding teachers that recorded versions of the shows were available.

Several other wartime radio programs were aimed at schools. The American School of the Air made broadcasts four times a week. Although some of its shows featured only patriotic music, others highlighted current events and science. The U.S. Office of Education sponsored the *Victory Corps Hour*, which informed highschool learners about the war. The *Handbook on Education and the War* (1943) identified several other radio programs, but it did not intend its list to be complete, because, the authors explained, "there isn't time for that."

Tuttle (1993a) agreed that wartime children were influenced by the educational films and radio programs that were aimed at them. However, he judged that they were also affected profoundly by the movies, newsreels, and radio broadcasts that were intended for adults. For example, one survey (Chase, 1943) of elementary school children indicated that more than 70 percent watched war movies or listened to war news on the radio. Another 50 percent read about the war in newspapers. In addition to getting information from these outside-the-classroom sources, children formed wartime impressions by reading comic books (Tuttle, 1993a). Lenroot (1942) observed realistically that urban children were attending to wartime information in "the store, the shop, the factory, street trades, the corner drugstore, the library, the movie theater, the pool hall, the ball game, the dance hall, the roadhouse, the tavern" (p. 137).

Slide film was another educational medium that conveyed wartime information. Figure 2.7 is part of an advertisement from a 1943 issue of *Progressive Education*. It described slides that had been designed to help students differentiate Allied planes from enemy aircraft.

In the September 1943 issue of the *Journal of the National Education Association*, the Hammond Company advertised a singular type of teaching material—a field marshal's war map. The map was mounted on cardboard and accompanied by flagged pins with which students could mark the movements of armies. The advertisement explained that "as regions are captured, or battle lines change, you move the flags." The March 1944 issue of *Educational Leadership* contained an advertisement for a map that displayed "the progress of the war up to the present time, indicating the

48   Wartime Schools

In modern air combat, lives depend on *instant* recognition of a friend or foe. Teach pre-flight students how to identify planes *instantly* with the S.V.E. Kit of 336 miniature 2" x 2" slides. It covers 110 different types of planes of **U. S. Army and Navy, Royal Air Force, British Fleet Air Arm, Russia, Japan** and **Germany.**

The slides in the S.V.E. Kit are authentically correct and up-to-date. They were made under the direction of aeronautical experts of FLYING magazine. There are six introductory slides, and three silhouettes of each plane — side view, bottom view, and front view. The slides are 2" x 2" and can be projected by any S.V.E. or other miniature slide projector. *Mail Coupon for Details!*

FIGURE 2.7. A 1943 Advertisement for Slides Designed to Help Students Spot Enemy Airplanes (*"Teach Instant Recognition with This SVE Aircraft Identification Kit." Progressive Education*, copyright 1943. Reprinted by permission of the publisher. All rights reserved.)

Moscow, Tehran, and Cairo conferences, and the Allied gains in Russia, Italy, and the South Pacific." The publisher assured teachers that "this dated war map furnishes a fine exercise in Geography for pupils, who can follow the progress of the war and the gains of the allies by marking these in with a red pencil."

The special patriotic music that was written for school bands, orchestras, and choruses constituted another wartime resource. The *Victory Song Book* (Frey, 1942) was subtitled 93 *Patriotic and Popular Song Favorites for Community Singing in Camps, Recreational Groups, Schools and in the Homes.* Another collection (Goldsmith & Morgenstern, 1942) was titled *Win-the-War-Ballads: Twelve Timely Songs for Children and Everybody Else.* One of these ballads began with the lyrics "we built a cozy shelter place, underneath the table, and there I play at Indian whenever I am able, and when the air-raid whistles blow, into my wig-wam we go, ma and pa, and me and Rover, till the air-raid is over" (pp. 15–16). Other songs from the same collection included *Junior Aviator*, *My Ration Book*, *Blackout*, *My Victory Garden*, and a piece about domestic espionage entitled *Old Man Rumor*.

The January 1943 issue of the *Music Educators Journal* contained an advertisement from the Broadcast Music Company for a band book entitled *Patriotic America*. That same issue included many other ads for stirring, patriotic music. An ad from the Church Company for "timely and practical music" featured special arrangements of *The Stars and Stripes Forever* and *The Glory of the Yankee Navy*. The Fillmore Music House highlighted "new band music of the times" that comprised marches such as *America's Defenders*, *The American Flyer*, and *American Legionnaires*. The Marks Music Corporation suggested "music for victory" that included *I Hear America Singing*, *Anthems of the United Nations*, and *Win-the-War Ballads*. A report indicated that "governmental and allied cultural agencies" had subsidized the composing of this music in order to provide "incentives to stir young people to creative undertakings in connection with their war efforts" (Pitts, 1943, p. 7).

Distinctive Wartime Programs

In a report about special military training in World War I high schools, Small (1917) noted that some of his contemporaries had already made up their minds that such programs would "stimulate the martial spirit," "make boys lovers of war," and "make trained soldiers of high-school graduates" (p. 567). Disagreeing, Small used the opaque style that was typical during this period when he pointed out that the true "purpose of such training is to capitalize on the ancient, fundamental, and ineradicable fighting instinct; to exercise, train, and educate it; to make of it a productive educational investment, and compel it to yield adequate dividends in physical and moral discipline."

Twenty-five years later, the arguments supporting special wartime programs were certainly being presented less pretentiously. However, the social dynamics that were driving these programs had not changed substantially. As an example, the members of the National Council for the Social Studies resolved that teachers had a responsibility to "lay a large part in building and maintaining a healthy morale" (Babcock, Jeffery, & Troelstrup, 1942, p. 3). They concluded that "perhaps the greatest need of teachers is for materials which will provide the means for fulfilling their role as accurately as possible and with maximum conservation of time and effort."

The federal Office of Education and the Treasury Department (United States Treasury Department—War Savings Staff, 1942) defined wartime educational programs in a pamphlet entitled *Schools at War*. This publication had two subtitles, *A Program for Action* and the *Handbook of Suggestions*. Their suggestions clustered in thee areas: savings, service, and conservation. As an example of the specificity within this pamphlet, the section on conservation advised students to earn money for war stamps by collecting fat drippings and selling these to butchers.

Judd (1942) wrote that it had become necessary to increase students' awareness of their wartime responsibilities. The school programs that were endorsed by the federal Office of Education and the Treasury Department nurtured the qualities that Judd specified. However, such wartime programs had been anticipated by Depression-era economic initiatives that were transformed easily into national defense programs.

A prime example was the Civilian Conservation Corps (CCC), which had been established in 1933. The participants in this program received a $30.00 monthly check, 80 percent of which was sent to their families. Griffing (1935) wrote that CCC was designed to redirect the lives of the unemployed young men who "tramped the streets, then the roads" and who had begun to develop "antisocial attitudes." The writer of another early report ("Is the CCC Educational," 1934) agreed that the original goal for the program was to recruit 300,000 young men from the "jungles and hangouts" where they were being "constantly tempted to criminal acts." Writing six years later, Weidman (1940), who was affiliated with the CCC, wrote that the organization's primary goal had been to promote behavioral changes through instruction about democratic values.

Even though the CCC was one of the archetypal social projects that a liberal administration had engineered, some liberals criticized its excessive formality. One former CCC worker (Lanigan, 1940) thought the organization was so regimented that it had been unable to inculcate a genuine understanding of democracy. In contrast, the conservatives, who may have been dismayed by the unwieldy federal bureaucracy that the CCC represented, prized its regimentation. They argued that its structured format helped participants experience "some of the habits and routines which soldiers must follow" and "the discipline of living in a camp similar in character to any army post" ("CCC's Contribution," 1942). After criticizing the CCC as an out-of-control bureaucracy, Holland and Hill (1942) did acknowledge that its programs could be adapted readily for defensive training.

The educational materials that were used in the CCC reflected the complex character of the organization. This is evident in Figure 2.8, which is a page from a *Camp Life Reader and Workbook* (United States Office of the Interior, 1940a). In addition to teaching literacy skills, this lesson highlighted the need to follow regulations. Figure 2.9, a page from another book in the same series (United States Office of the Interior, 1940b), simultaneously featured information about careers and Christian values.

As another example of an economic recovery program that complemented national defense efforts, a 1940 presidential act allocated over $60,000,000 to train defense workers. It also provided vocational training for out-of-school youths, persons enrolled in federal work programs, and adults who required refresher courses.

Although organizations such as the CCC had begun to prepare persons for jobs well before the war, this training became more important as the likelihood of war

```
                TO LEAVE CAMP
To leave camp you have to get a pass.
You must sign out.
You must sign in.
There is a late leave for week nights.
There is a week-end leave.
We can get a leave of six days.
This is called annual leave.
On some holidays we get leave.
On Sunday we may go to church.
We also may have leave to attend school.
```

FIGURE 2.8. A Passage That Taught Reading Skills along with Appropriate Attitudes Toward the CCC

increased. An eleventh-hour report from the Educational Policies Commission (1941c) described the prewar activities of males and females in the National Youth Administration (NYA), another massive, federally subsidized economic recovery program. In a list of the areas to which the NYA participants had been devoting significant amounts of time, this report singled out "vocational subjects in the trade and industrial, agricultural and commercial fields . . . homemaking and health . . . civics and public affairs . . . [and a] variety of other subjects from elementary language and arithmetic through the high school level" (p. 13).

A report from the National Education Association (Educational Policies Commission, 1941c) warned that robust federal funding, even though it was essential for education, could take away control of educational programs from states and local school districts. Joyal (1941) was more explicit when he warned that federally subsidized programs were leading inexorably to a nationalized system of education. Writing that same year, Norton (1941) criticized political liberals for deliberately funding the CCC and the NYA with budgets that were larger than required. He thought they had done this to ensure that these interim organizations would become permanent features of a burgeoning federal bureaucracy. The liberal Commager (1945) later riposted that massive federal support for education was not a dangerous departure from tradition but an initiative similar to those earlier government acts that had financed land-grant colleges, the agricultural experiment stations, and vocational schools.

Many of the educational programs that government agencies sponsored during the war had an overtly military character. The Treasury-sponsored Junior Salvage Army was "led into the field by student officers with well-earned 'commissions,' each

How long do you suppose men have been making useful articles from wood? There are stories about wood-carving and carpentry in the Bible. Solomon was a wood-carver. He carved images of trees and flowers from wood. Jesus was a carpenter. The Bible tells us that when Jesus was a small boy he watched the carpenters at work. When he grew to be a man he became a carpenter.

Carpentry is still an important trade. There are thousands and thousands and thousands of carpenters in the world today.

Carpenters and wood-carvers need more tools than whittlers. Many of the tools used today are like the tools used by the men in the days of the Bible.

FIGURE 2.9. A Page from a CCC Reader That Simultaneously Promoted Career Education and Christianity

soldier realizing that he is participating in a major campaign for victory" (National Education Association, 1943c, p. 34). The Civil Air Patrol Cadets program (National Education Association, 1943c) also had a distinctive military character. It introduced high-school students to military discipline so that they would be prepared for the severe training that would follow graduation. The participants were trained "in all branches of aviation, except actual flying" so that they would be ready for military flight school.

The High School Victory Corps (National Education Association, 1943c) was a nationwide program sponsored by the U.S. Office of Education. Like the Civil Air patrol Cadets program, it was designed to engage students in immediate, home-front service and prepare them for the war responsibilities that they would assume after they had graduated. The following passage ("Victory Corps," 1942) from *Life* magazine described the activities of the students who had enrolled in this program at a Maryland high school:

> The student body is organized into one battalion, divided into companies, platoons and squads. Corps members must spend an hour a day in military drill and calisthenics. The

curriculum includes intensive courses for boys and girls in metal work, blueprint reading, airplane riveting, and drafting. At noon daily, 60 seniors leave classes to work in factories, stores, restaurants and on farms. Other students act as school janitors, bake and cook, run nursery schools, collect scrap, learn first aid. (p. 53)

One of the books that was developed for the students in the Corps was entitled *Our Armed Forces: A Source Book on the Army and Navy for High-School Students* (United States Office of Education, 1943d). In addition to detailed sections that informed students about the armed services, this book included sections that prepared them for military duty. The authors advised students to join the High School Victory Corps and enroll in those courses "from which military men tell us spring the most important of all qualifications for success and usefulness in the Army and Navy" (p. 101). The recommended courses included physical education, mathematics, science, vocational education, business, communication, and civics.

Grigsby (1943) wrote that the Corps had been designed as a curriculum for "all legitimate demands that can be made upon the secondary schools of the Nation in wartime" (p. 73). Although the Corps emphasized citizenship, career guidance, community activity, science, mathematics, physical fitness, pre-flight training, and military drilling, Loomis (1943) defined its primary goal as the training of soldiers and defense workers. As an indication of the diversity of the services that became entwined with the Corps, one report (Jessen, 1944b) gave details of dentists who treated the participants in order to increase their readiness for military or industrial service. During 1943, the Office of Education published a special set of pamphlets to assist school personnel in organizing Victory Corps programs. After the release of the introductory pamphlet (United States Office of Education, 1943c), subsequent issues emphasized community service (United States Office of Education, 1943a), job opportunities (United States Office of Education, 1943b), physical education (United States Office of Education, 1943e), health education (United States Office of Education, 1943f), armed service careers (United States Office of Education, 1943g), and communication (United States Office of Education, 1943h).

Not all of the attention directed at the High School Victory Corps was positive. Largely because he judged the influence of the Corps to be inordinate, Johnsen (1943) warned that the war was in danger of becoming "more total in the schools than in life." He was especially critical of the federal government for using this program to distribute wartime propaganda to students. He observed that "it would be better for all concerned if the United States Office of Education would somehow develop an interest in *Education*" (p. 35).

White (1943) was also critical of the High School Victory Corps. He disapproved of a recruitment pamphlet because it emphasized that the participants would be taught "the habit of immediate and unquestioned obedience to proper authority" (Passage from a High School Victory Corps pamphlet, quoted by White, 1943,

"But Admirable Hokyyaki, aren't they carrying that V for Victory just a little too far?"

FIGURE 2.10. A Cartoon That Accompanied an Article about the High School Victory Corps (*Reprinted by permission of The American Legion Magazine, copyright January 1943.*)

p. 499). He also objected to a pamphlet that was "full of insignia, *esprit de corps*, and organizational charts—rectangles connected by straight lines, illustrating those subtle dependencies so pleasing to the bureaucratic heart" (p. 499). Even though membership in the Corps was promoted as voluntary, White questioned this contention because "somehow the word 'Victory' leaves a boy or girl little choice in the matter." In a monograph for teachers (Indiana Department of Public Instruction, 1943), the authors acknowledged that some critics had belittled the Corps. Without reprising the denigrating remarks, they responded that this criticism was part of a campaign to discredit organizations with "broad implications."

The High School Victory Corps was especially popular in southern states. Aderhold (1944) reported that it was admired to such a degree in Georgia that nearly 90 percent of the schools in that state participated. This estimate included the segregated schools attended by African Americans. The Corps proved so popular that the federal government provided correspondence courses for students who were attending schools without on-site programs ("Correspondence Study," 1943).

In an article that appeared in the pro-war *American Legion Magazine*, Shumaker (1943a) wrote that the Victory Corps promoted "practical education" by "training youth for the war service that will come after they leave school" and by "active participation in the community's war effort" (pp. 16–17). Shumaker's article included before-and-after photos of high-school students who at first had slumped about in T-shirts but who subsequently were transformed by American Legionnaires into a disciplined, uniform-clad team. The cartoon in Figure 2.10 accompanied Shumaker's article.

Pre-induction

Ugland (1979) wrote that the need for pre-induction training seemed especially urgent during the summer of 1942. A lowering of the draft age had reduced the postgraduation time during which high-school students could prepare for the armed services. Although military preparation programs such as the High School Victory Corps addressed this situation, many schools responded with less structured forms of pre-induction training.

A report in *Education for Victory* ("War Facts Schools Should Know," 1943) indicated that the navy viewed pre-induction training as "basic education in reading, mathematics, science, and knowledge of what the war is about." The army expanded this definition to include "such subjects and fields as machines, shopwork, electricity, automotive mechanics, radio code, driving automobiles, clerical work and preflight aeronautics" (p. 29). Identifying the pre-induction traits needed by females who wished to serve as WACS, Hobby (1943) included physical ability, mental ability, and the "personality qualifications for army success." The personality qualifications involved self-discipline, "ability to restrain oneself even under trying conditions," and demonstrated "adjustment to authority" (p. 87).

The *Handbook on Education and the War* (1943) specified three levels of pre-induction training. The foundation level included those high-school courses that provided background information about the armed services. The second level, which comprised introductory classes about radio operation and automotive mechanics, prepared students for the specialized training they would receive in the armed services. The third level, which was even more precisely aligned with armed services training, included advanced instruction about radio repair, radio codes, and intermediate automotive mechanics. Another reporter ("Best Kind of High-School Training," 1942) agreed that high-school students should develop radio and automotive proficiency as well as the skills they would need for aircraft maintenance, machining, photography, map reading, and nursing.

Rather than modifying existing courses, some educators established entirely new wartime courses. Robinson (1943) provided the outline for a novel course that would help students understand democracy, the causes of the war, and reasons for supporting the war. The actual content of his course covered information about military personnel and aircraft, air raid defense, war production, and wartime conservation. In other cases, state legislators introduced bills that required special courses in physical conditioning and military drilling (Karelsen, 1942). Convinced that the optimal type of pre-induction training could vary according to the scholastic philosophy in each school, Sykes (1943) responded that the many competing approaches were worthwhile because they all advanced vital wartime goals.

Women

In a pamphlet about the impact of war, Ogburn (1943a), a professor of sociology, lamented that the war was "especially disturbing" to women, who had begun "living a much more active life beyond the confines of the home than ever before" (p. 19). Singling out bobbed hair and flapper-styled clothing as by-products of an earlier war, he identified the increased number of women wearing slacks as one early effect of the current war. He also observed a "great expansion" of women's activities, some of which were part of a growing feminist movement.

Ogburn was accurate in his observation that the war was changing style, fashion, and many deeper aspects of women's lives. Even though the armed services initially had aimed pre-induction programs at males, they eventually began to recruit females. Treadwell (1954) wrote that the Army, which had employed civilian female nurses during World War I, had not been able to fully integrate them into its military structure. Dissatisfied with this inefficient arrangement, it later established the *Women's Army Corps* (WAC). Morden (1990) explained the transition in World War II public attitudes that accompanied the decision to recruit women for military service.

> In early 1941, "Never!" was a typical reaction to the idea of women serving in the U.S. Army. The subject conjured up pictures of women wearing helmets, carrying rifles, and attacking an enemy in a war zone. But after the Japanese attack on Pearl Harbor, these ideas and images did seem somewhat less outrageous. . . . The crisis changed the nature of the questions about women in the Army: What could women do in the Army? Would they ever be in combat? What weapons would they fire? Would they be giving orders to men? How would the army, a traditional male society, accept women into its midst? (p. 3)

Some of these questions were specifically addressed within the marketing materials that appeared toward the end of the war. Green (1989), who wrote a book about her service as a World War II WAC, attached an advertisement that had appeared in a 1944 copy of the *Minneapolis Journal*. The ad contained pictures of WACs "recording the returns of wounded men," "receiving messages from combat planes," and "moving up to new posts behind enemy lines." The accompanying text praised the WAC for "her fresh, cool poise, her air of quite confidence . . . her gallantry and her spirit . . . her way of getting things done, quickly and without fuss" (Text from an ad that appeared in the *Minneapolis Journal* on August 24, 1944, reproduced by Green, 1989, p. 6).

The WAC was not the sole opportunity for women to serve in the armed services. Seeley (1992) noted that the Navy formed the *Women Accepted for Voluntary Emergency Service* (WAVES), and the Coast Guard Reserve created the SPAR, which was an acronym representing its motto, "Semper Paratis—Always Ready." Women pilots could join the *Women Airforce Service Pilots* (WASP) or the *Women's Auxiliary Ferrying Service* (WAFS). Some women joined the Marine Corps, which dispensed with acronyms and simply referred to them as Women Marines.

De Pauw (1998) hypothesized that some women did not wish to be associated with military units because they were worried that they would be seen as promiscuous. Others feared that they would be viewed as the recipients of gratuitous appointments. Sherrow (1996) wrote that military leaders also had fears about women joining their units. However, their fears were different from those of their female recruits. They were primarily concerned that a public backlash against the military would result after women were killed or taken as prisoners. Sherrow judged that these fears were exaggerated because only 16 female soldiers were killed and less than 100 imprisoned during the entire war.

Although the public displayed mixed emotions toward females serving as soldiers, it was less ambivalent about those who worked in the factories that had once been restricted to males. Even before the United States had entered the war, the U.S. Commissioner of Education wrote that "increasing employment needs will call shortly for the recruiting and training of" minority workers, including "many more women for defense jobs" (Studebaker, 1941, p. 164). The illustration in Figure 2.11, which was placed in an NEA booklet, was accompanied by an explanation that "age, parentage, sex, or inexperience no longer stand in the way of people seeking work" (National Education Association, 1943a, p. 62).

Newspaper advertisements emphasized women's increased access to jobs. Within her detailed analysis of the women working in wartime Alabama, Thomas (1987) included a 1943 newspaper ad that featured a soldier with a machine gun. The heading read "Women of Mobile—He's on the job . . . Are you?" The accompanying text contained information about the types of jobs and job-training opportunities that were available to women.

> We are building ships faster than they have ever been built before on the Gulf Coast. But we must employ many more workers if we are to reach peak production. Many of the new workers must be women. Jobs are open now for women who have finished training courses. If you have had the training you can be sent to the shipyards by the United States employment Service. If you haven't had the training and want to do your part in the war, you will be referred to a training course. (Text from a 1943 advertisement that appeared in the *Mobile Press Register*, reproduced by Thomas, 1987, p. 18)

58   Wartime Schools

FIGURE 2.11. Newspaper Advertisements Indicated Women's Increased Access to Wartime Jobs (*Consumer Education Study of the National Association of Secondary-School Principals*, "My Part in This War. Helping on the Home Front," copyright 1943.)

The text of this ad continued that "women can build ships, yet never see a shipyard" if they were willing to provide the materials and services that the shipyard workers required.

Numerous newspaper advertisements corroborated the public visibility of women employees. The unprecedented volume of reports about women's wartime service also substantiated the high public profile of this issue. The U.S. Office of Education (Moore & Zapoleon, 1943) published a 66-page annotated bibliography of materials about "wartime work for women and girls." The 540 citations in this bibliography comprised just those materials that had been published between 1940 and 1943. The authors explained that many other materials on this topic had been excluded because they had not been distributed nationally or placed in public libraries.

Some educators (National Education Association, 1943a) argued that the United States should follow the pattern set in Germany and Great Britain, where large numbers of women had been aggressively recruited for industrial work. Addressing the British defense industry's reliance on women, Higham (1942) wrote that "many thousands are making tools, fine instruments, parts of airplanes, tanks, guns, and ammunition" (p. 293). To introduce a report about opportunities in industry for American women, Rosenberg (1942) declared that "it does not require any argument" to demonstrate that "women have a much more vital role to play in national defense today than at any other similar period in our country's history" (p. 287). Rosenberg's point became quite clear as 300,000 females became employed in the wartime aircraft industry alone (Sherrow, 1996).

Rupp (1978) investigated the degree to which government-sponsored propaganda influenced the attitudes of women toward defense industry employment. Although she agreed that the government's sustained information campaign did help mobilize the women's workforce, she concluded that this propaganda campaign was less motivating than the opportunities for increased earnings.

The total number of women in the labor force grew by approximately 50 percent between 1940 and 1944 (Campbell, 1984; Winkler, 1986). At the peak of this trend, 18,000,000 female employees constituted 36 percent of the civilian workforce (Winkler, 1986). Although Gregory (1974) made a comparable estimate, he pointed out that most of them had been working before the war and therefore only several million additional women entered the workforce. However, Gregory did concede that an important change transpired when they assumed wartime responsibilities that formerly had been restricted to males.

Hartmann (1982) was struck by another critical aspect of the wartime workforce, namely that an unprecedented percentage of the female employees were mothers. Attempting to minimize the family disruption that followed when mothers accepted defense jobs, the War Manpower Commission had encouraged employers to hire only those women whose children were at least 14 years old ("War Production Training," 1942; "Policy on Recruitment," 1943). However, this adjuration was difficult to follow. Employers needed younger workers in addition to mature women; and they needed women with selective skills, irrespective of the ages of their children. To deal with this problem, Fredericksen (1943) suggested that working women leave their children with volunteers, foster families, or specially designated childcare homemakers. Because such plans were not widely implemented, the success of government and industrial initiatives to increase the number of women defense workers depended on the availability of daycare.

A postwar reporter ("Postwar Planning," 1946) observed that most parents had never used nursery or daycare programs prior to World War II. Another reporter (United States Office of Education, 1945) noted that many of these programs had been initiated because of the perception that "children growing up in war years are deprived of many things essential for a happy childhood." This writer added that virtually all nursery programs, including those that had been established before the war, had been adapted for wartime conditions. For example, their hours of operation were expanded to include mornings, evenings, weekends, and even holidays.

Despite its novelty, daycare quickly became a success. This was indicated by several developments within the federal government. A national office was established to promote and provide information about daycare (National Education Association, 1943c). The federal government also published materials about daycare, including a series of leaflets entitled "School Children and the War." Each of these leaflets, which included a cover picture with a group of well-dressed, robust, and smiling youngsters, underscored the need for facilities in which children would be safe and loved. The initial leaflet acknowledged that each mother "cannot work efficiently in America's all-out production of war equipment when she is worried about the well-being of her children" (Federal Security Agency, 1943, p. 1). Succeeding leaflets reviewed topics such as all-day childcare centers, nurseries, lunch programs, and recreation at childcare centers. This series also included information for administrators and caregivers about specialized topics such as reducing juvenile delinquency, caring for children with special emotional needs, and training high-school students as staff for childcare facilities.

Acknowledging that the federal government was placing pressure upon schools to support daycare, one reporter ("All-Day School," 1942) observed approvingly that this federal intervention would simultaneously ensure the safety of children and the productivity of women workers. Schools were viewed as particularly suitable sites for nurseries and childcare programs because of their specialized personnel and facilities. They were also attractive because of opportunities to persuade teachers to extend their workdays and become wartime caregivers. The workdays of teachers could be lengthened "before school for an hour or so, after school until 5 or 6" as well as "on Saturdays and holidays" ("Extended School Services," 1942).

The availability of training programs for women was a key indicator of the importance assigned to their wartime contributions. A reporter ("Information for Women," 1942) who was writing after the first months of American involvement in the war was able to list agencies that already had begun to provide information to women about training programs. This training led to employment in factories, the Women's Army Auxiliary Corps, or the government. It also prepared workers for nursing, engineering, science, or management. Because girls between the ages of 14 and 19 constituted more than 17 percent of the additional wartime women workers who were being recruited, special training programs were needed for them (Amidon, 1942; Anderson, 1981). Schneider (1942) reported that 50,000 girls and young women were enrolled during 1942 in "regular federally reimbursed industrial and trade classes." Another 200,000 were trained that year by the National Youth Administration to be machine operators, metal workers, mechanics, radio operators, or electricians.

African Americans

The *Annals of the American Academy of Political and Social Sciences* published a 1942 series of reports about racial prejudice. The editors (Shallow & Young, 1942) highlighted the injustices that numerous ethnic and racial groups were sustaining "at the hands of the old-American white majority." The marginalized groups included Latin Americans (Crasford, 1942), Italian Americans (Corsi, 1942), German Americans (Wittke, 1942), Puerto Ricans (Pattee, 1942), Filipinos (Kirk, 1942), American Indians (Collier, 1942), Jews (Kallen, 1942a) and Japanese Americans (Warren, 1942; Miyamoto, 1942). Although reports about many groups were featured in this series, the largest number of reports (H. M. Bond, 1942; Hastie, 1942; C. S. Johnson, 1942, Weaver, 1942; White, 1942b) contrasted the heroic wartime service that African Americans were providing with the abusive treatment they were receiving.

Like women, African Americans had been categorically excluded from many prewartime jobs. A 1942 survey of the attitudes of 10,000,000 high-school students indicated the degree of prejudice against them. In a *Life* magazine article about this survey ("18-Year-Old," 1942), the author noted that 31 percent of the respondents disagreed with the statement that "co-workers of any color, race or religion are acceptable." The fact that the author interpreted these frightening results as an indication that "youth is remarkably free from prejudice" and "far ahead of its elders" reflects the severe racial prejudice of this era.

A resolution by the American Federal of Teachers ("High-School Students and the Manpower Shortage," 1943) urged employers to stop raiding the high schools for laborers and rely instead on underemployed groups, "especially the Negroes." An article (Britt, 1942) that appeared five months after Pearl Harbor included a photograph of three young African Americans who had been trained in a federal program to perform defense work. However, the caption indicated that "many young Negroes remain in the [training] shop" because of a "lack of job openings" for which they were racially eligible.

Granger (1942), the executive secretary of the National Urban League, argued that "rigid anti-Negro policies" in industry had created barriers that were preventing African Americans from securing factory jobs. Even the federal training programs had been only somewhat helpful because "most of these opportunities are closed to Negroes." Despite his frustration, Granger noted that the number of African Americans employed in shipyards had doubled during the five-month period after Pearl Harbor. He thought that these and other data were signs of "important progress" in the struggle for racial equality. Figure 2.12, which was included with Granger's article, showed African American and white workers laboring together at an industrial forge.

Reminiscing about her experiences as an African American in the WAC, Earley (1989) reported that she had been subjected to systematic discrimination, even

FIGURE 2.12. This 1942 Depiction of an African American and White Worker Revealed Changing Racial Attitudes

though she was a commissioned officer. For example, she and other African Americans were racially segregated and allowed to pick up their military clothing only after the other soldiers had been equipped. White (1942a), the executive secretary of the National Association for Advancement of Colored People, also wrote candidly about the pervasive discrimination against African Americans in the armed services.

Although the racial discrimination that White detected may have been patent, he did find some evidence of wartime social progress. For example, he noted that the Army exhibited less racism than the Navy when considering African Americans for appointments as officers. He also applauded national magazines for publishing articles opposing racial discrimination. Within a landmark book entitled *What the Negro Wants* (Logan, 1944), Wilkerson wrote a chapter describing the social progress that African Americans had made. He pointed out that "the Jim Crow cafeterias in federal buildings in the nation's capital are being eliminated" and that "steps are taken toward the entrance of Negro players into organized baseball" (Wilkerson, 1944, pp. 204–205). However, he described with special pride the advancements that African Americans had made in the armed services.

> A black man holds the post of Brigadier-General. Black men and white—in the good state of Georgia, mind you—pursue *together* their studies for officer's training on a basis of complete equality. Negro heroes are driving tanks and manning the great guns which spell disaster for our enemies. Negro pursuit flyers are giving a brilliant performance in the air, and other black men are now being trained as bombardiers. The Army's laggard Judge Advocate has relaxed, at long last, the traditional bans against Negro lawyers. In the United States Merchant Marine, white and Negro crews sail their Liberty Ships through submarine-infested seas under the command of Negro captains. Even though with reluctance and ill-grace, the Secretary of Navy has been forced not only to admit black men into the ranks of fighting seamen, but also to train them as officers. (p. 205).

Professional organizations published books and pamphlets to help eliminate racial stereotypes. Writing a pamphlet for an educational institute devoted to social policy, two anthropologists at Columbia University (Benedict & Weltfish, 1943) pointed out that the blood of African Americans was indistinguishable from that of white persons. They also noted that educated African Americans in northern cities scored higher on intelligence tests than poor southern whites. In another effort to reverse racial stereotypes, the NEA (Caliver, 1944) published an annotated bibliography of 186 articles, books, films, and other types of information that could be used as "instructional material on Negroes."

Publications by the federal government chronicled and promoted the changing attitudes toward African Americans. In a 1944 issues of the government-published *Education for Victory*, an article ("Schools-at-War," 1944) listed six different sets of free posters teachers could request for their classrooms. One category was identified in a matter-of-fact manner as "Negro posters." Other articles ("Army Experience," 1945; "Office of Education Services," 1944) gave information about special training programs available to African Americans. Caliver (1944) wrote a government-published pamphlet about *Education of Teachers for Improving Majority-Minority Relationships*. A year later, he wrote an Office of Education monograph (Caliver, 1945) that gave detailed information about training programs for African Americans. Caliver emphasized that the innovative practices that had been started during the war were "worth salvaging" for the postwar era.

Persons with Disabilities

During the Depression, able and trained workers had failed to find work. This situation changed as industrial production increased. Although industry and the armed forces competed with each other for recruits, national conscription gave a decisive advantage to the armed forces. Unable to find an adequate supply of personnel, ingenious employers searched for workers among those applicants they had once dismissed.

Unlike the publicized efforts to recruit women and African Americans, those directed at other groups were not written about extensively. Nonetheless, examples were discernible. Bailey (1977) pointed out that airplane manufacturers recruited little people to work within the cramped spaces of bombers on assembly lines. A wartime report from the National Education Association (1943c) noted that some industrialists were relying increasingly on workers with physical disabilities. The author added that many of these workers were supported through federally subsidized vocational rehabilitation programs.

The types of disabilities that had formerly excluded workers from employment were not solely physical. The Educational Policies Commission (1942a) judged that school personnel could expand the pool of work applicants and armed service recruits if they would correct the "educational deficiencies" of the many individuals who were being rejected. The remedial schoolwork that was needed would be managed "under the most skillful educational leadership that can be mustered." Recognizing that some of the persons with learning problems were immigrants who did not speak English and who had not become American citizens, the Commission proposed that instruction about English and American government supplement academic instruction.

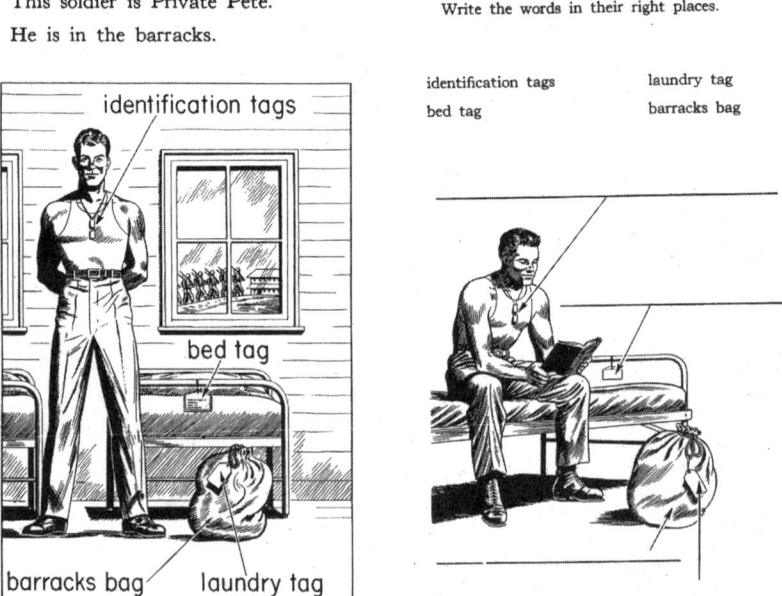

FIGURE 2.13. Material from an Army Literacy Program for "Academically Retarded Men"

Special Materials and Programs 65

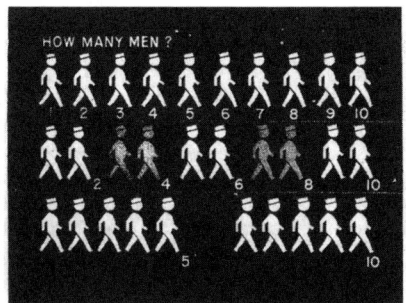 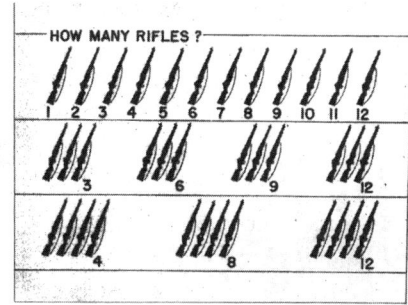

FIGURE 2.14. Material from an Army Mathematics Program for "Academically Retarded Men"

The United States Office of Civilian Defense (1943) published a manual that encouraged "an intensive program of training" for the mentally retarded during wartime. It estimated that every community had workers with mental disabilities who could perform "routine tasks" in agriculture and industry. Many of the persons of "border-line" intelligence could even be found "among young people at school." The authors wrote that this training was appropriate because "there has been no time in the history of the Nation when manpower and womanpower were so urgently needed" (p. 4). They pointed out that the employment of laborers with disabilities could have multiple benefits because it would address immediate labor problems and release "able-bodied men" for the armed services.

In a booklet about *Education in the Armed Service* (National Education Association, 1944a), the authors indicated that the army was training "educationally retarded men" to be soldiers. It had instituted programs that were academic as well as military, that involved 18 hours of instruction each day, and that could last for four months. These programs were designed to raise participants to the scholastic level of fourth-grade students. If they did not show a reasonable sign of improvement after 12 weeks, individuals would be discharged from the army. Some of the materials used in these programs are illustrated in Figure 2.13 and Figure 2.14.

Whitmer (1943) highlighted valuable practices that had emerged in the wartime schools and that needed to be sustained during the postwar period. One of these was instruction of the "pupil of low intelligence or physical disability." Whitmer concluded that students with disabilities who were taught to be academically and vocationally successful would stay in school and then go on to make contributions to either the armed services or industry.

Whitmer was concerned about the fate of marginally qualified war workers during that inevitable period in which they could no longer compete effectively for their current jobs. Concerned about this problem, educators such as Bowen (1943) and Fitzpatrick (1944) argued that displaced postwar workers should have access to the same career counseling, training, and placement services as returning veterans.

Noting that the field of "rehabilitation education" had been established to aid the returning World War I veterans, Gwynn (1943) predicted that similar programs would follow the Second World War.

Rural Youths

The government and industry inevitably turned to rural youths to help with the extraordinary wartime demands. Marsh (1942) noted that "in a number of states the public schools have cooperated with the state employment services in registering pupils for farm work" (p. 26). He concluded that "there seems to be no other choice than to take young people out of school for part of the year at least."

The possibility that rural youths would serve as workers became greater after the 1940 census revealed that a majority of persons under 16 lived in rural areas. Aware of these demographics, the Educational Policies Commission (1942a) encouraged special programs that would expand the involvement of high-school students in rural farming. Realizing that 4,000,000 supplementary workers were needed to plant, cultivate, and harvest the 1944 crops, Boord (1944) estimated that only 1,000,000 would be women. To solve this labor shortage, he recommended the hiring of 1,000,000 "youngsters who normally do not do farm work."

Lenroot (1942) warned that "increased pressure for children to help in farm work at the expense of their educational opportunity began in 1940, and this pressure has been growing monthly" (pp. 148–149). She observed that "children work under conditions entirely different from the healthful outdoor life of many farm boys and girls a generation ago." Characterizing rural farms as "factories in the field," she was distressed that "young children work from dawn to dark in the fields with their parents" and that "many are deprived of education and are subject to most unfavorable living and working conditions."

Two years later, Magee (1944) reported that many American children were still engaged in "premature work." As a demonstration of the size of the group, she noted that the work certificates issued to 14-year-old and 15-year-old children had increased by 156 percent from 1940 to 1943. Writing that same year, Rife (1944) was alarmed by those employers who were using "the camouflage of patriotism" to recruit workers who were 14 years old or younger.

Worried that the extensive use of adolescents and children on rural farms was leading to abuses, the U.S. Department of Labor developed policies to govern their hiring and employment. One of these guidelines stipulated that children under 14 "should not be employed in agriculture outside the home farm except when it has been established that unforeseen and extraordinary public emergencies exist" ("Safeguards for Wartime Recruitment," 1942, p. 14). This report added that employers should make every effort to hire children who were 16 years old before they recruited youngsters of 14 or 15. In those instances where young children were employed, their academic programs were to be adjusted so that they could stay in school. A later report (Groves & Groves, 1944) warned that the children working on wartime farms needed to be protected from sexual as well as physical exploitation.

As the end to the war became apparent, the federal Office of Education pledged to continue and extend its agricultural education programs. As one would expect, these programs were especially popular in rural areas. The February 3, 1945, issue of *Education for Victory* contained statements from the "Charter of Education for Rural Children." The result of a White House conference, this charter specified that "every rural child has the right to an educational program that bridges the gap between home and school, and between school and adult life." Six months earlier, a report ("Vocational Education," 1944) in this same journal had described a special program that exemplified one of these rural educational "bridges."

Student Workers

Unable to find sufficient adult laborers, the managers of factories and farms turned to students. The benefits of student workers for the industrialists and farmers were obvious. However, the advantages for the youths themselves were not as clear. This uncertainty was evident in a report about children who were dropping out of school for "reasons not legitimately connected with the war effort" ("Wartime Adjustments," 1944, p. 2). These dropouts had caused "labor standards to be lowered or violated" and "juvenile delinquency to increase at an alarming rate." The report concluded that "all national authorities are agreed that every effort must be made to persuade the largest number of children possible to continue their school work" (p. 2). Flexible scheduling turned out to be one of the most effective strategies for keeping child workers in school.

One reporter ("Wartime Counseling," 1943) noted that the tendency to raid schools for child workers, although a serious problem, was not "incurable." This author suggested that those school personnel who managed student work programs should consider flexible scheduling as well as "splitting up a job between two or three pupils, all of whom go to school, instead of giving one job to one boy or girl who must quit school entirely in order to take it" (p. 20). A year later, Joyal and Carr (1944) judged that the "school as work experience" programs were so successful that "hundreds, if not thousands" of schools were participating. They predicted confidently that these initiatives would continue after the war. Although such programs had always impressed them as "sound in theory," they judged that the war had "established them in practice."

Flexible scheduling was seen as particularly effective for retaining students and filling critical war jobs. After describing different models of flexible scheduling, Jessen (1944a) concluded that all of them were helping the nation, the schools, and the students themselves. In a subsequent review (Jessen, 1945), he revealed the enormous size of these programs when he observed that more than one-third of Chicago's high-school students were working, that 36,000 Philadelphia students were employed, and that Los Angeles students were completing more than 1,000,000 hours of labor each week.

Another reporter ("Problems of School Administrators," 1943) gave examples of school districts that had initiated six-day school weeks during the winter so that the students could be released later for the planting and harvesting seasons. This author did acknowledge that many educators were hesitant to endorse such procedures because of the strain they placed on both the pupils and their teachers. However, the author retorted that "in this emergency, all must keep in mind that while health must be protected, inconvenience and special effort even to the limits of endurance may be the price which all must pay" (p. 8). The guidelines (Indiana Department of Public Instruction, 1943) for Indiana's High School Victory Corps, which were based on a different strategy, allowed children to "participate actively" as workers, provided that career counselors carefully monitored their aptitudes, interests, and training.

High-school administrators cooperated with businesses to ensure a steady flow of student workers. Forbes (1942) indicated that his industrial plants would have been unable to meet their 1941 defense production goals had it not been for high-school apprentices. Even though the National Youth Administration had been designed to help out-of-school youths, this organization arranged industrial apprenticeships under the auspices of the public schools as well as the unions and employers (National Education Association, 1943c).

The author of an interesting report ("Training Schools," 1943) indicated that many incarcerated juvenile delinquents were engaged in relatively unproductive activities. This author recommended that reform school administrators modify their programs so that they were more like those in public high schools. For example, teenagers could work in the defense industries rather than quarry rocks. This reporter noted that some reform school administrators were paroling inmates if they would join the armed services.

CHAPTER 3

Influencing Educators' Attitudes

*The National Education Association is serving America at war
with every resource at its command.*
—ASHBY, 1942

Various groups found ways to advise educators about the war and simultaneously improve their own interests. For example, the leaders of educational organizations advanced national loyalty while trying to procure more members, higher teachers' salaries, and larger federal appropriations for education. Government officials took advantage of propaganda strategies to change the public's attitudes toward political as well as wartime issues. Businesspersons used comparable strategies to promote the war and their own fortunes.

Professional Educational Organizations

Prior to America's entry into World War II, some professional educational organizations had provided forums for antiwar rhetoric. For example, NEA editorialists had demonstrated their prewar reluctance to participation in the war. One editorial written nine months before Pearl Harbor had encouraged "loyalty to country" while simultaneously lamenting any initiative that would "underwrite the British empire with its class system at home and its exploitation of weaker peoples abroad and its domination by the London bankers" (Morgan, 1941, p. 65).

Several months before Pearl Harbor, the NEA had established the Commission on the Defense of Democracy thru Education. The president of the NEA wrote that this commission was intended to ensure that the schools did not lose additional federal funding to national defense programs. Furthermore, the Commission was designed to change negative views about "the efficiency of the public schools and of the loyalty of the teaching profession" (DuShane, 1941, p. 162). It was to accomplish this goal through an aggressive effort "to catalog the various groups opposing education, to investigate the sources of their funds, and to make résumés of their activities available to local and state teachers organizations" (p. 162). In an article that it published less than a month before Pearl Harbor, the commission reminded critics that it represented 900,000 NEA members, who were committed to preventing "unjustly attacked" teachers from becoming victims of "the destructive effects of the critical period which the nation is now entering" (National Commission for the Defense of Democracy thru Education, 1941, p. 247).

Several months after Pearl Harbor, Ashby (1942) tried to depict the NEA as a politically moderate organization that was "serving America at war with every resource at its command" (p. 36). He also attempted to soften the political image of the Commission on the Defense of Democracy thru Education, which he defined as a group concerned "with national issues and movements inimical to education" (p. 36). Although he conceded that it had focused its attention on the inadequacy of educators' salaries, he thought the commission had done this to increase the supply of teachers and thereby prepare America for war.

Organizations Support the War

Although not all members of professional organizations endorsed the war, some did so enthusiastically. A portion of this support could be attributed to the armed services, which had begun to communicate and cooperate with the educational organizations before the war. As an example, members of the American Council on Education (1940a) explained that they did not wish to repeat an earlier experience, when "the need for definite preliminary planning in event of war was effectively demonstrated by its very absence prior to and during the early months of the last World War" (p. 8). The Council proposed that President Roosevelt formally recognize a national defense committee. This committee, which had already begun to meet, included members from the armed services, the government, and 12 professional educational organizations. The educational organizations included the American Association of School Administrators, the American Vocational Association, the National Association of Secondary School Principals, and the National Education Association.

In an NEA journal that had a larger circulation than any other educational serial, the editors wrote that their organization, even though it had condemned "unwarranted optimism and demoralizing pessimism," believed that it was "the duty of the schools, as it is of all agencies, institutions, groups, and individuals, to make an all-out effort to win the war" ("Education and the War," 1942, p. 191). This doubly qualified remark was one of the closest statements of support for World War II that the NEA put forth.

The NEA's Educational Policies Commission (EPC) developed a series of policy statements before America's entry into the war (1937a; 1937b; 1938a; 1938b; 1939a; 1939b; 1940a; 1940b; 1941a; 1941b; 1941c) and afterwards (1942a; 1942b; 1943a; 1943b; 1943c). However, in the foreword to a post–Pearl Harbor publication, the Commission indicated that, because "the events of December 7–9 marked a turning point in American history," winning the war became "the most critically important matter with which it has been concerned" (Educational Policies Commission, 1941a, p. 1). Echoing the rhetoric of its parent organization, the EPC transformed its onetime opposition into cautious espousal. This change was highlighted when Morgan (1942a) indicated that the post–Pearl Harbor Educational Policies Commission assigned "immediate priority" to school activities that would prepare soldiers, train industrial workers, produce war goods, conserve resources, raise funds, promote democracy, inform students about the war's progress, maintain school morale, and bolster community spirit.

In addition to issuing policy statements, the EPC developed materials for classroom teachers. In the February 1942 issue of the *Journal of National Education Association*, the editors used patriotic allusions from the American Revolution to market their pamphlets. They also published a directory ("Wartime Teaching Aids," 1942) of the wartime teaching materials that they were developing. During the second year of the war, the NEA published its 64-page *Wartime Handbook for Education*, which was designed to skim the "cream" from the many other guides to wartime materials ("Wartime Services," 1943).

The Department of Elementary School Principals, which was affiliated with the NEA, made special wartime appeals to its members. As an example, the cover photograph for the October 1942 issue of *National Elementary Principal* displayed a young boy in a sailor uniform who had filled his wagon with discarded toys. The editors indicated that this photograph, which had been supplied by the Treasury Department, was intended to remind "school folks to clear your district of all available scrap." They added emotionally that "the elementary schools of this nation have never failed to help in an emergency" and "let's not fail now."

Some of the smaller professional organizations also displayed support for the war. The president of the extremely liberal Progressive Education Association warned his members that they risked becoming "an innocuous and vaguely helpful remnant of a once-powerful organization" if they did not accept "the great responsibilities that confront us in winning the war" (Washburne, 1942, p. 355). Childs (1942a) was another veteran member of the Progressive Education Association who was well aware that most of the liberal constituents had vocally opposed America's entry into the war. Although he conceded that the members were "not inclined to regard this war as a romantic adventure or an altruistic crusade," he adjured them to support the war "because we realize that our way of life would have no future in a world subordinated to the tyranny of the Hitler regime" (p. 142). In a similarly calculated fashion, the editors of *Progressive Education* inserted a declaration into the November 1942 issue about the need to cooperate with the National Resources Planning Board, which had asked the editors to distribute a wartime poster. Although they complied with this request, the editors assured subscribers that the poster was only "one of many documents" that teachers might use when studying "war and peace aims" and the reconstruction that would follow the war.

A spirit of wartime support was discernible in some of the educational organizations that represented teachers in specialty areas such as physical education, science, mathematics, and vocational education. The personnel in these organizations circulated wartime instructional materials, wrote supportive editorials within their periodicals, and made positive presentations at conferences.

Organizations Retain Their Self-Interests

New York's commissioner of education stated with pride that organized education had "acquitted itself well" during the war and that "never before has education stood higher in public esteem" (Austin, 1944, p. 12). In the minds of many critics, his assessment was too flattering. A year earlier, the chairman of the NEA War and Peace Fund Committee had advised teachers that they should be more attentive to their own self-interest. He reminded them that "our profession must again meet the challenge presented by war conditions" (Strayer, 1943, p. 187). He used the adverb "again" because he judged that World War I had been a period when teachers, schools, and professional education associations had made great progress. Despite the pressing demands of the war, teachers' salaries had increased, teacher preparation had improved, high-school enrollments had escalated, and the curriculum had been individualized. He insisted that all of these changes were "due in no small measure to the activity of the NEA."

The preceding remarks typified the professional writing that peppered the *Journal of the National Education Association*. Although the wartime remarks from leaders in this organization addressed the need for patriotism, they simultaneously echoed their association's prewar professional motifs. In a publication entitled *My Part in This War: Helping on the Home Front* (National Education Association, 1943a) the editors included a picture of German adolescents wearing Nazi regalia. The accompanying caption explained that "in Fascist schools, instruction is stern and rigid" and that "one must ask no questions, raise no doubts." This argument was designed to denigrate Nazis as well as those American conservatives who wanted teachers to convey uniform patriotic messages. The NEA editors also underscored the shortcomings in America's economic, social, and political systems. For example, the same book contained a photograph of migrant workers in a squalid tent. The caption explained that "workers can not do their best for the country when they must live in a home like this" (p. 21).

Writing before the war, the archliberal George Counts (1938) had adjured educational organizations to prepare for "the rising battle for democracy in America." One way to influence this battle was to ensure that each teacher was "more than a technician, more than a skilful practitioner of the art of pedagogy" (p. 346). To achieve this goal, teacher preparation programs were to "go beyond the techniques of the classroom and place large emphasis on the social, cultural, and philosophical foundations of education." Counts then added that "more important than the mode of training are the conditions under which the teacher lives and works." The teachers' organizations were charged with enlarging "the opportunities and responsibilities of the calling" because this would in turn "enlarge the intellectual and moral stature of the individual teacher."

If educational organizations had the impression that they were losing the ground they had gained prior to the war, this was a viewpoint shared by other labor groups. Anderson and Rogg (1942) noted that, under a banner of total war and the "extraordinary responsibilities" that this entailed, the federal government had increased its authority over both labor and industry. Responding to "complaints that unions are using the war emergency to strengthen their organizations," the government had placed unprecedented restrictions upon union activities. Union officers, who were fearful that this disturbing trend would continue, had reacted by intensifying their efforts to recruit new members.

Morgan (1943), the editor of the major NEA journal, may have exhibited some of the self-serving reactions to which Anderson and Rogg had alluded. Morgan indicated that the NEA could best meet its war goals if every teacher joined the national organization and became active in one of its local chapters. She set a target for recruiting 330,000 new members in 1943. A year earlier, she had warned that the nation was "starting down the same path" that it had followed during World War I, even though this had resulted in abuses "so flagrant that thousands of schools were closed" (Morgan, 1942b, p. 1). Continuing this theme after the war, she wrote that local chapters of the NEA could help to ensure peace by assiduously collecting the dues that the organization needed to promote its national agenda (Morgan, 1946a).

Recruiting new members and expanding organizational funding were not the only self-serving prewar themes that reemerged in the NEA's wartime publications. For example, Kilpatrick (1943) warned that teachers were being hindered by "rigid" wartime curricula and by "textbooks and materials unfit for any adequate openminded study" (p. 127). One editorial, which reminded members that the Association supported "Education for Victory" as the theme for American Education Week, also reminded them that it was concerned about low salaries "at a time when far higher salaries are being paid for almost ever other type of work and when the increase in the cost of living has so far outrun teachers' salaries" ("Education for Victory," 1943, p. 176). Ashby (1944) instructed NEA members that it was their "vital task" to help the public understand that teaching was a legitimate war service that required priority funding. Another editorialist ("NEA fights," 1943) chided those teachers who failed to give the NEA the credit it deserved for increasing teacher salaries and preserving tenure.

The postwar NEA editors removed all restraints on authors who supported politically liberal programs. For example, just a year after the war had ended, Morgan (1946b) underscored similarities between circumstances in post–World War II United States and those in post–World War I Italy, Germany, and Japan. Concerned about "the beginnings of the same pattern in America," she warned that small groups "with too much power" dominated industry and labor, that control of mass communication had been centralized, and that "big industry is supporting moves for an enormous military machine" (p. 111). The smaller Progressive Education Association had published comparable admonitions during the war. For example, a member of the Progressive Education Association's board of directors had urged teachers to "salvage what remains of free public education" by reversing the "failure to provide for and to protect teacher welfare" (Butler, 1944, p. 139).

Although professional associations offered advice, some of their constituents questioned the political motives of their leaders. Writing in the yearbook of the John Dewey Society, the politically liberal Axtelle (1940) did not conceal his own skepticism toward the power these leaders were attempting to wield. He wrote that the administrators who dominated the associations "generally maintained such autocratic relations with their staff that both they and their staffs look upon independent professional organizations as disloyal if not subversive" (p. 402). Axtelle advised teachers to demonstrate their self-determination by affiliating themselves with labor unions, which he thought were based upon more respectful, worker-centered philosophies.

Propaganda

The information from professional education associations was eclipsed by the government's bounteous wartime propaganda. Writing in 1948, Linebarger (1972) explained that propaganda was a form of psychological warfare designed "to win military gains without military force" (p. 37). He counseled his readers that the benefits of propaganda, "though incalculable, can be overwhelming," and that their failure, "though undetectable, can be mortal" (p. 1). Even though he saw propaganda as a military technique intended for the residents of enemy countries, Linebarger thought it could be directed at a "neutral or friendly foreign group for a specific strategic or tactical purpose" (p. 39). Linebarger admitted that the United States had actually developed wartime propaganda campaigns for allies, friends, and its own citizens. Although he thought that the domestic propaganda had been largely innocuous, he did note in passing that several campaigns had been tailored around caustic themes such as "slap a Jap" and "fight fascism at home" (p. 39).

Linebarger was not the only citizen who seemed embarrassed to admit that propaganda was a political tool that the United States government had employed on the home front. This was undoubtedly because the government had censured those countries that had relied on domestic propaganda. In his book on *Propaganda and Dictatorship,* Childs (1936) reinforced this impression. He explained patiently that "in a dictatorship, there prevails the tacit, if not the explicit assumption, that, inasmuch as truth cannot be discovered in its final and complete form, it is better for the masses, present and to come, to give up the futile and wasteful search, and accept a single and unified leadership" (p. 5). He contrasted this with the dissemination of information in a democracy, where one could find "a sort of protestant unwillingness to give up the personal search for truth, and complacently accept official edicts in matters of opinion." Childs added that "the democratic adherent prefers a variety of creeds and propagandas from which to make his own selection." Based on these convictions, Child limited his examples of propaganda to cases in which foreign governments had employed it. When Margolin (1946) later wrote his history of psychological warfare, he did document the use of propaganda by the United States. However, he described just those American efforts that had been aimed at foreigners. Believing that even these needed to be justified, he lectured critics that "thousands of American fighting men are alive today, thanks to little pieces of paper and words and ideas penetrating into the heart of enemy territory" (p. 101).

Not all citizens were embarrassed because their country had used propaganda. Lasswell (1951) asserted unabashedly that psychological warfare was actually a political activity, that it was appropriate even in times of peace, and that it "includes operations in relation to allies, neutrals and the home audience" (pp. 265-266). In the introduction to the book in which Lasswell had made the preceding remarks, Lerner (1951) noted that the British had historically referred to propaganda as an instance of political rather than psychological warfare. He added that the resistance of Americans to this type of characterization was "perhaps another illustration of that pervasive American antipathy to theory and generality which often misleads us into preferences for whatever can be made to seem technical and 'empirical'" (p. xiii). Also underscoring the differences between the American and British attitudes toward propaganda, Balfour (1979) contrasted the secrecy of America's wartime leaders with the relatively open manner of British officials.

Writing before World War II about changes in the prevailing methods of communication, Tomlinson (1940) had noted that political propaganda was becoming progressively more difficult to resist. Although he acknowledged that propaganda and commercial advertising employed the same strategies, he wrote eloquently that propaganda appealed to the "mysterious deeps" that were "stirred by cunning words dropped into the soul, words that do not show their origin and purpose as candidly as the trademark of a cosmetic" (p. 63). Also recognizing its immense power, White (1940) noted that propaganda, which once had been designed to deprive persons of relevant information, had been transformed into an insidious technique to suppress "the ability to discriminate between facts or the feeling of a need to do so" (p. 92).

Underscoring the potency of anti-American propaganda, Bernays (1940) warned that the United States was in danger because "at this very moment attempts directed, financed, or encouraged from Europe, Asia, and even from within our borders are being made to destroy our national unity and morale, to create and enlarge differences among us which might make for confusion, panic, and collapse, if we were attacked by an enemy" (p. vii). A year later, Williams (1941) wrote at length about the misinformation circulated by the American Destiny Party, which "was patterned after Hitler's National Socialist Workers Party" and which "had won a following not only among New York Germans, already trained in the Nazi salute by the German-American Bund, but among native born Americans as well" (p. 5). He calculated that the American Destiny Party was only one of "800 groups, societies, organizations, and political parties [that] are promoting Nazi, Fascist, and Communist propaganda in America" (p. 75). A photograph of a capacity crowd at Madison Square Garden was captioned, "The Nazis Lure 25,000 New Yorkers Toward the Robot State" (p. 20). In the unlikely event that his readers did not fully appreciate this portentous scene, he placed it next to one showing "45,000 robots" parading before Hitler at a Nuremberg rally. In the preface to this book, the U.S. Commissioner of Education alerted readers that they should "be prepared to defend their own heads and hearts from the barrage of totalitarian propaganda that has been loosed upon the world" (p. 2).

Cromwell (1941) urged Americans to scrutinize "all the facts and figures available" in order to dissolve the confusion that Nazi propaganda had created. In a book entitled *Axis America: Hitler Plans Our Future*, Strausz-Hupé (1941) provided additional evidence of the danger from Fascist propaganda. He pointed out that France, which had thought itself to be "secure behind the Maginot Line and one of the finest armies in the world," had discovered too late that "forces other than military had already sapped the vitality without which nations cease to be" (ix). Due to Nazi propaganda, "France had already been defeated before a single tank or dive bomber crossed her frontiers." From a sympathetic perspective, Williams (1941) opined that "Nazism in its propaganda, as in its military science, has developed, above all, the technique of infiltration" (p. 44). Using a simile with multiple embeddings, Williams extended this insight to the fall of France.

> Just as in the Battle of France the German mechanized columns nosed their way along the French defensive lines, testing here, testing there, until a point of weakness was found and then concentrated all their force in breaking through the line at that point, to spread out fanwise immediately a break through had been accomplished with the object of creating dismay, disorganization and disunity behind enemy lines, so German propaganda feels its way along the social and political structure of democracy, seeking a weak point here, a weak point there, through which it may be able to break through on identically the same errand. (p. 44)

Carlson (1943), who had investigated domestic Fascists during the early 1940s, subtitled his book *My Four Years in the Nazi Underworld of America—The Amazing Revelation of How Axis Agents and Our Enemies within Are Now Plotting to Destroy the United States*. As with other contemporaries who were conducting exposés of Fascist propaganda, Carlson intended this book to be "a warning to America of those factors which have led to the development of a nativist, nationalist, American Nazi or American Fascist movement, which, like a spearhead, is pointed to stab at Democracy" (p. 9). In just the short period between June and August 1943, this popular volume went through seven printings. On the page facing the table of contents, Carlson wrote about himself in the third person that "as investigator of subversive activity, the author joined or became affiliated with many self-styled 'patriotic' groups, some of which are listed below." The first 10 organizations in a list of more than 30 were the American National-Socialist Party, the German American Bund, the Christian Front, the Ultra-American, the Nationalist Party, the American Nationalist Party, American Women against Communism, the Gray Shirts, the America First Committee, and the No Foreign War Committee. Carlson warned that the members of these organization included not only "foreign agents" but also "many otherwise fine Americans" who had been duped into "propagating the lies and the 'party line' originally advanced by Hitler's agents and doing it sincerely in what they believed to be good Americanism" (p. 9).

Kris and Speier (1944) began their analysis of German radio propaganda with chilling observations about the objectives of the Nazis' information campaigns. They noted that "a ruthless and powerful man would be foolish if he killed opponents he could use for his own purposes." Having recognized the wisdom of this premise, the Nazis had decided that "words may achieve what bullets do not accomplish, because words do not kill" (p. 3). Although the Nazis committed innumerable murders, they did this in a calculated fashion, combining their killings with propaganda in ways that would "frighten others, equally powerless, into yielding in order to keep alive." In a book that he published in 1942, Bernard (1972) shared a similar view about the unethical use of propaganda by Germany and the Axis powers. Although he was heartened that citizens around the world were exhibiting "a great popular uprising against war," he cautioned that "this trend may not continue, for we have learned from European experience of the generation now closing that a people can be made war-minded almost without significant exception by the employment of skillful and persistent propaganda to that effect and by a close censorship of contrary ideas and ideals" (p. 6).

American Propaganda

Although they may have judged that the use of propaganda by its World War II enemies was pernicious, America's government officials did not hesitate to employ it. This decision replicated the one they had made during World War I, the era when countries recognized that propaganda could be an invaluable military device with which to control morale (Fraser, 1957; Mock & Larson, 1939; Taylor, 1983). Although he documented the use of propaganda during earlier conflicts, Fraser (1957) judged that World War I transformed it from a somewhat spurious art into a systematic science. This new status was accompanied by the establishment of wartime agencies to monitor, coordinate, and execute national propaganda campaigns. Fraser assessed that the propaganda efforts of World War I were part of a discipline that was still in a rudimentary stage of development. By the Second World War, the allied nations clearly had become much more sophisticated. Their sophistication was evident when they established propaganda agencies to disseminate common messages between their countries as well as within them.

A significant portion of the propaganda that the United States developed was spread abroad (Krugler, 2000; Shulman, 1990; Sorensen, 1968; Spykman, 1942). Although not abundant, testimonials from the American propagandists of World War II provided insights about their own and their peers' attitudes toward these activities. For example, Short (1983) cited remarks by Barknouw, who had broadcast American radio propaganda during the 1940s. Even though he was working as a propagandist, Barknouw referred to himself as a person involved with education, public service, morale building, or the distribution of information. He avoided the term *propagandist* because it had such negative connotations. Less inhibited, Fraser (1945) admitted that he wrote propaganda. He had done this in the spring of 1944 "at the invitation of persons officially concerned with the occupation and administration of Germany after the end of the Second World War." The material he wrote "was primarily intended to be read by Germans—as a means of showing them how they had been misled by their own propagandists both before and during the Nation Socialist regime" (p. iii).

The American distribution of propaganda abroad was complemented by massive domestic campaigns. As was the case with the persons who supported the foreign use of propaganda, the testimonials by contemporaries provide insights into their attitudes toward their home-front activities. Numerous persons argued in support of these efforts. Day (1941) had observed that Fascist propaganda was making democracy appear like "an outmoded form of society" that had been left "stranded on the dry sands of the dead past." He recommended that "the forces of counter propaganda" be "brought effectively into play" (p. 11). Davidson (1941) disagreed with the "general feeling that propaganda is evil, that it arises from undesirable motives and interests that its methods are dangerous, and that its results are bad." After documenting that the American colonists had relied on propaganda in the eighteenth century, he concluded that it was "simply an attempt to control the actions of a people indirectly by controlling their attitudes" (p, xiii).

Although Williams (1941) was one of those persons who did not conceal his opposition to Fascist propaganda, he admitted that the United States was widely disseminating a different type of propaganda. Because it was critical that persons not be confused by the two genres, he advised them to detect Fascist propaganda, which was designed "to make each person more dependent until at last he becomes a slave," by its association with the symbol of American Nazi groups (Figure 3.1). Williams differentiated this form of propaganda from the democratic type, which appealed "to the highest emotions and especially to reason" (p. 85). One of his samples of healthy domestic propaganda is reproduced in Figure 3.2.

Writing in 1940, Lavine and Wechsler (1972) had developed an extensive analysis of America's domestic information campaigns. In the introduction to this book, Lindeman and Miller (1972), who were respectively the President and Executive Secretary of the Institute for Propaganda Analysis, advised readers that "we live in a propaganda age" and that "in our time public opinion is primarily a response to propaganda stimuli" (p. vii). As another illustration of how they attempted to justify the use of propaganda, they reassured their audience that propaganda, which was simply "a device for conditioning behavior," could promote positive as well as negative outcomes. Because the Institute for Propaganda Analysis was a politically liberal organization, these two officers acknowledged that their remarks were out of synchrony with the thoughts of prominent liberals such as John Dewey. For this reason, their rationalizations are particularly interesting.

Carroll (1948) was another liberal who attempted to justify his involvement with the enormous propaganda campaign that the Roosevelt administration initiated. That Carroll later remained sympathetic to this effort was clear from his book's title, *Persuade or Perish*. Because he was aware of the public's enduring "confusion" and "hostility" to propaganda, he wrote defensively that "President Roosevelt had established the Office of War Information to carry out the American program of information and psychological warfare abroad" (p. 6). With regard to this unit's domestic activities, Carroll wrote in a matter-of-fact style that these were intended "to keep the American people informed of the progress of the war." Although Carroll conceded

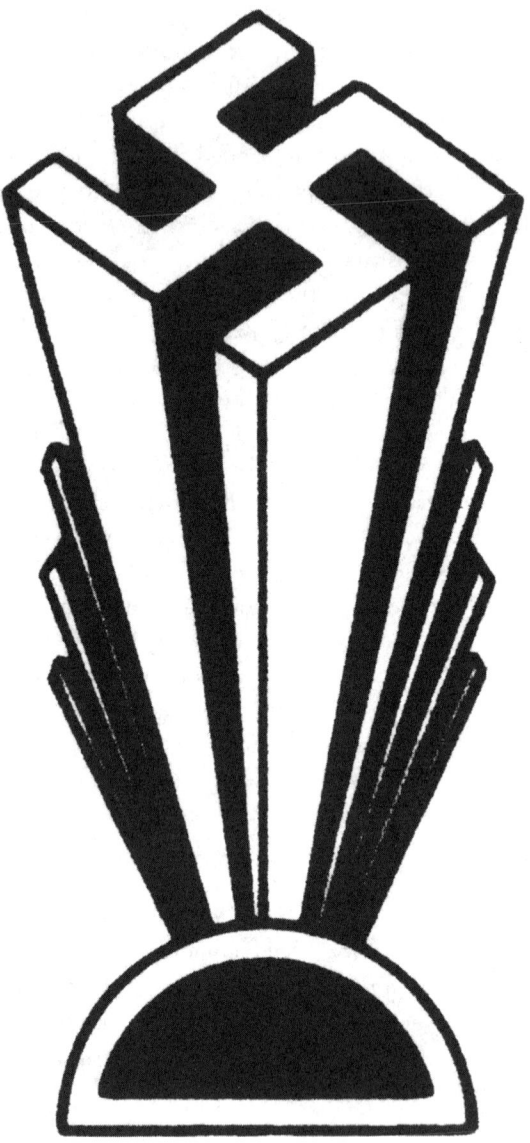

FIGURE 3.1. A 1941 Warning Directed Readers to Look for This Symbol, which Accompanied Propaganda from American Nazi Organizations

that Roosevelt used misleading propaganda in his public speeches, he was more disconcerted by the fact that the president had created an agency to restrict wartime information from his own people. Attempting to reconcile his liberal image of Roosevelt with the incontrovertible evidence of the president's antiliberal propaganda initiatives, Carroll observed that Roosevelt "had been opposed to the creation

Influencing Educators' Attitudes   81

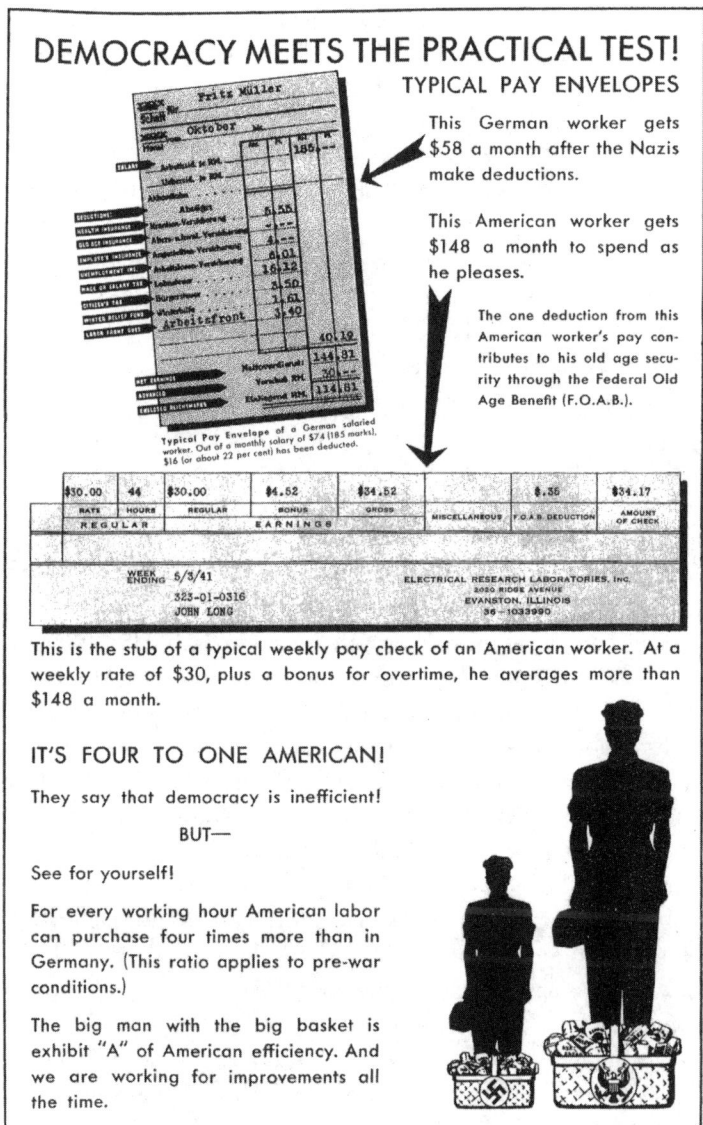

FIGURE 3.2. This 1941 Instance of "Democratic Propaganda" Was Intended to Appeal "To the Highest Emotions and Especially to Reason"

of a propaganda service and had established [the Office of Wartime Information] with considerable influence under pressure from his advisors" (p. 7).

Exhibiting considerably more sophistication than Carroll, realistic prewar analysts of American propaganda recognized that an effective domestic information campaign required citizens to abrogate some of their democratic rights. Even with this liability, the advocates of this strategy were convinced that the distribution of domestic propaganda was worthwhile. Writing in 1938 about domestic propaganda, Rogerson (1972) concluded that "it is because I do not want to risk [democratic privileges] being lost permanently that I recommend we should surrender some of them temporarily" (p. 184). Herring (1941) observed supportively that "freedom of speech is closed off quickly enough when men feel that it presents a clear and present danger to their way of life." However, he reassured Americans that freedom of speech and ideological tolerance were so endemic to their society that "the average citizen is amused rather than alarmed by deviations from the social and political norm" (p. 282).

After the United States had entered the war, Dodd (1942) noted an historical peculiarity that he thought justified Roosevelt's use of domestic propaganda. He observed that during previous conflicts between democratic governments, "the military handicaps of a government resting on discussion and consent have been cancelled out by similar conditions among our enemies" (p. 703). Because the current conflict, though, was between democratic and totalitarian governments, he concluded that propaganda was needed so that the United States could "act as one man."

Melby and Benne (1943) formed a syllogism of sorts to justify Roosevelt's use of propaganda with teachers. Because teachers were unprepared for the new communication age they had just entered, they were bound to have difficulty forming accurate opinions. Consequently, the wartime information presented to them had to be regulated. In fact, Melby and Benne thought that restrictions should be extended to classroom discussions and school materials.

Some World War II contemporaries probably expected the liberals to remonstrate against their president for distributing propaganda or restricting freedom of expression. However, this was generally not the case. Roosevelt's ultraliberal vice president urged that "we must be especially prepared to stifle the fifth columnists in the United States who will try to sabotage not merely our war material plants, but even infinitely more important, our minds" (Wallace, 1942, quoted by Sayers & Kahn, 1942, in a passage that is opposite the title page). The preceding remarks by the vice president were quoted at the beginning of a book with the title *Sabotage? The Secret War against America* (Sayers & Kahn, 1942). The authors of that book advised their readers to "bring about the banning of all seditious publications . . . stop the spreading of every kind of defeatist propaganda. . . . [and] use the polls to eliminate all defeatist and obstructionist Congressmen" (Sayers & Kahn, 1942, p. 254).

One of the reasons that liberals became confused about their political values may have been the inconsistent behavior of their leader, President Roosevelt. The liberals applauded Roosevelt's unprecedented social and economic reforms of the 1930s. However, Roosevelt's wartime decisions demonstrated that he was a pragmatist rather than an ideological purist. Fleming (2001) judged that Roosevelt's liberal followers became politically disoriented during the early 1940s because the president's actions promoted America's war interests at the expense of the fundamental ideological principles in which liberalism was grounded. Fleming noted that Roosevelt's mutating political identity was revealed when his initial support for American military intervention evolved into an intransigent insistence that the Axis powers surrender unconditionally. Roosevelt demanded unconditional surrender despite warnings from liberals and some conservatives that this would increase the enemy's will to fight, extend the war, and multiply American casualties. Fleming also documented Roosevelt's endorsement of domestic propaganda and his personal use of patently misleading information. Promulgating propaganda with the aid of advertising strategies may have seemed especially unsettling in view of the disdain with which Roosevelt had treated the advertising industry prior to Pearl Harbor (Fox, 1975). Other Roosevelt actions that flew in the face of the liberal philosophy included restrictions on freedom of speech, the funneling of defense contracts to a select group of industrialists, and the confinement of Japanese Americans in detention centers. Fleming summarized that, because "the war was an entity with its own rules, its own imperatives . . . realism—often brutal realism—almost always prevailed over idealism" (p. 126).

Other historical revisionists who had analyzed the politically partisan behaviors of this period had anticipated Fleming's conclusions. For example, Winkler (1978) had judged that "liberal propagandists accepted at face value the democratic pronouncements of the Roosevelt administration" (pp. 1–2). Washburn (1986) concluded that "most historians have failed to recognize the government's strong antilibertarian feeling during World War II" and that "Roosevelt believed in protecting constitutional rights, including First Amendment freedom, in peacetime but not necessarily during a war" (p. 206). Jeffries (1996) also judged that political liberals, including American Communists, were remarkably supportive of the Roosevelt administration's restrictions on freedom of speech. Their approbation became particularly noticeable once the Soviet Union became an American ally and was depicted more favorably by the American press. Jeffries decided that "the administration and its liberal supporters were not always solicitous of freedom of expression" and that "to the degree that worrisome dissent might impair the war effort, it came largely from the right" (p. 140). Agreeing with Jeffries observations, Steele (1999) noted that, "the Roosevelt administration investigated suspects for their 'un-American' associations, and employed a variety of legal devices to harass the dissenters" (p. 1). He added that most of the dissenters whom the administration pursued "emanated from what we might now call the 'Radical Right.'"

Propaganda through Radio

The World War I advocates of domestic propaganda had been particularly intrigued by new communication technologies. Winkler (1978) judged that these early propagandists recognized that the new media "opened up vast new possibilities." George

Creel, the chairman of the federal Committee on Public Information, had estimated that cinema could be as effective as printed materials for spreading the government's wartime messages (Rhodes, 1983a; 1983b). Looking back on the First World War, Taylor (1983) agreed that, even at that early date, "technological developments in the field of mass communications . . . provided the basis for a rapid growth in propaganda" (pp. 19–20).

Two decades later, when American involvement in another world war appeared likely, propagandists reexamined the possibilities for profiting from innovative media. Writing in 1938, Lasswell (1972) differentiated propaganda from logic. Whereas one was a technique for achieving specified political objectives, the other was an aid in the search for truth. In order to use propaganda effectively, one had to rely on plausible rather than truthful information. However, this approach had become more difficult because newer media had accelerated the rate of communication to a point at which persons could readily dispute the accuracy of information. The Machiavellian Lasswell reminded practitioners that "the truth about the relation of truth to propaganda seems to be that it is never wise to use material which is likely to be contradicted by certain unconcealable events before the political objective of propaganda is attained" (p. 208). Also writing originally in 1938, Rogerson (1972) emphasized the opportunities rather than the liabilities that the new media created. Predicting that America would become involved in another major war, he thought this would present an unprecedented chance to influence citizens through radio-based propaganda. He reasoned that government propagandists would find radio irresistible as a means of molding opinions toward world events before they had fully transpired.

In another prewar analysis of enemy propaganda, Williams (1941) advised Americans that a key defensive strategy for persons on the home front was to be "especially critical of what you are told late at night over the radio" (p. 87). In his book about Nazi propaganda, Strausz-Hupé (1941) was sympathetic to this warning. Within a chapter on "Offensive by Radio," he provided the following estimate of the impact of the 1941 German shortwave radio campaign:

> The words projected through the ether from Berlin are reaching a sizable audience in the United States. Approximately 7,000,000 radios in this country have short-wave facilities, and the number of American-born listeners to Berlin broadcasts is now estimated at somewhere between 150,000 and 300,000. The extent of Dr. Goebbels' foreign-born audience in the United States is considerably greater. . . . and in that section of New York City known as Yorkville, in which the population is largely German, listening groups gather each evening around loud-speakers tuned in to Berlin or Hamburg to hear the voices of the fatherland. (p. 253)

After the United States had entered the war, testimonials about the effectiveness of radio-based propaganda became more abundant. Although most of the propaganda that was analyzed came from enemy countries, some of it had been created by the United States. Rolo (1942) wrote that radio was "a weapon of *war waged psychologically*" that had "been streamlined from a crude propaganda bludgeon into the most powerful single instrument of political warfare the world has even known" (p. 11). Within another book written during the early days of the war, Dryer (1942) agreed that radio was "one of the most potent weapons of psychological warfare." Melby and Benne (1943) worried because radio could "exert a powerful educational influence in shaping the minds and conduct of our people" (p. 35). A year earlier, an editorialist ("Radio and the War," 1942) had observed that reporting about the war over radio was subject to distortion through nuances that might not be consciously detectable. These subtle but effective techniques might be as simple as changing tones of voice while announcers discussed different topics. Zeman (1978), who later evaluated the impact of radio-based propaganda, still agreed with the many wartime analysts who had concluded that broadcasting was "the most powerful propaganda weapon of the Second World War" (p. 11).

In his reminiscences about his work as a wartime radio reporter, MacVane (1979) observed that World War II was the first time in American history that most citizens turned to radio as their primary source for information. As a result of concerns about the need to regulate this new medium, the Federal Communication Commission, the Defense Communication Board, and the Office of War Information all identified radio programming as their domain. Dryer (1942) indicated that the influence of these agencies was so pervasive that their unquestionable authority should have been "obvious" to contemporary audiences. He concluded that "initiative in broadcasting has passed from the industry to Washington" and that the radio industry "plans nothing and creates nothing without watching the government out of the corner of its eye" (p. 8).

Byron Price, the federal government's official censor during World War II, developed a *Code of Wartime Practices for American Broadcasters*. Although the code was technically voluntary, many persons saw it as prescriptive. Journalists may have formed this view after they were directed to contact the censor's office if they disagreed with the code or even had questions about it (Sweeney, 2001). The code was also extremely precise. For example, it directed radio producers to prevent the possible dissemination of encrypted messages by canceling any live radio programs in which audience members would have access to microphones. Although they were permitted to recapitulate material that had been released by the government, journalists were to be cautious when providing unscreened information about troops, ships, planes, fortifications, production, weather, military casualties, or presidential travel. Pre-broadcast reports were to be reviewed so that controversial items could be deleted from them.

To garner support for radio censorship, Price lectured broadcasters that their "stations must be as actively behind the war efforts as merchants or manufacturers"

(Price, quoted by Collier, 1989, p. 145). In a postwar analysis, Price's deputy assistant concluded that "radio stations voluntarily withheld an amazing amount of news that would have helped the enemy" (Koop, 1946, p. viii). Although he admitted that some "thoughtful Americans" had questioned the imposition of censorship by a democratic government, he was not sympathetic to those "disdainful" and "flippant" Americans who were "irked because their mail was read" or who regarded "censors as prey for joke-writers and cartoonists." He responded authoritatively that "in time of war we do not always do what we like" (p. vii). He also lectured his critics that some of the censored information about which they had complained included "results of Germany's U-boat campaign; detailed preparations, in both men and equipment, for the great battle of Europe and the Pacific; the exact date and place of D-Day in Europe; President Roosevelt's wartime travels; Japan's fantastic balloon-bomb attacks on North America; Allied scientific achievements, from radar and the proximity fuse to plans for germ warfare (fortunately never needed) and, as a climax, the atomic bomb" (p. 191).

Propaganda through Cinema

Although the government's interest in wartime radio was discernible, its concern about cinema was more evident. The Roosevelt administration assigned such a high priority to film because it clearly understood the new medium's immense power. Its actions were different from those of earlier administrations, which had been quite obtuse in their attempts to influence citizens through movies. For example, specially trained speakers had delivered government-sponsored speeches at World War I movie theaters (Cornebise, 1984). Because a span of four minutes was thought to be the limit of the audience's attention, the length of each speaker's presentation was restricted to that exact amount of time. Hamlin (1973) reported that this early propaganda program eventually encompassed 75,000 speakers in 5,200 communities. Even though the speeches from the "four-minute men" may have had value, World War I filmmakers recognized that their messages could be delivered more effectively through the medium that was attracting audiences to the theaters in the first place. Consequently, producers began to release short propaganda films that would inspire support for conservation, savings, enlistment, and other wartime initiatives (DeBauche, 1997). Government propaganda also seeped into mainstream World War I movies. Although he did detect propaganda within commercial films, Butler (1974) judged that most of them were Hollywood romances into which some propaganda had been gratuitously interjected. The precise amount of propaganda in each film depended on the judgments of studio executives about the way this would influence box-office revenue.

The relationship between cinematic art and propaganda changed noticeably during World War II. Evaluating the war films from the second conflict, Hyams (1984) concluded that the amount of propaganda in them was so excessive that they quickly became outdated. Butler (1974) had made this same point. He dismissed these films as a "fairly worthless crop" with "moderately accurate backgrounds against which is played out a propagandist story of stock characters . . . involved in situations of uninspiring predictability" (p. 66). Kane (1982) judged that the World War II filmmakers resorted to stereotypical plots in obsessive attempts to justify America's participation in the war. Basinger (1986) agreed that the recurring plots in these films were so simplistic that they could be codified through just a handful of formulas.

Rhodes (1983b) reported about the use of propaganda within military documentaries. He gave the example of *The Battle of Midway*, a 1942 film that was directed by John Ford and that was "expertly edited to move emotions rather than convey information."

> For action, Ford chose to emphasize the Japanese attack on Midway Island while the main battle took place between the ships and planes of both sides far at sea. The portrayal of the rescued American flyers, also featured in the film, was drenched in patriotic sentimentality, with no information furnished about what they had been through or had accomplished. Ford shows instead an idealized relationship between pilots and their friends and relatives back home. (p. 293)

Rhodes was equally critical of a documentary about Pearl Harbor that Ford had directed. Rhodes judged that Ford had displayed a "cavalier" attitude toward "photographic authenticity" when he inserted professionally dramatized scenes into the historical film footage.

Dick (1985) concluded that the propaganda-filled works of World War II had been preceded by a decade of movies that were politically restrained but still anti-Fascist. Dick wrote sympathetically that "the industry moved cautiously, veiling fascist aggression in allusion and metaphor" (p. vii). Although Shindler (1979) could point to a small number of early anti-Nazi films, he reproached cinema executives for limiting their production. Like Dick, Shindler was convinced that industry executives had been reluctant to promote anti-Fascist movies. However, he judged that this decision had more to do with profits than politics. Doneson (1987) echoed this criticism when he recounted the difficulty that Charlie Chaplin had making *The Great Dictator*, a dark comedy that acknowledged Hitler's oppression of the Jews. Chaplin faced challenges from American isolationists and Nazi sympathizers who had advised the studios to stay away from this politically controversial film. Doneson added that "the most revealing complaint, made to the Motion Picture Association, came from a high Nazi official who said that Chaplin's playing Hitler will 'naturally lead to serious troubles and complications'" (pp. 31–33). German nationalists found this picture extremely distasteful because it ridiculed Hitler by depicting a "Jewish protagonist against the background of the Nazi world" (Avisar, 1988, p. 134).

Confessions of a Nazi Spy was another prewar film that called attention to the danger that American citizens faced from Nazis. Steele (1985) described this early 1940s film as a "melodramatic exposé of Nazi spying in the United States based on revelations at a recent federal trial." It incorporated "newsreel clips, a narrator, and other devices intended to give it documentary character" (p. 154). Jewish executives at Warner Brothers persuaded their studio's director, who was also Jewish, that this film would uncover Nazi threats within the United States, entertain audiences, and make a profit.

Morella, Epstein, and Griggs (1973) documented some pre–Pearl Harbor changes in Hollywood. One of these was the formation of the Motion Picture Committee Cooperating for National Defense, which distributed defense films from federal agencies. Despite this prewar cooperation of filmmakers, Koppes and Black (1987) noted a dramatic increase in the government's expectations from them after the United States entered the war. They observed that "the government, convinced that movies had extraordinary power to mobilize public opinion for war, carried out an intensive, unprecedented effort to mold the content of Hollywood feature films" (p. vii). To illustrate this point, Chambers and Culbert (1996) pointed out that the United States exploited German propaganda films for its own purposes. Whereas movies featuring thousands of uniformed, marching Nazis had been produced by Germans to convey national might, American filmmakers took these scenes out of context and used them to illustrate Germany's disdain for individualism and its obsession with militarism.

Taylor (1979) noted that the use of films for propaganda had a major weakness that, paradoxically, turned out to be one of its strengths. The weakness was the relatively high cost of film production and distribution. Taylor noted insightfully that "this also meant that the number of points at which films could be made was severely limited, and thus easier to control" (p. 31). The Office of War Information played a central role in regulating cinematic propaganda. Believing that a political backlash might ensue if films were to accurately depict the high number of American soldiers who were dying in battle, the personnel in this office initially limited the ways that Allied casualties could be depicted in war films. However, Fleming (2001) reported that the government later became worried that domestic audiences might conclude that enemy troops were more willing than Americans to die courageously. Consequently, the government actually began to distribute photos and film footage of wounded, dying, and dead American soldiers.

Although the Office of War Information was undeniably a propaganda agency, the executive order that established it explained artfully that it was created "in recognition of the right of the American people and all other peoples opposing the Axis oppressors to be truthfully informed about the common war effort" (Executive Order signed on 13 June 1942, quoted by Culbert, 1986, p. xi). Koppes and Black (1987) indicated that this office "issued a constantly updated manual instructing the studios in how to assist the war effort, sat in on story conferences with Hollywood's top brass, reviewed the screenplays of every major studio (except the recalcitrant Paramount), pressured the movie makers to change scripts and even scrap pictures when they found objectionable material, and sometimes wrote dialogue for key speeches" (p. vii). Koppes and Black concluded that "blatant morale-building propaganda" became the standard feature of the films from wartime Hollywood.

Combs and Combs (1994) decided that movie executives had eagerly purveyed propaganda not only because of patriotism but also because it benefited them. Although these authors did not identify their precise ulterior motive, Kagan (1974) had suggested one 20 years earlier. He pointed out that the film executives, who wished to avoid the financial ruin that would have followed had their industry been classified as a "non-essential" wartime activity, had no realistic alternative but to join the government in its domestic propaganda campaign.

Hyams (1984) documented that propaganda, though readily apparent within combat films, was not restricted to this genre. For example, Sherlock Holmes and Watson were transported to the modern era so that they could uncover Nazi subterfuge in two 1942 films, *Sherlock Holmes and the Voice of Terror* and *Sherlock Homes and the Secret Weapon*. Even a movie about Lassie had a plot in which "the brave collie wanders from home, serves in the army as a killer dog, suffers shell shock, and finally finds her way home" (p. 75). In an earlier movie, Laddie, who was the son of Lassie, had helped his military master outwit Nazis in Norway.

After his exhaustive analyses of American World War II propaganda, Rhodes (1983a; 1983b) concluded that every popular art form became a wartime medium for government messages. The major studios even used cartoons with wartime themes. Shale (1982) chronicled those that the influential Walt Disney Studios produced. Renzhofer (2002) reported about propaganda-laden "Looney Tunes" that relied on animated characters such as Bugs Bunny, Elmer Fudd, Porky Pig, and Daffy Duck. These characters "were drafted into the war effort as a way to keep morale high by selling war bonds, aiding with conservation, rationing, scrap-metal drives and lampooning the enemy." Some of the wartime cartoons included Daffy Duck "singing a song about recycling scrap metal, than tangling with a goat that resembles Adolf [sic] Hitler," "three little pigs facing a treaty-breaking wolf with a German accent," "a plane of Russian gremlins attacking a bomber piloted by Hitler," and "Bugs Bunny taking on Nazi Hermann Goering in the Black Forest" (p. E-1). Although Renzhofer acknowledged the explicit use of racism, especially in the ways the cartoons depicted the Japanese, he added his personal opinion that this was "justified at the time by the intense, take-no-prisoners style of fighting in the Pacific" (p. E-1).

Woll (1983) reviewed the cinematic musicals that were produced during the war years. He acknowledged that many critics had castigated these films as instances of unpatriotic escapism. Sure that this accusation was unfair, he retorted that "after Pearl Harbor, winning the war became the number one priority of the musical film, as escapism swiftly became an impossibility" (p. xi).

Advertising in Education Journals

Although he judged that propaganda was much more influential than advertising, Tomlinson (1940) pointed out strategic similarities in the communication paradigms on which these two techniques relied. A year earlier, Chakotin (1939) had also observed that political propaganda had been "borrowing more and more from the methods of commercial publicity" (p. 31). That Zeman (1978) later thought these insights to be valid was evident in the title of his book, *Selling the War*. Within this volume, he documented "a close link between the technical level of commercial advertising and political propaganda" (p. 7). Renov (1988) provided multiple examples of the government's use of commercial advertising strategies during an extensive wartime propaganda campaign that had been designed to increase home-front service by women.

Impact of Advertising during World War I

The early connection between propaganda and advertising had been quite clear to government officials. Goodrum and Dalrymple (1990) concluded that the impressive propaganda achievements of World War I advertisers enhanced their reputation for a decade. One postwar editorialist wrote confidently that World War I had had been "won by advertising." As a result, advertising had "proved itself an instrument of unmeasured power" ("Advertising as a Weapon," 1918, p. 143). Even though some critics thought that the advertisers were "claiming too much," this editorialist retorted that the advertisers themselves were quite sure of their decisive contribution to victory.

Although they had been used for decades to market commercial products, posters became an effective means of distributing wartime messages (Higonnet, Jenson, Michel, & Weitz, 1987; Rawls, 1988; Ross, 1996; Rudolph, 1990; Zeman, 1978). While the government did commission some of the 2,000 propaganda posters that were circulated in the United States during World War I, advertising firms voluntarily created the others. These posters relied on propaganda strategies that were sophisticated enough to be used again during the next war. Rudolph (1990) noted that emotional nature of their messages and potency of the illustrations distinguished the World War I posters from those that had preceded them. These posters were not so much printed proclamations as elements within strategic campaigns to promote enlistment, women's war efforts, fund-raising, conservation, war savings, and awareness of foreign espionage (Rawls, 1988). Even at an early point in World War I, the author of an article about European war posters could observe that the emerging materials demonstrated the "official government use of modern commercial advertising methods" ("Britain's War Posters," 1915, p. 675).

Later in the war, a leading advertising journal published an uninterrupted stream of articles about the value of wartime advertising. Some of these articles ("Bringing the Sales," 1918a; 1918b; Geisinger, 1918; Updegraff, 1918; "When War Shatters," 1918) reassured the businesspersons who read *Printer's Ink* that they should continue to advertise even if the war restricted their products' inventories. Other articles ("Advertising Stimulates," 1918; Bliven, 1918a; 1918b; 1918c; Jones, 1918) highlighted businesspersons' obligation to kindle patriotism. A healthy portion of the reports (Beers, 1918; "Illustrations with War-Time," 1918; Lambert, 1918; "Nailing Down," 1918; "National Biscuit," 1918; "Selective Draft Way," 1918) reviewed practical strategies for enhancing wartime advertising campaigns.

Each issue of *Printer's Ink* was filled with advertisements about the value of marketing. As influential as the editorials and reports that accompanied them, these ads reinforced long-term planning, the strategic opportunities in the postwar market, and the benefits of maintaining a link between corporate image and patriotism. For example, a 1918 promotion from an advertising firm called attention to the similarity between military operations and advertising campaigns. It included an illustration of allied commanders sitting at a field table covered with maps. The accompanying text stated that "behind the firing line sits the real brains of the army—the staff that plans the battle." The text continued that in advertising "the completely-planned, judiciously-planned Campaign is the one that wins." In another issue of *Printer's Ink,* a commercial art firm placed a breathtakingly realistic depiction of an aviation dogfight. The accompanying message indicated that this firm had formed a new division with artists specially trained to render battle scenes. Such personnel were needed because "an ever-increasing number of national Advertisers have found it expedient to use vivid illustrations of the many phases of War."

Although they did not occur in educational magazines as frequently as they did during the Second World War, World War I advertisements appeared in some educational journals, especially in the 1918 issues of the *American School Board Journal.* These advertisements used patriotic themes to increase support for the war as well as to promote sales of educational products. For example, the Sheldon Company encouraged teachers to buy their efficient chemistry tables to avoid waste, which was "a treasonable act." The Berger Company described their steel lockers as "a splendid line of defense—against petty pilfering, rats, mice, vermin, dirt, infection, confusion and fire." The Wayne Company suggested that teachers buy their horsedrawn or motorized school wagons because of "patriotism, war economy, and preparedness." Figure 3.3 is a portion of a Wayne Company advertisement.

The Holtzer-Cabot Company urged administrators to purchase their electrical school bells because these would "protect the children by providing a distinctive and absolutely reliable fire signal which is always heard and obeyed." The Caxton Company asserted that the "war time economy" should persuade teachers to purchase their brand of chalkboard eraser, which was the one that would last the longest. The Weber Costello Company urged that "war time conservation" should persuade

FIGURE 3.3. A 1918 Advertisement That Appealed to Teachers' Patriotic Convictions (*Reprinted from American School Board Journal, July 1918.*)

teachers to buy their chalkboard, which they had nicknamed *The Old Reliable*. The Eberhard Faber Company adjured teachers to avoid foreign-made materials and use their brand of pencils because the firm "counts its Americanism as its greatest asset."

The employees of the Empire Seating Company attempted to influence the market with a syllogism. They argued that "the war has brought the thinking men of America face to face with the fundamental truths which affect the building of a nation." Some of these truths centered about "the child—the future citizen—the greatest asset of America." The company marketers concluded that "you, Mr. Schoolman, must face this problem" and that "the Empire movable and adjustable chair desk stands as a volunteer offering its service in this noble cause."

As part of a sales campaign that was as disingenuous as it was clever, the G. Arnold Shaw publishing company included a postcard within its wartime books (Fraser, 1918). Marketers advised the wartime reader that this company, which was not widely known, produced books that "are intended for the discriminating few as our trademark, 'Aere Perennius'—'more lasting than brass,' indicates." Because the reader was expected to "agree with the Publisher that [this book] ought to have an immediate and wide distribution," he or she was encouraged to help the publisher "eliminate wasteful advertising by sending the post card enclosed, giving your opinion of the book to one of your friends" (p. i).

The Luther Shade Company used multiple premises to associate advertisements with positive postwar goals. Its marketers noted that "after all is said and done and the roaring sound of the long range cannon is heard no more" that "the great work after the war will be the training of the boys and girls in the schools." They added that this educational effort would be successful "provided the surroundings of the children will be the best available on all sides." This goal could be accomplished with shades that promoted "light and airy classrooms" and that shut out the "strong, glaring rays of the sun, without shutting out the light."

Although wartime issues may have been reflected in educational journal advertisements, they were also discernible in the promotional campaigns that relied on

Influencing Educators' Attitudes 93

FIGURE 3.4. An Advertisement Devised in Response to Woodrow Wilson's Acknowledgment of "The Generous Offers of the Advertising Forces of the Nation to Support the Effort of the Government"

public speakers, pamphlets, daily newspapers, special societies, exhibits at state fairs, motion pictures, and even stereopticon slides. Many of these campaigns were reviewed in the 1927 *Creel Report* (Committee on Public Information, 1972). This report also provided examples of government-sponsored advertisements aimed at foreign audiences as well as those intended for domestic spectators. With regard to the advertisements for foreign countries, Bliven (1918d) reported that the federally subsidized Committee on Public Education had distributed 30,000,000 pamphlets in seven different languages to numerous countries. These foreign advertising campaigns were intended to rebut German misinformation about the United States and transform America's tarnished international image.

George Creel, who had compiled the 1927 eponymous report, had been the chairman of the government's Committee on Public Information during World War I. This committee had been appointed by the president "for the purpose of receiving and directing through the proper channels the generous offers of the Advertising forces of the Nation to support the effort of the Government" (Woodrow Wilson, quoted by the Committee on Public Information, 1918, p. 1). The committee's members (Committee on Public Information, 1918) illustrated advertising campaigns for several important wartime organizations, including the Shipping Board, the Treasury Department, the War Department, and the Red Cross. Figure 3.4 is one of the advertisements featured in their wartime report.

Advertising's Stature Declines between the Wars

Advertising reports that were published at the end of the First World War or soon afterward restated a common theme: The public needed to be continually reminded of the advertising industry's role in the American victory. Bliven (1918a) advised his readers that they would make "a grave mistake" if they assumed that German wartime propaganda would die because of the recently signed armistice. He encouraged his clients to aggressively maintain their own propaganda campaigns as a type of defensive readiness against future belligerence by Germany or any other country.

Most of the articles supporting postwar advertising were less confrontational than the one by Bliven. The majority recommended the continuation of advertising because it was in the best interests of industrialists. For example, an advertisement from the McCann Company in the first 1918 issue of *Printer's Ink* advised industrialists to begin "preparing for peace" because "war's work is not all destruction." The ad noted that "manufacturers with vision" were "planning for post-war prosperity" by identifying potential markets. One of these markets could even be Germany, which "reliable information" indicated was looking to postwar industrial reconstruction after it had seen "the face of inevitable defeat in the present struggle." Numerous articles ("Advertising to Bridge," 1918; Lane, 1918a; "Reconstruction," 1918) assured businesspersons that postwar advertising would influence public attitudes with the same precision that it had demonstrated during the war.

In the midst of World War I, advertisers had continually advised their clients to market their products, including those that were scarce. They had emphasized that patriotic wartime advertising campaigns helped to maintain the positive public image that was essential for success in the postwar economy. As an example, Updegraff (1918) used this argument when he warned businesspersons that they could not "afford to stop advertising during this period when demand is running ahead of supply" or else their customers would "begin to forget *why* and *which* and *what*" (p. 10).

Geisinger (1918) was even more explicit, telling businesspersons who "could not at present supply the demand" that they should "damn the torpedoes" and "advertise consistently and persistently to keep that trade-mark before the public" (p. 54).

Advertising executives should have taken to heart the advice they were dispensing. Despite the high regard in which they were held during World War I and the decade that followed, their reputation deteriorated during the 1930s. Euphoric with success, they underestimated the need to remind the public, industry, and government about their industry's wartime accomplishments. The authors of a post–World War II report ("How the 100 Best War Ads Came to Be Written," 1946) noted that during the 1930s advertising's reputation had devolved to such a point that it became a "public whipping boy" that was "excoriated" and "debunked" by consumer organizations. Lengthy reports ("Case for Advertising," 1940; "Case for Distribution," 1940) in a leading advertising journal chronicled these attacks and even recapitulated passages that had been penned by hostile editorialists.

In an address to advertising executives, Young (1946) agreed that advertising had "very little standing" before the war. He observed that the government officials in the Roosevelt administration publicly denigrated it. An earlier report ("Public Is Not Damned," 1939) noted that even many of the businesspersons of the 1930s had forgotten advertising's accomplishments during the First World War. However, this author judged that the public's attitude had changed by 1938, when "there was scarcely a convention that did not feature an address on public relations, scarcely a trade magazine that did not devote some space to the subject, scarcely a board of directors that did not deliberate weightily on the powers of the new goddess" (p. 83).

Kendall (1943) observed that "much of the advertising immediately after Pearl Harbor lacked realism and direction." He indicated that those advertisers who had attempted to resurrect advertising campaigns from World War I found out that "the yardstick did not fit." They learned eventually that "an effective wartime advertisement is one that *informs* and *inspires* the people on the home front. . . . contributes to the readjustment of our whole pattern of living. . . . but, above all . . . promotes some phase of an essential, government-designated home-front campaign" (p. 62). Young (1946) agreed that the negative attitudes toward advertising were altered during the war, when advertising executives demonstrated that they still could decisively influence the public's opinions. He identified five marketing devices on which he and other World War II advertisers had relied to make this demonstration: "consumer opinion surveys," "a planned program of attack," "making facts simple, understandable and interesting," "repeat[ing] these facts until they stuck," and "emotionalizing facts" (p. 34).

Once advertisers had convinced the government of the value of their services, they still had to persuade businesspersons. The incentives for American businesspersons had to be distinct from those motivating British business executives. To understand the difference, one can consult a report by Waller and Vaughn-Rees (1987), who investigated the advertisements in the women's magazines of wartime England. After discerning a huge trove of patriotic ads, they noted that British magazine publishers were disposed to support government policies because government-sponsored advertising was their principal source of income.

In contrast to their British colleagues, American businesspersons did not rely on government subsidies. They used patriotic advertising during the Second World War because it simultaneously promoted the war effort and their own business interests. A monograph about American wartime advertising (Associated Business Papers, 1942) stated this case succinctly. It recommended patriotic strategies because they would "help re-establish a free world in which to do business, and help maintain a sound foundation upon which to base our business recovery" (p. 3). In addition to solving "some of the war-borne problems that harass the readers," businesspersons who followed this advice would increase their profits. As a result of their persuasive power, the extensive advertisements that were featured in this 1942 monograph were re-christened "aditorials."

Advertising Devices

Several hundred economics professors wrote a letter to the Secretary of the Treasury in 1943. Featured in a popular advertising journal, this letter ("Text of Open Letter," 1943) discouraged advertising because it stimulated home-front consumption and provided unprecedented *pro bono* support for the government's wartime initiatives. Especially concerned about the latter point, the professors recommended that the federal government pay for any advertisements supporting its policies. In a scathing response, the journal's editors dismissed the "amazing" letter as the confused ramblings of "Never-Never-Land" academicians who were "unrealistic in their conception and understanding of the relation of many phases of modern business to the economic world" ("Professors Do Their Bit," 1943, p. 15). They advised the professors to return to their campuses to write "something more sensible than this letter."

Clapper (1943) amplified the confrontational rhetoric from advertisers. He lectured government officials that the ideas of industrialists and advertising executives were not only ahead of those from professors but also "quite a bit ahead of our politicians." To substantiate this point, he highlighted advertising campaigns that had called for world transformation through international cooperation, global marketing, accelerated communication, and innovative technology. He wrote that "being conscious of these changes, industry is able to have a vision to build a new world" while "politicians live by playing to prejudices and by muttering the old words and phrases" (p. 16).

The brash confidence of the advertising industry was substantiated by its indisputably masterful manipulation of an arsenal of marketing devices. Cowles (1943) wrote that advertisers were helping to win the war on the home front because they knew how to measure attitudes, popularize initiatives, nurture public relations, and "persuade the public to act in accordance with determined plans." Tuttle (1942) remarked that "total war" had spawned "total advertising," which had as its goal to persuade "a *complete* audience, not merely a *large* one" (p. 15). He predicted that industry, government, labor, and even social reform movements would rely increasingly on the advertisers who had demonstrated their skills in the "all-out effort on behalf of the war." The concept of *total advertising* emerged again a year later in a report ("60 Million," 1943) about a campaign that the Advertising Council was implementing in 240 magazines. This effort confronted 60,000,000 readers with "messages to enlist maximum civilian support in winning the war." Several months later, the War Advertising Council ("War Message," 1943) proposed an even more ambitious drive, the goal of which was to place "a war message in every ad."

Hand (1943a) was a liberal educator who worried that new media such as radio, cinema, and "the vastly brightened and illustrated printed page" were developing into a "vast educational enterprise" under the "powerful stimulus of advertising." He feared that his fellow liberals were allowing "the new devices to fall into the hands of many agencies that either do not understand education or are antagonistic to its purposes" (p. 133). He compared his technologically unsophisticated contemporaries to the fifteenth-century monks who had underestimated the power of the printing press and continued to transcribe Bibles by hand.

Although Hand may have been worried that his contemporaries did not fully comprehend advertising devices, information about them was readily available. Almost every issue of the major advertising journals contained practical advice about wartime advertising. For example, *Advertising & Selling* serialized a column about the impact of war on advertising. This column was invariably accompanied by a patriotically rendered illustration of an eagle. As an indication of the specificity of the information in this series, the nineteenth installment recapitulated advice from government officials and business leaders about "business men and advertising executives who are trying to handle their Washington contacts intelligently" ("Impact of War on Advertising," 1943, p. 19).

Printer's Ink was another journal that regularly contained expositions of wartime advertising. Norton (1942a; 1942b; 1942c) wrote a three-part series that analyzed popular marketing devices. Although his examples were not selected from educational journals, they were grouped into categories that generalized to the ads in educational journals. For example, under the category *Ads for Plentiful Merchandise*, he recommended that unrestricted merchandise be connected to wartime themes, such as conservation. Figure 3.5 and Figure 3.6 contain portions of advertisements that are from educational journals and that illustrate this tack.

The following statement, which accompanied a *Parents' Magazine* story about vocational education, is another illustration of how wartime conservation was combined with marketing.

98   Wartime Schools

The paper we are using in this magazine is of a much lighter grade than the paper we used to use. As a result, the type and the illustrations suffer somewhat. But we don't apologize. For we are using this paper as a war measure, and as our way of cooperating with the Government in paper conservation. We know you will accept the situation cheerfully and with understanding. Saving paper is just one way in which we can help to win the war. (Brodinsksy & Nathan, 1944, p. 23)

In a report that surely caught the attention of marketers, Wachtel (1943) presented data to prove that advertisements with war themes promoted patriotism and increased the attention that those ads received. In agreement, Wilkinson (1943) used case studies to demonstrate that consumers recognized and remained loyal to products marketed through patriotic war advertisements. Due to regulation by censors, some of the marketing devices associated with patriotic advertising changed during the course of the war (Roeder, 1993). The primary example was the use of images of dead American troops. Once the government became convinced that these images actually strengthened home-front support, it rescinded the restrictions that it had imposed during the first 21 months of the war. As an indication of the extent of this turnaround, it actually supplied photographs and films of dead Americans to advertising firms and news agencies.

In 1942, the December 7 issue of *Life Magazine* contained an ad that depicted a Christmas wreath with a "V" in its center. Ambiguously entitled "Sprit of 43," the accompanying text assured readers that the Schenley Distillers Corporation's "gift to free peoples everywhere is the high spirit of sacrifice." This distillery's sacrifice was indicated when "many a *Schenley* man . . . left us to do his share in the war ef-

FIGURE 3.5. Wartime Ads for Plentiful Merchandise Still Emphasized Conservation (*Underwood Elliott Fisher, "How Long Will Your Typewriters Last?" Journal of the NEA*, copyright 1942. *Reprinted by permission of the publisher. All rights reserved.*)

FIGURE 3.6. An Attempt to Promote the Sale of Toilets with a Popular Wartime Message

fort." Another indication of the corporation's sacrifice was the fact that it had assumed "a war footing—turning out vast quantities of essential war alcohol." The ad reminded readers that the whiskey currently being marketed had been "drawn from our reserves—the largest in the U.S.A.—made and laid down in years gone by."

Distillers who were no longer producing alcoholic beverages were able to sell items from their reserves. Norton (1942a; 1942b; 1942c) pointed out that other industries, which lacked massive inventories, were hesitant to advertise once they had diverted their total production to the war effort. He assured firms that they would remain in the forefront of the public's consciousness if they continued to market their products. One way to do this was by publicizing their commitment to the war. The Conn Musical Instrument Company employed this maneuver within an ad that it placed in the January 1943 issue of the *Music Educators Journal*. The illustration depicted soldiers loading ammunition onto a bomber. The accompanying text indicated that "all band instrument manufacture for civilian needs was stopped on June 30 by government order" and that "now Conn precision manufacturing facilities are devoted 100% to war production." The ad concluded that "some day Conn will again go back to work building better instruments for a world at peace" but that in the meantime "when Adolph, Benito, and Hirohito hear that 'Americans are coming over with Conn instruments' they had better take to their dug-outs because when *these* Conn instruments are functioning they are going to help play tunes the Axis won't like!"

100   Wartime Schools

FIGURE 3.7. When One Corporation's Steel Educational Products Were No Longer Available, It Used This Illustration to Explain the Shortage

Figure 3.7 is a portion of another educational ad that attempted to position an unavailable item in the forefront of the public's consciousness. The supplementary text indicated that no steel pencil sharpeners would be available for the duration of the war.

In a separate category of wartime advertisements, Norton included ads that promoted high morale among home-front citizens. In the January 1943 issue of the *Music Educators Journal*, the Ludwig and Ludwig instrument manufacturing

FIGURE 3.8. This World War II Advertisement Promoted High Morale among Librarians and Their Patrons (*Gaylord Bros., Inc, copyright 1943. Reprinted with permission.*)

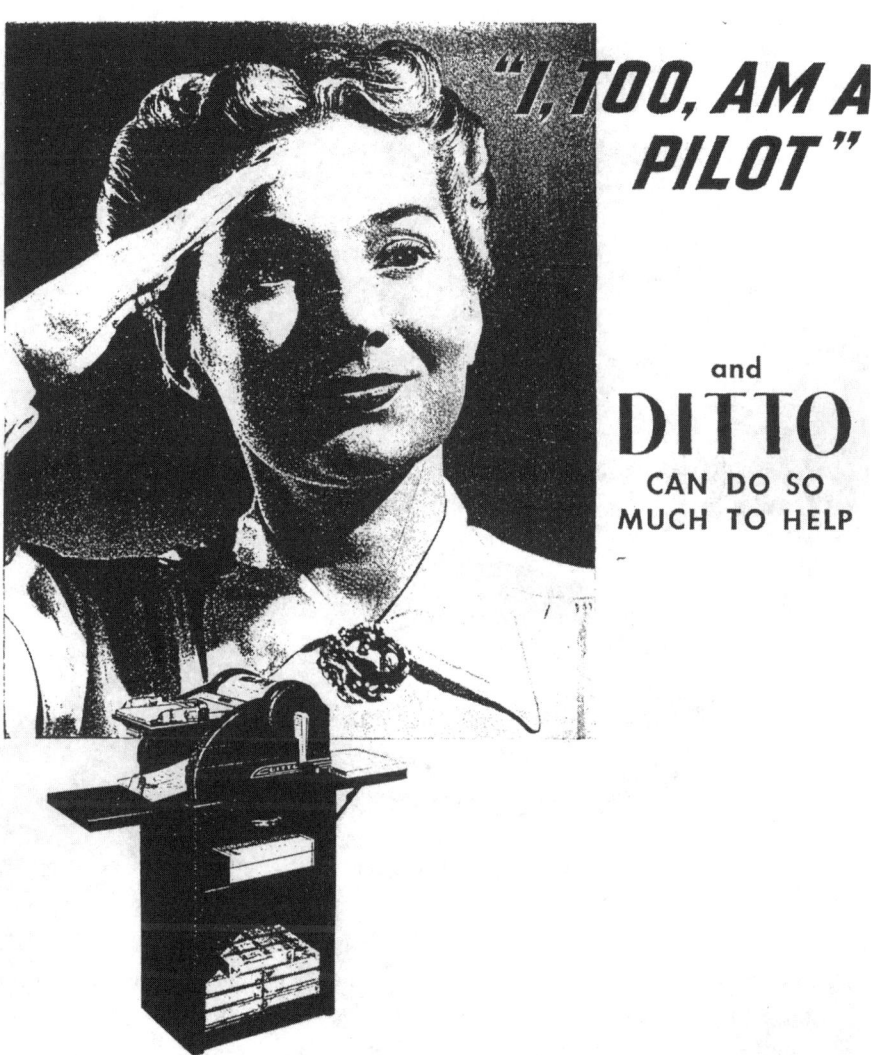

FIGURE 3.9. An Effort to Nurture Pride among the Persons Who Manufactured and Purchased School Equipment (*Reprinted from American School Board Journal, March 1943.*)

company used this approach. The company advertised a new type of "Victory" snare drum that represented "patriotism in a Drum Shell." This Spartan model had been "shorn of critical materials" with "no chrome nor nickel to dazzle the eye, it's strictly a blackout." The manufacturer assured band directors that the drum was "all the more beautiful in its smart simplicity" and that "with it the drummer on Bond-bardment parade knows that he is 100% in keeping with the spirit of the occasion."

102   Wartime Schools

He won't dodge this-

Don't *you* dodge this!

FIGURE 3.10. War Bond Advertisements Were Unqualifiedly Patriotic and Extraordinarily Effective (*Reprinted from American School Board Journal, July 1944.*)

Figure 3.8 and Figure 3.9 are portions of other educational advertisements that illustrate this same approach. Figure 3.8 assured library furniture patrons and their staffs about the value of their contributions to the war. Figure 3.9 had the identical effect on the persons who manufactured and used school reproduction equipment.

Sometimes ads were intended to develop select wartime behaviors among a broad national audience. Norton referred to these as public morale ads. For example, the Planters Peanuts Company used advertisements in educational journals to inspire loyalty to the nation and their product. The following passage accompanied one of its advertisements:

> Today *loyalty* if the biggest word in our language. It was written in the steaming jungles of Guadalcanal—on the hot sand of Africa—and on the shell-scarred beaches of Salerno. . . . And it is the common bond which is shared by. . . . boys and girls whose

FIGURE 3.11. Portion of an Ad That Associated the Brand Name of a School Seating Company with a Critical Wartime Career (*American Seating Company, copyright 1945. Reprinted with permission.*)

> loyalty is helping make the home front a bastion behind the battle front. Speaking of loyalty, "Mr. Peanut" is proud that millions of people are loyal to Planters because they are the choicest, freshest and meatiest salted peanuts, and because this vitamin-rich food is helping supply energy when energy counts. (Passage from a Planter's Peanut advertisement, 1943, p. 21)

The teachers who read this ad were directed to contact the company to obtain "pledge-for-victory" posters for their students.

Some advertisements were unqualifiedly patriotic. Norton referred to these as ads backing the government. The plentiful educational advertisements for war bonds and war stamps, such as the one depicted in Figure 3.10, demonstrated this approach. Figure 3.11 is another advertisement that "backed up the government." However, Figure 3.11 was part of a series prepared by a seating manufacturer. In each ad, the company linked its name with some patriotic initiative, thereby benefiting the initiative as well as the company itself.

Not all of the ads that backed the government were positive. Some of them duplicated government propaganda that had been designed to create distrust and hostility toward the enemy. A particularly striking ad from American Locomotive was accompanied by a photo of three attractive females who were being inspected by a lascivious, overweight, bald-headed Nazi officer. The accompanying text contained the following passage:

> The Nazis look upon us as a degenerate nation. But they have a great respect for our accomplishments. And, if they win, they may decide that we have something in our blood which they can use in building their master race. For they're great believers in eugenics, these Nazis. They're strong for selective breeding. You they may cast aside and put to some ignominious task, such as scrubbing the sidewalks or sweeping the streets. But your daughter . . . well, if she's young and healthy and strong, a Gauleiter with an eye for beauty may decide she is a perfect specimen for one of their experimental camps. (Passage from an American Locomotive advertisement, reproduced by Fox, 1975, between pp. 50–51)

CHAPTER 4

National Threats from Within

The war does many things to children, most of them bad.
—"CHILDREN LIKE," 1943

World War II Americans were as fearful of internal threats as they were of global dangers. Two of the most publicized domestic threats were those from juvenile delinquency and subversive textbooks. When teachers were directed to confront juvenile delinquency, they resorted to preventative programs. Although many liberal educators had joined the national campaign to check delinquency, they hesitated about restricting textbooks. They thought it would be better if students learned to read all types of materials critically. In fact, they believed teachers had an obligation to present students with the full range of politicized information on war issues.

Juvenile Delinquency

Although government officials were frightened of foreign armies, they also worried that the war could permanently disrupt the country's social foundations. The Director of War Services within the Federal Security Agency made this point when he chose the following metaphor with which to describe his agency's attitudes toward domestic juvenile crime:

> In our fight on juvenile delinquency, I should say that we have reached December Eighth, 1941. We have declared war. We know our enemy. We are ready to mobilize for the attack. We know that success requires teamwork of the finest kind. (Taft, 1943, p. 485)

The wartime public shared the government's dread. Alarmist predictions from educational leaders further exacerbated these fears. In one instance, the director of a state reform school forecast that the behaviors of young criminals would be "much more destructive in their effects on this country and its future than any of the bombings which the Japs and Germans will give us" (Special Committee on Juvenile Delinquency, 1943, p. 165). The accelerated wartime rate of juvenile delinquency seemed to corroborate the accuracy of such predictions. Evjen (1942) expressed this assumption when he wrote that "we are interested in learning to what extent delinquency and crime are by-products of war, how war produces crime, what types of crimes are on the increase and decrease, what steps we can take to prevent delinquency and crime, and what to expect in the postwar period" (p. 136). A year later, Abbott (J. D. Abbott, 1943) responded to Evjen's questions by identifying the precise social conditions that were causing wartime delinquency. These conditions included "poverty-broken homes and poor living and recreational facilities . . . migrant populations, women in industry, Army and Navy cantonments encroaching on already overburdened communities, racial hostilities, newly developing caste systems, changing social mores, and poor parental standards" (p. 93).

Wartime anecdotes and statistics seemed to confirm a perilous increase in juvenile delinquency. For example, one report ("Morale of High-School," 1942) described "alarming" increases in the number of juveniles who were drinking, fighting, and stealing. The author observed that promiscuity had increased to such a point that it comprised a special category of "sexual delinquency." Fisher (1942) noted that several reporters had estimated that the increase in juvenile delinquency had been as high as 50 percent. She provided the following descriptive remarks about the types of juvenile offenses that were being perpetrated:

> Young boys are being arrested for breaking into cars and parking meters, for holdups, for burglarizing homes, for running away. Tardiness, truancy, petty stealing, inattention and disorderly conduct in class rooms [sic], and trouble in the schools. Young girls, thirteen to sixteen, are staying out late, running away from home, being picked up by soldiers or defense workers, and engaging in sexual relations without knowledge or realization of the consequences. (p. 39)

Chute (1943) noted that Oakland, California, had reported a 41 percent increase in juvenile delinquency during 1942. Oklahoma City reported a 54 percent increase and Phoenix registered a 77 percent jump during that same year. With regard to Phoenix, a local probation officer stressed that nearly half the cases involved young females. Not very cryptically, this officer attributed the "girl cases" to the "popularity of the soldiers."

In a summary (New York State Board of Social Welfare, 1943) of testimonials about the effects of the war on children, the authors reported that 13 heavily industrialized

New York counties had sustained significantly increased juvenile delinquency court cases during the first half of 1942. Just the cases of juvenile neglect had risen by 39 percent. These reporters were especially concerned about the increased number of young female "sex delinquents." Although they felt that educators who were limited by inadequate budgets and shortages of personnel should not be held accountable, they were less sympathetic to distracted guardians, whom they referred to as "delinquent parents."

Also attempting to document the increase in wartime delinquency, a Connecticut investigator ("Juvenile Delinquency Survey," 1944) conducted a survey about the frequency of delinquency and the societal conditions with which it correlated. The respondents, who thought that juvenile delinquency had become a significant problem, identified the three most frequent instances as truancy from school, disrespect for teachers, and disillusionment about the value of education. They thought these correlated with opportunities for youths to earn lucrative wages and become independent.

Assuming a national perspective, Kandel (1948) noted that the prosecuted cases of juvenile delinquency had increased by approximately 15 percent between 1940 and 1942. Common charges against the males were stealing and "acts of mischief." Girls were being accused of running away, sex offenses, and "being ungovernable." Kandel did caution that these statistics might be inaccurate because they were confined to youths involved in legal proceedings.

A researcher from the National Probation Society (Bell, 1944) concluded that reports from numerous communities during 1943 had substantiated an increase in juvenile delinquency. Merrill (1948) later observed that variability in regional laws and social values invalidated conclusions that had been based on composite statistics. Some researchers, such as Wiers (1945), had attempted to deflect this criticism by examining juvenile court cases within a single state. Whereas the number of juvenile cases in Michigan had increased by only 550 between 1935 and 1939, Wiers documented an additional 2,000 cases by 1943. He concluded that the increase was primarily the result of wartime conditions.

In a booklet about community-based programs, the United States Department of Labor (1943a) noted that juvenile delinquency had been "intensified, aggravated, and given new emphasis under the pressure of war." As a result, it had been assigned high priority "among the social problems requiring special consideration and prompt action" (p. 1). Professional educational organizations agreed with the government that juvenile delinquency was a high priority issue. For example, the National Education Association developed a reform agenda ("Program of the NEA," 1943) that comprised "a constructive program to counteract those forces which are contributing to juvenile delinquency." Figure 4.1, which appeared in the February 1943 issue of the *School Board Journal,* symbolically depicted "the law" and "the school" collaborating to reduce wartime delinquency.

THE SCHOOL: "THIS IS MY RESPONSIBILITY, TOO!"

FIGURE 4.1. A 1943 Depiction of "The Law" and "The School" Confronting Wartime Delinquents (*Reprinted from American School Board Journal, February 1943.*)

Unprecedented media coverage helped to convince the public that juvenile delinquency was a growing menace. During the first year of the war, Glueck (1942b) observed that "there seems to be no need at this time to press home the fact that juvenile delinquency has been increasing since Pearl Harbor." She added that "on every hand evidence to this effect is pouring in" (p. 86). In another article that she published that same year, she scolded "those among us who believe that 'it cannot happen here' and are blinding themselves to the signs of the times" (Glueck, 1942a, p. 119). Although Chute (1942) was less passionate on this issue, he did acknowledge that "many newspapers are warning of an expected large increases in juvenile delinquency on account of war conditions." He demonstrated his personal skepticism by identifying cities with decreasing rates of delinquency. He concluded that the newspaper reporters had chosen to ignore these cities and instead publicize those with increasing problems.

During the second year of American participation in the war, multiple forms of evidence corroborated the extensive reporting about delinquency. For example, Gilliam (1943) noted that stories in newspapers, reports on radio, and feature articles in magazines revealed a "national awakening to the juvenile problem." Castendyck and Robison (1943) detected a positive correlation between the public's awareness of juvenile delinquency and the "numerous news items and articles in the daily press and popular magazines of today; in the reports of studies, investigations, and recommendations for programs appearing in scientific and professional literature; and in the requests for information and advice received almost daily by the Children's Bureau from individuals and community groups" (p. 253). Killian (1943) fretted that the uninterrupted newspaper reporting about the delinquency "wave" had created a national "scare." The executive director (Chute, 1943) of the National Probation Association reported that "never before has there been so much discussion" of juvenile delinquency in newspapers and magazines. Everett (1943) observed that the massive newspaper and magazine coverage was amplified by melodramatic movies such as *Youth in Crisis* and *Children of Mars*.

Stepped-up reporting about juvenile delinquency continued throughout the war years. Harris (1945) pointed to letters in newspapers, public discussions, speeches, and research studies as evidence of the public's continuing "great concern." Neumeyer (1945) agreed that "so much publicity has been given to this problem that the average citizen is inclined to believe that a veritable epidemic of juvenile misbehavior is spreading over the nation" (p. 262). Bogen (1944; 1945) used a comparable simile when he noted that extensive media attention, reports from investigative committees, and increased spending on juvenile delinquency programs were persuading observers that delinquency was spreading "like an epidemic." Werner (1945) indicated that "sensational" writers were referring to the problem as the "Junior Crime Wave."

In a postwar book about juvenile delinquency, Tappan (1949) was convinced that the threat from juvenile delinquency had been real during the war and still remained a menace. He firmly assured readers that "the war and its aftermath have served to accentuate the magnitude of the problem and to reveal its significance in the maturing of unregenerated delinquents into chronic adult criminalism" (p. vii). In another book published originally in 1949, Neumeyer (1961) assumed a different stance. Noting the difficulty of interpreting incomplete and heterogeneous statistics about juvenile delinquency, he concluded shrewdly that "perhaps the most significant development during the war was not the fact that delinquency increased but that there emerged an increased awareness of the problem" (p. 60).

Causes of Delinquency

Delinquency among youths had been an enduring concern since World War I. Writing during that period about female juvenile delinquents, a Massachusetts superintendent (Everal, 1917) noted that school truancy was the garden in which delinquency took seed. He encouraged concerned teachers to look for physical causes such as "adenoids, defective sight and nervous conditions." With regard to other physical factors, he noted that "we cannot hope for an adequate solution of the problem of delinquency until feeble-mindedness and its consequences are properly met" (p. 841). Also addressing physical problems of youths during that same year, Coleman (N. F. Coleman, 1917) called for a preventative program of "social hygiene" because venereal diseases had left 250,000 young males ineligible for military service.

Although critics continued to search for the physical causes of juvenile delinquency in the years after World War I, Germain (1945) reported that politically liberal scholars eventually shifted attention to social factors. This changed attitude was apparent in a World War II pamphlet (United States Department of Labor, 1943b).

> We know that most of the delinquents who come before the courts are underprivileged children from impoverished, overcrowded homes in deteriorated neighborhoods where demoralizing conditions, such as low-grade poolrooms and taverns, cheap dance halls, gambling "joints," and houses of prostitution are rampant. Many of these children run about in gangs and have learned from others in the neighborhood how to steal a car or rob a drunk.... A large proportion of delinquents come from miserable homes—homes that have been broken by death or desertion of a parent; depraved homes, where the mother may be immoral and the father alcoholic or criminal; homes where the foreign-born parents' old-world culture clashes with that of the community to which the child is constantly exposed; homes where social values are cheap or altogether lacking. (pp. 6–7)

Since the causes of delinquency were complex and variable, the authors of this pamphlet thought that the examination of a troubled youth required the assembling of comprehensive data "from the time that he was born." They added that "above all, we must know how he *feels* about things" (pp. 7–8).

The changed attitude among wartime liberals had been signaled in some of their prewar writings. In fact, quite a few of these prewar writings were unrestrained. As an extreme example, Frank (1937) published an article in the *Communist* in which he explained that delinquency in capitalist societies was inevitable. Furthermore, teachers should expect to become targets of violence because delinquents would recognize them as "the immediate agents of the school system for indoctrinating the minds of the children with bourgeois ideology" (p. 440).

Addressing the connection between economic problems and delinquency, the liberal Kilpatrick (1940) wrote that "any who have to do with youth must understand how economic conditions peculiarly concern adolescents." He employed a simile to explain that "an unhealthy economy insistently upsets social life much as an unhealthy body insistently upset individual life" (p. vi). Picking out conservative education as a cause of both juvenile delinquency and despotism, some liberals (Amidon, 1940; Gellerman, 1940) speculated that conservative education was actually predisposing youths toward fascism.

Like their liberal prewar opponents, politically conservative educators believed that rising delinquency portended societal disaster. They even agreed that educators had contributed to problem. However, they predictably blamed liberal teachers rather than themselves. Conklin (1939) castigated progressive educators, with their disdain for "old fashioned discipline," as "one of the reasons why we see undisciplined youth leading irrational mobs." Prewar speculations about the origin of juvenile delinquency in dysfunctional schools continued during the course of the war. Howell, Ryerson, and Stullken (1942) admonished the educational community that "the schools themselves must accept certain responsibilities in connection with the problems of delinquency." Although they questioned the value of the progressive schools, they also were skeptical about truncating academic schedules and other prevalent wartime practices.

Adducing a host of causes for rising delinquency, Abbott (J. D. Abbott, 1943) listed "the glamour of the uniform, the sophistication and accelerated maturation of the teen-age girl, the lowering of communal and familial standards, the attempt on the part of many girls and women to adopt one sex code—that of men—the mistaken patriotic theme of the so-called 'victory girl,' and the sudden increased earning power of youth and parents engaged in war work" (p. 93). Although all of these factors were contributing to juvenile delinquency, Abbott added her own "deep conviction" that aberrant juvenile behavior was primarily "the price being paid by the children for the sudden emancipation of women into industry and war efforts" (p. 93). A monograph from authors with complementary attitudes noted that "universal experience" substantiated the truism that "achievement in life is the product of orderly, persistent, unremitting effort," "control of one's emotions," and "respect for the rights of others and for law and order in general" (Michigan Education Association, 1944, p. 22). Although the authors of this book may have overstated the prevalence of their assumptions, there is no question that many Americans did agree with them.

Some World War II educators thought that social dysfunction could be traced to child labor and early employment. This explanation conflicted with that of the prewar educators who had connected delinquency to unemployment. For example, one analyst (Chamberlain, 1939) had urged educators to ensure that the 3,000,000 jobless youths who were "just hanging around" became invested in democracy "before it is too late." As the approaching war fueled the economy, unemployment became implausible as the explanation for the simultaneously accelerating juvenile delinquency problems. Searching for an alternative explanation, Sargent (1942) focused on child labor. Since the prewar pundits who were searching for social explanations for delinquency had connected it directly to "the deleterious effects of poverty and privation," Bogen (1944) concluded that the only viable social explanation left to them during the war was some type of connection to "prosperity and economic expansion."

Paralleling the analytical shift by scholars, educators began to shift their attention to the relationship between juvenile delinquency and home-front prosperity. They looked for a causative relationships between delinquency and poor school attendance ("Wartime Adjustments," 1944), disrespectful attitudes toward authorities (National Education Association, 1943a), inadequate recreational activities for females (Zeller, 1943), the absence of suitable adult models ("Schools Called Upon," 1943), and even "youthful awareness of [the] bad adult example" set by some of the persons on the home front (Thurston, 1942).

The ease of finding employment or joining the armed services persuaded some youths that schooling was irrelevant to high-salaried work or military service ("Schools Called Upon," 1943). Educators worried that some of these attitudes were often "not legitimately connected with the war effort" ("Wartime Adjustments," 1944). Bigelow (1942) noted that the impressionable high-school students who resided near military camps had become "distracted" by trainees with low morals. Observing that females were especially susceptible to "men in uniform," he wrote that even "nice girls" were being victimized at dances where "the trainees far outnumber the local girls with desirable social connections." This had produced "physical strain of the excessive social life for the relatively few girls who may participate" (p. 440).

During the war and the period that followed, many persons remained convinced that wartime delinquency was associated with disrupted social conditions. Although many causes had been ascribed to delinquency, Simon (1944) was sure that "none of these stand out more conspicuously than disrupted home life" (p. 7). To substantiate this hypothesis, he pointed to the divorce rate, which had climbed to 15 percent. Two years later, Burrows (1946) opined that the "phenomenal war increase in delinquency" had resulted from "'Boom towns,' 'big pay days,' 'mushroom' communities, 'honky-tonks' and 'hot spots,' roadhouses, glamour and thrill, mobility, lonesomeness, and the absence of any community *espirit de corps*" (p. 387). Viewing delinquency from a comparable vantage, Banay (1948) concluded that the "increased prosperity resulting from the war industries places too much money in adolescent hands, leading to a premature freedom from control, a premature sense of all-importance, a disordered picture of social relations and economic reality" (p. 27).

Many conservatives relied exclusively on emotional rhetoric to convince their readers that juvenile delinquency was connected to ineffectual parenting. In the unlikely event that his readers would fail to understand the significance of a chapter that he entitled "Manufacturing Criminals," Sargent (1943) explained that "our Puritan forebears believed that children should be seen and not heard. . . . [and] the child that they would have considered delinquent, we would today praise for his initiatives" (p. 327). Also attentive to the effects of disrupted social patterns, Miller and Miller (1942) warned parents that mothers who worked outside the home should expect their children to be delinquents. Lessner (1944) quoted an executive from the Boy Scouts who had concluded unequivocally that "total blame should be placed on the parents" for all "maladjustments of youth."

Unlike those who relied on emotional rhetoric, some authors did consult scholarly research in their efforts to explain juvenile delinquency. Even during the first year of American involvement in the war, these investigators (Burgess, 1942; Dunn, 1942; Hoehler, 1942; Hoyer, 1942; LaRocca, 1942; Reckless, 1942; Taft, 1942a; 1942b; Thompson, 1942) suspected that juvenile delinquency was only one component within a broader social syndrome. Nonetheless, they still judged that delinquent behaviors did interrupt traditional familial functions, which created situations that led to more delinquent acts. In spite of the professionalism and restraint with which some researchers had conducted their analyses, the disproportionate publicity assigned to juvenile delinquency probably persuaded the public to equate their conclusions with those of less sophisticated writers.

Intervention Programs

Because no single agency had sufficient resources for dealing with the high number of delinquent youths, civic and social organizations began to collaborate. Nutt (1943) reported that prewar juvenile delinquents had been handled by "the police, the juvenile court, the probation office, the child-guidance clinic, the detention home and the institution for delinquent children" (p. 4). However, some critics judged that this alliance could not accommodate the current cases, let alone the increased numbers that were predicted.

More juvenile delinquents seemed inevitable after social analysts concluded that disrupted home life was the unavoidable by-product of war and the primary cause of juvenile delinquency. Taft (1943) explained that it was "unrealistic" to blame the youngsters themselves when they were merely "reflecting their environment." Having reviewed the case of "an angelic-looking boy of 12 who killed a four year old child by throwing bricks from his roof," Doshay (1944) rationalized that the miscreant "came from a broken home" and "had been undisciplined and unchecked in previous exploits" (p. 335).

Since a coalition of liberals and conservatives acknowledged social explanations for delinquency, few educators were courageous enough to disagree. However, some of them did dispute whether they should accept the responsibility for suppressing, or even controlling, delinquency. Disgruntled because educators had been "saddled" with this new responsibility, one teacher argued that the expectation was "thus far proving too great to be discharged efficiently" (Cottrell, 1943, p. 231).

Another reason that educators felt frustrated was the inconsistency with which the phrase "delinquent child" was used. Even within a single state, the range of meanings assigned to this term could be staggering. Kluchesky (1945) provided the following example:

> In Wisconsin the words "delinquent child" mean any child under the age of eighteen years who has violated any law of the state, or any county, city, town or village ordinance; or by reason of being wayward or habitually disobedient, is uncontrolled by his parent, guardian or custodian; or who is habitually truant from school or home; or who habitually so deports himself as to injure or endanger the morals of health of himself or others; or, if below twenty-one years of age, shall unlawfully and carnally know and abuse any female under the age of eighteen years, or assault intending carnal knowledge and abuse. (p. 3)

Although educators may have been exasperated by a task that was defined so imprecisely, most of them displayed the same resigned attitude that they had shown toward their other wartime duties. In fact, some may have been relieved when they merely were required to implement programs that would deter diligent students from delinquency. Smith (1945) addressed this preventative approach when he wrote that mammoth increases in wartime delinquency had necessitated a "shift of emphasis from apprehending and rehabilitating the offender to outright *prevention* as a long-term policy" (p. 442).

Preventative programs ranged from those that reduced the pretext for unacceptable behaviors to ones that rechanneled subconscious drives. With regard to the former, Sorenson (1944) had described the development of teen recreational centers that went by names such as *teen canteens, ranch houses, coke bars, coops,* or *Saturday-Nighters*. In contrast, Gardner (1944) assumed a Freudian vantage to explain educators' critical role in curbing delinquency. Concerned that wartime delinquency entailed homosexual as well as heterosexual activities, he suggested that teachers restrict acts of homosexual delinquency by encouraging each male youth to "make an 'identification' with the members of his own sex." Although he did not give precise instructions, he did add that "this identification must be established in such a manner and with such rigidity that he overcomes (insofar as is possible) the inherent bisexuality with which all of us are endowed" (p. 60).

Another reporter recommended preventative programs because "all children, normal as well as delinquent, need more direction and guidance than when conditions were normal" ("Schools Called Upon," 1943, p. 25). This reporter suggested two levels of preventative action. The first consisted of "stabilizing" programs to foster appropriate student behaviors. The second level would train teachers and administrators to detect the physical, social, and emotional symptoms of delinquency. School personnel were also encouraged to collaborate with public and private social agencies to meet the needs of any students not affected by these programs.

Believing that the public had overestimated the impact of home and school supervision, Gilliam (1943) argued that the fundamental reason for misbehavior was insecurity. Consequently, he advised teachers and administrators to refrain from severe discipline, which could exacerbate student insecurity. Although he did not elaborate on how teachers might develop security, Gilliam assured them that the cultivation of this trait was the only effective means for reducing wartime misbehavior and crime.

Werner (1945) suggested a compact and easy-to-implement program to prevent juvenile delinquency. One of the provisions was that adults persuade children to avoid "blood-curdling radio programs" and disturbing comic books. Instead, they were to guide youngsters toward "good literature." He also endorsed hobby clubs and "mass athletic programs." With regard to the latter, he judged that children would benefit physically if they participated in competitive sports. In fact, he was sure they would profit to some extent even if they only viewed them, because "wholesome American games . . . [are] the most fascinating leisure-time diversion in our land" (p. 409).

Lieutenant Colonel Thom (1944), a member of the Army Medical Corps, drew a parallel between juvenile delinquents and soldiers with psychiatric disabilities. In the case of the soldiers, he thought that wartime service was merely a "factor exaggerating an already existing weakness" and not the true cause of their psychological problems. He explained that a more likely cause was the "impersonal and military attitude characterized by discipline and regimentation . . . and the continual necessity of patterning one's behavior to fit the demands of the organization rather than the individual" (p. 452). He reasoned that juvenile delinquency followed a similar pattern in that it resulted less from the war and more from eccentric social conditions. Had they been properly staffed and funded, guidance clinics, juvenile courts, and social agencies could have prevented the major problems that the country was experiencing. However, the personnel shortages had necessitated an alternative solution, such as "indoctrinating teachers, particularly those in the elementary schools, with some of the fundamental concepts of mental hygiene" (p. 455).

When schools failed to deter errant youths, state correctional schools were available. However, liberal critics thought that the managerial personnel at these facilities did not properly understand long-term reformation. They counseled them to use character development and value clarification to transform their prisoners into productive citizens ("Training Schools," 1943). In contrast, the conservatives thought that service in the armed forces was a key opportunity for rehabilitating miscreant young persons. In an editorial about "war's corrective influence," Miller (1942) argued that the war could be salutary for troubled male youths. He saw compulsory wartime service as a means of coercing "the undisciplined generation" to finally accept the "military discipline" they needed. The structure inherent within military service would "have an educational value of lifetime importance" and help the inductees become "better fathers than they would have made without the effect of the temporary discipline of war" (p. 189).

Conservatives Lobby for Patriotic Students

During the decade preceding World War II, some educators worried that those schools that had devised effective juvenile delinquency programs were still failing to prepare students to respect, love, and defend democracy. In the preface to a collection of patriotic materials (Robinson, 1940), the editors expressed these sentiments when they wrote that "children in a democracy, who keenly follow the thinking of their elders and so encounter a barrage of criticism of our institutions—that we do not have *complete* freedom of the press, *full* freedom of speech or *invariable* rights of assembly, may . . . gain the impression that we do not believe in these rights *in any degree*" (p. v). A year later, Ross (1941) stated these feelings more confrontationally when he wrote that the primary threat to the United States came from discontented revolutionaries "within our own fold." He observed ominously that these discontented intellectuals were persuading educators to support their cause.

Also concerned about disgruntled educators, Steele (1935a; 1935b; 1935c; 1935d; 1935e) had published a series of articles to expose the "subtle conspirators" who were using Communist duplicity to alter the "plastic youth mind." Figure 4.2, which accompanied one of his articles (Steele, 1935c) about "school Reds," depicted the deleterious activities of subversive college professors. Figure 4.3 accompanied a subsequent article (Steele, 1935d) and highlighted the training that Russian Communists were providing to American academicians.

In another report, Steele (1936) reported that Communist revolutionaries had depicted themselves as workers victimized by an oppressive establishment. He rejoined that the Communist leaders were actually academicians. He wrote pointedly that Marx himself was "not a worker, but an educated theorist." Despite the fact that he had railed against the bourgeois intelligentsia, Trotsky was a university graduate. Lenin was a university graduate and the son of a Russian nobleman. Stalin and his cadre of "educated revolutionists" all came from middle-class and upper-class backgrounds. Steele made these points to discredit Russian Communists and to highlight their similarity to contemporary American intellectuals.

Steele (1936) had emphasized that public education was one of the primary tools

National Threats from Within 117

Moody Bible Institute Monthly

Our Educational Institutions Once Believed the Above — How Many Do Today?

FIGURE 4.2. A 1935 Cartoon Illustrating the Deleterious Activities within American Universities (*Reprinted by permission of Moody Press.*)

American academicians used in their attempt to achieve their seditious objectives. To substantiate this point, he cited a passage from a Russian basal reader that was "circulated in the United States as well."

> Jimmy is a little American boy. Jimmy is a newsboy. Jimmy sells newspapers on the street. Jimmy's father is a worker. He has not worked for a long time. Jimmy has many brothers and sisters. When their father does not work, they have nothing to eat. That is why Jimmy must work. That is why he cannot go to school. (Passage from a Russian basal reader, quoted by Steele, 1936, p. 16)

Writing about the political dynamics of the 1930s, the president of the University of Wisconsin judged that political liberals were using the schools to help implement

FIGURE 4.3. A 1935 Cartoon Highlighting the Influence of Russian Communists on Liberal American Professors

"their particular brand of new social order, based upon some measure of collectivism" (Frank, 1936, p. 104). However, he was equally suspicious of the political right for advocating a "conservative concept of the traditional social order." Although contemporary liberals may have disagreed with Frank's characterization of their own movement, they concurred with his appraisal of their opponents. In fact, they wished to publicly castigate those conservative organizations that had fostered an uncritical commitment to the traditional social order. To accomplish this, they focused their attention on organizations they found particularly offensive, such as the American Legion.

The Legion's national commander had written a prewar article that typified those

National Threats from Within   119

confrontational pieces that infuriated the liberals. In it, he promised that the Legionnaires would defend traditional values and "wage this battle against un-Americanism in every field in which the enemies of America operate" (Belgrano, 1935, p. 16). Figure 4.4 is an illustration from this article that graphically complemented its rhetorical timber.

Figure 4.4 had been printed in the *American Legion Monthly*. Writing not in the Legion's own magazine but in the *Journal of the National Education Association*, Miles

FIGURE 4.4. A 1935 Illustration That Accompanied an American Legion Article about Un-Americanism (*American Legion Magazine*, copyright 1935. *Reprinted with permission.*)

(1936) reproached those critics who were misrepresenting the Legion's commitment to American ideals. Remonstrating that "we of the Legion are progressive, not reactionary," he pointed out that the "vast majority" of the 1,000,000 members were opposed to joining a second world war. As another indication of their independence, the Legion's members had never officially censured progressive education.

Although American Legionnaires may not have been officially opposed to progressive education in 1936, they did examine it more carefully as the United States escalated its preparation for war. Their examination intensified even more once the United States entered the conflict. Unable to conceal their respect for the efficiency with which Germany, Italy, and Japan had trained soldiers and developed national solidarity, they questioned the efficiency of democratic education. To allay their doubts, they and other conservatives demanded an appraisal of the nation's educational system.

Democratic, Patriotic, and Nationalistic Education

Even before America had entered the war, political conservatives and many liberals agreed that instructors should highlight the merits of democracy in their classrooms. Erica Mann (1938) wrote a popular book in which she characterized the Nazi educational system as "a school for barbarians." Believing that the failure to teach about democracy had been a critical miscalculation by Germany's pre-Nazi educational establishment, she scolded it for refusing "to influence its citizens one way or the other, or to convince them of the advantages of democracy" or "carry on any propaganda in its own favor" (p. 45). Reckoning that the "atonement" of the German people for this error would be terrible, she provided extensive observations about the degree to which Fascist propaganda had saturated the once politically pristine German curriculum.

> Every child says "Heil Hitler!" from 50 to 150 times a day, immeasurably more often than the old neutral greetings. The formula is required by law; if you meet a friend on the way to school, you say it; study periods are opened and closed with "Heil Hitler!"; "Heil Hitler!" says the postman, the street-car conductor, the girl who sells you notebooks at the stationery store; and if your parents' first words when you come home to lunch are not "Heil Hitler!" they have been guilty of a punishable offense, and can be denounced. "Heil Hitler!" they shout, in the *Jungvolk* and Hitler Youth. "Heil Hitler!" cry the girls in the League of German Girls. (p. 21)

Terrified by such accounts, many American educators supported Mann's advice to saturate students with propaganda about democracy. In an article that he published in a 1940 issue of *Harper's Magazine*, Adler (1988) reported that "faith in democracy" became a motif permeating that year's college commencement addresses. Even though the ceremonial speakers may have deplored the training of Nazi youths, they pointed out that the Fascist youngsters had sustained an education that made them "loyal and resolute." They asked Americans to set similar goals for their own children, eliciting a commitment to democracy as strong as the one the Germans had extracted for autocracy.

An editor at Macmillan Publishers advised prewar educators to boldly underscore the value of democracy because "it is absurd for us as educators to blind ourselves to the fact that we are already at war" (Michener, 1941, p. 342). A high-school principal in New Jersey (Spalding, 1941) agreed that the schools had not made the changes that were needed to protect democracy during a world war. Another principal had warned teachers that they should reexamine their entire approach to education to ensure that it was instilling "a dynamic zeal for the American way of life" that could compete with "the amazing indoctrination of youth in other lands to their national ideologies" (Hawk, 1940, p. 19). The editors of the annual yearbook of the California Elementary School Principals' Association (1942) devoted that entire publication to the promotion of democracy through education. They approvingly cited a quotation urging that "the American people should give as close attention to the moral quality of their educational program as the dictatorial regimes of Europe have given to theirs" (Educational Policies Commission, quoted by the California Elementary School Principals' Association, 1942, p. 13).

The preceding statement was issued by the Educational Policies Commission, which was a unit within the National Education Association. This commission published an extended series of materials (Educational Policies Commission, 1937a; 1937b; 1938a; 1938b; 1939a; 1939b; 1940a; 1940b; 1941a; 1941b; 1941c; 1941d; 1942a; 1942b; 1943a; 1943b; 1943c; 1946; 1948; 1951; 1952) that affirmed the need to teach the principles of democracy. These materials appeared well before America entered the war, continued throughout the war years, and did not taper off until afterward. The gist of the content within these reports could be discerned from titles such as *Purposes of Education in American Democracy* (Educational Policies Commission, 1938a), *Structure and Administration of Education in American Democracy* (Educational Policies Commission, 1938b), *Learning the Ways of Democracy* (Educational Policies Commission, 1940), and *Policies for Education in American Democracy* (Educational Policies Commission, 1946).

Most of the articles, pamphlets, and books about democratic education were written as formal exhortations. Examples of articles with this style were "Building for New Understanding of Healthful Living in a Democracy" (Lammel, 1943), "Carriers of Freedom" (Adamic, 1943), and "The Direct Emphasis on Democracy" (Hullfish, 1943). A relatively small number of articles about democratic education included classroom activities. Carr (1941; 1942), who was a member of a commission that had written stuffy NEA pamphlets about democracy, presented a set of articles that reviewed materials, lessons, and samples of "direct instruction" for "civic education."

Maskel (1943) was a teacher who described lessons about democracy that had transformed the anti-Semitic prejudice that some of her students had formerly exhibited toward her. Cressy (1943) developed a "character alphabet" that used each letter to introduce historic, patriotic quotations. In another instance, NEA staff members ("Selections for Memorizing," 1943) collected inspirational passages for students to memorize. This NEA collection was one of 16 "Personal Growth Leaflets" that encompassed patriotic speeches, poems, and prayers.

In a review of a book with the title *Education in a Democracy*, Essert (1942) complimented progressive authors for writing about liberal issues such as "the threat of social tensions in American life to social cohesion," "structure of simple, direct lines of meeting the emotional problems of youth in facing failures and frustrations," and "the principles of functional form by drawing upon new materials of educational services which are emerging from our social needs" (pp. 180–181). Essert hoped that the book he was reviewing would introduce a series of similar materials about democratic education. Other politically liberal educators (Edison, 1945; Penhale, 1944) argued that teachers could effectively instill an understanding of democracy by managing their classrooms in decentralized fashions. This approach would enable the students to model the collaborative decision-making used by voting citizens. Progressive educators were especially enthusiastic about such recommendations because they combined wartime themes with the classroom approaches that they had been espousing for decades.

Conservative educators dismissed the liberal advice as unrealistic and dangerous. The conservative Stude (1943) buttressed this opinion with writings from early American patriots who distrusted "the conduct of the general public" and saw unrestrained democracy as the road to anarchy. He concluded that constraints on democracy were politically expedient as well as congruent with the ideals of the country's founding fathers. Andrews (1943) agreed that educators should teach democratic education by helping students understand that "in a democratic society it sometimes becomes necessary for the government to exercise certain restrictions over its people" (p. 26). Liberal extremists were upset when many of their colleagues agreed with this advice. Even more unsettling, so did President Roosevelt and the members of his liberal administration.

Patriotic Education

As the wartime threats to the United States increased, educators argued that the schools should introduce topics that went beyond knowledge of democratic government, values, and institutions. Tuttle (1993b) reported that President Roosevelt had made national pleas that effectively transformed democratic education into patriotic education. In a letter addressed to the "patrons, students and teachers of American schools," Roosevelt (1941) had advised them to turn away from "hoarding" and direct their lives toward "sacrificial giving." He adjured children to "achieve the satisfaction of the good life and to eliminate evil from the world" (p. 226). Although Roosevelt had made this supplication in an NEA journal, he restated the same points in his popular radio broadcasts.

Even teachers who disagreed with the prevalent methods for nurturing patriotism recognized that the public supported these practices. Prior to America's entry into the war, Klapper (1940) wrote that the United States had already become embroiled in "the present war crisis." He lectured teachers that the inculcation of patriotism was an important strategy for defending the country. One editorialist ("Responsibility of Education," 1941) directed educators to wake up to their direct responsibility for "the building of national unity and morale."

Another report (Staff of Springfield Missouri Public Schools, 1942) contained detailed advice about ways to transform democratic education into patriotic education. For example, teachers were to ensure that their instruction involved "symbols, principles and emotional expressions," that it reinforced "specific values," and developed national "pride." The writer also warned that patriotic education should not be confused with nationalistic education, which discouraged international alliances and promoted "excessive military emphasis."

Most educators believed that the presence of militarism within school programs transformed them from patriotic to nationalistic education. Although he recognized this distinction, Mills (1943) still concluded that schools had no choice but to stimulate patriotism through "direct participation" in war activities. A high-school principal agreed that "a little shift of school activities" could accommodate student involvement in "fire-prevention, scrap conservation, and an occasional contact with the public in rationing and registration" (Rich, 1943, p. 39). One guidance counselor (Dyer, 1943) observed that schools had relinquished their prewar objectives as well as entire programs so that they could "concentrate on education for defense."

Nationalistic Education

Just as supporters of patriotic education expanded the scope of democratic education, the advocates of nationalistic education extended the limits of patriotic education. Writing years before the United States had joined the global conflict, Lindeman (1939), who had taken note of special interest groups that were trying to enrich curricula with coursework linked to employment, science, or the humanities, warned of those nationalist individuals who believed that "the chief objective of education is to produce patriots" (p. 570). He observed that the nationalistic educators, who agreed with other teachers about the schools' responsibility for strengthening democracy, disagreed with them about the best method for achieving this. In fact, Lindeman concluded that the politicized communication between these two groups had been less effective than that between the multilingual builders at the biblical tower of Babel.

Also writing before America's entry into the war, the president of General Electric (Wilson, 1941) asked his readers to recognize that the "period of chaos" through which the country was moving necessitated "total security." Assuming that his audience would concede that total security included educational programs for protecting democracy, he encouraged them to think more expansively and recognize that the nation also needed educational programs for safeguarding America's free-enterprise system of economics. A year later, the author of an Office of Education pamphlet (Federal Security Agency, 1942) agreed that instruction about democracies and dictatorships should stress the vital connection of national defense to America's economic processes and institutions.

In an article that they published in the popular *American School Board Journal*, Bruce and Bruce (1940) had reported about legislation intended to terminate the armed service deferments for male teachers. The Bruces thought that the logic behind this initiative was "well taken" because "many patriotic people" judged that schools should be staffed only by "loyal and patriotic" instructors. Although they questioned the practicality of eliminating the deferments, the Bruces would tolerate "no quibbling" about the value of male teachers demonstrating their national loyalty through military service. In a report that was written after the United States became involved in the war, Cocking (1943) proposed comparably close scrutiny of female teachers, since each one was "the cynosure of all eyes from the time she accepts a position in a community, until she retires." He added that "if she has a particular political philosophy, she must subordinate it to that of the town rulers" (p. 45).

In a history of the American Legion that he completed in 1937, Gellerman (1938) pointed out that the Legion had already begun an attack upon the schools' "revolutionary radicalism," "extreme pacifism," and "total ruin" of the American spirit. This confrontational stance became stronger during the war. It was evident in an article written several years later by the group's assistant director (Shumaker, 1943b) and entitled *Our Fighting Men Are Coming Back Some Day—Not to Collectivism*. Worried that this title might not adequately convey his attitude, Shumaker attached a byline noting that "the ridicule of educational 'progressives' prevented a strong national defense of the United States between the last war and the Pearl Harbor attack." An accompanying illustration of a soldier in a foxhole was captioned "some of us will get back, and God help those on the home front who have let [Lady Liberty] down."

The Legion's national Commander (Waring, 1943) introduced an editorial about wartime education with the assurance that "the great battles" in America's history were won "through the teaching of patriotism and good citizenship." Urging patriotic educators to resist the "open" challenges from "social-science extremists," he directed them to emphasize mathematics, science, vocational training, and "preinduction basic military training." Writing in the *Social Service Review*, Towle (1943a) remarked ruefully about the damage that had resulted after "a generation of adults repudiating war as a futile social measure had indoctrinated their children with a pacifist ideology" (p. 67). She advised readers who disagreed with the liberals to personally prepare their children for wartime combat.

Even within articles about classroom practices, conservative educators sprinkled remarks that appealed to readers with nationalistic sentiments. For example, Mayer (1943) gave examples of ways in which parents should deal with children who had begun to vent wartime emotions. The editor included a footnote indicating that "many teachers will recognize in the approach here presented principles applicable to the classroom."

> Perhaps it disturbs you to see your child playing with guns and toy tanks. Perhaps you shudder when you see him throw his knife into the ground and hear him tell you that he is "killing Japs." You think there is already enough brutality loose in the world and his mind should be turned in another direction. You are wrong about this because the games he is playing are his *release*. They are his way of getting rid of his bottled emotions and his confusions about the war. They are cleansing and wholesome activities. (p. 227)

From an equally militaristic perspective, Fisher (1943b) wrote that total war had "positive emotional value" because it gave teachers an opportunity to instill nationalistic insights within their students. Ream (1943) advised accounting instructors to tell their students to strive for accuracy because, "when the bomber is ready to drop his load, he must have absolute accuracy" (p. 19). In a recitation that was to precede the flag salute, Caskey (1944) asked students to model their home-front fortitude after that of the soldiers who had fought at Guadalcanal, Corregidor, and Normandy.

Seditious Textbooks

Cole (1939) observed that post–World War I Americans developed a concern over textbooks, especially those intended for history and social studies courses. While assuring his readers that he could name numerous organizations that had demonstrated this concern, Cole provided an abbreviated list that included the Carnegie Endowment for International Peace, the National Council for the Prevention of War, the Association for Peace Education, the Daughters of the American Revolution, the Daughters of the Confederacy, the American Legion, and the American Association of University Women.

Kandel (1941) was not convinced that the prewar inspections of textbooks were worthwhile. He pointed out that the political attitudes of students could be predicted more accurately from those of their parents rather than those of their teachers, let alone those of their textbooks' authors. Despite Kandel's skepticism, many teachers, administrators, and politicians endorsed the popular adage that textbooks and teachers together determined student learning. Giordano (2003) provided extensive evidence to establish the prevalence of this assumption. In fact, many Second World War citizens still agreed with Cast's (1919) earlier observation that the textbook was "a substitute for the teacher." As a result, Americans worried that politicized textbooks constituted a genuine peril. Although he acknowledged the prevalence of this fear, Ross (1941) dismissed it as "naïve if not adolescent." He retorted that "a textbook is, after all, a pretty dry compilation of facts and will mean to pupils just about what a teacher makes it mean" (p. 243).

Writing during the Depression, Walters (1934) reported on the anti-textbook remarks made by Hayes, the commander of the American Legion. Recalling the liberal "intellectuals" who had dismissed allegations of a school-based movement to undermine the government, Hays responded that these intellectuals were "not sneering now" (Hayes, quoted by Walters, 1934, p. 273). In the preface to a civics textbook written six years later, Broome and Adams (1940) expressed similar sentiments. They described their book as a response to "organized efforts to discredit our country, to belittle the principles upon which it was established, and to undermine, if not overthrow, its institutions" (p. v). Katz (1966) surveyed social studies textbooks from the 1930s to ascertain whether they actually demonstrated the politically liberal biases for which contemporary conservatives faulted them. Although he was personally sympathetic to the "passion and commitment" in these books, Katz did detect a strong "interventionist" viewpoint intended to make "education a vehicle of social reform."

Many conservatives worried that liberal textbooks weakened patriotism as well as capitalism, which they saw as the indispensable economic foundation for democratic government. Rippa (1958) reviewed reports from the American Legion, the Advertising Federation of America, and the New York State Economic Council that reflected this apprehension. The National Association of Manufacturers (NAM) also produced reports to showcase the antiestablishment threats embodied within textbooks. This organization hired a professor of economics to examine 800 social studies textbooks so that its members could "move against any [books] that are found prejudicial to our form of government, our society or to the system of free enterprise" (NAM executives, quoted in "NAM to Judge," 1940). As for Ralph Robey, the professor hired by NAM, liberals warned that he "long has been one of the foremost critics of the 'socialism of the New Deal'" ("NAM to Judge," 1940). Robey responded that he would ensure the objectivity of his analysis by appointing conservatives, liberals, and even Marxists to assist him in his textbook reviews ("Textbooks Brought," 1941).

Most politically liberal editorialists reserved their most concentrated vitriol for NAM itself rather than Robey. One editorialist noted that "if any other organization than the National Association of Manufacturers had initiated the scrutiny of public school textbooks to see if any subversive teaching lurks with their covers, the project could be haled with more enthusiasm" ("Looking for Red Tinge," 1940, p. 1604). A year later, another editorialist ("Finds Textbooks Tend," 1941) who was writing in the same magazine could not suppress annoyance with NAM because it had the temerity to investigate threats to democracy when it was "one of the least democratic organizations in the country." In a similarly caustic manner, the *New Republic* dismissed NAM as "a whip for reactionary business men in the area of economics and government" and an organization that had begun to place "its heavy hand on American education" ("Burning of the Textbooks," 1941, p. 296). The author of the latter editorial decried NAM's hypocrisy for castigating socialist propaganda at the same time that it was purveying its own conservative brand of misinformation. In an open letter to NAM members, Price (1941) wrote acidly that the propaganda from American Fascists was as damaging to students as that from Communists. Miller (C. G. Miller, 1941) agreed that some of NAM's leaders did not merely oppose Communism but that "down deep in their hearts, might favor fascism" (p. 507).

Even though the education dean at Harvard, several of his predecessors, and a group of that university's education professors ("Manufacturers' Association," 1941) acknowledged that the vilification of NAM was unfair, they still warned readers to be cautious of biased studies from this association. In a series of articles written for the conservative *National Republic*, Gilbert (1941a; 1941b; 1941c; 1942a; 1942b; 1942c) agreed that the attacks on NAM were unwarranted. However, he also questioned the motives of the critics who had assailed Robey's character, his investigative approach, his data, and the conclusions that he had drawn. Gilbert applauded Robey's conclusions that many textbooks demonstrated poor writing, poor scholarship, "a very low level of competence," failure to stress "what has been accomplished in this country," and an emphasis on "defects of our democracy" (Robey, quoted by Gilbert, 1941a, p. 17).

Although contemporaries disagreed about the validity of the NAM study, none denied the inordinate publicity it generated. To make this point, Hunt (1941) examined popular newspapers and then quoted from the extensive editorials and "letters to the editor" the NAM study had attracted. An article in *Publisher's Weekly* ("NAM Textbook Survey," 1941) also documented the "storm" of responses and counterresponses that the report spawned.

Textbooks by Harold Rugg

The tempest of publicity associated with the NAM textbook survey did not exceed that generated by a single professor at Teachers College. During the 1920s and 1930s, Harold Rugg (1928; 1931; 1933; 1936) published a series of professional books to help teachers understand "industrial-democratic culture." All of these books had an unmistakably liberal orientation. For example, Rugg (1936) had advised his readers that the "uninterrupted production and distribution of goods and services cannot continue without the definite control of government" and that the country required "a giant plan of made work ... the vast expansion of public services ... attempts at the setting of minimum purchasing power and hours of work ... critical forms of social insurance ... control over speculation ... and the building of a mechanism for financing the whole enterprise" (p. 445).

In the foreword to the volume in which Rugg (1936) made the preceding comments, he revealed that he had matched his books for teachers with ones aimed at schoolchildren. The student materials depicted a corresponding "portrait of industrial-democratic culture for our young people" (p. v). An editorial ("Does This Smell," 1940) in the conservative *Forbes* magazine cited a passage about school governance from a Rugg textbook. After emphasizing that American principals, teachers, and students deferred to superintendents, school boards, and state educational personnel, Rugg had written that the "school is not an example of self-government.... because in a truly self-governing school the students, teachers, principals, and other officers as a group would be the government" and "the students would play a large part in discussing and deciding the problems of the school" (Rugg, quoted in "Does this Smell," 1940, p. 10). The editorialist concluded that Rugg's book, which had been "widely disseminated among schoolchildren," was designed "to cause pupils to rebel against all authority."

Within an exposition of "treasonous textbooks" written for *American Legion Magazine*, Armstrong (1940) analyzed Rugg's professional writings and schoolbooks. He cited passages to demonstrate that Rugg minimized "the heroic characteristics of the early American patriots," broke down "respect for individual effort and initiative," showed "contempt for the Constitution," instilled a sense of "class consciousness," and depicted the United States as a country rife with "unemployment and economic distress." Although Armstrong identified 39 "subversive" textbooks in his report, he attributed 19 of these to Rugg. An accompanying illustration depicted a slime-drenched teacher leering at a group of innocent students. The repulsive instructor had written on the chalkboard that "America is NOT a land of opportunity."

A subsequent editorial ("Battle of the Books," 1940) in the *American Legion Magazine* reported that the Armstrong article had elicited "an avalanche of congratulations." Although the article had also provoked some "bristling criticism," the editorialist promised that the Legion would "scrutinize every book and every issue of every magazine" used in the schools. Another article (Shumaker, 1941) in the same journal was accompanied by an illustration of worms with swastikas on them (Figure 4.5). The revolting worms were eating through books entitled *Textbooks of American Ideals*. The caption for this illustration noted that Rugg's philosophy encouraged "the totalitarian borers-from-within who would destroy our democracy" (p. 5).

The *American Legion Magazine* was not the only conservative journal that was critical of Rugg's textbooks. A report in *Nation's Business* noted that Rugg had found

FIGURE 4.5. A 1941 Depiction of Textbooks Infested with Un-Americanism (*American Legion Magazine*, copyright 1941. Reprinted with permission.)

"the heat turned rather uncomfortably on himself" because parents were "discovering chunks of unamericanism insinuated here and there in the pages of his textbooks" ("Through the Editor's Specs," 1941, p. 13). An article (Sokolsky, 1941) in *Liberty* magazine referred to Rugg's textbooks to illustrate the subversive propaganda prevalent in the schools.

Although Rugg's books attracted critical attention because of their strident liberal rhetoric, they also became special targets because of their immense popularity. An article ("Book Burnings," 1940) in *Time* magazine had characterized Rugg's "lively and readable" school materials as "the most popular books of their kind." The report indicated that over 2,000,000 copies of Rugg's books had been adopted in 4,000 schools. Without identifying Rugg by name, an earlier report ("Treacherous Teaching," 1939) in *Forbes* magazine had referred to extremely popular textbooks that were "reputedly used in over 4,000 schools." This author added that they had been written by a person who was "viciously un-American" and "in love with the way things are done in Russia" (p. 8).

The liberal Myers (1940) judged that some of the persons who had challenged Rugg's textbooks had done so because of their irreconcilable political philosophies. He implored them to halt their attacks and substitute a scholarly dialogue about the relationship of political convictions to school materials. Myers was especially distressed that the conservatives who wished to depict Rugg as a communist propagandist had used propaganda-like strategies to make their case. Even though Rugg's faults had been publicized in major magazines and newspapers, Myers alleged that a small group of New York political activists had "manufactured" this misinformation.

A writer ("Textbook Tempest," 1941) from the *New York Times* took a more dispassionate view of this controversy. Although agreeing with those liberals who had suggested that children could benefit from reading controversial materials, this editorialist reminded the liberals that children required instruction about how to be "constantly vigilant and critical," especially when the portrayal of Communism in textbooks written five years earlier had become "shockingly misleading." The editorialist then suggested that students employ diverse materials so that they would not be unduly persuaded by the political views embedded in any textbook.

In an address at an American Legion Convention, DuShane (1940), who was the president of the National Education Association, confronted the accusations that had been made against teachers and textbooks for undermining patriotism. He admitted to the audience that his remarks on this subject had already been "somewhat determined" by an article that had been published earlier that month. The article to which he was referring was Armstrong's influential report (1940) on "treasonous textbooks." Attempting to deflect some of Armstrong's accusations, DuShane observed that few persons were "unduly alarmed by exaggerated statements about schools being controlled by radicals." DuShane also tried to win over the Legionnaires with an inelegant syllogism. He argued that teachers and textbooks had nurtured the patriotism that had been evident during the First World War, an era when students had spent less time in the schools. DuShane reasoned that the current students, who were experiencing increased exposure to teachers and textbooks, would develop patriotic sentiments that were even more intense than those of their World War I peers.

In his history of textbooks, Giordano (2003) documented the entanglements that occurred between politicians and textbook authors throughout the twentieth century. Although conservatives had disapproved of textbooks that undermined patriotism, liberals had been just as censorious of materials that glorified nationalism. Giordano cited remarks from educators and passages from widely adopted textbooks to demonstrate the burgeoning popularity of the liberal viewpoint during the Depression. This popularity diminished as the public became preoccupied with national security. Nevertheless, examples of the liberal viewpoint were apparent even during the heaviest fighting of World War II. Although other issues such as civil rights, religion, and gender equity exerted a stronger influence on textbook publishers during the latter half of the century, Giordano demonstrated that the opposing demands of liberals and conservatives still persisted throughout succeeding periods. This was especially true during the Cold War, when each group lobbied to be the exclusive censor of textbook content.

Liberals Lobby for Peace

Prior to World War II, liberals and conservatives had debated about the need for a large standing army. After compiling reports and editorials from popular magazines and newspapers, Johnsen (1941) employed an understated writing style when she concluded that "military training has been more or less subject to controversial discussion throughout the period during which it has been part of the curriculum of educational institutions," "its values, military and otherwise [have] been called into question," and "its compulsory feature . . . has been subject, more or less, to attack" (p. 4).

A portion of the articles compiled by Johnsen had been published in professional education journals. Although some liberal educators had used these journals to express their cynicism about conscription, they also indicated why the United States should avoid intervening in World War II. For example, an editorialist in one NEA journal (Tyler, 1939) advised readers to stay away from the "European War" because "people in other countries . . . may have to fight before they can think." In contrast, he assured Americans that "we can wait" (p. 270). A month earlier, another editorialist had cited an NEA commission's recommendation that "the American people will make their greatest contribution to the protection and survival of democratic values by refraining from military participation in the struggle in Europe" ("American Education," 1939, p. 225).

Some liberals attempted to portray the reasonableness of pacifism by discrediting the arguments of prowar conservatives. For example, Counts (1939) counseled his readers to refrain from categorical judgments about the wickedness of European fascism and the righteousness of America's own government. He especially deplored those conservatives who attributed the emergence of fascism to "evil and ambitious men" rather than to decrepit societies. He lectured them that "in America the gradual decay of the old economic basis of our democracy, the passing of free land, the decline of agriculture, the growth of economic dependence, and the spread of those twin destroyers of free institutions—poverty and riches—have excited the suspicion among many that the fair promises of the early days of the Republic have in some way been betrayed" (p. 17). Counts predicted that even "ardent democrats" in the United States might embrace autocracy as an alternative to "starvation or frustration."

Some elementary school teachers attempted to enlist their fellow educators as advocates for pacifism. Bowman (1938) conceded that some believed that "a plea for education in international affairs or for peace seems absurd and useless" in the face of a "mad armament race." Nonetheless, she was optimistic that teachers could arouse "the peaceful fighting spirit of the world." Barker (1938) intensified Bowman's suggestions by urging teachers to counteract the influence of nationalistic and militaristic propaganda in the schools. She reminded fellow teachers that "our militaristic society is our own creation" and that a peaceful society could be created "day by day in the schoolhouse and in the schoolroom" (p. 121).

Bowman and Barker were pacifists who thought that schools had the power to prevent war. Writing two years later in *Progressive Education*, the liberal Ryan (1940) lashed out at those school boards that were restricting "the teaching of war facts."

Ryan judged that such prohibitions, along with the textbook restrictions, were harming students. He cited remarks by the editor of an NEA journal who alleged that those students who failed to discuss the peaceful resolution of international disputes had missed "an unusual opportunity to develop the habit of tolerance" or to witness "a scientific approach to problems of the day" (Editor of *Secondary Education*, quoted by Ryan, 1940, p. 8).

Mead (1939) had used poetry instead of prose to express his support for pacifism. His poem concluded with a verse in which the personification of war said, "I fear only those who believe I can be destroyed" because those persons "are my enemies, and when their doctrine is taught unto man, I am undone" (p. 6). Winter (1939) also tried to bolster the morale of pacifist teachers, especially those who were feeling that their antiwar protestations were not effective. He reassured them that their influence was limited not because their suggestions were inappropriate but because the peace movement was "haphazard and informal." He promised them that the goals of pacifists would be achieved if teachers carefully orchestrated appropriate activities within the schools. A year later, Goldenweiser (1940) also attempted to reassure pacifist teachers that they were actually altering the course of international events. Guaranteeing that their power was immense even when it was not readily detectable, he told them to resist the national pressure to endorse war "and substitute a constructive program of peace propaganda" (p. 145).

Despite declarations by pacifists about the continuing viability of their movement, Hartmann (1940) acknowledged that a chorus of nationalistic and militaristic sentiments had drowned out their voices. Although he was a staunch pacifist, he recognized that even the members of politically liberal educational organizations were disavowing their ideological principles. These recantations had appeared in numerous journals, including those published by the Progressive Education Association. Conceding that many liberals had gone several steps further and actually adopted militaristic philosophies, he counseled the remaining loyalists that "temporary rejection does not mean that pacifism is wrong." He reminded those who were preserving their pacifist principles that they would have the satisfaction of attacking wrong ideas rather than human beings.

Pacifists Are Labeled Antiestablishment

During World War I, prominent pacifists had railed against militarism. Many of these were women who had integrated their opposition to the war with a broad range of social issues such as the unfair treatment of females, immigrants, and laborers. Interested in the reason that so many of the World War I pacifists had been women, Elshtain and Tobias (1990) dismissed the canard that they were less militant than the men of this period. In fact, they were able to identify numerous militaristic females, most of whom had a greater impact on society than their pacifist counterparts. Kennedy (1999) judged that the waning political influence of early female activists was connected primarily to the increasing frequency with which they were depicted as antiestablishmentarians or even anarchists.

After World War I, conservatives continued to allege that pacifism was connected to political radicalism. This sentiment was especially true during the Great Depression, when pacifism, which had initially been viewed as the fascination of college professors, was attributed to school administrators and teachers. Conservatives documented this association through Communist entreaties directed at teachers, controversial textbooks adopted in the public schools, and socialist credos written by the teachers themselves.

Professional educational journals contained numerous examples of the politically inflammatory entreaties that had been directed at teachers. Addressing English teachers in *Education Worker*, Montgomery (1932) had adjured them to study the fundamentals of Marxism and to "carry the revolutionary point of view into your teaching." Kilpatrick (1932) had urged them to help change the minds of any citizens who were still clinging to the "impossible individualism of the past" and who had not recognized that collectivism represented the only genuine egress from the Depression.

Kilpatrick was a professor at Teachers College, the institution where the dean had suggested that teachers adapt education so as to compensate for the "good and evil found in a society operating under laissez faire in a fiercely competitive world" (Russell, 1933, p. 101). Another professor (Reisner, 1933) at the same college had exhorted teachers to reject the "dull, slogging task-work" that characterized traditional schools and instead embrace "militant humanitarianism" and its "gospel of social reform." Carlson (1933) had tried to persuade teachers that American education, which was being eroded by unfair taxes, bad banking, and obsolete government, required a new generation of teachers who would "wreck our educational system in order to get an intelligent tax system and a decent social order" (p. 714).

Antiestablishment rhetoric continued throughout the middle 1930s. Politically sophisticated readers should not have been surprised when an article (Frank, 1937) in the *Communist* characterized the schools as tools with which the bourgeoisie was attempting to suppress the "toiling masses." Books by Langford (1936) and Slesinger (1937) contained comparable Marxist accusations. However, even some of the articles that appeared in mainstream educational publications questioned the viability of American education, economics, and government. An editorial by Kilpatrick (1936) in an NEA journal stipulated that "our sense of economic security is greatly shaken" and the economic system had "forfeited our confidence." Looking back on the socially incendiary literature that he and his colleagues had written during the 1930s, Counts (1951) depicted the Depression as a time when "revolutionary doctrines spread through the land" (p. 77).

Liberal Ambivalence about War

During the late 1930s and the very early 1940s, some liberals continued to champion social activism, opposition to participation in the Second World War, pacifism, and Communism. When Edman and Schneider (1941) assembled an anthology of writings by the "fountainheads of freedom," he followed passages by Thoreau, Lincoln, and Whitman with the *Communist Manifesto* by Marx and Engels. He reminded his audience that Marx should be read because "he was a scholar, and his great work 'Capital,' based on a long study of economic history and problems, is an important contribution to economic science" (p. 507). A selection from Engels was included because it illustrated "the Marxian emphasis on the need for economic equality and justice as a basis for social and political freedom."

Despite the sustained support for Communism from some liberals, Briggs (1940), who was a professor at Teachers College, reported that an overwhelming majority of persons believed that American communists should be jailed, deported, or, at the very least, prevented from further political activism. Another professor at Teachers College had noted that "the whole liberal tradition" was under attack and that "schools and teachers are now subjected to constant pressures by individuals and groups seeking to control education" (Newlon, 1939, p. 5). Carr (1940), the associate secretary of the NEA, wrote that the "influential groups in American life" were using national magazines to indict liberal educators for antidemocratic practices. He personally disagreed with these accusations, especially those that equated alternative educational practices with treason.

A reduction in public tolerance became more discernible when the wartime threats to the United States increased. As a result, many liberals began to scale back their radical rhetoric. Writing in *Progressive Education*, Redefer (1940) observed to his fellow liberals that "ever since the invasion of Denmark, Norway, Belgium, Holland and the fall of France, the national temper of the United States has been changing rapidly" (p. 452). Writing in the same journal a year later, Geer (1941) encouraged the liberal members of the Progressive Education Association to start emphasizing citizenship within their courses because "everything we value is being threatened" (p. 104).

Melby (1942) was the editor of a book that a group of liberal authors had planned before the United States entered the war. Because it was not published until 1942, he wrote in the preface that Pearl Harbor had "altered the setting in which the book would be prepared" to reveal "a greater awareness of the real nature of the current national and international scene" (p. ix). Melby recognized that an increasingly conservative public would be unsympathetic to those suggestions in which some of his contributing authors had urged the federal government to control, monitor, and subsidize the schools. To appease the conservatives, he warned about "uncritical resort to federal control and support of education" or any proposed remedy that was "worse than the ailment" (p. x). At the same time, he reassured liberal readers that education had a vital role in the attainment of long-term peace.

Ambivalent Trends in a Radical Journal. The *Social Frontier* was the most politically liberal educational journal from the period preceding World War II. Brameld (1936), a Marxist educator, wrote that the *Social Frontier* exemplified "the most progressive trends in educational thought" and that it was one of the most widely circulated academic journals. Both of these remarks were erroneous. Even the liberal Progressive Education Association was embarrassed by its association with this journal. Furthermore, this magazine's largest circulation, which was only 6,000 subscribers, was reached during its initial year, 1934. More than a thousand persons canceled their subscriptions at the end of that year. For the remaining three years that it was published, the attrition of subscribers continued. In his history of the *Social Frontier*, Bowers (1964) attributed this decline to readers' discomfiture or outright revulsion at the journal's Marxist tone.

The front cover for the initial issue of the *Social Frontier* displayed the following quote from a committee of the American Historical Association: "The age of individualism and laissez faire in economy and government is closing and a new age of collectivism is emerging." The revolutionary suggestions within the journal's articles were prefigured by titles such as "Education—The Tool of the Dominant Elite" (Dennis, 1935), "Karl Marx and the American Teacher" (Brameld, 1935), and "Education as an Instrument of Sovereignty" (Marshall, 1938).

Giordano (2000) documented the demise of the *Social Frontier* and then its rebirth as a politically moderate and rather establishmentarian journal. Re-christened the *Frontiers of Democracy*, it was published from 1939 until 1943 under the sponsorship of the Progressive Educational Association. As an indication of the journal's shift in philosophy, Kefauver (1942) wrote an article for it that he entitled "Education in a Democracy at War." In this piece, he counseled the new journal's readers to recognize "the probable necessity of a reduction in the amount of social criticism in the schools of the country in wartime" (p. 115). Some of the less controversial issues explored in the journal included advocacy for international education (Kilpatrick, 1942c), identification of social problems in ways that still nurtured faith in democratic government ("Democracy and Education," 1940), and methods for demonstrating opposition to totalitarian countries while still showing respect for the citizens of those nations (Childs, 1940). Although some confrontational articles were still published, the frequency with which they appeared decreased. This trend was especially true after Pearl Harbor.

In a statement within the final issue of *Frontiers of Democracy*, Rogers and Tibbetts (1943) reported that the Progressive Education Association's directors had voted to discontinue the magazine's publication because of "a necessary program of economy." The directors reassured members that their other journal, *Progressive*

Education, would "increasingly reflect the new direction in which the Association will move" and "promote all constructive endeavors that make for better education and for a democratic society" (p. 70). Writing in the identical issue of the journal, Rugg (1943) scorned the Association's leaders and warned them of the "contempt" that young educators would display toward them. Rogers (1943), the Association's president, retorted coolly that a portion of the Association's members had always opposed the *Social Frontier,* even before it had become a "liability."

Liberals Advocate for Democratic Learners

Throughout the early 1940s, the impending war caused shifts in the public's attitudes. Aware of these changes, liberals reappraised their own political attitudes. Beck (R. Beck, 1943) wrote an article entitled "Progressive Education in Transition" in which he admitted that the Progressive Education Association had become "a clearing house for liberal opinions in education." He challenged the Association's members to revitalize themselves and demonstrate that their recommendations were relevant to a dire war that threatened democracy. Liberals who had shown outright opposition to America's entry into World War II could respond to Beck's challenge in four ways. They could staunchly continue to oppose the war; they could reverse their opposition; they could qualify their opposition so that it seemed less severe; or they could reformulate their political position in ways that made them appear to be the genuine guardians of patriotism.

With regard to the first option, some prewar liberal educators disregarded pressure from the public and persevered with their politicized approach. Porter (1940), who insisted that liberal educators continue to employ progressive practices, noted that only Fascists demanded "obedience without understanding." He encouraged liberal teachers to "be more militant about their personal rights." These rights included the freedom of teachers to "bring up in their classes any vital subject" and "express their own opinions frankly and fearlessly" (p. 158). Pulliam (1940) argued that the true "democrats" were insisting that students display "responsible critical citizenship" and that only the "politicians" were calling for technically trained students. Barnes (1940) agreed, warning those prewar teachers who did not "arouse themselves to the social responsibility of education" to anticipate that "some form of regimentation, roughly similar to European Fascism, will settle down upon us" (p. 260). Rosenthal (1939) wanted students to learn about political propaganda so that they could "understand and to evaluate the force and ideas shaping their lives."

Newlon (1941) dismissed conservative-sponsored education programs as instances of "super-patriotism" that actually suppressed a true understanding of democracy. Kilpatrick (1941a) believed that efforts by conservatives to promote indoctrination were irreconcilable with democracy. He endorsed cooperative experiences to shepherd children from individual play "to small group play, to larger play groups, to team play, to the work in the community, to the larger community, to the state, to the political nation, to the social-economic system and its injustices, to ethics as a matter of conscious study, to institutions in general and how they work, to international relations, to war, to collective security" (Kilpatrick, 1941b, p. 230).

Although most liberal teachers recanted or became silent, some of them used patriotic rhetoric to rephrase their philosophical principles. In general, these efforts did not meet the expectations of their fellow citizens. As an example of an early political adaptation, Frank (1940) wrote an article in the liberal journal *Progressive Education* in which he warned that children were being threatened by the "world of violence" that surrounded them. To emphasize this point, he attached alarmist newspaper headlines and terrifying wartime photographs. He counseled teachers that only classroom activities focusing on "human values" could halt the further degeneration of society. The editors of *Progressive Education* also featured practices with which classroom teachers could protect their students from "compulsory this-and-that's to match totalitarian 'efficiency,' rote civics courses to build 'patriotism,' narrow vocational programs to speed 'defense,' curbs on thought and discussions to insure 'Americanism'" ("Nine Teachers," 1940, p. 385). Instead of such regimented initiatives, the editors recommended classroom activities to "help students understand democracy and to help people love it, and to understand people and to help them to grow." Bachrach (1940) agreed that democracy, because it "cannot be imposed upon a people unprepared to receive it," had to be nurtured through democratic education, which would ensure that students were "capable of understanding the principles of democracy and living in conformity with those principles" (p. 95).

Zyve (1941) referred to the many amorphous suggestions for promoting democracy as "implied" strategies. However, he indicated that the educational literature did contain examples of "actual" strategies. Wartime liberals such as Holmes (1940) adduced democratic decision-making as an "actual" strategy and pleaded with progressive educators to resist the pressures to scale it back. Stone (1940) counseled educators to retire the "shibboleths" with which some of them were attempting to advance democratic education and instead rely on the power of democratically organized classrooms. Billett (1940) stated that each high school in a democracy should "be organized and administered as a miniature democracy" (p. 41). Also addressing classroom organization, Watson (1940) asked teachers to examine their approaches to classroom management and determine whether they were based on the principles of dictatorship, laissez-faire governance, or democracy. He argued that only democratically organized classrooms genuinely prepared students to understand and assume democratic responsibilities. Cooper (1940) approved of democratically managed classrooms because they would help students appreciate the interrelation between committees, parliamentary procedures, and democracy. Even though she admonished liberal teachers for their excessive criticism of American government, Geer (1941) complimented them for their democratically organized classrooms.

Liberal Education Continues Its Wartime Transition. Before the United States had entered the war, critics were urging progressive educators to realign their programs with national defensive priorities. The frequency of these exhortations increased noticeably during the war. Some progressive educators who initially had been reluctant to restructure their practices eventually realized that they could display a commitment to patriotism and still rebuff conservative educators. Wakeham (1942) documented this development when he observed that those progressive educators who had been "jarred" by criticism after Pearl Harbor were "beginning to move again" and "revert to the teaching practices and traditions which had proved so satisfactory during the progressive era" (p. 554). The dean at liberal Teachers College (Russell, 1942) advised progressive educators to adapt their philosophical stance so that they could take advantage of wartime and postwar opportunities. He suggested that they model themselves after Sergeant York, a famous World War I hero, who never abandoned his pacifist principles.

Wishing to demonstrate their patriotism, politically liberal educators resurrected several of their prewar themes. They insisted that the democratically organized classrooms were the optimal wartime learning environments because they fostered morale (Watson, 1942), self-discipline (Caswell, 1944; Davidson, 1944; Green, 1943), independent decision-making (Schneideman, 1945), individualism (Anderson & Krug, 1943), and preparation for democratic living (Agard, 1942; Shuck, 1942). In order to highlight the entwining of democracy and progressive education, Shuck (1942) redefined progressive education as "that process of guiding the young in the ways of self-government and individual action which prepares them now and in the future to adapt easily to complex democratic social fabric" (p. 447).

In addition to using the war to justify progressively organized classrooms, liberal educators used it to rationalize critical thinking, which was another of their favorite prewar pedagogical objectives. The editors of *Frontiers of Democracy* (Board of Editors, 1942) urged educators to employ strategies that developed critical thinking so that American children would not replicate the automaton-like behaviors of German and Japanese youths. Contrasting the tolerant philosophy of liberal educators with the proscriptive approach of the conservatives, Douglas (1942) characterized the conservatives as "shrewd schemers" who wished to "Hitlerize the schools." Skard (1943) made this same point when he praised Norwegian teachers for having "vigorously repelled" attempts to "natzify" their students.

Some liberal educators tried to find novel opportunities for teaching critical thinking. For example, McSwain (1943b) thought that critical thinking could be facilitated through reflection, fact-based problem solving, thought processes that promoted change, sharing, cooperative planning, strategies that highlighted the collective nature of international security, and activities that impressed students with their responsibility for building a new society. Chase (1943) suggested that students learn to think critically about the war data with which they were being barraged.

Soffner (1943) advised teachers to repel "Hitlerism" in American schools by promoting interactions between nonminority students and "students of, say, German or Italian origin, or with Chinese or Negro youth." Mumford (1942) supported activities that would help students recognize and condemn the "machine-centered, power-driven, lopsided system that Western Man had created during the last four hundred years" (p. 359).

CHAPTER 5

Wartime Curricula

*[The curriculum should include] whatever education future soldiers,
sailors, and marines, or WAACS, WAVES, and SPARS get.*
— FITZPATRICK, 1943

Valued for their wartime efficiency and ease of implementation, accelerated, vocational, and skills-based curricula earned approbation and financial sponsorship from the government and industry. In contrast, support for progressive curricula declined because of their expense, reliance on elite teachers, inability to train large numbers of students for military service or wartime employment, lack of responsiveness to home-front priorities, and connection to political radicals.

Defining Curriculum

The prewar author of a federal bulletin (Mackintosh, 1940) commented that educators were unable to agree on a definition for the term *curriculum*. Traditionalists focused their attention upon academic organization, format, content, and learning materials. Their straightforward approach was apparent when Frost (1943) infused special wartime information, tasks, and materials into traditional, skills-based curricula. The National Education Association (1943c) was equally pragmatic when it adapted established academic curricula by interjecting wartime content into them. Although these types of adaptations were efficient, the most easy-to-implement curricula changes simply accelerated the rates at which high-school students completed their studies.

In contrast, progressive educators' approach to curriculum was circuitous. This is because they thought it encompassed nonscholastic experiences as well as academic matters. New York City's progressive educators defined curriculum as "all of the experiences which the pupil has in the realization of the aims of education" (Bristow, 1943, p. 76). Some progressive educators were even less precise, defining their curriculum as the alternative to the approaches that they found objectionable. As an example, Fowler (1944) applauded persons who were concerned "with the intangibles of the mind and spirit" and who were part of a "widespread reaction by educators against the overemphasis of the technical and the vocational" (p. 306). The progressive Mitchell (1942) was attracted to curricular activities that were not "too academic," "fragmentary," or "broken into short units." Mitchell's proclivity was based on a nebulous conviction that "life is continuous." Many educators who maintained comparable attitudes eventually became part of the Life Adjustment Education movement, which enthusiastically promoted the integration of scholastic and extrascholastic experiences (Giordano, 2000; Kliebard, 1986).

After the United States entered World War II, progressive educators lost a good portion of their audience. Having witnessed this change, Devane (1943) observed that "before the war came upon us, the American educational world had its affairs almost entirely in its own hands" and that "its leaders prescribed what students should study, and in large part how they should study" (p. 35). Noting the absence of accountability, he concluded that "it was an easy market, and a great deal of shoddy was sold with the good." Even educators who disagreed with these bitter remarks would not have denied that school accountability assumed unprecedented prominence during World War II.

Accelerated Curricula

The accelerated high-school programs that became popular during the Second World War were based on a narrow, course-focused view of curriculum. The military and industry supported these programs because they trained the personnel on whom they depended. In fact, the U.S. Commissioner of Education (Studebaker, 1940) acknowledged that the prewar defense industries had exerted pressure to reduce the periods for training workers. This pressure increased significantly after America entered the war.

Responsive to these pressures, the U.S. Office of Education became a strong proponent of measures to accelerate academic programs. It appointed a commission (War-Time Commission, 1942b) to suggest ways for accelerating programs in vocational schools and colleges. These adaptations increased the availability of graduates for armed service and defense jobs as well as the many other jobs that were unfilled due to the wartime disruption. The Office of Education ("Wartime

Acceleration of Secondary School," 1942) even published criteria to help educators predict which students would be successful in accelerated programs. One measure was the special situation in which a student was "planning to leave school anyway, on his own initiative for work, [vocational] study, or enlistment" (p. 7). Other measures included age, strength, maturity, learning speed, mental abilities, and personal organization.

Most of the suggestions for accelerating high-school curricula were straightforward and simple. For example, one report ("Acceleration," 1942) recommended that June graduations be rescheduled in May to advance the dates on which student workers and conscripts would be available. The Consultative Committee on Secondary Education (1942) proposed that schools change any requirements that limited the number of courses for which students could enroll during an academic year. Because technically trained students were especially needed, the federal War-Time Commission (1942a) recommended that vocational schools remain in session 24 hours each day, seven days a week. The chairman of the War-Time Commission (McNutt, 1942) agreed that high schools should follow the lead of the vocational schools, which had posted signs to indicate that they would never close. The NEA's Educational Policies Commission (1943a) recommended that high schools stay in operation throughout the year.

Some procedures for accelerating programs required a reduction in their curriculum's scope of content. This measure struck many school administrators as regrettable but expedient because of the relatively few instructors that remained on their staffs. Rappleye (1942) advised administrators who were scaling back curricula to preserve those elements that had the greatest wartime value. In agreement, King (1942) argued for the elimination of internships, such as those required by most high-school business departments.

Some models for academic acceleration were in the form of adjurations rather than practical proposals. For example, the Educational Policies Commission (1943a) advised colleges to accelerate their programs by making "adjustments of curricula as may be consistent with national needs and with educational standards" (p. 45). The National Education Association (1943c), which was the organization to which the Educational Policies Commission answered, made comparably vacuous suggestions. It urged educators to expedite graduation and to allow those youngsters who did not qualify for acceleration to engage in part-time work. The Stanford University School of Education Faculty (1943) also supported accelerated programs. Because they wanted to increase the supply of servicemen with backgrounds in science, they urged educators to integrate science-based training into accelerated programs. Although Worth (1943) agreed about the need for specialized support programs, he singled out physical education and industrial education as higher priority supplements.

A huge amount of publicity was an indication of the popularity of accelerated curricula. Although advocates of these curricula benefited from most of this publicity, passionate opponents did attempt to attract sympathetic audiences. Osborne (1942) was concerned that the accelerated programs, even though they were endorsed by "men with outstanding names in the field of education," were often "ill-considered" responses to wartime hysteria. He questioned whether they were superior to the progressive curriculum, which had been belittled "for its lack of emphasis on adult-imposed discipline, for its failure to insist that all study higher mathematics, and for a variety of real and imagined weaknesses of modern youth" (p. 359). Kallen (1942b) advised those schools that had implemented accelerated curricula to keep in mind that they were to "return to normalcy" after the war. Some of those persons who expressed support for accelerated curricula were extremely cautious. For example, Mulford (1942) saw them as expedient practices suitable only for colleges and universities.

The *Handbook on Education and the War* (1943) contained a report that the schools had "responded wholeheartedly" to the governmental requests for accelerated programs. Melchior (1942, 1943a, 1943b, 1943c, 1943d, 1943e) provided numerous examples of accelerated curricula and identified districts throughout the United States that had implemented them. One of his examples alluded to California, where the state government had formed a Committee for the Study of Education Regarding Acceleration for the Emergency (Melchior, 1943e).

Because statistical data were disparate, the number of students who graduated early as a result of accelerated wartime curricula was difficult to calculate. As a consequence, Cornell (1946) and Latimer (1958) were able to document decreasing numbers of wartime high-school students but not the degree to which accelerated programs had been a cause. Although he reviewed similar data, Kandel (1948) assumed that accelerated high-school programs, along with conscription of 18 year olds and reduced birth rates, did influence the wartime decline in students.

Vocational Curricula

Referred to as *manual training* at the beginning of the twentieth century, the World War II programs that prepared students for specific, practical careers had been rechristened *industrial arts education, school-shop training,* or *trade education.* However, the most frequently assigned term was *vocational education.* A committee of the American Council on Education (Special Committee on the Secondary School Curriculum, 1940) judged that early enthusiasm for these curricula had come from a desire to find educational programs for the "new type of pupils" attending secondary schools. However, Bossing (1955) concluded that vocational education's stature had grown dramatically during World War I when proponents depicted it as a critical component of home-front defense. He added that vocational education remained "such a rage" after the war. Smith (1943) agreed that the expansion of vocational curricula, which was impressive during World War I, became completely astonishing afterward. He described the postwar period as a golden age during which vocational programs comprised "huge numbers of trained personnel, enormous physical facilities, and well-established plans and techniques" (p. 480).

Rippa (1964) reported that businesspersons temporarily lost interest in vocational education during the depths of the Depression. Nonetheless, the vocational curricula continued to prosper because the federal government made them key elements of a policy to restore national economic health. When the war in Europe began to stimulate American markets, businesspersons rekindled their interests in vocational education. However, it was not until vocational education exhibited its wartime value that it regained the unqualified approval of the general public. Vasché (1945) replicated the rhetoric from the end of the previous war when he adduced vocational education as the collaborative type of curriculum that all educators should pursue to prepare schools for a "new age."

A reporter ("High School Teachers and the War," 1942) had highlighted the urgent need for high-school programs that would prepare graduates for industrial, clerical, and civil positions. In addition to the contributions that they would make after graduation, these students could support the war while they were in training. One instructor (Thompson, 1945) recounted that 45 percent of the students at her vocational school held out-of-school jobs. Ray (1944) reported that the classroom shops at his high school had been transformed into "war plants" at which the students worked on subcontracted defense projects from local factories. That same year, Bacon (1944) estimated that 6,000,000 American high-school students were doing some type of work in their communities.

The many changes in warfare increased the battlefront value as well as the home-front value of vocational curricula. Even though he was an opponent of vocational curricula, Clifton (1942a; 1942b) recognized this point. He wrote that the liberal-arts curricula were "under fire on all sides" because they were unable to respond as effectively as vocational curricula "to the technological demands of war" (Clifton, 1942a, p. 113). Educators applauded vocational educators for training the high-level workers who could produce modern weapons and the sophisticated soldiers who could operate them (Engelhardt, 1942; Kyker, 1941; Stephan & Wigen, 1942). Johnson (W. H. Johnson, 1942) noted that the importance of vocational education should have been self-evident when one considered that more than 40 different types of specialists were needed to operate a single battleship.

Changing Attitudes about the Value of Vocational Curricula

Many pre–World War II parents had dismissed vocational education as appropriate only for academically inferior students. Making this point in the *Atlantic Monthly*, Friedrich (1934) observed that most of the children attending elite progressive schools, such as the Lincoln School in New York City, came from wealthy and politically liberal families. Although he acknowledged the right of individuals to espouse socialist doctrines about the emergence of a homogeneous working class, he pointed out that wealthy liberals were sending their own children to progressive schools that would not prepare them for this fate. Mischievously suggesting that progressive schools might be suited for children "who can look forward to a life of leisure and comfort," he described the type of education that would be best for his own children.

> My children . . . will have to work for a living and the likelihood is that they will be professional men like myself. Now the competition in all lines of professional work is daily more severe. If we go further in the direction of a socialized community, that competition will further increase, because opportunities will be given to gifted children of impecunious parents who will struggle the harder, since their chance to get an education will depend upon their proficiency. (p. 422)

A decade later, Brodinsky and Nathan (1944) were still adjuring parents to recognize that vocational education was not restricted to "slow students" or the "children of the people on the other side of the tracks." They argued that it was an indispensable component of a wartime effort that required 9,000,000 new defense workers. The fundamental premises of this argument were presented pictorially in the April 1942 issue of the *School Board Journal*. Reproduced in Figure 5.1, this illustration represented vocational studies as a formidable piece of artillery in "the first line of civilian defense."

Vocational educators had to change the attitudes of parents and many male students who had been denigrating them. Even more difficult, they had to change the perceptions of the females that industry now wished to recruit. One patronizing report ("High School Teachers," 1942) indicated that women who wished to work should apply for the clerical and sales positions that males had vacated. Despite some deprecating essays of this sort, many writers genuinely tried to persuade women to seek industrial positions. The author of one report ("Vocational Schools Training," 1942) identified supplementary vocational schools that had been established to educate women for the defense industries. Another reporter ("Vocational War Production," 1942) described new safety regulations that protected women workers. For example, women were encouraged to wear slacks, blouses, and clothing that was "conservative in color and tailored in style."

Even the tenor of the articles in vocational educational journals revealed increasing respect for female industrial workers. Although he had acknowledged that a

THE FIRST LINE OF CIVILIAN DEFENSE

FIGURE 5.1. This Illustration Represented Vocational Education as a Formidable Component of "The First Line of Civilian Defense" (*Reprinted from American School Board Journal*, April 1942.)

"vast vocational training program" had been established before the war, Bedell (1943) asked his readers to recognize that the expanding requirements of the war still made it "necessary to recruit labor from the ranks of women." Less apologetic, Silvius (1942) judged that the war had made it "imperative" to train female high-school students for industrial work. A high-school principal extended this argument further, directing females to accept the fact that they would not have "the kind of lives which they would have chosen under more normal circumstances" (Threlkeld, 1943, p. 56). A reporter (Metz, 1942) in *Industrial Arts and Vocational Education* followed a more positive tack, assuring women that they should undertake industrial tasks because they could discharge them "as well or better than men ever performed them."

The covers on educational journals provided additional indications of the changing attitudes toward the vocational training of females. For example, the cover of the June 1942 issue of *School Shop* displayed young females using massive factory machines. The September 1943 cover of the same journal featured a female plumbing instructor. The January 1943 cover of *Industrial Arts and Vocational Education* displayed a woman student learning about industrial tools.

Models for Vocational Curricula

Vocational educators proposed relatively simple methods with which to increase the compatibility between the existing vocational curricula and wartime defense goals. For example, Zelliott (1941) identified opportunities for business education instructors to use classroom problems that had wartime themes. Bedell (1943) and Wilson (1942) both provided wartime examples with which to enrich welding courses. Some reports focused on general topics that had wartime relevance, such as tool use (Williams, 1943), shop safety (Parkes, 1943; "Wartime Safety," 1944) or the fundamentals of electricity (Agren & Massey, 1943). Other training reports provided specialized information about drafting (Shay, 1942), radio repair (Ferris & Parker, 1944), or the production of camouflage screens (Bailey, 1943a; 1943b; 1943c; 1943d; 1943e). Some reports (Bauder, 1942; Olson, 1942a; "Q & A," 1942) recommended that administrators adapt high-school programs for special wartime clients, such as the many laborers who required refresher, supplementary, or retraining courses.

Tarbell (1942) suggested that industrial arts instructors adapt their courses by employing some of the same techniques that were being used in other portions of the high-school curriculum. For example, he recommended that they distribute patriotic information, use it to supplement textbooks, and employ it as a pretext for motivational discussions. Additionally, he recommended that they share information about defense during enemy air raids and other practical topics.

Vocational educators structured courses around special wartime issues, for selective industries, and in ways that would appeal to certain types of students. However, some educators went further. For example, Olson (1942b) thought that training could be streamlined to avoid "long expositions on theory" or "the reading of involved textbooks." Instead, instructors could "summarize the field of knowledge and the basic education points" and then rely on the "learn by doing" approach. Westerberg (1942) advocated a conservation-centered model that would increase the effectiveness of wartime vocational programs and divert natural resources to the war effort. He also encouraged the administrators who were in charge of vocational programs to rely on fewer teachers, so that employees could be released from their instructional responsibilities to fill critical industrial jobs. Fenn (1943) urged students in woodworking classes to create tool handles, tent pins, clothes lockers, bomb racks, benches, and other supplies that would be useful to members of the armed services. Newkirk (1943) gave examples of games and puzzles that soldiers would appreciate. He also illustrated military training materials that apprentice pilots and gunners needed. Some educators (Bedell & Gleason, 1943; Means, 1943) recommended that students complete their vocational training by signing up for internships at wartime factories.

Success of Wartime Vocational Programs

Even at the beginning of the war, one editorialist ("War and Industrial," 1942) noted that vocational programs had extended their curricula to more than 10,000 schools, provided more than 50 percent of the workers for the aircraft industry, and trained more than 1,500,000 defense workers. This writer noted proudly that vocational programs had greatly exceeded the goals that had been set for them and were secure "in the schools of today and tomorrow." A federal report claimed that during a three-year period beginning in the summer of 1940 "more than 5,000,000 trainees attended preemployment and supplementary courses in public vocational schools" ("Preemployment Trainees," 1943, p. vii). Jacobson (1944) estimated that vocational programs had made it possible for hundreds of thousands of inexperienced laborers to work in industry. He added that "millions more were given refresher or single-skill courses which enabled them to fit into war production" (p. 5).

Although Wells (1943) observed that "vocational education has been pushed to the front in this war as never before," he worried that the gains later might be lost. Because the achievements of vocational educators depended on federal subsidy as well as public confidence, his concerns were foresightful. Vocational educators calculated that governmental sponsorship would continue only if businesspersons demanded it. To elicit their support, they highlighted the expanded labor force that postwar consumer demands would require ("American Vocational Association," 1944; Arlin, 1944; Craigo, 1943; Dalton & Jay, 1943; "Responsibilities of Vocational," 1944). They also predicted high personnel needs for the many industries that would continue producing military products.

Skills-Based Curricula

Hopkins (1941) was disposed to progressive curricula because they deferred to "a series of purposeful life experiences grown out of pupil interests and guided by all learners." Conversely, he was not enamored of skills-based curricula because they made academic subjects "the means through which the individual becomes educated" and because "learning of the subject matter" was then recognized as "proof that the end has been achieved" (pp. 20–21).

Although Hopkins's characterization of skills-based curricula may have been partisan and self-serving, it still did capture the spirit of these approaches. In a book that he had published originally in 1945, Eisenhart (1949) wrote that the skills-based curricula assumed that academic content could be clearly identified, sequenced within each grade, and then coordinated between grades. He explained in a matter-of-fact manner that "contrary to the belief held by some that the educational process should be different at the various levels, I hold that it should be essentially the same, differing only in content and degree" (p. iv).

Writing in the *Scientific Monthly* about wartime physics instruction, Compton (1942) underscored the need for the "presentation of our material in a form that can be clearly and quickly grasped" (p. 372). For many persons, skills-based lessons seemed to be the perfect solution. A Los Angeles superintendent (Kersey, 1944) characterized the wartime basic-skills curriculum that he had implemented as one stressing "precision, speed, accomplishment and discipline." He emphasized that "youths must be trained to *read* intelligently, *spell* correctly, *think* systematically and *live* effectively" (p. 44). He noted that some subjects, such as "typing, swimming, conversational Spanish, mathematics, reading, writing, speaking and manual skills are 'musts.'" He also required all the schools in his district to hire special counselors to advise them about the military and vocational training that had become so critical.

Jones (1943) was a teacher who recounted the transformation of his traditionally organized Oklahoma high school into a skills-based institution. In addition to highlighting new wartime courses in aeronautics, mechanics, and commando training, he described ways in which existing courses had been revised to stress "fundamentals and accuracy." The school's personnel regularly administered tests that were in the same format as those used by the armed services. Wartime topics such as patriotism, conservation, home-front defense, emergency first aid, and progress of the war were extensively integrated into all courses. As an example of the far-reaching curricular adjustments that had been made in just the English department, Jones noted that these teachers concentrated on "accuracy in fundamentals of punctuation and composition, conducted essay contests, and publicized, through the creative writing class, the war effort activities in two newspapers weekly" (p. 33).

The curriculum that Jones illustrated stressed "fundamentals and accuracy" in academics. This type of curriculum responded to an adjuration from Clark (1943), who affirmed that the "military and naval authorities have emphatically stated the need for competency in the basic skills of reading, arithmetic, and language" (p. 555). The *Wartime Handbook for Education* (National Education Association, 1943c) gave detailed examples of skills-based curricula in science, mathematics, and physical education, subjects that had been traditionally taught in this format. However, this handbook also included examples of skills-based curricula in English, foreign language, and the fine arts. The sections on the arts directed teachers to make patriotic materials, highlight wartime issues, and arrange concerts or performances that supported home-front defense. One specific activity encouraged "members of the marching band to instruct civilian defense units and members of the home guard in the fundamentals of formal drill" (p. 26).

Skills-based curricula were popular because they could be implemented without educational specialists. One of the explanations for this was their reliance on textbooks, films, supplementary materials, tests, and worksheets. The American Council on Education (1944) reported that the educational branch of the Army had developed "self-teaching courses" for 63 vocational and high-school subjects. These courses relied on special materials to such an extent that the instructors, who had initially served as facilitators, eventually became completely dispensable. Although these courses were designed for military personnel, the fact that they could be used without instructors demonstrated the simplicity and versatility of the format in which they were arranged.

Because they did not require technically sophisticated teachers, skills-based lessons appealed to public school administrators who had hired untrained replacement teachers. They were especially attractive to rural administrators because of the extreme teacher shortages in their communities. Marsh (1942) described the wartime plight of the rural school districts.

> A recent release from the United States Office of Education stated that the country faced a shortage of 50,000 school teachers for the coming term. In some states there never has been an adequate supply of rural teachers and the situation is now made even more acute by the war. The rural districts have always lost many teachers to the larger communities. Now experienced teachers are going into war and the number of potential recruits is declining. Rural education is confronted with a serious shortage of teachers affecting all educational levels and the varied fields of specialization common to the rural schools. (p. 9)

Another reason that public school educators were enthusiastic about skills-based courses was the ease with which wartime information could be plugged into them. As an example, Bryan (1942) suggested that high-school chemistry curricula could be supplemented with "practical information on explosives, war gases, incendiary bombs," or that "gas masks and anti-gas protection can be stressed in the study of acids, bases, and salts" (p. 60). Cardall (1943) provided military career information that could be integrated with skills-based courses. The federal government ("Packets Popular on Aviation," 1942) provided aviation education materials that could be

Can You Learn These Planes by Name?

Students making model planes will think of P-38s as "Lightnings." On January 4 the Army and Navy jointly announced a plan to follow the English practice of giving names to various classes of ships. To talk intelligently about United States military airplanes students will need to become familiar with the following list:

With a few exceptions, where manufacturers have not yet submitted suggested names, the following will be applied to American aircraft:

Heavy Bombers

Army, Navy, and Marine Corps	Original Manufacturer	Name
B-17	Boeing	Flying Fortress
B-24 PB4Y	Consolidated	Liberator

Medium Bombers

B-18	Douglas	Bolo
B-23	Douglas	Dragon
B-25 PBJ	North American	Mitchell
B-26	Martin	Marauder
B-34 PV	Vega	Ventura

Light Bombers

A-20 BD	Douglas	Havoc (Attack)
A-24 SBD	Douglas	Dauntless (Dive)
A-25 SB2C	Curtiss	Helldiver (Dive)
A-29 PBO	Lockheed	Hudson (Patrol)
A-34 SB2A	Brewster	Buccaneer (Dive)
A-35	Vultee	Vengeance (Dive)
SB2U	Vought-Sikorsky	Vindicator (Dive)
TBD	Douglas	Devastator (Torpedo)
TBF	Grumman	Avenger (Torpedo)

Patrol Bombers (Flying Boats)

OA-10 PBY	Consolidated	Catalina
PB2Y	Consolidated	Coronado
PBM	Martin	Mariner

FIGURE 5.2. The Federal Government Published Materials to Help Students Learn about Military Aviation

incorporated into traditional courses. Figure 5.2 contains a portion of a list ("Can You Learn," 1943) that students were to memorize to "talk intelligently about United States military airplanes."

Chambers (1947) recounted that the American Council on Education had appointed a special commission in 1945 to study the skills-based lessons and materials that the armed services had developed. Believing that the army training programs had been validated by their success, the American Council on Education commissioned other postwar studies to determine whether the same model could benefit public education. They were particularly interested in those programs that had trained women, improved textbooks, and facilitated rapid mastery of technology.

Although high-school curricula received most of the attention, the wartime curricula in elementary schools were also scrutinized. Writing immediately after the war, Cole (1946) articulated the opinions of the many teachers and administrators who supported skills-based curricula when she wrote that "the core of academic work in elementary schools consists of reading, simple arithmetic, spelling, handwriting, geography, and the beginnings of English composition and history." She added that these critical subjects were "basic for work beyond the sixth grade" and "necessary in all walks of life" (p. vii).

Some teaching magazines, such as the *Instructor,* regularly carried materials designed for skills-based curricula within elementary schools. For example, Ledbetter (1943) provided a multiple-choice test with which to assess students' understanding of the "V" home. In this test, students were asked about the priority that occupants of "V" homes should assign to the instructions that might be issued respectively by air-raid wardens, city clerks, or postmasters. Another test (Beck, 1943) questioned students about the colors, values, and uses of war stamps.

The author of an article that appeared in *Newsweek* at the beginning of the 1942 school year noted that "war had wrought a revolution in the curriculum" ("Schools in War," 1992, p. 54). Some widely adopted elementary school changes were the use of aviation problems in mathematics, globes in geography, newspapers in current events, and synthetic rubber in science. The reporter added that "even kids in kindergarten will be drilled on how to act during air raids and how to collect scrap" (p. 54).

Mathematics and Science Curricula

Mathematics and science assumed greater prominence during the war. State leaders from school offices and teachers' associations formulated a list of critical curricula programs ("Statement to the U.S. Office of Education," 1942) that they urged the U.S. Office of Education to approve. The first item on this list recommended "courses in arithmetic, algebra, geometry, general mathematics, and in some cases trigonometry where many of the problems will be drawn from the field of aviation, navigation, mechanized warfare, and industry" (p. 7). Woods (1942) observed that "it was amply evident" that industry and the armed services had an "acute" shortage of "men and women trained in specific skills and basic school subjects, especially science and mathematics." As a consequence "the schools set about revising curricula and revamping teaching methods to aid in the emergency" (p. 16).

The relationship of mathematics to the technical responsibilities of the new type of war today seems self-evident. Nonetheless, Curry (1942) reassured skeptical contemporaries that "the firing of projectiles, the design of airplanes, the construction of secret codes, and countless other activities require large amounts of mathematics which is sometimes highly technical" (p. 337). Providing examples of wartime problems that he had incorporated in elementary algebra instruction, Anderson (G. L. Anderson, 1943) wrote that "rectangular coordinates employed in graphing the algebraic equation were extended into the concept of the *grid*, a device used by the artillery to direct fire at an enemy position" (p. 5). Anderson described additional problems that involved military transportation, aerial maps, and global air travel.

One report ("Preinduction Courses," 1943) demonstrated that the federal government concurred with these recommendations. The U.S. Commissioner of Education wrote that his office had "received urgent and repeated requests from individuals and organizations throughout the country to give the secondary school detailed suggestions of the teaching of mathematics" (Studebaker, quoted in "Preinduction Courses," 1943, p. 12). This report contained curricula that specified topics and competencies for courses in arithmetic, geometry, and algebra.

The U.S. Office of Education regularly published mathematical materials that introduced wartime themes. One report gave examples of verbal problems, such as the following one:

> In the manufacture of one of our 50-ton, heavily armored tanks, rubber equal to the amount found in 68 average size automobile tires is used. The average "life" of an automobile tire is 30,000 miles. There are about 30,000,000 automobiles in the United States. If in a year each automobile owner in the United States drove 500 miles of unnecessary driving, the amount of rubber used up in this unnecessary waste of vital war material would have provided for how many tanks? ("Teaching Arithmetic through Defense," 1942, p. 6)

Brueckner (1943a) endorsed this type of problem because it not only helped students learn mathematics but also provided "a wealth of information of value to prospective soldiers" and established "a sound foundation for the more advanced specialized courses that are included in the active training program following induction" (p. 564).

In another report, Brueckner (1943b) indicated that the problem of making mathematics relevant to future soldiers had been compounded because fewer students were enrolling in wartime algebra courses. This fact was particularly startling when one considered the high number of mathematics courses that had been introduced into high schools. As one example, a survey ("Impact of War on the Schools," 1943) revealed that 77 percent of new high-school courses emphasized mathematics or technology. Latimer (1958) observed that declining interest in mathematics had actually begun in 1934, a period when progressive programs were at the peak of their popularity. Judging that progressive teachers had been responsible for the diminished interest in mathematics, the proponents of skills-based instruction depicted their own approach as the academic antithesis.

One report ("Alleviation of Wartime Weaknesses," 1943) recommended the strengthening of high-school mathematics requirements, more frequent testing of mathematical achievement, wider dissemination of data about the national need for mathematically skilled graduates, and the aggressive implementation of governmental measures to ensure an adequate supply of wartime mathematics teachers. The severity of this national problem eventually necessitated additional measures, such as the development of special remedial mathematics courses to supplement the standard courses. As an example of this remedial approach, a curriculum ("Essential Mathematics," 1944) in *Education for Victory* listed the "essential mathematics for minimum army needs." The precise competencies in this curriculum were organized under categories such as whole numbers, fractions, decimals, mathematical notations, counting, ratios, powers, roots, graphs, maps, tables, formulas, equations, positive numbers, negative numbers, measurement, geometry, and simple arithmetic operations. Another government report ("Preinduction Courses," 1943) contained a remedial curriculum that identified not only mathematical topics that were important but also ones that were irrelevant. Some of the unnecessary topics were quadratic equations, equations with artificial fractions, and fractions lacking monomial denominators. Many of the remedial, skills-based mathematical curricula (Fehr, 1943; National Council of Chief State School Officers, 1942; Reeve, 1943) that were developed during this period were referred to as "essential" or "emergency" programs.

Physical Education Curricula

Because most of them were already using skills-based curricula, the teachers in fields such as mathematics, science, and technology responded eagerly to the calls for expanded skills-based learning. This was also true of physical educators. In fact, no scholastic group exhibited greater enthusiasm for skills-based instruction than the physical educators.

Immediately before America's entry into the war, the U.S. Secretary of the Navy warned that "our educational institutions have tended to neglect the physical education of American youth" (Knox, quoted in "Athletics: An Aid," 1941, p. 32). After the United States entered the war, this admonition was echoed by others. The executive secretary of the NEA (Givens, 1942) supplicated school administrators to develop essential physical education skills such as swimming to save the lives of future soldiers. An army survey ("Soldier Opinion," 1944) revealed that soldiers judged physical conditioning to be the most important skill developed in preinduction programs. The public agreed with government officials, educators, and soldiers that physical conditioning was essential to modern warfare.

Military Curricula. Even before the war, Staley (1941) reported that numerous school boards had been petitioning the War Department to certify their physical education programs as official military training units. Once the United States was at war, school boards assigned even higher priority to physical training. They began to search for ways of integrating physical education with military or military-like activities. Special programs such as the High School Victory Corps seemed to provide a convenient opportunity for achieving this goal. In fact, some school administrators assumed that the drilling within the High School Victory Corps and comparable programs could even replace traditional physical education activities. After all, the High School Victory Corps was designed to "redirect the health and physical training programs" and "to provide voluntary and properly conducted military drill" ("High School Victory Corps," 1942, p. 6). Since the armed services needed persons who were able "to give orders and to obey them," Jessen (1942) endorsed physical education curricula that would develop discipline as well as strength. Stoddard (1942) recommended a daily regimen that included five minutes of "military facings" (e.g., right face, left face, about face, and mark time) as well as five minutes of marching.

McGilvey (1942) was ambivalent about militarizing physical education. Although he conceded that physical fitness programs should develop patriotism and wartime preparedness, he argued that educators needed to carefully evaluate any programs that accentuated discipline or nationalism. An article with an unambiguous title, "Military Drill Should Not Take the Place of Physical Education" (1943), included a letter from the Secretary of War. This official noted that "the amount of military drill which can be given in schools and colleges can also be given after induction into the Army, in a relatively short period of time." The Secretary instead gave precedence to physical conditioning, which "cannot be developed in so short a space of time" (Secretary of War Stimson, quoted in "Military Drill Should Not," 1943, p. 7). Weible (1943), the director of military training for the armed services, agreed that schools should not attempt to replicate army training but instead develop general physical aptitudes such as endurance, strength, posture, and agility. However, he did advise instructors to also nurture teamwork, a fighting spirit, and an understanding of war issues.

Some physical educators argued that those programs that did not resemble army training should nonetheless prepare students for the physical tasks that were predictably associated with soldiering. Geiges (1943) recommended a "power building" regimen to increase strength. Antonacci (1943) and Otopalik (1943) highlighted hand-to-hand combat exercises. Many educators (Hewitt, 1943; Shea, 1943; Silvia, 1943; Vansant, 1943) recommended swimming practices that were patterned after realistic war scenarios, such as maneuvering underwater while fully clothed, jumping from diving towers while fitted with complete military equipment, or using trousers as flotation devices. Torney (1942) gave details of a skills-based swimming curriculum that included tasks such as underwater movement, bobbing, swimming at right angles to the strafing fire of approaching enemy airplanes, swimming in rip tides, swimming with only arms, swimming with only legs, swimming while using combat debris for flotation, and swimming in water with oil burning on its surface. Although he had developed a curriculum comparable to that of Torney, Wehring (1942) augmented the competencies with night swimming, boat handling, and aquatic leadership.

Curricula for Women. Campion (1942) recommended that physical educators prepare high-school females for the strenuous wartime tasks that they might have to discharge while working in the defense industries. Schuck (1943) agreed that "the American girl, in her later teens, should be trained for doing physical work for the war effort" (p. 301). To help female students develop strength, endurance, flexibility, and time-space relationships, one report ("Suggestive Materials to Supplement," 1944) provided a "rhythmic" curriculum that encompassed stretching and calisthenics.

Education for Victory depicted sports activities as opportunities for females to acquire the physical skills they might need during war. This journal also featured a special physical education test to measure the performance levels of female high-school students. The test consisted of "the standing broad jump, the basketball throw for distance and the modified potato race . . . sit-ups, modified pull-ups, and modified push-ups . . . the 10 second squat-thrust . . . [and] the 30 second squat-thrust." Although the editors recommended that all high-school teachers administer this exam, they cautioned them to "not permit any girl to take the tests during her menstrual period" ("Physical Performance Levels," 1943, p. 3).

Halsey (1942) described a survey that was designed to discover whether physical education programs for female college students had been altered during the first year of America's participation in the war. She indicated that 123 surveys were returned, of which 46 percent indicated curriculum changes and 17 percent documented increases in the minimum number of physical education credit hours in which students were required to enroll. She noted that many college administrators had claimed that they were promoting increased female participation in physical education through "speeches, papers, assembly programs, faculty meetings, committee work, and the like." Halsey added insightfully that "the most convincing evidence of support, however—more money and more staff—was cited in only 8 institutions" (p. 283).

Sports Curricula. Griffith (1942) reviewed editorials, articles, and reports from World War I to demonstrate that the nation's young men had been physically unprepared for that earlier war. He judged that competitive school sports could have helped, had these not been discouraged by progressive educators. He lectured the progressive educators that "real Americans have never thought it wrong to want to

FIGURE 5.3. A 1943 Political Cartoon That Emphasized the Importance of Active Participation in Competitive Sports (*Reprinted from American School Board Journal, November 1944.*)

win at sports" (pp. 18–19). Griffith was scolding those progressive educators (e.g., Ainsworth, 1943; Bonney, 1943; Moulton, 1943) who had modified physical education curricula to engender psychological security, cooperation, critical thinking, and democratic classroom management. Figure 5.3, a political cartoon that appeared in the November 1944 issue of the *American School Board Journal*, depicted the unenviable fate of students who observed rather than participated in competitive sports.

FIGURE 5.4. A World War II Advertisement That Associated Athletic Fabrics with Wartime Defense (*Athletic Journal*, copyright 1941. Reprinted by permission of the publisher. All rights reserved.)

Rogers (F. R. Rogers, 1944) reviewed physical education during World War I, a period when 30 percent of armed service inductees had been classified as physically unfit. Although state and local school boards had resolved to correct this shocking situation through mandatory physical education activities in the high schools, the number of inductees who were physically unfit had increased to 50 percent by World War II. Rogers explained this paradox by noting that many of the required physical education courses were taught by progressive educators who emphasized "moral" development instead of "muscle," "sweat," and "strength." Rogers urged physical educators to return to the skills-based curricula that had been espoused by prominent World War I academicians such as Franklin Bobbitt. Bobbitt himself later recapitulated some of his earlier generalizations when he wrote that any competitive sport

FIGURE 5.5. A World War II Advertisement That Linked the Skills of Athletes to Those of Soldiers (*The Bike Web Company. Scholastic Coach, copyright 1943. Reprinted by permission of the publisher. All rights reserved.*)

"is enjoyable, of course, since humankind loves the job of battle and finds its supreme ecstasy in rejoicing over a fallen foe" (1941, p. 309). However, he also demonstrated that he had matured when he cautioned that "in both players and spectators it whips up the antagonistic emotions and attitudes of the fighting spirit, rather than the friendly emotions of generous play."

Porter (1943), who was a strong supporter of high-school athletics, predicted that the war would finally cause physical education "to receive the attention which is its due" (p. 34). Although he was correct, much of that attention was restricted to competitive athletics. Possibly because of their personal backgrounds and experiences, many physical educators found the rationalization for competitive athletics quite convincing. Their commitment was strengthened by assurances that competitive

Figure 5.6. A World War II Advertisement That Associated Sporting Nets with National Defense (R.J. Ederer Company. *Athletic Journal*, copyright 1944. Reprinted by permission of the publisher. All rights reserved.)

sports developed essential wartime skills. Both Veenker (1943) and Griffith (1941a; 1941b; 1941c; 1941d) wrote that sports should be encouraged because they developed team cooperation, tactical maneuvering, and physical conditioning.

Some enthusiasts highlighted the similarities between football and combat. One report ("Military Drill Should," 1943) about soldiers playing a football game overseas contained a picture that was captioned "a neck tackle, slightly rough, but effective when needed" (p. 7). An advertisement from the Wilson sports equipment company in the September issue of *Athletic Journal* contained an illustration that superimposed football players and other athletes on a combat background. Beneath the picture was General Douglas MacArthur's remark that "in the fields of friendly strife are sown the seeds which, in other years on other fields, will bear the fruits of victory." Although the basis for a comparison may have been weaker in baseball, basketball, volleyball, and soccer, proponents of these sports were as opportunistic as the football supporters. Figure 5.4, Figure 5.5, and Figure 5.6 are portions of advertisements that appeared in physical educational journals. Although each ad was from a different company, they all used the connection between athletics and war to market their products.

Progressive Curricula

Writing in 1897, John Dewey (1940) had articulated a "pedagogic creed" that was to be repeated often by fervent followers as well as irate opponents. His disciples restated it because they thought it was cogent; his adversaries repeated it to highlight its outrageousness. Arguing that the traditional notion of curriculum failed to defer to the "primitive unconscious unity of social life," Dewey judged that the subject of education was not "science, nor literature, nor history, nor geography, but the child's own social activities" (p. 9). He dismissed skills-based curricula because "progress is not in the success of studies, but in the development of new attitudes" and that "there is, therefore no succession of studies in the ideal school curriculum" (pp. 11–12).

Although he eventually tempered these opinions, Dewey was unable to dissuade many of the zealous advocates who had been inspired by his early remarks (Giordano, 2000). The accurate depiction of Dewey's opinions was complicated even further because his opponents found it politically advantageous to cite either the early remarks or injudiciously paraphrased versions of them. Armentrout (1939) made these points in a progressive educational journal when he observed that the controversies between progressive and skills-based educators were based largely on stereotypes. He thought that progressive educators had unfairly dismissed traditional instructors for supporting "teacher-imposed-adult-view-of-subject-matter." Just as unfairly, the traditionalists had criticized progressive educators for catering to "the impulses, desires, whims, and ever changing interests of the child" (p. 275).

Although Armentrout correctly noted that the two sides had been typecast on the basis of the extremists within their movements, he failed to note that recent shifts in criticism had placed the progressive educators in a precarious position. A year earlier, Bode (1938a), a veteran progressive educator, wrote that his movement had "started as a protest against regimentation and the 'imposition' of adult standards." Bode noted derisively that "the sinfulness of such imposition has long been a favorite theme wherever the faithful were gathered" and that "as in the case of the Mother Goose rhymes, endless repetition, curiously enough, seemed to enhance the charm" (p. 38). After remarking that "no thoughtful observer of American education can have failed to notice that a significant change is taking place," Bode reported that concern about curriculum had ceased to be the raison d'être for progressive educators. The leaders of the progressive movement had turned instead to "the social implications of education." In a book that he published that same year, Bode (1938b) wrote that the unsuccessful search for the social and political implications of progressive education had "burdened the progressive movement with a heavy load of trivialities and errors" (p. 113).

Although the radical political stances of progressive educators may have elicited much of the initial hostility that was directed at them, political and pedagogical issues merged. Bowers (1962) concluded that critics of the radical social reconstructionists of the 1930s had superimposed the political perils of communism onto the progressive curricula with which the reconstructionists were associated. As a result, progressive academic activities were seen as calculated strategies with which disloyal educators were attempting to dismantle America's national security.

Many liberal educators did not deny these accusations. Responding to criticism that Communists had infiltrated teachers' unions, the liberal Hendley (1939) agreed that "whatever Communists there are in the schools are probably in the Union" (p. 239). However, he thought the resulting problem was complicated by the lack of a test with which to differentiate Communists, socialists, and those who were just "muddle-headed." Consequently, he recommended that all union members remain vigilant, respect democracy, and tolerate fellow members, including the Communists. Needless to say, such a response was hardly reassuring to suspicious conservatives.

Conservatives were incensed by the confrontational comportment of progressive educators. As an example, Lamson (1940) was a progressive educator who sterilely identified the skill-based approach as the "formal curriculum." She differentiated it from the progressive approach, which she affectionately referred to as the "rich vital school curriculum." Stead (1940), another progressive educator who employed provocative language, equated the alternatives to his approach with "totalitarian dragooning of children into standardized activities and modes of thought." Childs (1940) discerned "many disturbing signs that the forces which believe in authoritarian morality" were preparing an assault on public education. Rugg (1941) characterized the attacks on progressive education as a manic form of "witch-hunting." The Committee on a Democratic Method of Education (1941) demanded that "organs" be established with which to defend the teachers who were being harassed because of their "loyalty" to progressive principles. Hand (1943b) berated nonunionized teachers for supporting "an antidemocratic tradition of associating only with the upper economic classes whenever and wherever possible." He also scolded them for responding to "the pressures of those powerful minority interest groups who so far have had such great success in shaping the school curriculum to conform to their own self-interest" (p. 80). Clayton (1945) excoriated the popular vocational curricula, which he characterized as expedient but nonetheless "Fascist."

Not all progressive educators supported this type of antagonistic language. Writing in *Frontiers of Democracy*, an editorialist who was personally militant still acknowledged those milder members of the Progressive Education Association "who in the privacy of their living rooms, with shades drawn, will concede their acceptance of the philosophy but shun like a plague any forthright public acceptance of it in the bold clear light of day" ("Rose Is Not a Rose," 1941, p. 100). As an indication of the attrition to which this editorialist had alluded, Bowers (1964) reported that one-sixth of the 6,000 subscribers to the politically inflammatory *Social Frontier* did not renew their subscription after the first year. Several years of additional declines eventually forced an end to the publication of this activist educational magazine.

The members of the NEA's Educational Policies Commission (1944) concluded that the schools had demonstrated resourcefulness and flexibility by making far-reaching wartime changes. As examples, they identified the pre-induction and vocational programs that had already prepared millions of persons for the armed services or the defense industries. Progressive educators were aware that their own curricula had not been credited for such achievements. Due to their circuitous, student-centered way of approaching issues and their reliance on highly experienced teachers, their curricula could not respond to wartime priorities as efficiently as the accelerated, vocational, and skills-based curricula. Nonetheless, progressive educators thought that the government, industry, and the public had unfairly devalued their approach. Attempting to adduce convincing reasons for using progressive programs during the war, they had to resort to subtle and long-term effects, such as those that had been used by supporters of the liberal arts and the humanities. English education struck them as a portion of the curriculum that might be particularly well suited to winning this argument.

English Education Curricula

A group of prominent educators pleaded with teachers to pursue "English as it should be even if there were no war" and "not abandon their permanent functions for temporary ones" ("Function of English," 1942, p. 227). The only wartime concession these educators would make was an allowance that progressive teachers could encourage students "to read with emphasis on ideals." However, they immediately added that "international brotherhood is regarded as one of these ideals."

The deliberations from this group were reported in a 1942 issue of the *English Journal*, which was a forum for high-school teachers. During that year, other articles were published that echoed its recommendations. Hatfield and De Boer (1942) urged colleagues to resist campaigns similar to those that had been mounted during the previous war, when teachers of English were pressured "to turn their classes into mere propaganda agencies" (p. 67). Reichart (1942) reminded teachers of "the blunt fact" that their roles were "the same as . . . during peacetime" (p. 657). Grey (1942) lectured teachers that those who implemented pedagogy logically rather than emotionally would endorse progressive practices. Farmer (1942) concluded that progressively conceived English education, because it dealt with life's "most abiding values," required few wartime changes.

Like the *English Journal*, the *Elementary English Review* published the dialogue from a symposium ("What Shall We Do," 1942). However, its report centered about reading education. Some of the participants in this discussion exhibited the same type of defiant loyalty to progressive programs that their high-school colleagues had shown. In response to a question about the appropriate reaction of the schools to the high number of illiterates that they had sent to the Army, one of the contributors answered pugnaciously that "the schools should keep on doing just what they are doing and do it more widely and energetically" (p. 229). Another contributor disputed the accusations that the military's literacy problems were the result of "'pseudo-scientific bungling' and the innovation of so-called progressive methods of teaching" (p. 235). Still another participant called the attack on progressive curricula a "Hitler tactic" that was designed to divide the educational community. In a separate article about the recent pressure to emphasize grammar, Miller (H. R. Miller, 1942) simply exclaimed, "Oh what mad thinking that was!"

Several years after the United States had entered the war, a reporter ("Curriculum Changes Evolve," 1944) who was looking back on the early wartime pressure to transform the English curriculum concluded that the "general aims" of high-school English had not truly changed. The author thought that these aims, which encompassed reading, speaking, and writing, still included cultural sensitivity, personal adjustment, character development, understanding of common welfare, and appreciation of human values.

Just as progressive educators found multiple examples of English curricula that they supported, they discerned many that they opposed. For example, they certainly frowned on one recounted in a report from the U.S. Office of Education. This report ("Pre-induction Needs in Language," 1943) described a basic-skills program to help participants learn simultaneously about language and military issues. Another report supporting basic skills explained a program in which "creative expression will also be fostered as an outlet for the emotions and as a means of reflection upon and synthesis of the experiences which young people are facing" ("English Instruction and the War," 1942, p. 90). Other reporters (Broening, 1942; "Literature as a Resource," 1943; H. R. Miller, 1942) recommended that teachers use their literature programs to promote an understanding of democracy, patriotism, and wartime issues.

Life Adjustment Curricula

Progressive curricula were attacked unrelentingly during the war. A prewar NEA report had indicated that superintendents already could discern "wide circulation of criticism of school programs thru newspapers and magazine articles and also thru public discussions" (Committee on Certification of Superintendents of Schools,

1940, p. 23). Some of this criticism was directed at the amorphous and almost mystical attitudes of the educators who propounded progressive curricula. These attitudes were evident in a prewar curriculum book by Dobbs (1939), who dedicated her volume to "the task of revealing to our little citizen that he 'still is nature's priest.'" She assured her readers that her progressive curriculum was not based "*on a subject but an emphasis* in education upon a way of living by which is approached 'wholeness' and its physical equivalent, health" (p. ix). She added that her curriculum was pointed toward "the pupil's life activities where information, care and supervision are aimed at co-operation with his impulse to grow in all ways, one of which is in self-awareness."

Critics also complained about incompetent progressive teachers and the ineffective practices they employed. The president of the Progressive Education Association (V. M. Rogers, 1944) conceded to the members that "powerful forces outside the profession" were denigrating their organization. A year earlier, Tibbetts (1943), a former president of the same organization, had urged the members to turn away from "the cry for more formal discipline and for the glorification of the R's." Ravitch (2000) cited additional criticism that must have been especially styptic because it came from the general public as well as rival educational factions.

Lindeman (1943) chronicled that progressive education "had been almost destroyed" prior to the war by a "pincer" maneuver in which radical elements from the political left and right had simultaneously assaulted it. He added that the movement's leadership nearly collapsed and that the "situation has become worse rather than better as we have gone deeper and deeper into total warfare" (p. 4). Pounds (1944) noted that some progressive educators did fight back, making "frantic efforts to maintain things as they were." However, most decided not to resist the tidal wave of curricular reform. This passive resistance could have misrepresented the percentage of teachers actually supporting those special wartime curricula that emphasized classroom discipline, vocational training, basic skills, and scholastic nationalism. Pounds was convinced that many shrewd progressive educators were maintaining an underground resistance and that they planned "to 'go back' as soon as the war is over" (1944, p. 55).

Progressive educators clustered into four wartime groups. One of these defied the popular educational schemes of that period. Another abandoned liberal principles so that it could support widespread wartime initiatives. The third group, which expediently supported the wartime curricular changes, waited for the conflict to end so that its members could safely express their genuine liberal convictions. The fourth group searched for curricular initiatives that embodied long-established liberal values but to which they could assign novel names. The sentiments of this fourth group were clearly in the mind of Mursell (1946), who observed metaphorically that "judging by the din of recent bombings, progressive education ought to be lying with its upper works in the mud and its keel in the air" (p. 248). However, he thought that progressive education was quite alive, with "its name . . . changed, its silhouette altered, its course modified."

As an example of the type of strategy to which Mursell referred, Bennett and Laws (1943) had changed some of the conventional names for progressive educational goals. Because the war had accelerated the ages at which females were assuming adult responsibilities, they initiated a wartime program to help females "achieve perspective," "keep feet on the ground and heads in the air," and "see their responsibilities." Needless to say, these goals were actually the same as those within the preparation-for-life units that had been standard features of progressive educational programs before the war.

As another example, Gambrill (1943) had quoted remarks from an anonymous progressive educator who was resisting the advice that "more conservative patterns of education should be followed during the period of the war." Instead of a "return to the old days of formal discipline, much drill in the fundamentals, and emphasis on subject-matter," this teacher helped his students form "well-developed personalities, excellent powers of judgment, and real self-respect" (p. 213). The instructor achieved these newly christened goals through critical thinking and democratic decision-making, two customary prewar practices that progressive educators had repackaged for the war.

The life skills adjustment curriculum provided another opportunity for progressive educators to depict their standard practices in a novel fashion. Kearney (1940) had recommended a truce in which progressive educators and their critics would set aside "philosophical problems" for the duration of the war. Attempting to honor the terms of that truce, progressive educators had become preoccupied with new types of curricula that would aid students in "the process of seeking out a true personal end of life and corresponding valid social objectives" and "synchronizing the schools to them" (p. 16). Like Kearney, Flick (1943) recommended that progressive educators step beyond the preparation of students for immediate wartime responsibilities and ensure that "curriculum really makes possible preparation for life" (p. 222).

The substance of the life skills curricula was hardly distinct from that which progressive educators had been pursuing for decades. As just one example, Bonser (1920) had written a book after World War I in which he observed that it was possible to "organize a curriculum wholly upon the basis of *activities of life* in which children actually engage rather than in terms of *subjects* in which, as such, few are engaged" (p. vi). Although Bonser thought that the implementation of such an "activities of life" curriculum was "ideally desirable," he cautioned that "the whole organization of the schools, and the experience and training of teachers, supervisors, and administrators are so thoroughly established for work on a subject basis that change must be gradual rather than abrupt."

Writing after the Second World War, Douglass (1949) noted that the life adjustment curricula that had been proposed during that recent conflict were intended to redress some of the allegations that had been made against earlier progressive initiatives. The preface to a report from the National Commission on Cooperative

Curriculum Planning (1941) revealed one of these earlier faults. The editor noted proudly that this publication, which concluded with a chapter on "Our Emerging Life-Centered Curriculum," had been written by a group that "consists exclusively of representatives of organizations of teachers in various school subjects" (p. vii). Within the book itself, the Commission's members lectured teachers and the public that the "subject-matter areas are no longer vested interests" but rather expedients that might "contribute to the orientation of boys and girls themselves and to the democratic problems of their society" (p. 170).

Instead of being developed by elitist academicians, new life skills curricula were to be planned and coordinated with community members. Furthermore, they were to be designed for integration within existing school practices. Nickell (1949) characterized them as community-wide efforts that would produce "healthy and patriotic citizens who are good husbands, good wives, good fathers, good mothers, good neighbors, good workers, good employers, wise spenders of income, wholesome users of leisure time and so forth" (p. 154). Tyler (1949) agreed that "the day-by-day environment of young people in the home and in the community generally provides a considerable part of the educational development of the student" and that therefore "the school's efforts should be focused particularly upon serious gaps in the present development of students" (p. 8). These gaps might occur in areas such as health, individual social relationships, group social relationships, civics, consumerism, occupation, and recreation.

The progressive educational philosophy had clearly influenced the "curriculum for modern living" that Stratemeyer, Forkner, and McKim (1947) published. In an accompanying teachers' guide, the authors presented a set of commandment-like statements about effective curricula. For example, the following statements summarized that portion of the curriculum that dealt with democratic government.

> The schools must therefore provide the learner with experiences which will (1) help him become sensitive to problems of common welfare in the family, the school, the community, the nation, and the world; (2) teach him to work with others in the solution of these problems; (3) develop his feeling of individual responsibility for the common welfare; and (4) help him to act in harmony with what he says and believes. (Stratemeyer, McKim, & Sweet, 1952, p. 3)

The authors added that their curriculum was one in which "learners and their teachers work together on the problems and interests of everyday living" (Stratemeyer, McKim, & Sweet, 1952, p. 9).

Kliebard (1986) observed that proponents of the life adjustment curricula had attempted to ward off criticism by selecting social commitment as their ideological centerpiece. After all, the social activists who had been identified with progressive education during the 1930s had been censured for failing to imbue students with the societal commitment needed to sustain and protect democratic government. Despite their precautionary maneuvers, the progressive educators of the 1940s were accused of manipulating education to advance their vested political interests. Undaunted by these accusations, Benne (1949) summoned sentiments from the social reconstructionists of the preceding decade when he advised latter-day progressive educators to defend "social engineering" as an essential feature of sound education.

Pragmatic Curricula

Many educators were compelled, or at least felt compelled, to adapt their curricula to the war. Spears (1943) judged that these adaptations were extensive and immediate. He wrote that "the 26,000 public high schools of the country have revealed a remarkable inclination to swing their programs over behind an all-out war effort" (p. 359). After looking back at textbooks, editorials, and professional reports, Nelson (1986) concluded that pervasive and rapid wartime changes were made within the secondary social studies curricula. Field (1994) judged that government-sponsored savings and conservation campaigns had a noticeable impact on the elementary schools. Writing during the war itself, Wade (1943) concluded that the wartime changes, although they were affecting both elementary and secondary schools, were influencing the secondary schools to a much greater extent.

Although most of the curricular adaptations were voluntary, some were required by legislation. The NEA's Educational Policies Commission (1941) had published a set of guidelines for the "emergency" teaching of American history. The Commission's members pointed to the need for guidelines that would relate course content "more closely to current national issues and trends" during a period when democracy was under attack. The Commission's members added that their own guidelines were especially useful in those American history courses for which state legislators had mandated the content. A later report ("Wartime Legislative," 1944) outlined state regulations that pertained to physical education, vocation education, civics, and military training—the four core subjects that legislators considered critical for an American victory.

Whether prodded by state regulations, personal commitment, or the social pressures within their communities, teachers did make adaptations to their curricula. Many of these adaptations were expedient. In the case of teachers who were employing skills-based curricula, they could supplement their current courses with the numerous activities, problems, books, worksheets, films, or radio programs that had been designed to promote specialized wartime learning. Responding to teachers who were wondering "whether to substitute war-centered lessons for the usual school work," Taylor (1943) counseled them to consider instead the many "excellent suggestions" for integrating wartime issues into their traditional lessons.

Expedient curricula adaptations could not be incorporated as facilely into progressive curricula as they could into those that were skills-based. For this reason, some progressive educators tried to assimilate wartime goals within hybrid curricula. For example, Caswell (1943) was worried about academic fields such as physical education and industrial education because "proposal after proposal asks for more time in the curriculum." He advised teachers to deal with this problem by employing curricula that would win the current war but simultaneously expedite postwar peace. Although physical education and industrial education might expedite victory, he did not think that they would help solve postwar problems as effectively as progressive educational activities. Believing that educators would become exasperated by continuing requests for additional wartime instruction, he suggested that "it is the job of local leadership to study this situation and to develop for its own schools programs which contribute to the war need to a maximum extent and which are balanced and sensible" (pp. 278–279).

Cottrell (1943) was a professor at Teachers College who lauded instructors for having "put every ounce of energy into the war effort." Still, he warned that America could be entering an era during which decisions would be made by "brute force" and in which "personal degradation" would become common. He counseled teachers to continue to work for victory but simultaneously begin to help students understand the link between war and "the moral standards of the community" (p. 232).

Wiles (1945) recommended that every secondary school become accountable for citizenship, patriotism, vocational proficiencies, and fundamental academic skills. These were the precise wartime attributes that had earned public approbation for the vocational and skills-based curricula. However, Wiles identified six progressive educational goals that were equally important to every high school. These comprised critical thinking, knowledge of international culture, participation in democracy, information gathering, access to personal guidance resources, and contact with educational counselors who would mentor students about personal philosophies of life.

Some progressive educators suggested pragmatic adaptations for progressive courses of study. For example, Eurich (1942) and Blackwell (1942) both wrote articles for *Progressive Education* in which they highlighted opportunities for teaching about wartime consumer issues in a manner that was compatible with the progressive philosophy. Fowler (1942) and Glicksberg (1942b) illustrated ways in which progressive English teachers could use literature-centered approaches that highlighted patriotic literature. In a similar manner, Abbot (J. W. Abbot, 1943) advised progressive educators to use units with wartime themes. For example, children might research the chain of events through which the metal scraps from conservation drives were transformed into weapons. Abbot recommended that progressive teachers address such issues not only to answer children's questions about the war but also to ensure that their interests did not devolve into an insidious form of nationalism.

In a book about American culture, Blum (1976) noted that many liberal-arts and creative arts teachers had felt unappreciated during the Depression, a period when the courses they taught were seen by the public as irrelevant to the nation's overshadowing social and economic problems. These teachers became even more despondent as the national preoccupation with socially useful training expanded during World War II. Although wartime liberal-arts and creative-arts curricula were unable to achieve the same community stature as vocational education, some liberal-arts educators did suggest techniques with which to enhance their wartime value. For example, within a book on wartime education (Stanford University School of Education Faculty, 1943), the authors emphasized the importance of selecting appropriate wartime music. They warned that "popular music still retains much of the blue defeatism of the pre-Pearl Harbor period, when crooners received fabulous salaries for singing 'Someone's Rocking My Dream Boat,' and 'I Don't Want to Set the World on Fire'" (p. 293). They added that "the French were singing just such stuff when the wave of the future engulfed them."

Many educators suggested simple techniques with which to make wartime adaptations to music and art programs. The *Handbook on Education and the War* (1943) endorsed musical selections and performance venues that would inspire positive morale, patriotism, and insights about the war. Rothenbush (1945) recommended that drama classes foster high morale, transmit wartime information, and provide the "proving ground for democracy." Kirby (1942) gave examples of useful, wartime items that students could construct in their art classes. He also suggested strategies for boosting morale and patriotism through art. Roy (1942) and Young (1943) recommended that the training of art teachers prepare them to instruct persons in the community about democracy and wartime issues.

CHAPTER 6

Educational Patterns Set during World War I

During the [First] World War and afterward . . . vindictiveness toward Germany began to creep into the teaching of history.
—WALWORTH, 1938

The First World War foreshadowed the Second. This symmetry was evident in education, where earlier campaigns to promote savings, gardening, and conservation were hardly distinguishable from those that followed decades later. National preoccupations with basic academic skills produced explosions of courses in mathematics, science, and physical education. Fierce feuding between liberals and conservatives provided another striking parallel. Their quarrels centered about foreign-language instruction, pre-induction training, nationalistic textbooks, patriotic activities, the promotion of international cooperation, accelerated curricula, vocational education, pre-induction military training, and teachers' freedom of expression.

Assessing the Significance of World War I

In his 728-page book about the "War of 1914," Stowell (1915) acknowledged the difficulty of writing an historical account of a conflict that had not been resolved. He therefore limited his inquiry to the "beginnings" of the war. Believing that these origins could be documented well before the single year of fighting that had transpired, he pointed out that "it is impossible to understand the causes of the outbreak of the present war without some knowledge of the salient features of history," one of the most important of which was the 1815 Congress of Vienna. As a result of this post–Waterloo meeting, "modern Europe, as we know it to-day was patched together" (p. 3). Stowell was convinced that this century-old gerrymandering had created the pretext for the current war.

Stowell's investigative approach, in which he looked for historical antecedents to explain the origins of war, was replicated later by most historians when they ruminated about the causes of the Second World War. As one example, Roth (1967) judged that the Second World War resulted from earlier events to which it was inextricably connected. These events included the Treaty of Versailles, the Great Depression, the Manchurian War, the rise of Communism, and the spread of totalitarianism. Although other twentieth-century historians debated the degree to which World War I itself had determined the subsequent war, they all agreed that some causative relationship connected the two events.

Even during World War I, some scholars had begun to anticipate that their current fight would determine a succeeding one. Assuming that conflict was the result of universal human traits such as pugnacity and gregariousness, Eastman (1917) delineated steps for moderating their effects. For example, he advised persons to reduce provincial instances of patriotism and the pretexts for belligerence that these created. They could do this by expanding their social identities to include regional, national, and international groups.

Some of Eastman's contemporaries followed in the same direction. Referring to the traumatic experience of the Civil War, they tried to discourage chauvinistic state loyalties and replace these with national allegiance ("Patriotism," 1917; Winship, 1918a). Many of those who were urging teachers to use the current conflict to develop broad social sentiments thought the study of geography provided the ideal opportunity for promoting international sensitivity (Andrews, 1916; G. W. Coleman, 1917; Norton, 1919; Purcell, 1918; Sisson, 1917a; "Step Toward," 1918). Several decades later, the members of the Educational Policies Commission (1943b) concluded that post–World War I educators had transformed the annual 1919 NEA meeting into a "peace convention" supporting the League of Nations and an international commission on education.

Even teachers who questioned whether international loyalties would promote peace believed that the schools could influence the future. Brown (1943) looked back and agreed that most teachers had truly believed that World War I could be the "war to end all wars." Blake (1917) had expressed these sentiments when he advised teachers that the war, terrible as it was, had actually presented them with a chance "to prevent a like catastrophe in the future" (p. 147). On a post–World War I cover of *School Life*, the journal of the U.S. Bureau of Education, the Commissioner of Education wrote that the war had been fought for democracy, freedom, and "possibly, for permanent peace."

Conservatives and liberals concurred that World War I would influence the future. Both political groups also agreed that the schools should actively prepare learners for the postwar era. However, the two factions conceptualized this preparation differently. For example, the conservative Horn (1917), who recognized that patriotism was difficult to nurture in a country as heterogeneous as the United States, endorsed programs to increase the national loyalty of recent immigrants. He suggested that "special emphasis ought to be laid on those things which tend to make Americans out of those who are not already Americans" (p. 270). From similar perspectives, Stone (G. L. Stone, 1917) and Stone (H. E. Stone, 1918) judged that children should be taught to recognize the centrality of the United States in world affairs, the importance of democratic forms of government, and the superiority of capitalistic systems of economics.

Scholastic Nationalism

The precise amount of nationalism in the schools prior to America's entry in the war is difficult to assess. The members of the Educational Policies Commission (1939a) looked back on the first three years of World War I as a period when the educational literature "contained little or no reference" to the European conflict. Writing during this period, the famous psychologist G. Stanley Hall (1916) investigated the practices of teachers rather than reports in professional journals. After surveying whether teachers were adequately educating their students about the war, he noted that some teachers were completely avoiding this topic. However, he did observe others who were pursuing it "to the heroic extreme of giving it a weekly and even daily place, and of utilizing to the uttermost, and in as many subjects as possible, the unprecedented wealth of interest it has everywhere generated" (p. 86).

Once the United States was involved directly in the war, the participation of educators became evident. A former senator from Indiana wrote unapologetically that nationalism should be part of every school program so that it could instill "steadiness, thoroughness, tolerance, discipline, unity of action, and exclusive devotion to the American nation" (Beveridge, 1917, p. 918). Also writing during the first year of American participation in the war, Ames (1917) agreed, emphasizing that teachers should use history and civics courses to inspire their students to become "loyal soldiers" who would recognize that "never were the opportunities for glorious achievement brighter than in the present hour" (p. 192). Other conservative educators spurred scholastic nationalism with comparable sentiments. Churchill (1917) specifically adjured teachers to view themselves as the "preparers of patriotism." Alley (1917) urged teachers to help their students view the current war as "a struggle of democracy against autocracy."

The public unquestionably viewed the sheer number of scholastic associations and businesses that supported the war as an endorsement of nationalism. As just one example of this highly visible support, the National Education Association (1918) printed a roster of the hundreds of clubs, professional organizations, social groups, and government offices that were demonstrating "what American schools are doing to win the war." Even this impressive list was qualified because it contained only a portion of the many educational units that were backing the war. The full number of units was so extensive that the NEA established special committees to coordinate the interactions between them.

Benefits of War

Writing in the *History Teacher's Magazine*, Eckhardt (1917) noted that many of the authors of history textbooks had characterized war as an inevitable by-product of human nature. However, he pointed out that some had "gone farther and have regarded it as a beneficial institution" (p. 43). To illustrate this point, he noted that war had been lauded for developing individual strength as well as "such moral qualities as patriotism, courage, self-sacrifice, efficiency, devotion to a lofty ideal, consideration for the welfare of others, willingness and ability to dispense with luxury." As one instance of an historian with this perspective, Gomery (1915) had written extremely graphic descriptions of the outrages that the German army had committed after it invaded Belgium. He thought that the subjugated Belgians, despite the violence that they had suffered, would recover because "our unfailing moral strength increases our material strength a hundredfold" (p. 238). Other reawakened wartime virtues that Gomery discerned were "a sense of honour [sic], the spirit of independence, courage, and patriotism."

Some educators believed that war had positive features. Howe (1916) did not conceal his admiration when he pointed out that numerous countries, including the United States "owe their existence to liberation by war." He wrote metaphorically that "as iron must be welded in the fire, so nationality has generally come out of the intense heat and turmoil of war" (p. 43). He concluded by urging teachers to "restrain any impatience or rebellious spirit that may arise with us and receive [war's] lessons."

Many educators (Barnum, 1917; "Education after the War," 1917; Lane, 1918b; National School Service, 1918; Seerley, 1917) viewed war as an opportunity to strengthen patriotism and national morale. Leighton (1917) wrote of the war in France that "sacrifice, ennobling the souls of the entire nation, from the budding soul of the child to the tired, ready-to-depart spirit of the aged, is the blessing war has brought" (p. 15). Grossman (1918) noted the war's "spiritualizing effect upon childhood." Bagley (1918a) adjured teachers to appreciate the "unprecedented opportunities" that the war had created for them to instill nationalism within their students.

An editorialist writing in *Educational Foundations* ("Appeal to the National," 1918) agreed that the war presented an obvious chance to foster patriotism, as well as "a rare opportunity for the promotion of industrial and agricultural education." Writing after the war, Allen (1919) observed that the French had been fortunate because, in the midst of devastation and suffering, they had demonstrated loyalty, courage, idealism, unity, and patriotism in a manner that "will be forever a beacon of light to all the nations of the world."

Although most of the educators who underscored the benefits of war were conservatives, some political liberals also did discern benefits. As one example, Hill (1918) noted that, just as every cloud has a silver lining, the Great War had produced "beneficent results," one of which was increased popular support for social reform. He especially applauded the Russian Revolution, which he thought could not have transpired without war.

Although American teachers deplored Germany's use of education as a cornerstone for its overall war strategy, many judged that systematic instruction about war was essential within wartime democracies. A *Journal of Education* editorialist decried Germany for "teaching her children falsehoods" but added that "it is time for America to teach her children the . . . truth about the war" ("Teaching War Lessons," 1918, p. 328). Another editorialist asked teachers to earnestly ponder whether "American schools teach democracy as thoroly [sic] as German schools teach Prussianism" ("Prussianism, Democracy, and Education," 1918, p. 140). Cleveland (1918) instructed teachers that "the world is waiting in almost breathless suspense" to see whether democratic education could compete with the wartime system of education of the "Prussian Autocracy."

Arousing School Support for the War

Educators helped embellish the rhetoric of the war hawks. For example, some of them described the war as an unprecedented opportunity to refute a perverse ideology. Abbott (1915) wrote that "following the first onslaught of the German advance, the world as inundated by a tidal wave of controversial literature, upholding, excusing, glorifying the conquerors of Belgium, it became apparent that we had to do not merely with a clash of arms but of beliefs" (p. 664). Angell (1915) judged that American teachers would "do a service to mankind greater than that yet performed by any people in history" if they instilled the faith and understanding that would enable future generation to guide international events. Many educators (Alderman, 1917; Aley, 1917a; Finegan, 1918; "Teachers as a War Necessity," 1918; West, 1918) tried to engender enthusiasm through flowery prose that portrayed America's involvement in the war as an altruistic attempt to protect the future of democracy, civilization, and mankind itself.

FIGURE 6.1. This 1918 Illustration Accompanied a Description of Patriotic Activities for Primary Schools (1918, *Primary Education Magazine*.)

Kendall (1918) urged teachers to use the war to foster "virtues" such as "intelligence, industry, self-denial, clear thinking, obedience to law, discipline, self-government and service" (p. 368). Abbott (1916) saw the war as an opportunity to create "a higher and nobler existence than the material prosperity which recent generations have so plentifully enjoyed, and which we have come to reckon as the chief if not the sole end of man" (p. 485). Adams (1916) viewed the war as a force that could dissuade males from questioning "how and when our country may exact from us our lives." The war might also deter independent women from the belief that they could "dissolve the family bond at pleasure" (p. 233). Providing a practical illustration of the educational contribution that the schools needed to make to America's "new nationalism," Bagley (1918b) reminded his audience that victory would be imperiled if schools failed to teach reading to the hundreds of thousands of young men who were being drafted. He hoped that teachers would recognize their own scholastic responsibilities and make their students aware that they also had special wartime responsibilities. Moore (1918) recommended that the United States model itself after Great Britain, which had the foresight to incorporate precise educational objectives into its national war plan.

Many educators suggested practical classroom activities that would inspire support for the war. These included instructional units ("Emergency War Courses," 1918; Wilson, 1918), special displays ("War Cabinet," 1918), loyalty pledges ("War Creed," 1918; "Work the Schools," 1918), patriotic art shows (Dow, 1917; 1918), wartime dramas (Smith, 1918), and war essays ("War and the Schools," 1918a). Students could make clothing and supplies for soldiers (White, 1918), posters that reinforced wartime themes (Grubb, 1918), and even dolls for French orphans ("War and the Schools, 1918b). An article ("How Can I Help," 1917) in the *Journal of Education* listed 37 activities through which students could help win the war. These diverse activities included expressing support for the President, attending patriotic rallies, praying for victory, loaning the family's "Ford" to the government, sewing bandages, recycling magazines, giving up chewing gum, and working "harder in schools so that [students] will not have to repeat and thus save the town the expense of an extra term." Figure 6.1 accompanied an article ("Work the Schools," 1918) about patriotic activities suitable for primary schools.

Special Programs

Although exhortatory rhetoric may have aroused emotional support for the war, precisely detailed programs were required to ensure that national educational goals would be met. To accomplish this, educators systematically promoted specific objectives, such as increased public consciousness of health, disease, and the critical role of national health in winning the war. One editorialist ("War and Health," 1917) reported that an "unprecedented desire" for sound health had been developing during the war. In fact, he judged that most citizens had come to accept the maintenance of good health as "a patriotic duty." Other school-centered health programs taught sexual hygiene. The need for this type of instruction was underscored by the rampant venereal disease that prevented a significant number of young men from discharging their military obligations (N. F. Coleman, 1917; Bigelow, 1918).

Russell (1917) and Wilson (1917) argued that the Boy Scouts of America maintained precisely the type of program that could meet educational needs during a "time

FIGURE 6.2. A 1918 Illustration Highlighting the Activities of "The Loyal Teacher" (*Reprinted from American School Board Journal, February 1918.*)

of unparalleled storm and stress, when the traditions of centuries are crumbling and ideals of civilization are being weighed in the balance of war" (Russell, 1917, p. 1). The May 1918 issue of *Primary Education* contained a cover on which Lady Liberty, arrayed in battle paraphernalia, accepted an enormous sword from a kneeling boy scout. Williamson (1918) identified the Junior Red Cross as another organization that already exhibited many of the features that the school programs were aspiring to replicate. One editorialist ("Bobbie and the War," 1917) pointed to Camp Fire Girls as one more opportunity for schools to join an existing organization to achieve their wartime goals.

Educational Patterns Set during World War I 179

FIGURE 6.3. Uncle Sam Commends Board Members Who Extend School Schedules to Support Wartime Activities (*Reprinted from American School Board Journal, July 1918.*)

The U.S. Commissioner of Schools highlighted the value of some of the federally initiated programs within the World War I schools. He wrote that the students participated in "drives for liberty loans, thrift-stamps sales, and Red Cross Aid, in increasing the production of food and the saving of it, and in harvesting of crops where labor supply was inadequate" (Remarks made by Claxton during World War I, quoted by Pounds, 1944). Numerous educators (Bradford, 1918; Harvey, 1918; Haughton, 1918; McCartney, 1918; Starkey, 1918; Vanderlip, 1918; "War Saving Stamps," 1918) indicated the importance of the Red Cross as well as the federally sponsored programs that promoted savings, conservation, and patriotism. They also

FIGURE 6.4. This 1918 Illustration Linked Home-Front Efforts with the Fighting at the Battle Lines (*Reprinted from American School Board Journal, October 1918.*)

supplemented their reports with practical school activities that could increase the impact of these programs.

In addition to nationwide initiatives, many local programs were available to educators. In fact, one reporter complained about the "never-ending requests . . . from various war-service organizations desiring the use of schools as a medium for their operations" ("Safeguarding War Appeals," 1918, p. 44). Many of the school-centered wartime programs were coordinated by local organizations such as farming clubs, women's groups, churches, and even community bands. Figure 6.2, Figure 6.3, and Figure 6.4, which appeared as covers on the *American School Board Journal* during 1918, were intended to inspire support for these types of programs.

Programs to Develop Patriotism

During World War I, educational administrators were genuinely worried that a financially strapped federal government would close the schools. Claxton, the U.S. Commissioner of Education, reported that "everywhere there seems to be fear les [sic] our schools of all kinds and grades, and especially the public schools, will suffer this year because of conditions growing out of our entrance into the war" (Claxton, quoted in "Great Campaign," 1917, pp. 79–80). Some legislators endorsed such closings so that the money saved could be used to subsidize battle-front campaigns. Additionally, vacated schools could be reassigned to the army, defense industry, or government. This had been the case in France, where closed schools were converted into military barracks or storehouses (Strickland, 1918).

Because they viewed education as an intellectual check on excessive nationalism, political liberals ("American Notes," 1917a) were particularly worried about school closings. Conservatives were also worried, although for a different reason. Phillips (1918) and his conservative colleagues thought that schools were needed to promote the patriotism that was essential to victory. An editorial in *School and Society* contained an emphatic statement from the U.S. Bureau of Education that "the war should in no way be used as an excuse for giving the children of the country any less education, quantity or quality, than they otherwise would have had" ("Use of Schools," 1918, p. 404). Another governmental statement (Council of National Defense, 1917) reaffirmed the schools' critical role in preparing leaders for the armed services and industry.

Since patriotic educational programs inspired students and trained future leaders, most conservative legislators viewed wartime schooling as essential. The most simple to implement types of patriotic programs were those that incorporated drama or oral reading. Professional educational journals published texts for dramas and group recitations on subjects such as war savings ("Over-the-Top," 1918), conservation ("Winning the War," 1918), detection of treason (Leighton, 1918a), the Red Cross (Greenawalt, 1918), the American flag (Whitmer, 1918), and military courage (Blair, 1918).

In addition to scripts for patriotic convocations, educational journals published practical problems that teachers could incorporate into different portions of their curricula. For example, the *Journal of Education* reproduced patriotic and practical mathematical problems such as the following one:

> By leaving butter in their plates and throwing away buttered bread Alice and John each wasted one teaspoonful of butter a day. If they used only the butter they needed how many teaspoonfuls of butter did they save for the little children of Europe in one week? ("War Problems," 1917, p. 581).

More ambitious educators developed entire sets of lessons for arousing patriotism. Dunigan (1918) outlined an extensive series of activities to help children read, speak, and write about past and current patriots. She judged that her activities would help children form "notions of nobility and heroic quality" and inspire them to give "service to society." Leighton (1918b) described early elementary school civics activities such as meetings with town leaders, joint events with veterans of former wars, viewings of war memorabilia, and visits to cemeteries. After engaging in these activities, children might discover that a patriotic death was "sweet and fitting." In a topical outline for the wartime teaching of civics, Barnard (1918) indicated that an appropriate goal was to help students understand the differences between democracies and autocracies. To ensure that wartime instruction was geared to changes in maturity, Lindley (1917) identified distinctive types of war interests that correlated with the stages of child development.

Pre-induction Training

Although they admired patriotic programs, many conservatives were attracted to the more militaristic programs that were adopted widely in colleges and universities. A report described the college-level Students' Army Training Corps as "one of the biggest big things in War Modification" (S.A.T.C., 1918, p. 261). Faunce (1918) recorded that all students at Brown University had been required to enlist in either the Students' Army Training Corps or the Reserve Officer Training Corps. They also had to pursue wartime majors in civil service, education, chemistry, medicine, engineering, or the armed services.

Stewart (1917) reported that "intensive courses for war service have been the rule all summer long at the colleges and universities, including Collegiate schools of aviation; balloon schools; signal corps instruction; wireless telegraphy schools; ambulance work; trench warfare training; courses in store keeping for the ordinance department, in military stores inspection and in cost keeping; practical work in munitions foundries, factories and on farms" (p. 269). Another reporter ("Problem of the Schools," 1918) concluded that the "colleges have been turned into armed camps." The influence that the armed forces wielded on university campuses was discernible when some administrators began to substitute military service for traditional academic coursework ("Academic Standards," 1918).

Throughout the war, the government subsidized many of the college pre-induction programs. In contrast, the funding to support high-school pre-induction programs did not become available until late in the war ("Draft and the Schools," 1918). An important reason for the delay was the opposition of many high-school communities. This conflict was evident in the account that Stever (1917) wrote about a prewar training program in Wyoming. The early initiative had produced "opposition on the part of parents who did not want their boys to be soldiers; opposition on the part of women's clubs; opposition on the part of labor unions, who feared a militarism which would be hostile to their interests; opposition on the part of school-teachers [sic]; and, most important of all, opposition on the part of the boys, who had their football, basket-ball [sic], and track games, but had no notion whatsoever of national-defense games" (p. 145).

Several years after the Wyoming experiment, the NEA published an editorial that indicated that "the Association deplores any attempt to militarize this country" and that it was opposed to "military training in the schools on the ground that this is reactionary and inconsistent with American ideals and standards" ("Danger: The Illogical Pronouncement," 1915, p. 71). The state educational superintendent of New Hampshire insisted that he would "strongly deprecate any headlong rush upon the part of our local authorities into plans for military drill, so called, in the high schools" (Morrison, 1916, p. 93). Two articles in the *Journal of Education* ("Military Training for School Boys," 1917a; 1917b) contained letters from educational leaders who strenuously opposed pre-induction education.

Those who supported pre-induction training were as intransigent as those who opposed it. The U.S. Secretary of War ("Should Our Educational System," 1915) wrote that he was distressed at those American citizens who had refused to reach the "wise, patriotic conclusion" to support pre-induction training in high schools. Field (1916) reported about the "numerous writers" who were arguing that "our public schools [should] offer an existing and well-organized machine by which military training can be given to practically all of the boys of America" (p. 5). An editorialist ("Militant Pacifism," 1915) observed that his initial resistance to the war changed after he realized that Germany and its allies would be unrelenting in their aggression. He concluded that "there is no excuse for us if we do not learn our lesson well" (p. 1). Although this editorial was suffused with arousing imagery, the accompanying illustrations of school children preparing for war were even more revealing (Figure 6.5).

Once the United States entered the war, the prevalence of pre-induction programs increased. The superintendent of the New York City schools ("Military Training," 1918) noted that 50 percent of the eligible boys participated in his district's military drilling programs. Ayres (1917) reported that military drilling programs had been "vigorously" implemented in several other major cities. In reality, the extent of military drilling went much further, because several state legislatures had mandated statewide pre-induction training (Bell, 1917). Figure 6.6, which appeared in a 1915 issue of *Harper's Weekly*, encouraged readers to view military readiness as a basic educational skill.

A principal in the District of Columbia (Small, 1917) attempted to walk on ideological middle ground when he suggested to the delegates at an NEA convention that military training be permitted in high schools, provided that it was voluntary. Although the emotional pacifists in the audience dismissed him as a "sinister militarist," the militarists themselves, who were annoyed at his restraint, characterized

FIGURE 6.5. These Illustrations Accompanied a 1915 Editorial That Encouraged Parents and Teachers to Prepare School Children for War (*Courtesy, The Butterick, McCall's, Vogue patterns archives New York.*)

FIGURE 6.6. This 1915 Cartoon Represented Basic Education Skills as a Form of Military Readiness

him as a "pacifist ass." One of the reasons that terms such as *high-school military training* or *pre-induction training* elicited such a wide range of responses is that they evoked completely different images in the minds of diverse political groups. As a consequence, it was difficult to ascertain precisely what an editorialist had in mind if he or she referred to school courses that were "peculiarly serviceable in pushing forward the war" ("Education and Citizenship," 1918).

Bliss (1917) noted that some of the advocates of pre-induction training equated these courses with lessons in physical education, discipline, self-control, courage, patriotism, and "the development of a man's powers as shall make him capable of rendering efficient service to his country, either as a private citizen, or, when this general training has been supplemented by technical drill, as an enlisted man" (p. 161). An NEA committee that was established to evaluate the benefits of pre-induction training opposed military instruction but endorsed "physical exercises, setting-up drill with emphasis upon posture and discipline, marching, organized and supervised play, recreation, athletics, gymnastics, summer camps and outdoor life" ("Report of the Committee on Military Training," 1917, p. 1018). Another reporter took an even more moderate tone, supporting military training only when it was "conceived as a *comprehensive program* of *physical, moral*, and *civic* education" ("Military Training in Public Schools," 1917, p. 470).

Bliss (1917) observed that some advocates of pre-induction education actually equated it with "training with a rifle, manual of arms, and close-order formation" (p. 161). Hall (1918) reported about high-school programs with "real rifle practice in trenches, long hikes and something like military manoeuvres [sic]" (p. 116). Several years earlier, the *American Review of Reviews* had published an article that expounded the benefits of Germany's military youth programs ("Compulsory Military Service," 1915). A companion report (Green, 1915) reviewed a military program that had been sustained for 15 years in one of South Carolina's school districts. Keller (1915) had proposed that the United States form a "school army" that would comprise 100,000 boys between the ages of 16 and 18. The participants would "live constantly under the strictest military discipline" and devote two to three hours a day "to military drill, army exercises, study of military science, and physical training and education, including sanitation, prevention of disease and like broad general information" (p. 485).

One editorialist reported that the President of the National Daughters of America had endorsed military training in the public schools for the simple reason that "the unpreparedness of the United States offers too tempting of an opportunity for foreign aggression" ("Military Training in the Schools," 1915, p. 184). Although he personally deplored the military types of pre-induction education, Garlock (1916) summarized their alleged advantages. In addition to security against enemy aggression, the benefits included physical conditioning, school discipline, patriotism, citizenship, and the inculcation of military interests.

An editorialist who characterized military education as "sound pedagogy and sane patriotism" believed that it discouraged "wanton assaults upon the peace of our land by rearing a prepared citizenry able to propound out principles and to defend our possessions without carrying old-world burdens of extravagant military establishments" ("Education for Peace," 1915, p. 135). This reporter concluded with four pages of remarks that various governors had made about military education. Although several expressed reservations, most of them endorsed the training enthusiastically.

The Committee on Militarism in Education published a pamphlet (Barnes, 1927) about the liabilities of the pre-induction programs that remained popular after the war. Barnes indicated that a primary objective of this committee was to oppose "all formal military training in high schools." Although the committee did not expect pre-induction programs to cease, its members were especially irate about those that were controlled by the War Department or funded by the federal government.

In the introduction to Barnes's pamphlet, John Dewey (1927) also acknowledged the popularity of the pre-induction training programs. A photograph of uniformed young boys in drill formation accompanied his remarks. This photograph also depicted an instructor arrayed in full military regalia. Dewey warned of "a well-organized movement to militarize the tone and temper of our national life" and an effort by the "vested interest to militarize the country... deliberately and knowingly through the medium of the schools" (p. 3). After observing that the proponents of pre-induction training had been trying to intimidate their opponents through vilification and "overt attacks," he adjured citizens to disregard "the reckless aspersions in which the militaristic crowd freely indulges" and rely instead on factual information, such as that within Barnes's pamphlet.

Programs for Women

Attempting to explain the "myth" about most World War II women working outside their homes, Kennedy (1999) referred to the disproportionate media exposure given to those females who did work in industry. The federal government's propaganda and its marketing of the extensive training available to women may have further enhanced this impression. In contrast, the women of World War I were not depicted persistently as home-front workers. Even so, World War I readers did confront histrionic writing about this issue. In the foreword to a book about the wartime contributions of British women, MacCracken (1918) wrote that the author's goal had been to educate "American women to a sense of what the mobilization of the entire citizen army of a democracy must mean" (p. ii). The frontispiece for this book, shown in Figure 6.7, depicted diminutive female factory workers surrounded by countless large pieces of ammunition. This photograph was identified by the remarkably understated title "A Few Shells."

Using language similar to that of MacCracken, Ruutz-Rees (1918) agreed that American women were to look to England for an indication of the military "mobilization" that awaited them. She wrote that, "as the effects of conscription made themselves felt and as the capacity of munition [sic] factories increased—in some cases twenty-eight times between 1914 and 1917—greater and greater numbers of [British] women were carried into industry, and above all in these factories, to take the place of men" (p. 803). She called attention to those valorous women who were "in constant danger from the materials in which they work and also because the factories are chief objectives of air raiders" (p. 803). In the following passage, Ruutz-Rees described the responsibilities of the munitions workers.

> Women equipped with fireproof gown and cap, green veils and respirators, the brave "canary girls," their hair and skin turned bright yellow, are working in the dangerous Trotyl. Fusemakers there are who must get their fuses correct to the thousandth of an inch. Women from the universities, specialists in science and mathematics, are working as tool-setters; others move six-pound shells with ease. Women, again, work in the tailor shops and canteens connected with the arsenals, or clad in leggings and mackintosh, do trucking and carrying like strong men. (p. 803)

A Few Shells

FIGURE 6.7. This Photo Was the Frontispiece for a 1917 Book about Women Workers

In the introduction to another report about Britain's women workers, Asquith (1918) wrote that they "have done and are doing things which, before the war, most of us would have said were both foreign to their nature and beyond their physical capacity." Asquith added that "these experiences and achievements will, when the war is over, have a permanent effect upon both the statesman's and the economist's conception of the powers and functions of women" (p. iv). In the book for which Asquith wrote the introduction, McLaren (1918) indicated that her primary goal as a writer had been to help "readers picture themselves working under similar conditions in similar fields of labour [sic]" (p. vi). She was particularly impressed by Britain's nurses, who deserved "the crown of women's war services" because "their selfless devotion, their courage, their unquestioning acceptance of any risk, and their willing sacrifice of personal comfort, health, even life itself, will stand for all time in the proudest memorials of these tragic years" (pp. 159–160).

An American who was also impressed by the labor of British women used emotional language to describe concomitant social changes that were taking place within the United States.

> Across the Atlantic I studied that proclamation in Old World cities. Women Wanted! Women Wanted! The capitals of Europe have been for four years placarded with the sign. And now we in America are writing it in our sky line. All over the world see it on the street car barns as on the colleges. It is hung above the factories and the coal mines,

the halls of government and the farmyards and the arsenals and even the War Office. Everywhere from the fireside to the firing line, country after country has taken up the call. Now it has become the insistent chorus of civilization: Women Wanted! Women Wanted! (Daggett, 1918, p. 82)

The book from which the preceding passage was taken was entitled *Women Wanted: The Story Written in Blood Red Letters on the Horizon of the Great World War*. Opposite the title page was a photograph of women's rights marchers carrying a banner with the words, "FOR MEN must FIGHT AND WOMEN must WORK."

Even the writing in American educational journals revealed changing attitudes toward women's wartime responsibilities. As an example, an article (Preston, 1917) about ways in which women educators could support the war indicated that their primary responsibility was to provide sons who would serve as soldiers. However, because most female teachers at this time were unmarried and without children, one instructor lamented that "we, many of us, cannot give sons to the war." This teacher still reassured her colleagues that "with true mother-hearts we will consecrate to [the armed forces] our dollars and our service" (unidentified teacher, quoted by Preston, 1917, p. 65).

Hitchcock (1918) recommended the coordination of women's activities through clubs or special service organizations such as the Red Cross, Navy League, or Emergency Aid. Gulick (1917) thought that young girls could make wartime contributions under the auspices of the Camp Fire Girls. She commended this group for designing special patriotic uniforms that its members were to wear for the duration of the war. Another report ("Scouting," 1918) identified the Girl Scouts as an opportunity for young women to prepare themselves for "the new conditions forced upon us by the war." It also described the beginning of a typical day at the Teachers College scouting camp.

> Lined up with military precision by patrols in the big gymnasium every morning at nine very sharp, by their commander-in-chief . . . [they] gave the girl scout promise of duty to God and country and community; recited the scout laws and pledged allegiance to the Stars and Stripes. Then retiring to their respective drill rooms, each troop with its captain worked intensively marching and counter-marching, tying knots and practicing the international code of signaling. Reassembling at ten o'clock each day they had various memorable demonstrations. ("Scouting," 1918, p. 405)

Trow (1918) reported that the women in some European countries had been "forced" to serve as soldiers. She also conceded that a Russian women's regiment had "performed deeds of great heroism." In spite of these incidents, she concluded that "women's war work is the same work she has always pursued, be she at home or abroad, the work of guarding the interests of those she loves best and of training them to uphold the honor of their country" (p. 409). To further underscore this point, she proclaimed that "I believe women will always be housewives and the more they develop, the better housewives they will be."

During World War II, more than 150,000 American women enlisted in the Women's Army Corps, the WAC (United States Army Center of Military History, 1993). Because comparable opportunities were not available during the First World War, women either volunteered or worked "under contract." However, even those who did receive salaries "had to obtain their own food and quarters, and they received no legal protection or medical care. . . . [or] disability benefits or pensions" (United States Army Center of Military History, 1993, p. 3).

While their chances for serving at the front may have been few, women did have opportunities to work in wartime industries. Writing in the conservative *American Legion Weekly*, Harting (1919) recounted that she had taken a wartime job that a soldier had vacated. She believed that most other women who had taken soldier-vacated jobs had no intention of disrupting the traditional employment patterns. Even though "the necessity for relieving the strain on the family budget was probably the primary motive, in the beginning," Harting opined that women workers soon learned that they could discharge their new jobs as well as men. For this reason, she predicted that women would remain in the labor force, where they would complement rather than compete with the returning soldiers. She also reminded readers that some additional increase in the number of women workers was inevitable because "not all women delight in the continual care of the baby and the baking of pies" (p. 19).

Rowell (1917) described the war as "a period of transition" during which "the girl is not under the same conventionalities as was her grandmother or even her mother" (p. 254). McNaught (1917) agreed that the teaching of "school lessons will appear to many [women] as tedious" and that they would experience "continually awakening impulses toward movements that go beyond the schoolhouse and the home" (p. 164). Rowell (1917) adjured the schools to nurture those impulses that were luring young women toward employment outside of the home. For example, she suggested that "school visitors" meet with girls to distribute information and answer questions about employment. Woolman (1918) recommended female vocational education programs because their "many-sided" advantages would benefit even "girls who are not forst [sic] to work."

Writing before America's entry into the war, Howe (1915) acknowledged that unprecedented industrial opportunities had emerged in the United States. Because this growth had created a labor shortage, competitive employers had tried to attract qualified male workers by shortening workdays and increasing wages. However, these inducements had not been extended to women, and Howe interpreted this omission as a sign that females would eventually be excluded from the labor force. This prediction did not eventuate because the number of males required by the military greatly exceeded Howe's estimates. As a consequence, opportunities for women workers and their pay increased. Lewis (1918) observed that "the greatest change in

American industry that has been seen for many years—the first fruits of the war—the employment of women not for merely a few occupations, but in every line, at every job which does not require great strength, and at wages absolutely equal to those of men" (p. 198). Trow (1918) agreed that the "seemingly unexpected but thoroughly efficient" work of women was the most significant development of the war. Like other feminists, she insisted that women's contributions be recognized with wages and working conditions comparable to those of males.

Garden Army

During World War II, local governments motivated, instructed, and even helped citizens raise crops. For example, they converted the lawns next to municipal buildings into garden plots so that even apartment dwellers could cultivate gardens (Bailey, 1977). The federal government supported these local efforts through its own home gardening initiatives. A senior administrator in the U.S. Department of Agriculture characterized the World War II home gardening programs as "one of the greatest civilian activities ever stimulated and organized by man" (Wilson, U.S. Director of Extension, quoted in "Victory Gardens and the Schools," 1945, p. 13). Although this estimate was hyperbolic, the enormous success of the program was undeniable.

Many World War II educational initiatives were built on earlier programs. However, none did this with more deference than home gardening. The personnel in federal agencies duplicated the school-centered paradigms of the First World War to help another generation of students learn about homegrown crops. Comparably robust federal involvement had been evident during that earlier campaign. For example, President Wilson wrote a letter urging each school to establish "a regiment in the Volunteer War Garden Army" (Wilson, quoted in "Gardening a Patriotic Duty," 1918). Wilson, who wanted homegrown produce to expand to a value of $500,000,000 (Lane, 1918c), allocated $200,000 to the federal Bureau of Education to stimulate educational projects ("United States School Garden Army," 1918).

A World War I elementary school civics textbook contained an entire chapter about the "Harvesting Boys and Girls Can Do." The author reminded children of the wartime changes that were transpiring.

> Last year, you went out to the cornfield and picked a fat, golden pumpkin. . . . climbed up in the old apple tree. . . . decided that you would rather play with other children than help grandfather clean the garden . . . [and] wanted to rake leaves and have a bonfire, or go off to the woods and fill your pockets with nuts. This year, though, Uncle Sam wants you to spend the crisp, sunny fall days very differently. He says that you are to stay outdoors just as much as you did last year, and you are to have the same fall fun but in a bigger, more useful kind of way. There are a great many things he wants you to do to help your country in field, and orchard, and garden. (Bailey, 1918, p. 28)

FIGURE 6.8. A Government Poster That Lured Students into the Garden Army

Accompanying photos depicted young children harvesting crops in meadows or small gardens. One illustration showed a group of boys wearing long aprons from their necks and scarves about their heads as they worked in a kitchen. It was captioned "Uncle Sam's Canning Club Boys at Work."

As a result of the school-centered initiatives, 1,5000,000 students eventually participated in home gardening programs ("United States School Garden Army," 1918). Figure 6.8, a government poster intended to lure students into the Garden Army, was reproduced in a 1918 issue of *School Life,* a publication from the federal Bureau of Education.

Benefits of the Garden Army. One obvious accomplishment of the Garden Army was a substantial increase in the amount of food available during the war (Hogan, 1918). The Garden Army was also successful because it made citizens aware of the importance of commercial agriculture (Hamilton, 1918; "Schools and the War," 1917b). However, it had several additional positive attributes. President Wilson claimed it was "just as real and patriotic an effort as the building of ships or the firing of cannons" (Wilson, quoted in "Gardening a Patriotic Duty," 1918, p. 643). Kolbe (1918) agreed that the Garden Army was "the most extensive and the most important" of the wartime school activities that stimulated student patriotism.

One report ("School Work Improved," 1918) maintained that the Garden Army improved the academic work of the participants. Their learning was enhanced when the classroom gardens were used to solve problems through reading, composition, mathematics, science, or art. Another reporter ("United States School Garden," 1918) suggested that classroom gardens provided practical insights about the applications of mathematics and economics.

The appearance of special textbooks seemed to validate the view that gardening was an academic subject. For example, a 1918 issue of the *American School Board Journal* contained an advertisement for a book entitled *Garden Steps*. The accompanying description assured teachers that this book would make "garden work both patriotic and profitable by eliminating delays, wasted effort, and costly errors." Although they acknowledged that free government materials were available, the publishers recommended that teachers buy their 238-page book because it was "more direct, more compact, more teachable."

Progressive educators saw opportunities to advance their philosophical goals through school-based gardening. Murdock (1917) advised teachers that school gardens could be managed "with the general purpose of satisfying the personal and social needs and interests of the children." Other progressive educators were likely to agree with Murdock's suggestion that "the social aim is to train children to be helpers to their families by the production of food and beauty, to be foresighted and economical as to efforts and products, and to respect the gardens and rights of others" (p. 349). The value of the Garden Army is graphically represented in Figure 6.9, which appeared on the cover of the *American School Board Journal*. It was entitled "The Best War Service Educators Can Render at Present."

Chamberlain (1917) had argued that school gardening developed insights about waste, thrift, and the "gospel of work." Although remarks about the importance of wartime conservation were not made as frequently as they would be during the subsequent war, some World War I educators did offer testimonials. They particularly highlighted the need for food conservation (Homan, 1917; United States Bureau of Education, 1917). A 1917 issue of *Teachers College Record* contained an advertisement for the "War Emergency Bulletins" that it was publishing. The materials in this conservation-focused series had titles such as *Economical Diet and Cookery in Time of*

FIGURE 6.9. A 1918 Illustration That Inspired Work in War Gardens (*Reprinted from American School Board Journal, July 1917.*)

Emergency, How to Plan Meals in Time of War—With Economical Menus and Directions for Marketing, and *Canned Foods: Fruits and Vegetables.*

Most of the conservation initiatives of World War I were based on recycling or voluntary rationing. The Garden Army stood out because it emphasized an alternative way of producing resources. Foresighted individuals viewed it as particularly worthwhile because it was a model that could influence current as well as postwar conservation (Carr, 1917; McNaught, 1918; Devoe, 1918; Rosenstein, 1918a; 1918b; "War and the Schools," 1917). Their predictions turned out to be accurate. Even though they were relatively modest, the conservation efforts of World War I prepared the way for the mammoth and extremely important initiatives of the next war.

Anti-German Initiatives

The intensification of wartime nationalism was apparent in the calls to "Americanize" the schools. Convinced that "complete democracy" could only be attained if the schools acknowledged a responsibility for expediting national unity, Weber (1917) identified "the general use of a common language" as the key to this unity. One report ("Americanization," 1918) described legislative bills that had been designed to promote school-centered Americanization. Another report ("New Plan," 1918) gave details about an endowed chair at Boston University that was established to ensure that "the heterogeneous elements of these United States shall be united into a homogeneous whole."

Even though the Americanization movement had preceded World War I, it assumed greater prominence during that conflict. As a result, citizens began to reappraise the basis for classifying countries as amicable or hostile. A report in the *Elementary School Journal* stated that "the war has made it very clear that it is necessary for the people to apprehend the national purposes, both of our own country and of others" ("War and Teaching History," 1917, p. 251). This political shuffling affected foreign language instruction. For example, Swiggett (1918) suggested that students study Russian because it would facilitate "bonds of mutual understanding and common sympathy in all economic, social and political programs" (p. 640). Goggio (1918) made a comparable argument for studying Italian, since Italy was "one of the great commercial powers of the world" as well as an ally.

In view of current international alliances, Americans revaluated their impressions of England. Winship (1918b) wrote that the prewar "prejudice against the English has been deep-seated in the schools and among the people because of the schools." Although this earlier disharmony had been regrettable, it became clear to Winship that "no stronger affection exists between America and any nation than between America and Great Britain" (p. 649).

Looking back on the First World War, Walworth (1938) agreed that American Anglophobia was reduced during this period. However, he judged that this change was made at Germany's expense. In a book that he had written in 1916, Jordan (1918) began a chapter on "pangermanism" with the following quotation: "If we hate Prussian and Prussianism now, it is because [the Prussians] have taught us to hate Prussians and Prussianism. Whom have they ever taught to love them?" (Vernon Kellogg, quoted by Jordan, 1918, p. 139). Writing in the *History Teacher*, McLaughlin (1917) admitted that many persons in the United States were skeptical when politicians and the press initially began to censure Germany for its global ambitions.

However, most of the public came to understand that Germans "believed in the superiority of German efficiency and of German culture," that they had attempted to extend this belief through political control of other nations, and that they "were determined that the world should live in awe of Germany" (p. 183). To ensure that America's entire population comprehended Germany's true character, Allen (1918) recommended that all schools be "deprussianized." Agreeing that American students should learn about "the poison growth of Prussiansim," Kahn (1918) confided that he would not have believed "that such a dreadful phenomenon could have possibly taken place were it not for the evidence of my own eyes and my own ears" (p. 583).

Blegen (1918) concluded that all American citizens eventually did recognize that the war was being fought to determine "whether the American or the Prussian standard of morality is valid" (p. 457). Using even more emotional language, a gubernatorial candidate urged that the war be won "so decisively that such a cataclysm as visited the world through German greed and arrogance can never threaten it again" ("Symposium: Education and Citizenship," 1918, p. 348). This politician insisted that students of all ages support the wartime efforts.

Attacks on the German Language. Not restricting their assaults to Germany's government and political philosophy, conservative educators attacked colleagues who had demonstrated "pro-German tendencies." Aley (1918a) demanded "outspoken loyalty" to ensure that "no opportunity be given in the schools of the country for the German propaganda that has produced the traitors and plotters that are now giving the government so much trouble" (pp. 176-177). Winship (1918b) worried in particular about the "Germanized men" on the faculties of colleges of education. He warned that "there was no Teachers College, or school of education, without Germanized men in the faculty" and that these politically biased professors had "carried the idolized glow and glory of German education into these institutions" (p. 649). He was somewhat comforted only because the war had finally "opened the eyes of the school people."

Conservatives broadened their criticism of disloyal educators by inculpating those who used German to teach German-speaking elementary school students. The NEA ("Educational News," 1918) resolved that all teachers should discourage "un-American and unpatriotic" attitudes by speaking solely in English. A report in *School and Society* supported laws "which will make it forever impossible for a boy or a girl in the United States to be taught in any tongue other than English in the elementary schools" ("Emergency in Education," 1918, p. 417).

Some educators wished to extend the German language prohibition beyond the elementary schools. Despite the fact that this debate revealed "a grave state of public hysteria," one author concluded that "for the period of the war, even if some schools and some teachers suffer, the less German . . . the better" ("Teaching German," 1918,

p. 459). An editorialist who was writing in an NEA journal agreed that "German should be promptly and emphatically eliminated" because its continuation might "be construed as a triumph for the enemy" ("German in Schools," 1918, p. 155). Observing that the movement to remove German as a subject in the curriculum was "fast becoming a nation-wide issue," Harris (G. W. Harris, 1918) recommended that high-school administrators cooperate by requiring their students to concentrate on English, which, after all, was "the greatest language ever used by man." Harris also suggested that higher education students restrict their studies to the foreign languages of "democratic peoples." He encouraged all school personnel, from the elementary through the college levels, to adopt the mantra "English, English, English everywhere required" (p. 458).

Dickie (1918) identified 14 states that had "abolished" the teaching of German and 16 others with movements to enact similar prohibitions. One reporter ("German in the Schools," 1918) observed that the National Security League was spearheading a campaign against "the Teutonic tongue." Todd (1918) judged that study of German, which had suffered "very noticeably" from 1914 to 1917, was weakened further by a "disastrous" decline in 1918. In his history of American Education, Good (1956) concluded that German language instruction had been "the first educational casualty" of World War I. Using a similar metaphor, Ravitch (2000) indicated that German instruction was "virtually wiped out."

Advocating Tolerance. Not all educators agreed that the study of German was unpatriotic, let alone seditious. The author of a report about textbooks ("Textbook Forum," 1917) questioned whether hostility to Germany had been abetted by the "erroneous impressions" conveyed through American school materials. The reporter asked educators to ascertain whether "scientific history" had been crowded out of the curriculum by "historical fiction." Harris (H. M. Harris, 1918) warned that the "passionate personal enmity" of extremists had engendered the national hatred of Germans. Foster (1918) agreed that teachers should resist the "blindness of race hatred" and become "dedicated to the discovery and preservation of truth." A year earlier, Handschin (1917) had argued that the restrictions on German language instruction were inappropriate because of that language's immense literary and cultural value. At a more practical level, he warned of the pedagogical pandemonium that followed when tenured German language instructors were reassigned to academic subjects for which they lacked training.

One reporter ("Teaching German in the Schools," 1917) challenged Americans to differentiate the German people from "their vicious and dangerous government." This person added that "least of all do we hate their language, or their contributions to the arts and sciences, to medicine, to poetry, to music, or any other department of human knowledge and culture" (p. 96). Hoskins (1918) adjured Americans to recognize that German language proficiency would be needed when postwar Germany emerged as "a formidable competitor in the world's commerce and a powerful factor in world politics" (p. 603). He characterized the prohibition against German in the schools as a "shortsighted policy smacking of that wisdom which cuts off its own nose to spite its face."

Special Resources

Although special instructional materials were available during World War I, their quantity was small compared to those published during the next war. The relative paucity was evident when the National Education Association Library Department (1918) resolved to publicize materials suited for wartime education but then was able to identify only four reference books. When Tuell (1917) decided to provide a list of the organizations that teachers could contact for wartime information, he identified only nine organizations.

Many of the materials that were available nurtured patriotism. For example, Dodson (1918) assembled addresses and speeches by Woodrow Wilson "to provide important documents of permanent value for school use." Dodson thought these presidential speeches had "aroused us from our indifference and thoughts of material success, and made us conscious of our purpose as a nation" (p. 3). The patriotic tone of the speeches was discernible in titles such as "The Meaning of the Declaration of Independence," "The Meaning of Democracy," and "To Make the World Free."

The *Liberty Reader* (Sheridan, 1918) was a collection of patriotic passages. One of its chapters, "The Human-Hearted Foch," described the exemplary behavior of a French general. Another chapter contained inspirational notes from the diaries of young French soldiers who later died in battle. The anthology's frontispiece, which showed a frightened waif, was entitled "Behind the Firing Line—A Sadly Bereft Child of the War-Zone, Graphically Expressive of the Tragedy that War Brings to Innocent, Helpless Children." Allen and Kleiser (1918) published *Stories of Americans in the World War,* a collection in which each selection contained "a message of entertainment or inspiration." Shurter (1918) assembled *Patriotic Selections for Reading and Speaking,* a book specifically designed to prepare "children in the schools" for the "brotherhood of arms" as well as the "brotherhood of peace" (p. i). Case (1918) chose comparable selections for his anthology of *Wartime and Patriotic Selections for Recitation and Reading.*

The president of the National Council of Teachers of English (Abbott, 1918) reassured his constituents that they should not feel depressed at remaining behind while students were leaving for war. He pointed out that home-front teachers were the "conservators of a great national tradition . . . embodied in our literature" (p. 2). The members of the Patriotic Service League of Indiana (1918) agreed that home-front teachers had opportunities to instill wartime values through "patriotic literature." Brewster (1918) outlined wartime magazine topics that students could investigate with the aid of the *Reader's Guide to Periodical Literature* or the *New York Times Index*.

Many commercial publishers supplied special materials for developing school patriotism. For example, Powell and Powell (1918) assembled an anthology of prose and poetry that was designed to match "the cosmic character" of the war and to exemplify "patriotism through literature." The October 1918 issue of *Primary Education* contained an advertisement for "patriotic books" on its back cover. Some of the featured books included *The Patriot's Parade: A Patriotic Play in One Act*, *Drill and Play for Patriotic Days*, *Military Drills for Schools*, *Patriotic Songs*, *What to Do for Uncle Sam*, and *The Stars and Stripes*.

Fowler (1917) identified books that illustrated a critical wartime principle, "American literature for American schools." Although Hulst (1918) also identified patriotic books, her list was based on less nationalistic criteria. It included authors from the United States as well as those "from all the races in Europe in our own age, and even from the Far East" (p. 342). Also assuming a liberal political stance, the director of the children's department at the Brooklyn Public Library (Hunt, 1918) worried that the children who were being "stampeded" toward patriotic materials were not receiving the instruction that they needed to evaluate them. Not limited to the schools, patriotic texts were distributed to armed services personnel through a program sponsored by the American Library Association. Each book was accompanied by an explanation of the program and an illustration of a battle-clad soldier with a tall stack of books (Figure 6.10).

Winship (1917) described a government-sponsored syllabus for promoting patriotism in the schools. Another patriotic syllabus (Cohen, 1918) was so explicit that it contained wartime mathematical problems about farming, the Red Cross, savings stamps, Liberty Bonds, and conscription. The *History Teacher's Magazine* regularly published syllabi to help with instruction about the war. The January and February issues from 1918 contained advertisements for wartime syllabi (Harding, 1918b) that originally had appeared in the magazine but that were so popular that they had been reprinted commercially. Some of the other syllabi within this journal were intended for courses in European geography (Linglebach, 1918; Tuell, 1917).

Primary Education was a journal that illustrated ways for schools to use wartime themes. For example, one of its columnists (Stevens, 1918) gave examples of mathematical problems that centered about the creation of quilts, blankets, and ambulance pillows for armed forces personnel. Even the politically liberal *Teachers College Record* published examples of lessons (Bement, 1917) that illustrated the integration of information about art and military camouflage.

Normal Instructor and Primary Plans published numerous patriotic lessons and materials. In addition, it supplied patriotic stories, pageant scripts, mathematical problems, art projects, wartime posters, and student-created military materiel. The cover

FIGURE 6.10. This Stamp Was Placed on Those Books Circulated through the War Service Library Program (*Permission granted by the American Library Association.*)

for the September 1917 issue featured a virile Uncle Sam who proclaimed that "I am more than the lank figure, clad in the uncouth garments of a by-gone age—I am the soul of a people." Exactly a year later, the magazine showcased a poster of a fierce eagle. The eagle's talons grasped a scroll with the following credo:

> I believe in the United States of America as a government of the people, by the people, for the people; whose just powers are derived from the consent of the governed; a democracy in a republic; a sovereign nation of many sovereign states; a perfect union, one and inseparable; established upon those principles of freedom, equality, justice, and humanity for which American patriots sacrificed their lives and fortunes. I therefore believe it is my duty to my country to love it; to support its constitution; to obey its laws;

to respect its flag; and to defend it against all enemies. (Statement on the cover of *Normal Instructor and Primary Plans*, September, 1918)

In addition to materials with a patriotic character, some journals provided general information about the war. Tuell (1917) recommended that high-school instructors consult *History Teacher's Magazine* for these types of data. The January 1918 issue advised readers that the journal was publishing "a series of War Supplements, designed to present to history teachers helpful material concerning the war" (*History Teacher's Magazine*, 1918b, p. 1). An introductory editorial in the February 1918 issue referred to a war supplement that was "devoted to a description and reproduction of war curiosities from Belgium, more particularly the clandestine press of that country" (*History Teacher's Magazine*, 1918a, p. 69). It also advised that "the Supplement for March will be devoted to a Bibliography of the war" (p. 69). The 28-page March bibliography (Dutcher, 1918) encompassed 69 subtopics. A year earlier, Dutcher (1917) had assembled a wartime "summer reading" bibliography that he published in the same magazine.

The federal government developed numerous materials to assist teachers. An advertisement in the September 1918 issue of the *History Teacher's Magazine* featured materials from the Committee of Public Information that had been "established by order of the President." This federal committee provided free pamphlets from the *Red, White and Blue Series* and the *War Information Series*. *American Loyalty by Citizens of German Descent*, which was one of the pamphlets in the former set, was available in German as well as English. Another pamphlet, *How the War Came to America*, was available in English, German, Polish, Bohemian, Italian, Spanish, and Swedish. The Committee of Public Information also published daily posters that recapitulated the wartime activities of government agencies. One reporter noted that, even at the beginning of America's involvement in the war, one could discern the influence of the Committee on Public Information and other federal agencies that were "striving to present to the teachers and public of the country the facts concerning the present world conflict" ("Schools and the War," 1917a, p. 231).

Although educators advised their colleagues about printed materials, they also informed them of opportunities to enrich wartime instruction through alternative materials such as maps, pictures, magazine articles, and newspaper stories (Harding, 1918a; 1918b; Rice, 1918a; 1918b). Other nontraditional materials involved the emerging technologies of that era. For example, the December 1917 issue of *Normal Instruction and Primary Plans* contained an advertisement for Flanagan and Victor record players. The accompanying text adjured teachers that "now is the time for all American children to hear and learn to sing the stirring patriot songs of our country, the music which is inspiring the boys of Uncle Sam's Army and Navy, who are helping to win the war." A companion photograph was captioned "High School Cadets Drilling to the Music of the Victrola."

Cinema became a popular medium for enriching wartime instruction. Ward (1985) recounted that the federal government produced more than 60 motion pictures, including weekly newsreels about the war's progress. The 1918 issues of the *American School Board Journal* contained advertisements for motion picture projectors as well as specialized devices such as the "stereopticon," a device that projected slides, and the "animatrograph," a machine that projected either slides or motion pictures.

Although home-front educators may have benefited from wartime instructional materials, entrepreneurial publishers also profited. In fact, many publishers were so successful that they decided to carry on their war-themed advertising campaigns even after the conflict ceased. For example, the editor of the *Boys' Magazine* (Hungerford, 1919) continued to depict this periodical as a tool of democratic leadership. He invited readers to contact him so that he could "gladly submit evidence" about the character traits his materials developed. Employing the same strategy, Broadhurst and Rhodes (1919) assembled an anthology of "verse for patriots" to sustain "the flame of patriotism which swept our country at the outbreak of the War" (p. iv).

Liberal Dissension

Some liberals did not conceal their displeasure at the rapid growth of scholastic nationalism. During the early phase of the war, Snowden (1915) had adjured American teachers to impress their students that the "gay and glorious exterior of war is but a mask to hide the grinning skeleton within" (p. 55). An announcement ("Peace Play," 1915) in *Playground* during that same year noted that the Junior Work Committee of the Drama League of America was offering $100 for the best play about peace. This announcement included the rhetorical question, "Why shouldn't a peace play win this prize?" (p. 17). Fahey (1917a) wrote in an NEA journal that patriotism was not a true force in education so much as "a plaything in the hands of demagogues" and "a device in the autocracy thru which secret diplomatists attain their ends" (p. 47). Writing in the same popular journal, Force (1917) adjured teachers to help students understand that love of humanity should exceed love of one's own country. Responding to those who were demanding national preparedness, Rugh (1917) insisted that religious lessons on the incompatibility of war and religion were the most effective means for promoting peace.

Holcombe (1941) identified the World Peace Foundation as an organization with a long-sustained commitment to the international peace movement. Writing decades earlier, Crowther (1916) had indicated that this foundation was associated with the "substantial peace movement [that] has existed in this country for many years and [that] has enlisted the best citizenship" (p. 9). A World War I issue of the *History Teacher's Magazine* featured a testimonial ("League to Enforce Peace," 1917) in which the members of this group expressed their support for a resolution to guarantee peace through "all known and available sanctions." The same issue contained a supportive statement from President Wilson about his willingness to promote peace through "any feasible association of nations" (Statement by Woodrow Wilson in 1916, quoted in "Historical Light," 1917).

Although the oratory from members of the peace movement was passionate and eloquent, the responses from pro-war partisans were equally compelling. A naval officer berated pacifists for deluding themselves "that peace, bought at the price of political supremacy lost, would be a noble aim" (Stikney, 1916, p. 91). Believing that the pacifists were "living in a fool's paradise," Stanley (1916) adjured them to realize that the war provided an opportunity to advance "humanity, justice and right." In view of the wide public support that the pro-war arguments were attracting, some liberals began to temper their suggestions. For example, Lange (1917) admitted that liberal initiatives should not exclude scholastic nationalism, because "we do not want our school system to be without a country; nor curricula, nor school life, nor mental discipline" (p. 366). However, he simultaneously insisted that nationalistic programs should be temporary, because no one wished to think "of preparedness for war as a permanent state" (p. 361). Employing a similar tactic, Dean (1918a) scolded those who were attempting "to bring the war into the schools" for crowding out "fundamental studies to meet the need of the temporary environment however urgent the need may be" (p. 1).

Liberal educators initially were perplexed about how they might express support for the war without compromising their traditional values or classroom practices. Wishing to avoid an artificial dichotomy of "democracy versus efficiency" when resolving this problem, Baldwin (1917) counseled teachers to reject those conservative educational practices that exhibited "definite, specific, accomplishment without waste for time, material or effort" unless they were integrally connected with democratic education. Bradford (1917) was worried that school boards had become too authoritarian. He condemned those "autocratic school boards" that had employed "weakness, fear, distrust, and indifference" to deprive teachers of their managerial and executive responsibilities.

Many liberal educators decided that they could exhibit support for the war and continue to use their standard classroom practices, provided that they connected those practices to democratic governance. For example, some of them (Kirk, 1916; Pearse, 1916) argued that teachers who used progressive forms of classroom organization were ensuring that their students would develop into citizens who could express divergent views. One editorialist defended these practices because they instilled a "new patriotism" in which students exhibited a "clean-cut distinction between knowing what best to do and how best to do it, and the why of the doing of it" ("New Patriotism," 1917, p. 658).

Some liberal educators expanded the arguments supporting democratically organized classrooms to include critical thinking, which was another of their staple practices. For example, Fahey (1917b) thought that liberal educational strategies helped students make ethical decisions in their lives. Her argument anticipated those of other progressive educators (e.g., Clark, 1918; Ogden, 1918b) who would conclude that only students who had learned to think critically could avoid future world crises. They reckoned that progressive curricula developed critical thinking because they encouraged students to defend or refute controversial assertions. Russell (1918), the dean at liberal Teachers College, wrote that the raison d'être for public education was to help students assess the standards to which political leaders deferred when they made decisions. From a sympathetic vantage, Boodin (1918) judged that the goal of education was "mastery of the material from the point of view of participating more effectively and more appreciatively in the social process" (pp. 451–452).

Academic Freedom

Although liberal educators argued for the rights of students, they were just as concerned about the rights of teachers. Looking back on World War I, Beale (1936) conceded that teachers' academic freedom had been in jeopardy well before that conflict. Nonetheless, he thought that the "war stimulated a particularly blatant brand of 'patriotism' and gave new impetus to the activities of 'patriotic' societies seeking to coerce others into their conception of loyalty to country" (p. 21). Ravitch (1985) agreed that a conservative wartime campaign, which then continued after the war, devolved into a "crusade to cleanse the schools of teachers and other employees who were suspected of being disloyal, subversive, or controversial" (p. 262).

The threats to academic freedom were revealed in the educational literature of that period. For example, the president of the University of Maine (Aley, 1917b) wrote approvingly about those school administrators who were dismissing teachers with "pro-German tendencies." A year later, he advised high-school administrators to "take advantage of the present opportunity to "weed out all teachers of doubtful loyalty" (Aley, 1918b, p. 634). The author of a lead editorial in *Educational Foundations* suggested that teachers "prove by word and act that they are worthy to be trusted" ("Teacher-Traitors," 1917, p. 523). Ackerman (1917) wrote that it was important for students to learn about patriotism from "teachers who themselves possess the elements of loyalty" (p. 60).

Cooper (1918) judged that administrators in rural schools needed to diligently recruit loyal teachers. He worried because "the minds of the country boy and girl is [sic] plastic wax that can be moulded [sic] at will . . . into patriotic men and women" (p. 288). If unpatriotic persons were allowed to teach in rural schools, the children would resemble their parents, who "use their small brain power to figure out ways to have [their sons] exempted from service" and who "cannot be made to see that this war is their war" (p. 287). An accompanying editorial advised readers that Cooper's report revealed the need for domestic propaganda to "enlighten the people regarding the war and international relations."

Rural administrators were not the only ones concerned about the loyalty of teachers. An urban superintendent recommended that every teacher affirm specific loyalty statements, the first of which was that "I will teach my children to love their country, and train them to see that no sacrifice is too great" (Chadsey, 1918, p. 10). Each teacher was also to acknowledge that "I will at all times be on my guard against disloyal propaganda" and "I will never forget that as a public-school teacher I must be aggressively and unmistakably loyal." The teacher would conclude by professing that "I fully realize that my greatest duty is to be a true American and to inculcate in others true Americanism."

Several years before the United States had entered the war, a member of the Chicago Peace Society wrote about the difficulty of opposing combat during a time when opponents knew that they would be labeled with "the stigma of 'moral flabbiness,' of 'degeneracy in moral fiber,' of 'physical and moral cowardice'" (Lochner, 1915, p. 222). After the United States had joined the combatants, the liberals were criticized even more fiercely. Thompson (1917) expressed the sentiments of defiant liberals when he wrote that governmental leaders were hypocrites who claimed to be fighting for democracy but who were curbing teachers' "liberty of thought and freedom of action."

An article ("Academic Freedom," 1918) in the *Journal of Education* contained a stern report from the American Association of University Professors. This report scolded the administrators at one university for dismissing a "distinguished man of science" who had protested the war. Although the committee members withheld their opinions about whether the individual deserved to be fired, they were outraged that the accused professor had been denied his right to due process. They insisted that this professor, even if he turned out to be guilty, was still entitled "to have the charges against him stated in writing in specific terms and to have a fair trial on those charges" (p. 377). They reminded readers that "the importance of maintaining these procedural safeguards against hasty or unjust action is, if possible, even greater at a time of popular excitement and heightened passions than under normal conditions." The editors of the journal in which this report had appeared may have provided an inadvertent example of the "popular excitement" and "heightened passions" of the period when they followed the report with a set of resolutions demeaning the German military. The credibility of these resolutions was certainly enhanced when readers noted that their author was the commanding general of the American forces in Europe.

Special Curricula

Education professors had become intrigued by progressive pedagogical practices during the first quarter of the twentieth century. Nonetheless, the actual frequency with which classroom teachers adopted those practices remains questionable

(Giordano, 2000). One factor restricting the spread of progressive curricula was their abstruse rationale. This intellectual obscurity was evident when Snyder (1917) reviewed a book by John Dewey, the most famous apologist for progressive education. Although Snyder described himself as a "warm admirer" of Dewey, he admitted that he had trouble discerning the precise message within many parts of the author's book. He counseled Dewey to "rewrite the book in half the space" in order to make it "more readable and more immediately convincing" (p. 483).

Because it was infused with an idealistic philosophy, even the pedagogical advice from progressive educators was at times impractical. For example, Slawson (1918) described a progressive approach to teaching in which the teacher "must first know the child, know what he knows and what he does not know, study his capabilities and his aptitudes, strengthen his weaknesses through the use of his strength, see that he is at work at that which he is prepared to do, determine the measure of success that he is achieving, and his consciousness of his power to achieve" (p. 63).

Even in those cases where progressive educators had clearly specified practical benefits for their recommendations, some of the alleged paybacks were exaggerated. For example, Dow (1917), a colleague of Dewey's at Columbia, wrote that progressive art activities in the schools encouraged individual expression and appreciation of art. These claims probably seemed reasonable to most observers. However, Dow went much further when he maintained that progressive art activities also spurred "better quality of industrial products" and "better city planning." Only zealots were likely to be convinced by such oblique assertions.

Farley (1940) observed that the World War I public had held educators accountable for responding to wartime priorities. Critics singled out progressive educators for flagrantly disregarding the nation's wartime goals. In fact, the harshest critics began to speculate that the reduced academic expectations set by progressive educators had been responsible for the widely publicized deficiencies of American soldiers. Disagreeing, Hart (1918) judged that their problems must have had social and cultural roots. To substantiate this point, he pointed to the disproportionate number of illiterates from "the hills in Missouri and Arkansas," which were hardly fertile grounds for progressive schools. Irrespective of the source of wartime illiteracy, many persons concluded that its solution would involve the relatively inexpensive and simple-to-implement skills-based programs. In fact, they saw skills-based programs as solutions for other educational problems such as poor physical conditioning, truancy, misinformation about the war, lack of patriotism, and the inability to communicate in English.

Vocational Curricula

Using abstruse rhetoric, Shoop (1916) assured his readers that the persons who were supporting vocational education were not to be dismissed as "aggressive promoters" or "forensic enthusiasts." Although he could have used emotional appeals to make vocational education more attractive to a citizenry preparing for war, Shoop proffered logical arguments instead. He noted that vocational education created opportunities to enhance learners' motivation, broaden their access to schools, advance their individual interests, and help them improve society. Redfield (1916) also resisted the opportunity to characterize vocational education as an explicit aspect of national defense. However, he did use a metaphor that may have had the same effect when he alleged that vocational education "makes it just so much the harder for the wolf to reach the door" (p. 121). Joyner (1916) ratcheted the rationale for vocational education a notch closer to nationalism when he characterized it as "a democratic right and obligation."

Once the United States entered the war, the defensive benefits of vocational education became readily apparent. In a postwar analysis, Judd (1919) wrote that vocational education had actually provided the prototype for the national educational system that the wartime nation required. This insight transpired because the government "made generous appropriation to the support of industrial education and created a federal board to manage this interest" (p. 559). An editorialist who was writing during the war observed that vocational education had provided a "jolt to all the ideals of the old cultural curricula and systems" ("American Notes," 1917c, p. 183). Another editorialist ("American Notes," 1917b) advised school personnel to train students for wartime responsibilities as mechanics, electricians, bakers, blacksmiths, steam engineers, gas engineers, riveters, saddlers, shipwrights, tent-makers, and wheelwrights. Even John Dewey (1918), the most famous liberal activist of the era, opined that the wartime vocational educator was as important as "the man behind the gun."

By 1918, the stature of vocational education had become impressive. Moulton (1918), a political science professor at the University of Chicago, argued that all factories making nonessential items should be required to shift their production to wartime materials. He recommended that federal legislation assure the supply of specially trained workers required to implement this conversion. He reasoned that "selective recruiting of this sort does not imply commandeering of private wealth" but that instead "it means merely that the government gives to certain business men the opportunity and the honor of rendering service in the common cause of humanity" (p. 106). Calling attention to the many high-school programs that were already training persons to be soldiers and army technologists, Snedden (1918c) concluded that wartime America had "embarked on vocational education on an heroic scale" (p. 752).

Snedden (1918c) used the term *vestibule programs* to describe the efforts to rapidly retrain workers for the specialized jobs in the defense industries. As an example of the interest in this topic, the NEA appointed a special committee to investigate ways in which schools could assist with "the training of hundreds of thousands of men in short courses" ("National Emergency," 1918, p. 351). One reporter

("Training of Mechanics," 1918) described a federally subsidized vestibule program that offered courses in the late spring, summer, and early fall, which were the periods when the buildings at the vocational schools normally would have been vacant.

As the public gradually recognized the value of vocational training, apologists became less deferential. In a book about vocational education for women, Leake (1918) recapitulated the usual supportive arguments and then extended their limits. As one example, he thought it was of "vital importance to the nation at large" that vocational education be promoted among females, including those who were only 14 and 15 years old.

Just as the ardor of its supporters indicated the popularity of vocational education, so did the unusually fierce resistance of its opponents. Some of these opponents resented vocational education because of its regimented, task-oriented pedagogy; others were annoyed because it failed to acknowledge the importance of the arts and humanities. Nutting (1918), who certainly represented the latter group, wrote passionately that the humanities had fallen into disfavor because of "prominent educational leaders who preach in season and out of season the virtues of applied and vocational education and exert all their influence to secure wider recognition for courses of this type in the high-school curriculum" (p. 83).

When they eventually realized that vocational education was not a fad, some proponents of the humanities attempted to strike a compromise. Hopeful that vocational and humanistic educators would collaborate, Ogden (1918a) counseled them to "ward off a rivalry between two systems which ought never to become divorced" (p. 663). Some educators pointed to business education (Lyon, 1918) and home economics ("Home Economics on a War Basis," 1918) as examples of longstanding vocational programs that had been successfully integrated with other areas of the curriculum.

The president of Columbia University (Butler, 1919) agreed with critics that those teachers who wished to teach the "classics" were having a hard time finding supporters. He reassured disheartened teachers that the newer types of curricula still presented opportunities for them to emphasize the morals derived from the classics. Also associated with Columbia University, Snedden (1918a) was more of a pragmatist. He suggested that those persons who wished to pursue traditional curricula should turn to foreign languages. However, they should anticipate a higher demand for modern languages with "probable vocational use."

Although vocational educational programs had been established prior to World War I, many of them did not emphasize the precise career fields for which the war had created needs. One reporter ("War and the School," 1917) correctly assessed that America's entry into the war would make great demands on engineering and technology programs. Camp (1917) made an early prediction that the wartime "demand for the products of industrial enterprise" would lead to a shortage of workers in wartime factories. A government reporter noted that "the problem of producing competent scientific and technical workers in large numbers is immediate and pressing" ("Government Policies," 1918b, p. 3). The War Department ("War Department Committee on Education and Special Training," 1918) organized a specific committee to expand "intensive training in technical subjects" for those students who aspired to careers in industry or the military.

Student Workers. Due to the severe shortage of trained adults, it was inevitable that employers would recruit student workers. The prevalence of student labor was revealed by the federal government's attempts to prevent the employment of children under the age of 14. After acknowledging that the shortage of adult workers was limiting wartime industry and farming, one reporter commended the government's protective efforts because "there appears to be nothing in the present or prospective war emergency to justify curtailment in any respect of the sessions of the elementary schools, or the education of boys and girls under fourteen years of age" ("Government Policies," 1918a, p. 476). Another reporter objected to the employment of children because "city boys, without farm experience are not generally useful under sixteen years of age" and even "the labor of [rural] boys under fourteen years of age is not a vital factor on the farm" ("Schools in War Time," 1918, p. 642).

Camp (1917) advised the citizens of the United States to emulate the wartime example of Great Britain, a country with "no exploitation of child labor." A conference of Pennsylvania's educational leaders ("Education and War Conditions," 1917) recommended the "continued enforcement" of that state's child labor laws. Such recommendations would not have been made if infractions of child labor laws had not been common. A year later, Ettinger (1918) confirmed that "shortly after our entrance into the war, it appeared that the safeguards thrown around our children, through the enactment of Compulsory Education and Child Labor Laws, were in serious jeopardy" (p. 269).

Innovative wartime programs were devised to deal simultaneously with the labor shortage and the attrition of students from schools. The U.S. Commissioner of Education advised that "for all boys and girls who cannot attend the day sessions of the high schools, continuation classes should be formed, to meet at such times as may be arranged during working hours or in the evening" (Claxton, quoted in "Educational Program for the War," 1917, p. 33). The Indiana State Council of Defense recommended that the schools adjust "curriculum, school terms, and vacations, so that the maximum of industrial work may be done with a minimum of interference in the essentials of that education which safeguards the future of the nation" ("Patriotic Service League of Indiana," 1918, p. 135). The federal Bureau of Education (United States Bureau of Education, 1917) recommended the extension of curricular and scheduling adaptations to African American students, including those attending segregated schools in the South.

Snedden (1918b) suggested that "a large proportion—perhaps not less than half—of the student's time available for vocational education can be given to the actual practice of its processes, even as these are carried on in commercially productive shops, offices, homes, farms, and salesrooms—and, ideally, so organized as to give him a wage" (p. 16). The attendants at the 1917 annual convention of the NEA endorsed a full range of educational changes to facilitate student employment. Their advice included "alterations in the lengths and dates of school terms, shortening of vacations and holidays, [and] adaptations of school days with provision for part time work" ("Resolutions," 1917, p. 122). One reporter indicated that the graduates of these adapted programs had sometimes competed for jobs with their own teachers, many of whom had "found it necessary to seek more remunerative employment because of the inexorable increases in the cost of living" ("Cooperation of the Schools," 1918, p. 1).

The World War I scholastic adaptations that enabled students to meet extraordinary wartime responsibilities resembled the accelerated curricular that became popular during the next war. One editorialist lamented that, before the war, "there was no conception of war speed in anything, least of all in education" ("War Modification," 1918, p. 490). This editorialist concluded succinctly that "we must put more of the 'go' in pedagogy." Another reporter had recommended "war-time efficiency" measures such as lengthened school days, decreased promotion and graduation requirements, and "the arrangement of courses in the manner calculated to emphasize the more important and to minimize the least important" (Sharpleigh, 1917, p. 20).

To discourage the view that schooling was irrelevant to employment, educational and industrial personnel devised collaborative programs. Although he endorsed these programs, Smart (1918) noted that they did not address a corollary problem created by the students who were quitting school to join the armed services. This second problem was particularly acute among high-school seniors. Some school administrators cooperated with the armed forces by accepting military service as the equivalent of high-school academic study. Sinclair (1918) observed these types of cooperative agreements in numerous high schools throughout Oregon. Smart (1918) reported that some persons were so optimistic about these initiatives that they recommended comparable agreements for those high-school seniors who were quitting school to work in agriculture or the defense industries.

CHAPTER 7

Dynamics of Wartime Education

> [Students should be taught to understand that] in the uncertainty of a 'divided world' where peaceful coexistence of conflicting philosophies of life may at any time be terminated by armed conflict, the individual must be ready to renounce for the good of the group even his wish to survive.
> —SHEVIAKOV & REDL, 1956

Liberal educators postulated that warfare would not stop until teachers inculcated international sensitivity, democratic decision-making, and critical thinking within their students. Although many of them had suppressed this view temporarily, they promoted it aggressively after World War II. Alarmed by the international belligerence of World War I, the subsequent rise of Fascism, and the postwar spread of Communism, the conservatives adhered to distinct assumptions. They thought that the most effective ways for the United States to prevent war were by increasing its own national security, forming defensive alliances, and influencing the balance of international power. They urged teachers to help their government by cultivating patriotism, rigorous academic achievement, and selective career learning.

Postwar Dynamics

In a book about American education, French (1955) noted that "frequently, during a major war, attention is focused upon existing need for educational reform" (p. 59). He immediately followed this remark with the observation that wartime educational leaders exhibited another common trait, which was a concern for "programs of education to be instituted after the war has been won." The conservative educators of World War II had certainly confirmed the accuracy of French's first observation. Responding to the most pressing issues of that period, they had prepared youths for military duty and wartime employment. As a result of their success, their public esteem rose to an unprecedented level.

In contrast, the response of progressive educators to the current crisis had failed to win the public's confidence. Confirming French's second prediction, they began to change their emphasis to postwar educational programs. Although they may have done this for idealistic reasons, they certainly recognized that their advice would be more popular if the public's attention were directed away from immediate wartime issues. They tried to identify forceful arguments that would speed up this process. As an example, they insisted that the Second World War had ensued largely because comparable warnings from liberals had been ignored 25 years earlier. They urged the public to avoid the mistakes made in the past and thereby prevent the third international war of the century from occurring. They promoted dialogue about postwar peace as a replacement for the prevailing one about wartime emergencies.

The liberals were disappointed with the meager support their proposals attracted. The American public, which was well aware that an earlier generation of liberals had given them comparable advice, exhibited the same disparaging attitude that it had displayed once before. The public judged many instances of liberal advice to be naïve. For example, Nash's (1940) may have been an archetype for disdained advice. Nash had pleaded with pre–World War II American citizens to refrain from entering the European conflict. Despite the "unprovoked attack on Poland, Norway, Denmark, Holland and Belgium" as well as the "barbarous oppression of the Czechs, Poles and Austrians," Nash argued against military intervention. He suggested instead that teachers "impress our young people . . . that they should be seriously interested in such conditions . . . [for] it is only by patient, friendly, unselfish vision that the world may be organized so that such conditions and events may gradually disappear" (p. 355). Recognizing that his idealistic recommendations might fail to deter armed aggressors, Nash thought the efforts still would be worthwhile because someday they might prevent a third world war.

The Committee on Educational Reconstruction after the War (1941) provided another prewar sample of the liberal advice the public received without enthusiasm. Headed by William Kilpatrick, a professor at Columbia's Teachers College, this committee published a set of principles to guide the actions of Americans while they were watching the war in Europe. The committee's members, who judged that "Hitlerism" was merely a symptom of European unrest, maintained that the true causes were "diseased" capitalistic societies. Instead of devoting their energy to repressing the overt symptoms of totalitarianism, American citizens were to reform their own far-from-perfect society and government. The contents of this report (Commission for After-War Educational Reconstruction, 1941), which were reproduced in the *Journal of the National Education Association,* were accompanied by an introduction in which that serial's editors congratulated the Committee for its attempt to check the "economic, political, social, and cultural" roots of Nazism. Referring to the report from Kilpatrick's committee, the liberal Babcock (1941) urged teachers and professors to join the university institutes that were planning for the comprehensive postwar reform of American society.

In a book about postwar planning that she published just nine months after Pearl Harbor, the liberal Johnsen (1942) predicted that persons would be looking forward to "a new order" characterized by extensive international cooperation. The director of the Pacifist Research Bureau touted his group's philosophy as one in which men "employ only love and sacrificial good will in opposing evil" and in which they recognized a "world brotherhood in which cooperative effort contributes to the good of all" (Paullin, 1943, p. iii).

Unnerved by fears of hostile armies, American citizens were not eager to implement these suggestions. Their skepticism was apparent to one liberal editorialist when he wrote ruefully that "the pattern of behavior which is modern total war and the pattern of the democratic way of life are in essential conflict" ("Educational Programs in a World," 1943, p. 227). Ahl (1944) acknowledged the practical difficulty of persuading students to adopt the liberals' political views when programs such as the High School Victory Corps had been "given over entirely to the promotion of the military struggle" (p. 61).

Elias (1942) recognized that many of his liberal colleagues wished to delay speculation about social and political reconstruction until the war had been won. However, he chastised them because "this attitude is wrong; for if we wait until the war is over, it will be too late" (p. 505). Sympathetic liberals counseled their colleagues to rebuke those who were demanding retribution for "Axis despotism" (Myers, 1942) or "the damnable tortures of Nazi and Japanese sadists" (Keliher, 1942). A lead editorial in the *School Board Journal* questioned whether educators could find "true satisfaction from success in battle and its destruction of life" ("Year 1943," 1943, p. 15). Havighurst (1944) wrote bluntly that "it is especially difficult to discuss education for peace in time of war" because of the "propaganda of hatred which a society at war imposes upon itself" (p. 162)

Revisiting one of their prewar classroom strategies, some wartime progressive educators (Childs, 1943; Hodson, 1943; Hopkins, 1943) encouraged teachers to turn students' attention toward the underlying social inequalities that had caused the war. The liberal National Council for the Social Studies recommended that students learn about the causative chain between post–World War I nationalism, the rise of fascism, and the subsequent war (Murra, 1943). Berman (1944) warned that the attention required by social and economic problems could be compromised by "postwar hysteria and jingoism with its concomitant appeal for 'good citizens'" (p. 347).

Some World War II liberals resuscitated additional arguments from the First World War. For example, Norris (1943) reminded his readers that the unfair Versailles treaty, even though it had been negotiated two decades earlier, was "the spawning ground for another world war." The members of the Fellowship of Reconciliation (1944) lectured the citizens of the Allied nations that pre–World War I Germany had made war in the first place because it "lacked the resources, territories, and colonies which represented political prestige" (p. 3). As a consequence, Germany "fought and lost a war against a group of nations that were substantially satisfied with the *status quo*." The resulting treaty "discarded the idealist concepts of Woodrow Wilson, and continued the system of power politics which had characterized the pre-war period." The Second World War became inevitable because "the victorious power-states refused to consider peaceable adjustment of international relationships in the interests of the peoples of states which were equally ambitious."

As the wartime prospects for an allied victory increased, liberal educators became bolder and more confrontational. Mitchell (M. R. Mitchell, 1944) wrote passionately that educators should interact with their students in ways to ensure that "man may never again wallow in human blood of his own killing, never so completely distrust any men as to set out with modern might and the devil's own passion to destroy them, their families, homes, recourses" (p. 285). Woody (1945) criticized conservative educators for the "*idée fixe* that military preparedness prevents war, and lack of it leads to them" (p. 191). One NEA editorialist noted sympathetically that military preparedness "cannot be defended on educational grounds" ("Peacetime Conscription and National Security," 1945, p. 87). Also writing in an NEA journal, Freeman (1945) discouraged postwar military training because he was skeptical about "what the military forces will attempt to teach" (p. 152). After examining government intrusion into the World War I schools, Todd (1945) concluded that the federal government had generated wartime support among adults by surreptitiously influencing their school-age children. He urged the new generation of World War II teachers to be watchful for duplicitous campaigns that exploited "the appeal of childhood to touch the hearts and purses of the adults" (p. 223).

The contempt that some liberal educators felt for many of the wartime educational initiatives may have been partially veiled during the early days of the war. However, their true feelings, which had become more apparent as the war progressed, were revealed completely afterwards. Publishing his thoughts about peacetime military training in *Progressive Education*, Johnson (1947) fulminated against the "Brass Hats" for refusing to rationalize why they were "pressing military requirements" on "beardless youths." After accosting conservatives as pretentious, stupid, dishonest, and disgraceful, he demanded that legislators "compel them to consult a psychiatrist."

Dynamics of Wartime Education 215

FIGURE 7.1. An Allegorical Depiction of the Diabolical and Heavenly Uses of Aircrafts

Sentiments as emotional as Johnson's were evident in an advertisement that the Air-Age Education Research Advisory Board published in the March 1945 issue of *Educational Leadership*. The text for the ad noted that "the dominance of the airplane in World War II is proved," that "it has achieved deadly effectiveness," and that "if another air war is waged, the resultant havoc may bring the collapse of our civilization." Figure 7.1, which accompanied this text, allegorically depicted two types of aircraft. While a devil-winged plane dropped bombs to symbolize the philosophy of "might," an angel-winged craft represented the ideology of the "right."

Conservatives Define Postwar Issues

As was the case with the writing by American liberals about post–World War II reconstruction, the prewar and wartime writing by conservatives embodied the attitudes that they would display during that postwar era. In the introduction to a book that he published less than four months before Pearl Harbor, Lorwin (1941) advanced the conservative case and expressed disdain for dissenting views. He stated bluntly that "the tragedy of the Second World War is that it need never have been fought" (p. xiii). He explained that most of the pretexts for the war "and the evil forces which unloosed it could have been nipped in their first stages of growth" had it not been for the "narrow-minded and confused leadership of the pre–1939 Western World." Instead of promoting a "new forward development in behalf of humanity," the liberals' timid and indulgent attitudes had contributed to the "increasing exploitation of small racial and social groups."

The members of the National Resources Planning Board (1943) succinctly articulated the conservative belief about the newly emerged role of the schools when they wrote that educators should "provide an understanding of the requirements of national security in all its forms and preparation for participation in national defense" (p. 19). In his final state of the union address, President Roosevelt seemed to concur with the position of the National Resources Planning Board when he pointed out that the war had "broadened our conception of the role that education should play in our national life" (Roosevelt, quoted in "President Speaks Up," 1945, p. 27).

Their enormous wartime achievements exceeded the goals the educational conservatives had set for themselves. Looking back on the war, the liberal Kirk (1948) had to acknowledge that the conservatives had been able to elicit unprecedented political support. As the end of the war became discernible, liberals decided to regain some of their lost political ground. However, the conservatives were just as resolved to protect their recent gains. Writing at the end of the war, the conservative Dodds (1944) reported that the liberals had "loudly proclaimed doctrines of pacifism" and accused the conservatives of fighting "for low and selfish motives" (p. 10). Even though he and his fellow conservatives knew these allegations were false, they had "feared that young men had become so indoctrinated by the cynicism of a few popular writers as to be blinded to the grave issues building up into a war that... would strain the very foundations of our civilization" (p. 10). However, Dodds wrote confidently that "the fog of cynicism rolled back as young men by the hundreds of thousands entered the services of their country, and freely offered themselves to sustain those same values to which they seemed indifferent a few years ago." The changed attitudes that Dodds detected represented the political opportunity that the conservatives needed to secure their wartime advances.

Using a tone similar to that of Dodds, Becker (1944) decried the prewar "theatrical despair of the sad young men, the disparagement of 'ideals,' the easy assumption that democracy was on the way out" (p. 386). He also detected changed dispositions that made the prewar cynicism about American democracy "look pretty thin and unrewarding." A year later, Sinnott (1945) judged that Americans were still embracing conservative attitudes toward "freedom, progress and the worth of individuals." Assuming a unique perspective, he argued that "the fundamental character of protoplasmic structure and activity" had biologically determined these emerging values. He was able to reassure himself and his fellow citizens that these singularly American biological structures made them "safe from totalitarian attempts to regiment us into an army of standardized robots who would march off the assembly lines of indoctrination as monotonously alike as a string of jeeps" (p. 66).

Sayers and Kahn (1945) wrote a book with the title *The Plot against the Peace—A Warning to the Nation!* They began with the disclosure that German leaders had "vast hidden economic and political reserves for future use, not only inside Germany but throughout the world" and that they were "already preparing for a new world war" (p. 10). They added that "having suffered a military defeat in the Second World War, Germany's rulers are plotting to win the peace." They would do this by pursuing a course comparable to that which they had followed after 1918. While Americans

FIGURE 7.2. A 1945 Representation of America's Altruistic Rationale for Entering Two World Wars

might have disputed the accuracy of these authors' predictions, many of them agreed that they still faced international perils. However, most of them saw the Soviet Union as the imminent and dire threat to their safety.

One of the most frequently cited advocates of postwar conservative education was Major Augustin Rudd, chairman of the Guardians of American Education. At the beginning of the war, Rudd (1942a; 1942b) recapitulated an argument that conservatives had used effectively for decades. He chastised the "progressive, the liberal, or the radical group" of educators who taught that "our American way of life has failed, that it should be reconstructed to bring about what they call 'more democracy' and that our present structure of society must make way for a form of collectivism" (1942a, p. 30). In contrast, he praised "conservative or traditional" teachers

"Some of us will get back, and God help those on the home front who have let her down!"

FIGURE 7.3. This 1943 Cartoon Warned Liberal Activists That They Would Eventually Have to Confront Returning Veterans (*Cassel, Jim. American Legion Magazine*, copyright 1943. *Reprinted with permission*)

who encouraged their students to respect the political and economic system that had "brought more happiness and opportunities to the peoples of all nations than any form of government in history" (1942a, p. 30). Rudd and many other conservatives dexterously employed the same logic for decades after the war.

Although conservatives judged that two recent wars had revealed essential lessons, they disagreed with the liberals about the nature of those lessons. Their attitude was expressed pictorially in Figure 7.2, which appeared in a 1945 issue of the *Education for Victory*. This illustration emphasized that America's postwar security would not have been procured without military victories.

Numerous other illustrations eloquently revealed the conservatives' attitudes about the postwar era. These illustrations occurred as political cartoons or advertisements in educational journals. Figure 7.3, which accompanied an article in the September 1943 issue of *the American Legion Magazine*, contained a caption advising

FIGURE 7.4. This 1943 Ad Predicted That Competitive Sports Would Always Be Needed for Defensive Readiness (*Wilson, copyright 1943. Reprinted by permission. All rights reserved.*)

liberal activists to be wary of that inevitable day on which they would have to confront postwar veterans. Figure 7.4, which accompanied a 1943 advertisement, reflected conservative arguments about the need to maintain military preparedness.

Although both conservatives and liberals devised political arguments with which to buttress their educational programs, the conservatives were able to demonstrate the wartime value of their recommendations in a more convincing fashion. While the liberals resorted to philosophical observations to alter the public's attitudes toward alternative school initiatives, the conservatives reversed this process, relying on already popular school initiatives to underscore the validity of their philosophy. Goldman (1960) documented the many liberal domestic programs that the Roosevelt administration had introduced and in which the postwar public maintained confidence. Nonetheless, the public, which was simultaneously preoccupied with questions about foreign affairs, resolved to "keep moving along the path marked out in the early Truman years, a path suggested by the words 'containment' and 'co-existence.'" This path departed radically from Roosevelt's amicable policies toward the Soviet Union. Although one might expect that the direction of education would have been determined by the broad domestic agenda, it was influenced more by foreign affairs.

Conservative educators had a considerable advantage over their liberal colleagues when they connected postwar education to foreign affairs. This position was apparent in their characterization of vocational education. For example, they pointed repeatedly to its success in preparing graduates for the armed forces and the defense industries. Even while the war was being fought, they were describing vocational education as an asset that would be just as useful after the conflict (Fowlkes, 1942; Spencer, 1942; "Victory thru Education," 1943).

Publishers adapted their marketing campaigns to take advantage of popular conservative motifs. For example, the Silver Burdett Company appealed to the prevailing public sentiments through a clever textbook advertisement in the December 1945 issue of *Educational Leadership*. This postwar ad was introduced with the oxymoron that "the war is not yet won." The text went on to explain that "in times of peace, as well as in times of war, we fight an unseen enemy in our midst." The enemy to which the publishers alluded was not Communism but poor hygiene. These publishers adjured teachers to "LEAD your high school students in the battle for a healthy life in a healthy nation" by equipping them with one of their company's health education textbooks.

Materials That Prepared Educators for Postwar Education

Just as wartime teachers had been deluged with materials to help them discharge their special responsibilities, they were covered with another wave of materials to help them with their postwar duties. Writing before the end of the war, Johnsen (1943) observed that "individuals, groups and organizations by the hundreds, governmental agencies and officials are attempting to make clear . . . blueprints proposing in detail plans for a new world order to come" (p. 3). In the first year of America's involvement in the war, Galloway (1942) had already assembled a 158-page report entitled *Postwar Planning in the United States*. Galloway apologized that this hefty report was "a mere reconnaissance, conducted under pressure of time," and that it did "not pretend to be thorough or complete." Despite this self-deprecating assessment, Galloway put together a 30-page "selected bibliography" within his report. A year later, the NEA also compiled a bibliography of materials about postwar planning. In the introduction to this 261-item, annotated list, the editors expressed regret that their inventory was "by no means complete" and that a comprehensive directory "would contain thousands of items" (National Education Association,

1943b, p. 4). Instead of attempting to list the many materials that were available, the Twentieth Century Fund (1944) created a directory of the several hundred organizations that were publishing information about postwar planning.

Many of the materials about postwar issues were written by members of professional educational organizations and then published by these societies. For example, Stoddard (1944) provided a list of postwar materials that had been written and published by the NEA's Educational Policies Commission. He also identified postwar materials written and published by organizations such as the Liaison Committee for International Education, the American Association for an International Office for Education, and the World Peace Foundation.

Like professional organizations and private agencies, the federal government provided materials and directories about postwar education. One of its pamphlets (Federal Education War Council, 1943) contained a list of 10 additional government pamphlets about postwar issues. The U.S. Office of Education created a detailed list of 255 publications about postwar issues. This bibliography was preceded by the qualification that the "titles bearing upon post-war problems are multiplying at a rapid rate" (Federal Security Agency, 1944, p. 15).

Commercial publishers joined with educational organizations and the federal government in developing postwar materials. The April 1944 issue of the *Journal of the National Education Association* contained a textbook advertisement that displayed the heading, "How Will We Re-Educate the Germans?" Although the Ginn Company did not provide the answer to the preceding question, it did counsel its clients to trust commercial textbook publishers to prepare suitable postwar books. In the January 1945 issue of the same journal, this company used wartime associations to market social studies textbooks.

> Ahead of us looms a grave problem. We are winning the war. But a problem just as vital—even more staggering—will face us when firing stops. It is, to win the peace! The collapse of Germany and Japan will not mean that peace is won. Peace is never won unless it is *maintained*. And one factor indispensable to the maintenance of peace is *knowledge*. (Passage from a Ginn Publishing Company advertisement, 1945, p. A-9)

In May 1946, the Iroquois Publishing Company marketed its arithmetic books in the *Journal of the National Education Association*. Although the war was over, the company used language that capitalized on the prevailing postwar sentiments.

> [There is] another thing the war has taught us. Today, too many Americans are very poor in arithmetic! The astonishingly low grades achieved on the arithmetic tests given to the men about to enter our armed forces clearly indicate that something is radically wrong. Far more attention must be given to the mastery of arithmetic than has hitherto been the case. (Passage from an Iroquois Publishing Company advertisement, 1946, p. A-105)

The Allyn and Bacon Company listed some of its books in an advertisement that appeared in the September 1946 issue of the *Journal of the National Education Association*. Teachers were encouraged to adopt these textbooks because they were "successful in the test of war," because they complemented "education for the atomic age," and because "all textbooks of Allyn and Bacon give special attention to aviation" (passages from an advertisement that appeared on the rear cover of the *Journal of the National Education Association*, September, 1946).

In addition to printed materials, alternative media conveyed information to postwar educators. The National Resources Planning Board (1943) recommended that teachers take advantage of the postwar information available in films, radio programs, visual aids, and phonograph records. One reporter ("Education for American Citizenship," 1944) described a series of radio broadcasts that had been developed by the federal Office of Education and that concerned postwar educational problems. A notice in *Progressive Education* ("Profits of War," 1946) advised those educators who were working in poor communities that "billions of dollars" worth of surplus military equipment was about to be distributed to them. This "virtually cost free" equipment included projectors, films, books, scientific instruments, electronic apparatuses, and industrial arts machinery.

An advertisement from RCA in the October 1944 issue of the *Journal of the National Education Association* marketed sound systems, record players, film projectors, FM receivers, and FM transmitters as "teaching tools in your post-war school improvement program" (p. A-107). This advertisement also advised teachers that televisions, electron microscopes, and other new devices "will be 'must' equipment for most schools after the war."

Many educators published lists of postwar materials within their articles or books. For example, Douglass (1944), who had included bibliographies within a report that he wrote for *Social Studies*, advised the journal's readers to consult his reference list for information about articles, pamphlets, and "short non-technical reliable books." Anderson (G. L. Anderson , 1943), who wrote a monograph entitled *Adapting the High School to Wartime and Postwar Needs*, included an entire chapter of annotated references to articles and books. These references were topically organized under headings such as technology, social problems, and world citizenship. The Stanford University School of Education Faculty (1943) concluded their book about *Education in Wartime and After* with a bibliography of books and articles as well as a four-page list of those organizations that supplied pamphlets about wartime and postwar issues.

Postwar Plight of Progressive Educators

As an end to the war came in sight, liberals challenged conservative claims about their critical role in winning the war and rejuvenating the economy. Mitchell (B.

Mitchell, 1944) made these points in the foreword to a pamphlet from the Post War World Council. He wrote that the war was not winding down but being replaced by "stabilized" conflict as a "normal condition." He concluded that the two world wars and the period of economic disaster between them were all interconnected. Convinced that the conservatives were not genuinely concerned with defending the United States, he accused them of sponsoring peacetime conscription to prolong the world crisis from which they were benefiting politically. He wrote scathingly that the conservatives who were using patriotism as an "economic disinfectant" recognized that "files of uniformed men on the parade field look better than broken figures in the breadline" (p. 3).

Although they resented their opponents, liberal educators did not underestimate their strength. In the booklet for which Mitchell had written the foreword, Thomas (1944) warned that the conservatives were especially formidable because they were backed by a "powerful press." A year earlier, Fisher (1943a) had counseled her progressive colleagues to respect the strength of the conservatives, who could summon enough political support to make progressive education the "scapegoat for the complex ills of a nation hard-pressed by war" (p. 140).

Fisher's prognostication about the conservatives' immense power turned out to be accurate. Recognizing this danger, the liberal Robinson (1945) tried to put a positive spin on it. He reassured his colleagues that progressive ideals, even though currently out of favor, were "determined" for eventual inclusion in the curriculum. Like Robinson, Hientz (1947) used the concept of social predestination to brighten progressive education's image. In view of the inevitable fate awaiting their students, teachers had an unavoidable obligation to provide them "with conditions permitting the free play of their intelligence in the construction of their own individual and meaningful patterns of life" (p. 271).

Liberal educators employed a full range of rhetorical ploys in their efforts to fend off the conservatives. They also wished to bolster the security of their remaining constituents. Acknowledging that politically liberal teachers were losing their jobs, Rugg (1948) demanded that the conservatives explain why the behavior of the liberals was more reprehensible than that of tradition-bound teachers who parroted "the 'line' of a Party—either that of the Republicans or Democrats." Stanley (1948) protested that the conservative philosophy placed such an emphasis on national loyalty that it was indiscernible from the oppressive Russian and German propaganda in which "devotion to the national state is the first, and the highest, duty of every citizen" (p. 61).

Undeterred by these maneuvers, conservatives insisted on the dismantling of progressive education. They took extraordinary delight in pointing out that the Progressive Education Association had fallen into such public disfavor that it was forced to change its name to the American Education Fellowship. Even the president of the renamed organization acknowledged that "the intellectual climate of our time has been so inhospitable" that many teachers had "taken pains to absolve themselves of any imputation of progressivism" (De Boer, 1947, p. 1).

Some progressive educators refused to admit that the selection of a new organizational name was an indication of political weakness. Beck (1948) wrote that "Progressive education is still 'quick'" and that the term progressive, even though it had been retired from the organization's title, would not become obsolete until "democracy, too, will have dropped from our vocabularies" (p. 83). An editorialist agreed that the renamed Association still preserved "all of its old time vitality" and that it was "forging ahead and that it has its mind and eyes focused upon the horizons and that it will remain as it has always been" ("Report on the National Conference," 1948, p. 29). Another liberal editorialist ("New Policy for New Times," 1948) did concede that the Progressive Association's initiatives had "by no means succeeded in transforming the entire traditional pattern" of education. Nonetheless, this partisan writer insisted that the association was still "bearing rich educational fruits" because some of its goals had been adopted by organizations that were larger and more influential than the Progressive Education Association.

Theories of War and Education

Looking back on the First World War, Roth (1967) opined that the war itself had not caused the nationalistic and revolutionary developments of that period. Instead, the war had hastened trends that had originated during the preceding century. MacNeil (1944), who made this same point about the Second World War, had concluded that "World War II accelerated the processes of change that already had been in motion for generations" (p. 27). If one extends this perspective to the schools, then the educational changes that were so evident during those wars represented the acceleration of earlier patterns.

However, neither this hypothesis nor its educational implications occurred to most educators when they initially began to ruminate about the relationship of war to educational change. For example, consider the assumptions that provided the foundation for a pre–World War II report from the American Council on Education (1940b). Attempting to establish the milestones in modern secondary school reform, the authors somehow failed to discern the remarkable changes that had transpired during the First World War. Instead, they drew their conclusions by examining the sterile deliberations and recommendations of professional educational associations. Despite the monolithic character of their own investigation, even the members of the American Council on Education eventually recognized the blinding conflict of interest that prevented most educators from discerning the true causes of school reform. This Council's members concluded dryly that "it is obvious that the general public, the professional publics, and even the tireless producers [of reports from professional educational associations] should inquire into the effect of this output upon educational practice" (p. 1).

Once the United States had entered World War II, changes to the schools became so evident that every educator had to be aware of them. Glicksberg (1944) remarked that "only in 'revolutionary' epochs such as ours do profound transformations take place in a relatively short time" (p. 299). Although he was a progressive educator who resented most of the changes that were transpiring, Gwynn (1943) urged his colleagues to realize that "sweet are the uses of adversity." Gwynn was sanguine because he thought that progressive educators would be able to turn the scholastic turmoil to their advantage. Although the conservative Hanson (1944) also recognized the astounding pace of scholastic change, he disagreed with Gwynn about which political faction would profit from it. He predicted tautologically that conservative educators, who were heading in the right direction, would win out because "advance in the right direction is always desirable . . . and the war is hurrying that advance" (p. 49).

Although numerous World War II theorists argued about which political groups benefited most from the wartime educational transformations, Merrill (1948) highlighted the difficulty of resolving this debate. Writing after the war, he noted that the rapid and pervasive wartime changes had affected individuals in subtle and disparate manners. For this reason, he thought it was impossible to appraise the aggregate impact of the changes on either political faction.

Liberal Theorists

Profound philosophical differences compounded the communication problems between liberals and conservatives. Partisan attitudes further compromised communication. The conservatives restricted their attention to the immediate wartime problems to which their own programs were so responsive. Although they were dismayed by the speed with which the conservatives were transforming the schools, the liberals preferred to focus on the matters for which they had an advantage. They thought these were general, theoretical, and long-term issues. The dysfunctional communication between the two groups was hardly redressed when they consistently directed their arguments and rebuttals to the general public rather than each other. Finally, their inability to communicate was aggravated after each group tried to gain political advantages by purposefully misrepresenting its opponents' arguments.

The liberals attempted to discredit the conservatives by depicting them as simplistic, nineteenth-century reactionaries. Young (1941) identified the conservatives' "ever-recurrent" psychological theory that "man is by nature an animal given over to struggle and pugnacity" (p. 4). He contrasted this with the more credible, liberal assumption that "war is the result of social-cultural conditioning, chiefly bound up with striving for political or economic power" (p. 4). In a book with the subtitle *A Study of the Social and Spiritual Conditions of Freedom*, Orton (1945) referred to the conservatives' patently fallacious position as the "peace-by-force illusion." Although their own social explanation for international conflict recognized the possibility of additional world wars, the liberals optimistically pointed out that such conflicts could be prevented if national leaders would adopt the liberals' political platform.

Nelson (1971) identified World War I as the period during which political theorists first predicted that war would be endemic throughout the century. With the passing of only 40 years, this prediction had been confirmed. Nelson wrote that early liberal and conservative theorists were limited in their ability to explain war because they restricted their analyses to the motives of the participants. He judged that not until the Cold War did theorists genuinely appreciate the societal consequences of war on all of the participants, the victors as well as vanquished, those on the home front as well as those at the battlefront.

Although Nelson's observations were generally accurate, several World War II scholars had shown an interest in war's pervasive consequences. In a book that he titled *Man and Society in Calamity*, the sociologist Sorokin (1942) had concluded that the length and severity of any war was correlated to "the disintegration of the value systems . . . in belligerent societies" (p. 304). His thesis correctly predicted that World War II would be waged until one of the sides was forced into unconditional surrender. However, his 1942 book did not anticipate the degree to which that war would substantively alter the societal values within the victorious nations.

While Americans were still contemplating the war, Rugg (1941) used sociological data to decipher how eventual participation could affect educational reformers. Convinced that dissatisfaction with schools had occurred in cycles, he attempted to predict whether progressive educators should brace themselves for wartime rejection. He documented that the assaults had not occurred during periods of national prosperity because "the promise of personal gain is so intense that people cannot be bothered with 'trivialities in the schools.'" He also demonstrated that fierce educational criticism had not appeared during "periods of great unrest, panic, [and] economic anxiety" because "the interest of the people in such campaigns just cannot be captured" (p. 107). Even though he made a serious omission when he failed to examine the plight of World War I educational reformers, the changing political attitudes of the contemporary public persuaded him that progressive education would suffer if the United States entered the war. Agreeing with Rugg's historical analysis, Hanna (1943) later judged that conservative educators had challenged progressive reformers during "every critical period in our national history" (p. 173). Hanna also confirmed the accuracy of Rugg's prewar prediction when he observed that the wartime public's displeasure with progressive educators was "probably more widespread than at any previous time."

Redefer (1948), a former director of the Progressive Education Association, was able to take advantage of the time that had intervened after the war to make relatively objective observations. Writing toward the end of the decade, he assessed that progressive education had been criticized so severely during the war that it was dying. Attempting to assign a cause for this fate, he noted that national and global events had persuaded most educational reformers to reevaluate their commitment to divisive, partisan issues. He wrote bluntly that "as the war clouds over Europe gathered, the interest in social reconstruction among the Progressives shifted to a concern for the preservation of democracy and the democratic way of life" (p. 348).

Many liberals and progressive educators had demonstrated ideological reversals. Prior to the American entry into World War II, the NEA's Educational Policies Commission (1939a) had published a monograph entitled *American Education and the War in Europe*. The authors accused conservative educators of using radio and cinema to highlight the advantages of American intervention. They also thought that they had used these media to denigrate political opponents, including the Educational Policies Commission and the NEA. They inaccurately contrasted this situation with World War I, a period in which, "during the years 1914-16, education literature contained little or no reference to the bearing, upon American educational policy, of the war then being fought in Europe" (p. iii). Since the members of the Educational Policies Commission were confident that American citizens could "make their greatest contribution to the protection and survival of democratic values by refraining from military participation in the struggle in Europe," they urged the public to distrust media campaigns that were intended to amplify nationalism. This late 1930s opposition to entering the war was not an isolated instance. Well before the beginning of World War II, Boeckel (1935) had referred to an NEA resolution opposing militaristic programs in the schools. The resolution had advised that all military training in the schools take place "under the direction and administration of regular school authorities" (NEA Resolution made in 1935, quoted by Boeckel, 1935, pp. 14-15). Some members of the NEA (Educational Policies Commission, 1943c) reversed their earlier attitudes once the United States was engaged in war, looking back on isolationism and its educational concomitants as a "tragic retreat" that had been caused by negative post–World War I experiences.

The most influential theories about the negative consequences of warfare may have been those that were simple and accessible. As an example, Morrison (1944) described militarism as a "cult" that would harm any country that subscribed to it. On the basis of this belief, he challenged American citizens to set higher ethical standards than those that had been adopted by the Germans. The editors of *Educational Leadership* devoted their October 1944 issue to a discussion of compulsory postwar military programs for youths. They introduced the issue with the unqualified assertion that "it is our conviction that legislation requiring such military service should not be passed" ("Shall We Have," 1944, p. 2). They explained that it would be "inconceivable" if Americans were "so unsuccessful in making a just peace that we will need to maintain indefinitely an army of such proportions as to require the services of *all* of the boys of the nation."

A report ("Educators Look beyond the War," 1944) in the *School Review* used a similarly straightforward rhetorical strategy. Acknowledging the popularity and usefulness of expedient wartime programs, the author reassured educators that the accelerated high-school curricula were "largely a result of social demands and that, when these demands disappear, acceleration will disappear with them" (p. 72). Conservative-sponsored programs of this sort would be replaced by liberal curricular strands that emphasized social adjustment, racial cooperation, and world peace. McLaughlin (1944) predicted that the conservative-sanctioned skills-based curricula would also be retired after the war. Instead of "more and longer drills and more coercion," he envisaged a return to progressive activities that would emphasize "generous application to everyday problems and to the local environment" (p. 273). McLaughlin even questioned whether the widely popularized mathematical deficiencies of wartime recruits truly had been the fault of progressive educators. Instead, these problems might have been caused by the progressive educators' opponents, the skills-based instructors with their "lack of goal, neglect of applications, and . . . purposeless drill."

Educational Politics during the 1950s

Thomas (1987) wrote that the United States and the Soviet Union engaged in undeclared, albeit metaphorical, combat after the Second World War. The deteriorating relationships between the two countries were evident in the three-paragraph preface that Major General Leslie Groves, the officer who had been in charge of the Manhattan Project, wrote for *Atomic Energy for Military Purposes* (Smyth, 1945). Groves reminded the readers that this book, which documented the "silent perseverance" of scientists and engineers, contained "all pertinent scientific information which can be released to the public at this time without violating the needs of national security." He followed this remark with the chilling admonition that "no requests for additional information should be made to private persons or organizations associated directly or indirectly with the project." He added still another warning that "persons disclosing or securing additional information by any means whatsoever without authorization are subject to severe penalties under the Espionage Act" (Groves, 1945, p. v).

The symbolic disagreements of the early postwar years escalated into actual combat during the 1950s. Addressing listeners at a national conference on curriculum development, Norton (1950) warned that the nation had entered "a period of mobilization" in which global education would undergo profound changes. Ruthless

FIGURE 7.5. A 1956 Illustration from a Federal Book about the Dangers Students Faced from Nuclear Weapons

Communists obsessed with world dominion would cause these changes. Recapitulating the conservative view about the role that educators should assume during the inevitable confrontations, Meyer (1949) advised them to create an "intellectual, moral, and military defense" against "a powerful and hostile nation which we shall have to endure for many years to come" (p. 36).

Already substantial in the late 1940s and early 1950s, fear and distrust of Communism increased demonstrably over the next ten years. When Sanford, Hand, and Spalding (1951) wrote their book about elementary and secondary curricula, they selected a title, *The Schools and National Security,* that indicated their preoccupation with Communist threats. Their actual advice was more foreboding. In a chapter about aviation education, they warned that aviation's potentialities had been "compounded with those of the atomic bomb." They added that "to ignore or to neglect its educational implications as thus compounded is, in sober fact, to invite catastrophe" (p. 238). Even an everyday issue such as testing was depicted as a technique with which to record students' "progress toward goals which are important for their own survival and the survival of the free nations" (p. 193).

Advocates of vocational education advised school personnel that their approach enhanced the nation's military security. Educators were adjured to use "every practicable means" to reinforce vocational education because this would ensure the nation's military security. The vocations toward which students should be directed were defined in the *Guide to the Evaluation of Educational Experiences in the Armed Services* (American Council on Education, 1954). Originally published in 1944, this volume listed and described the types of training available to servicemen and servicewomen. Academic counselors could use this information to attract students to the armed services, help high-school students complete curricula that complemented military training, and guide institutions that wished to award academic credit for military training. The authors indicated that the 1954 revision of this book addressed novel academic issues that had emerged during the Korean conflict.

230   Wartime Schools

A decade later, Shelburne and Groves (1965) wrote another book with the identical focus. The introduction indicated that high-school and college counselors could consult their book to advise a student about the "pleasure and the profit . . . from experiences in the armed forces" and to help that student recognize that military service was "a continuation of his education—not just an interruption of it, or a postponement of his plans for civilian life" (p. viii).

The federal Office of Education (United States Department of Health, Education, and Welfare, 1956) published a monograph with the austere title *Education for National Survival*. The book described preventative measures to ensure the safety of students. For example, it advised school personnel and students to rehearse the actions they would take during a school-time attack. Even though these simulated drills might frighten the children, as well as the staff and teachers, they were seen as essential because "the enemy's temptation to strike against the United States will shrink in proportion to the advance measures this Nation adopts to protect its peoples and its institutions, thus making an attack unprofitable to the enemy" (p. iii). Government officials pointed out that the schools, which contained 25 percent of the national population, would be irresistible targets to cold-blooded adversaries.

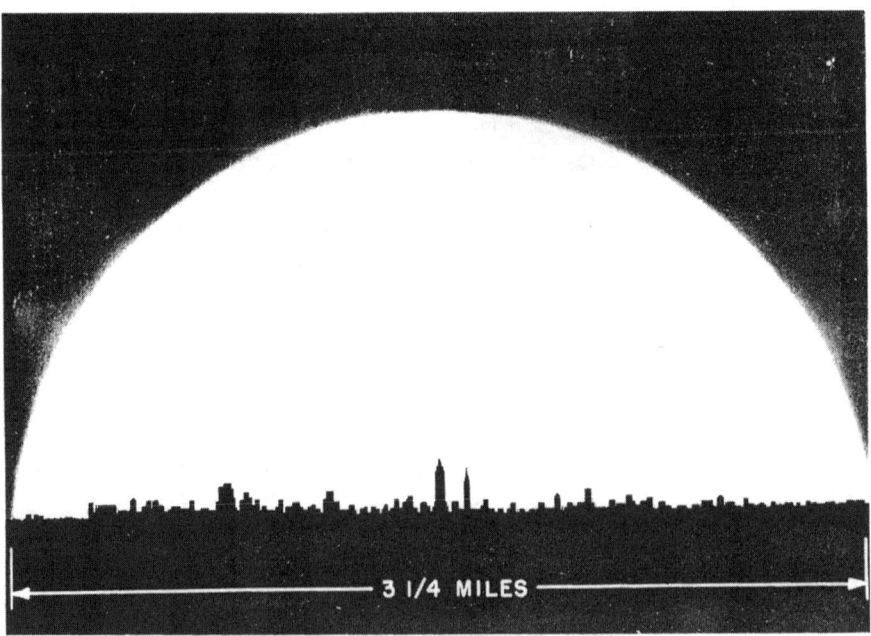

An artist's conception of a hydrogen bomb fireball over the skyline of New York City.

FIGURE 7.6. This 1956 Illustration from the U.S. Office of Education Indicated Damage from Hydrogen Bombs

Dynamics of Wartime Education 231

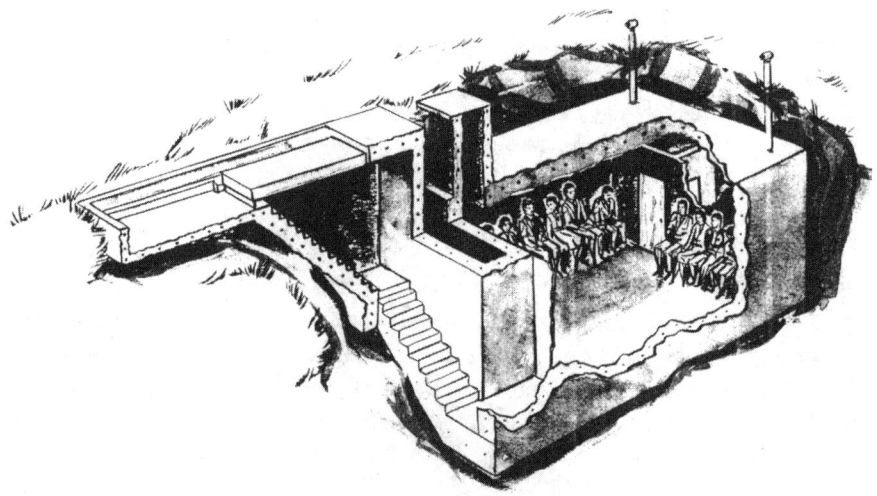

FIGURE 7.7. A 1950s Illustration of Defensive Measures during a Nuclear Strike

In addition to advice on surviving a nuclear strike, *Education for National Survival* contained curricula about biological warfare, chemical warfare, and sabotage. The book's illustrations reinforced this grim information. For example, Figure 7.5 demonstrated the relative size of the blasts from atomic and hydrogen bombs. Figure 7.6, which appeared in the same government book, used a model of New York City to indicate the scale of the damage caused by a single hydrogen bomb's fireball. Figure 7.7 depicted citizens searching for security in a fallout shelter.

Communism in the Schools

Mid-century Americans hoped that they could survive nuclear, biological, and chemical attacks. They also wondered how their political system would fare in the face of a confrontational political ideology. The authors of the annual yearbook from a major educational organization began their volume with a set of resolutions, one of which was to "understand that the ideals of freedom and justice that we call democracy are opposed by communism and fascism" (American Association of School Administrators, 1954, p. 8). They added additional cautions that the resulting conflict would determine "whether the free world's ideals and standards shall perish" and "whether the world as we have known it shall continue" (p. 14).

Conservative educators fretted not only about the Communists but also about those American citizens who covertly sympathized with them. Thayer (1954) documented that the widespread public dissatisfaction with educators had developed into the "serious charge that public education has become a conveyor of subversive ideas" (p. 4). Not attempting to conceal their suspicions, 32 states were requiring teachers to take pledges of national loyalty by 1952. This was a significant increase from the 21 states that had demanded oaths 11 years earlier (Fariello, 1995).

The NEA's Educational Policies Commission (1952) warned teachers that education's role had changed because of two threats. One was the atomic bomb and the other was "the ruthless and alarmingly successful postwar demonstration of the ambition of the Russian government to promote a policy of world dominion" (p. vii). Despite such overtly patriotic manifestations by members of the NEA, conservatives questioned the genuine political convictions of their leadership. In a book about Communist subversion, Kaub (1953) chose the subtitle *A Documented Study of the Role the National Education Association Is Taking in the Indoctrination of the Youth of Our Country with the Ideology of Communism-Socialism*. Needless to say, readers did not have to peruse this entire volume to discover the author's attitudes. Several years later, Jones and Oliver (1956) wrote a book that examined the national loyalty of progressive and liberal educators. Even the book's title, *Progressive Education is REDucation*, projected some of their conclusions.

This period's most notorious crusader against American Communism was Senator Joseph McCarthy. McCarthy's (1952) confrontational political style was revealed in a book in which he presented "documented answers to questions asked by friend and foe" about the "fight for America." In the foreword to McCarthy's book, McGovern (1952) observed that postwar Americans had stopped "living in a fool's paradise" when they began to realize that a "seriously weakened" United Stated was "headed toward disaster." Although catastrophes could be initiated by the Russians, they might also come from the Chinese, who were "clearly and admittedly wholehearted Communists, closely tied up with the Kremlin crowd, and aimed at the total communization of the whole of the Far East" (p. vii).

Some of the conservatives who were alarmed about Communist sympathizers concentrated their attention on liberal professors. In the *American Legion Magazine*, Kuhn (1952) published an exposé of "how a small but well organized minority is attempting to manipulate our public schools to condition our children for what they call 'a new social order'" (p. 18). Beneath the headline for this article, Kuhn displayed the photographs of four politically liberal professors at Teachers College. On the opposite page, the editors placed a picture of Hitler saluting a formation of uniformed German youths. The caption beneath the Nazi picture noted that "in a totalitarian country, perversion of education can be done openly [while] in the United States the methods have to be more subtle" (p. 19). In another article published in the *American Legion Magazine*, Root (1952) wrote about the "collectivist professors," "academic hucksters," and "left-wing super-sales-men" who were persuading idealistic youths to share a vision of "reaction, terror, purges, slavery, and spiritual darkness" (p. 18).

Social studies teachers and the professors who were preparing them fell under an especially dark cloud. In an article about the teaching of government, Karsch (1951) alerted high-school instructors that "instead of being arrested by the military outcome of World War II, the threat of totalitarianism has become vastly augmented, for it is now carried on in the Soviet ideology and policies, which because of their insidious nature and tremendous armed backing are more alarming than the programs of Hitler and Mussolini" (p. 16). Despite this foreboding message, Karsch complimented school administrators for their promptness in adapting social studies programs. Writing during that same year, Keohane (1951) made a different assessment of the schools' responsiveness. He observed acidly that "we await with as little impatience as we can the radical renewal of our educational system in general, and of the social studies in particular" (p. 104).

The extent of the public's skepticism about social studies instruction was evident in the foreword to a book by Hunt and Metcalf (1955). Readers might have suspected from this book's title, *Teaching High School Social Studies: Problems in Reflective Thinking and Social Understanding*, that the authors encouraged students to question traditional societal values. The editor asserted that such examinations were "the solid bedrock of genuinely democratic principles," even though social studies instructors who facilitated them were "particularly exposed to pressures and attacks by anti-democratic forces" (p. vii). Having predicted that teachers who employed this book would encounter a hostile public, the editor confided that "everything in the book is important, even the final and distinctly unusual chapter on academic freedom." Within this latter chapter, the authors acknowledged that many teachers were hesitant to employ "provocative types of teaching" because "it is frequently claimed that communities would fire teachers who provoked thinking in their students" (p. 431).

Although 1950s conservatives had been concerned about the inadequacies of American education, they became even more distraught after the Russians launched the Sputnik satellite. A former U.S. Commissioner of Education wrote that persons became worried about the "military significance of this epoch-making feat" and foresaw "hydrogen bombs being dropped from a similar instrument into the midst of our cities" (McGrath, 1958, p. 379).

Vice Admiral H. G. Rickover was an influential spokesperson for conservative educational interests during this period. In an introduction to one of Rickover's books, Murrow (1959) pointed out that the admiral was "no theoretical pedagogue" and that his insights had been formed through practical experiences. Within another introduction, the editors (Rickover, 1957b) of the *Saturday Evening Post* characterized Rickover as "a noted authority on atomic energy," "a brilliant engineer-scientist," and "the creator of the atomic submarine Nautilus." In an article (Rickover, 1957a) from *U.S. News & World Report*, Rickover was identified as the "Assistant Chief for Nuclear Propulsion in the Bureau of Ships." Needless to say, any person characterized in this manner was a difficult target for liberal educators to discredit.

In one of his essays, Rickover "bluntly" summarized education's primary problem as the "failure to train the nation's brain power to its highest potential." Believing that teachers were partially to blame for this failure, he pointed out that Russia had "no substandard teachers [because] she has set their scholastic standards very high . . . [and] honors them and pays them exceedingly well (Rickover, 1957a, p. 86). One of the consequences of the misguided American system was "an alarming shortage of trained professionals." This personnel shortage was weakening the recruitment of young men into the Navy's atomic submarine program. It also was limiting the talent for other critical military programs and the scientific fields on which they depended. In the wake of the Sputnik launch, Rickover's warnings seemed particularly unnerving.

Lansner (1958), an editor at *Newsweek*, was less concerned than Rickover about appearing objective and unbiased. He assembled a series of books with sensationalistic titles such as *Second-Rate Brains*, *The Challenge of the Sputniks*, and *Can We Meet the Russians Halfway?* The annotated table of contents for *Second-Rate Brains* highlighted disturbing aspects of Russian achievement such as "the alarming facts about soviet science education" and "the long-range goals of the Russian educational machine."

Lansner had tried to entice readers with an article in which "Professor Arthur Bestor directs his withering fire at most U.S. schools." Bestor was an eloquent and intellectually formidable adversary of progressive education. Even the progressive educators themselves acknowledged his impressive following. An article by Cunningham (1959), who was participating in a symposium of liberal educators intent on refuting the conservative Bestor, contained an editorial sidebar acknowledging that Bestor's opinions did "enjoy headway in the commercial press" (p. 158). Another participant in that seminar conceded that the anti-progressive Bestor had come to be regarded as "a leader in the movement for educational reform" (Susky, 1959, p. 173).

In an interview with this conservative scholar, the editors ("What Went Wrong," 1958) of *U.S. News & World Report* assured readers that Bestor could explain why American students were failing to compete with Russian youngsters. Bestor responded that American students and their teachers were responsible. While the students had not developed the work ethic to master rigorous lessons, their teachers lacked the skills to teach them appropriately. Bestor assigned much of the responsibility for this lamentable situation to progressive education. In one of his influential books about America's "educational wastelands," the witty Bestor (1953) used a train metaphor to characterize progressive education as a club car that "dispenses the amenities of life to persons bound on serious errands elsewhere" (p. 2).

Death of Progressive Education

Although dogs will usually spare the life of a wounded and submissive foe, sometimes bloodlust can make them continue their assault. With comparable cruelty, 1950s conservatives attacked their mortally weakened progressive colleagues. Terrified by the prospects of a nuclear strike, the conservatives were not in the mood to show tolerance to foreign saboteurs or the American sympathizers who might be abetting them. Sure that progressive educators were in the latter category, the conservatives were unmerciful.

Prewar conservatives had examined politically liberal textbooks to demonstrate that their authors were Communists. In a similar manner, World War II conservatives had ferreted though journals and books to portray liberal educators as Communists or Communist sympathizers. Because the conservatives of the 1950s preserved the conviction that Communist subversion remained a substantial menace, they continued to monitor the remarks made by liberal contemporaries. They focused on progressive educators who, they thought, were conspiring to reduce America's academic standards. This plotting seemed especially insidious at a time when Communists were increasing academic standards in their own countries. Just as Pearl Harbor had validated accusations that the conservative had made during the early 1940s, the Russian launch of Sputnik convinced many 1950s Americans that the conservatives' warnings were accurate again.

As a result of this vote of confidence, conservative educators were able to maintain the beneficial alliance that they had formed with the public during World War II. Albert Lynd (1950) showcased this alliance when he wrote that average citizens knew more about education than elitist progressive educators, some of whom were "the real 'enemies' of the public schools" (p. 3). Three years later, Lynd (1953) used a widely read magazine as the vessel from which to fire another broadside at progressive educators. Writing in *Atlantic Monthly*, he agreed with the progressive educators about the "unquestioned intellectual stature and integrity" of John Dewey, who was the philosophical architect of their approach. However, he differentiated Dewey from the "pedagogical boondogglers" who had misappropriated his philosophy to justify their own eccentric practices. He wrote that "precisely because Progressive Education dispenses so far with tradition and stakes so much upon the educational creativity of the teacher, it is a method which would require someone like a Dewey in every classroom" (p. 34). Instead, progressive education had been forced to use "the least fitted group in the community to assume the responsibility for recreating its cultural aspirations."

The conservative Mortimer Smith (1949) was another master of populist rhetoric. He characterized one of his influential books as a "layman's" attempt to examine the public schools. He decried the snobby attitudes of progressive educators who viewed the term *layman* as "something condescending and faintly derogatory." In a book that he entitled *The Diminished Mind*, Smith (1954) chastised progressive educators for eroding public education through a campaign of "planned mediocrity." Disagreeing with the liberals who had identified social reconstruction as the primary goal of education, he retorted that "education is a personal, individual experience" and that "its purpose is the improvement of persons and only secondarily the improvement of society" (p. 8). To substantiate this point, he referred to statements by early educational liberals such as Horace Mann and Henry Barnard. Smith (1956) wrote yet another critical book, *The Public Schools in Crisis*, as a response to "the preoccupation of the mass circulation magazines" with the troubles in public education. As examples of this preoccupation, he noted that "*Life* has devoted a whole issue to the problems of the schools, *Collier's* has carried a controversial series of articles, and the *Ladies' Home Journal* manages to find space for the subject in almost every issue" (p. 3).

Many other critics of education followed the same path as Albert Lynd and Mortimer Smith. Bell (1949) pointed out that a layperson's revolt was substantiated by "current trends in journalism, by radio, by our magazines of large circulation and by our best-selling books" (p. viii). Thompson (1953a) cited widely circulated books as well as articles in newspapers and magazines to demonstrate that progressive education was the center of unprecedented "acrimonious debate." Woodring (1953) agreed that "entire issues of popular magazines and journals of opinion have been devoted to critical examinations of the schools" and that "in each year more books are published which attack current educational practices" (p. 1). In one of those books, Scott and Hill (1954) concluded that an extraordinary amount of criticism was causing citizens to view education with "serious concern." Allen (1956) bragged that the powerful alliance supporting conservative education was a heterogeneous mixture of "businessmen, university professors, ministers, judges, politicians, commentators, doctors, writers, parents, and many others" (p. 9). She wrote that this diversified group of citizens was sounding "the bell of dissatisfaction."

The *Ladies' Home Journal* regularly published articles that found fault with education. In an especially acerbic essay, Thompson (1953b) attempted to undermine several of the defensive bulwarks that progressive educators had erected. For example, progressive educators had represented themselves as the initiators of "a revolt against previous conventions." Thompson retorted that the progressive educators were actually "so conventionalized and conformist that a teacher opposes them at the risk of his or her career" (p. 125). She dismissed as self-serving their claim that they exhibited unparalleled professional discretion and immense sensitivity to children. Instead, she suggested that progressive "'patterns' of education are set by teachers of teachers, rather than by teachers of children, with an administrative bureaucracy upholding what might be called a teaching *theology*."

Continuing to cut with the same analytical scalpel, Thompson dissected progressive educators' assertion that only those students who had learned in democratically organized classrooms were prepared for citizenship. She responded that "although children and youth can be drum-majored into blind obedience, the human stuff out of which totalitarian societies are made, they can be prepared for the same submissiveness by the total lack of authority, by moral and intellectual anarchy, whose offspring is tyranny" (p. 125). In his book, *A Program for Conservatives*, Kirk (1954) used a similar rhetorical feint. He discouraged progressive educators from criticizing conservatives when they themselves were the "true conservatives of stupidity." They had revealed this by transforming "the sentences of Dewey, Kilpatrick, and Counts into unalterable secular dogmas" (p. 62).

Just as conservatives denigrated liberals, so did the liberals disparage their opponents. However, the liberals did recognize that the conservatives had greater popular support. In an article that appeared in *McCall's Magazine*, the liberal Morse (1951) admitted that public education, because of its association with progressive educators, was "under the heaviest attack in its history" (p. 26). Brameld (1951), a leader in the progressive education movement, acknowledged that the conflict surrounding progressive education was unprecedented "in the history of American education." Writing in the journal *Progressive Education*, Molinaro (1952), who applauded the "brief revival" of educational liberalism during the 1930s, conceded that the conservatives had effectively displaced the liberals during World War II. By 1952, the remaining liberals had come to be viewed as "questionable evangelists."

In the early 1950s, Melby (1953) lamented that Communism had "frightened us to such an alarming degree" that administrators were radically modifying their schools. At the end of that decade, the mood of national terror was still present. As a consequence, conservatives continued their feverish attack on the moribund vestiges of the progressive education movement. Resigned to this fate, the liberal Koerner (1959) wrote dejectedly that the empowered conservatives, who maintained "access to audiences of substantial size," would not relax their assault until they had destroyed "every worthwhile accomplishment in public education since the turn of the century" (p. 245).

Postscript

> [Although] every social institution is subject to the tendency toward crystallization and inertia . . . the war and the period of reconversion after the war involve such rapid and marked changes that most social institutions are abruptly forced into change.
> —TYLER, 1945

Early twentieth-century reformers feared that educators had lost contact with their communities. They criticized their handling of curriculum, instruction, textbooks, funding, discipline, character development, extracurricular activities, and preparation for employment. They eventually contested everything they did. In the middle of these attacks, persons came forward to defend the schools. The aggressors and defenders faced a common problem as they appealed to a public that was less interested in education than in other matters. This problem dissolved during World War I, when government officials, military leaders, and industrialists demanded a home-front campaign to ensure national security. They asked educators to maintain morale, emphasize the righteousness of America's actions, increase the supply of food, raise money, protect wartime resources, prepare soldiers for the armed services, and train workers for wartime industries.

In response to these adjurations, educators made pervasive changes. They earned the admiration of the conservatives by promoting patriotism and vocational education. They also promoted liberal goals by supporting conservation and opportunities for women workers. Even programs that mixed conservative and liberal issues became attractive after they were portrayed as essential to America's war interests. For the identical reason, skills-based, vocational, and accelerated approaches were widely accepted.

Although the liberals might have profited from the public's pragmatic mood, they did not use this opportunity to their advantage. In contrast, the conservatives immediately saw an opening to advance their interests. They also saw a chance to discredit their opponents. They criticized liberal teachers, many of whom were progressive educators, for disregarding civic responsibilities, patriotism, and the menace of Communism. They censured them for their allegiance to the creative arts and the humanities rather than mathematics, science, physical conditioning, career training, and other critical wartime subjects. They disparaged them for relying on highly trained instructional specialists. They even blamed them for the academic and physical problems that their students later exhibited when they entered the military.

Although many of the educational changes of World War I foreshadowed the patterns of the subsequent war, the most striking similarity was the expansion of scholastic nationalism. It was evident in curricular bans against the languages of the foreign countries with which America was at war. It was apparent in the books, maps, posters, motion pictures, and course syllabi that the government and industry distributed. It was revealed in the proliferation of patriotic school activities, courses about wartime issues, and programs that prepared students for military service.

The Lesson Is Reinforced

Several decades later, pre–World War II government officials decided to replicate the earlier war's educational initiatives. They acted cautiously because they were politically less secure than their World War I peers. After all, the public deliberated at length before it endorsed entry into World War I. Furthermore, its territory, armed forces, and citizens were geographically isolated from combat during those deliberations. This was not the case in World War II. Even though they had years to contemplate international events, many Americans were not ready to begin warfare in 1941. A surprise attack on their territory and forces made them believe that immediate total war was unavoidable.

The anxiety created by Pearl Harbor was heightened by the federal government's dexterous use of propaganda. Even though the World War I government had employed propaganda, it had not taken full advantage of combat photography, cinema, and radio to convey a sense of impending danger. It also had underutilized potent psychological strategies that could alter perceptions, dispositions, and values. The Roosevelt administration established an extensive and sophisticated domestic propaganda campaign. It was augmented by wartime advertisements that used the identical strategies to convey complementary messages. It was also enhanced by news reporters who deferred to government censors.

Teachers and school administrators supported the war because of choice, mandate, or a sense of obligation. Many participated by gardening, conserving resources, raising finances, planning patriotic activities, or taking precautions to shield children during military attacks. In addition to making their own contributions, they encouraged their students to engage in wartime activities. By cooperating with the government, the armed services, and businesses, they discharged their most important responsibility, which was preparing students for military and industrial service.

As the federal government assembled specialized educational resources, it was able to build on its earlier wartime experiences. It also benefited from the late 1930s and early 1940s defensive programs for which it had tailored educational materials. Despite its prewar preparations, the wartime government had to massively expand its production of classroom texts, supplementary resources, instructional advice, and curricula. Textbook publishers and industrialists helped with materials that matched those from the government.

Professional educational associations produced wartime materials that complemented those from the government, textbook publishers, and industrialists. Before Pearl Harbor, the politically liberal leaders of these associations had spoken out against American participation in the war. Even though most of them later rallied for victory, they simultaneously used their journals, newsletters, and conferences to promote their traditional political interests. For example, they tried to increase union dues, the portion of taxes allocated to education, instructors' salaries, teachers' academic freedom, and the sizes of their organizations.

Most of the wartime instructional materials were books, pamphlets, or articles that supplemented established educational curricula or supported novel wartime courses. In addition to the countless printed supplies, the new materials included films, radio broadcasts, phonograph records, games, and war memorabilia. These resources were so practical that instructional scripts and student worksheets often accompanied them. Educators also used distinctive wartime programs to develop scholastic skills and nonacademic traits. The nonacademic traits comprised discipline, physical conditioning, national loyalty, altruism, knowledge of the war's progress, enthusiasm for military service, and career talents.

Most of the educational issues that became prominent during World War II were not novel. The war provided a forum from which groups could lobby for the scholastic changes to which they were philosophically disposed. As such, political groups were able to characterize their proposals as expedients that would protect America's territory, citizens, and democratic traditions. The shifting rhetoric was illustrated in the debate about juvenile misconduct. Although this had been a perennial concern of the conservatives, they portrayed deteriorating adolescent behavior as a national epidemic caused by wartime society. They demanded that educators solve the problem by assuming the roles of parents, counselors, and the police. Instead of following this impractical advice, most teachers and school administrators implemented preventative procedures to direct potential offenders toward military service and defense employment.

The deleterious effects of politically liberal textbooks had been another concern of prewar conservatives. The suspect materials depicted the United States as antidemocratic, untrue to the ideals of the founding patriots, and inferior to Communist societies. The liberal educators who espoused these materials pointed out that the books were antijingoistic rather than antidemocratic, internationalist rather than un-American, and egalitarian rather than Communist. They thought that students needed this exact type of instructional material to become independent and thoughtful citizens. They made the same case to support the right of teachers to speak openly in classrooms. Not persuaded by these arguments, the conservatives lobbied state legislators to restrict the content of materials and the speech of teachers. Even though they were able to enact prohibitions in several states, the conservatives relied primarily on parents, teachers, and school boards to take actions in their own communities.

Aware of the power that their critics wielded, most liberal teachers attempted to appease them. As one example, they changed the labels on classroom activities to highlight their commitment to diversity, independence, and democracy. Despite such reconciliatory actions, inexorable social pressures forced them to restructure their classrooms using conservative-approved practices. This restructuring extended to the selection of topics for their courses and the way this content was presented. The insistence to make such precise changes, especially at the secondary level, came from the military, the government, and industry. These groups supported scholastic practices that reinforced the war effort. As a consequence, they backed vocational curricula because they would prepare learners for armed service and home-front employment. Their enthusiasm rose further when vocational curricula were enhanced through accelerated learning schedules, individualized assignments, and flexible assessments.

Skills-based curricula, which also were endorsed, had several obvious assets. Like the vocational curricula, they could be accelerated to meet wartime deadlines. They benefited from their traditional connection to mathematics, science, technology, and physical education, all of which became more prominent during the war. They could be integrated easily with the bounteous wartime teaching materials. Finally, their modular format and easy-to-follow learning objectives made them accessible to novice teachers.

Because progressive education was associated with pedagogical elitists and controversial political activists, the wartime public eschewed it. Even after jettisoning the portions of their approach that had elicited the greatest hostility, progressive educators could not persuade politically moderate colleagues to remain in their organization. Unable to retain the confidence of professional peers and their own associates, they inevitably failed to win the approval of a public that demanded fervent commitment to home-front defense.

The Lesson Remains Vibrant

World War I demonstrated the power that educators could summon when they connected their initiatives to national security. Impressed by this lesson, the World War

II conservatives adopted a comparable educational campaign. As they responded to an international emergency that seemed greater than that of the First World War, the public's receptivity to their proposals escalated correspondingly. The liberals, who were less opportunistic than the conservatives, ignored the political lesson of World War I. As a result, their reputation declined even lower than it had during that earlier conflict. The liberals' recalcitrance was evident after the Second World War as well, when they urged citizens to reject the wartime educational initiatives that had relied on vocational learning, regimentation, classroom discipline, academic achievement in prescribed subjects, and nationalism. Convinced that the recent war never would have been fought if the public had acceded to post–World War I advice from political liberals, they urged it to recognize that progressive education constituted the only true egress from future cycles of armed conflict.

Formidable and empowered, postwar conservatives were not inclined to compromise. They viewed their opponents as idealists who had underestimated the dangers of aggressive nationalism in one war and Fascism in another. They thought they were equally uninformed about the current threats from Communism. They urged the public to resist liberal-sponsored reforms and rely on conservative educational programs in a dangerous postwar era.

During the second half of the twentieth century, conservatives continued to represent their educational program as a critical security measure. This strategy's efficacy increased in proportion to the danger of international crises. When alleged threats seemed genuine, the public's reception of the conservative program increased. On the basis of these political dynamics, the conservatives' power was propelled to its zenith during World War II, when international devastation had seemed imminent. Even excluding World War II, the conservatives' domination of education extended from World War I to the end of the twentieth century. The conservatives devised programs that had obvious practical advantages; but these advantages, by themselves, could not have accounted for their eight-decade rule. Their success came from their skill in depicting a coherent, efficient, and financially reasonable approach to education that was prudent in periods of peace and absolutely necessary in times of international conflict.

References

Abbot, J. W. (1943). Children's interest in the war and the curriculum. *Progressive Education*, 20, 111-113.
Abbott, A. (1918). The English teacher and the World-War. *English Journal*, 7, 1-6.
Abbott, J. D. (1943). I have seen the children. *Educational Leadership*, 1, 93-97.
Abbott, W. C. (1915). Germany and the Prussian propaganda. *Yale Review*, 4, 664-683.
Abbott, W. C. (1916). The war and American democracy. *Yale Review*, 5, 484-502.
Academic freedom in war time. (1918). *Journal of Education*, 87, 376-377.
Academic standards in war-time. (1918). *School and Society*, 7, 295-296.
Acceleration. (1942, March 3). *Education for Victory*, 1 (1), 31.
Ackerman, J. H. (1917). The normal school as an agency for teaching patriotism. *Journal of the National Education Association*, 2, 55-60.
Adamic, L. (1943). Carriers of freedom. *Educational Method*, 22, 152-156.
Adams, B. (1916). The American democratic ideal. *Yale Review*, 5, 225-233.
Aderhold, O. C. (1944). A state looks at its war program. *School Executive*, 63 (10), 42-43.
Adler, M. J. (1988). This prewar generation. In G. Van Doren (Ed.), *Reforming education: The opening of the American mind* (pp. 3-17). New York: Macmillan. (Original work published in 1940.)
Advertising as a weapon of war. (1918). *Printer's Ink*, 105 (7), 143-144.
Advertising stimulates enlistments in aviation section. (1918). *Printer's Ink*, 102 (1), 103-104.
Advertising to bridge gap between war and reconstruction. (1918). *Printer's Ink*, 105 (9), 16-20, 25.
Agard, W. R. (1942). Democratic education during the war. *School and Society*, 56, 393-397.
Agren, R., & Massey, E. L. (1943). Training in fundamentals of electricity, machines, radio, shop work, and automotive mechanics. *Teachers College Record*, 45, 176-182.
Ahl, F. N. (1944). Preparing for the post-war period. *Social Studies*, 35, 61-62.

Ainsworth, D. (1943). Our contribution to morale in times of war and peace. *Journal of Health and Physical Education, 14,* 67-69, 116-117.

Air raid protection and evacuation planning. (1942, December 1). *Education for Victory, 1* (19), 13-14.

Air raids and the schools. (1942). *Journal of the National Education Association, 31,* 57-58.

Alderman, L. R. (1917). The public school and the nation in 1917. *Journal of the National Education Association, 2,* 226-229.

Aley, R. J. (1917a). Cooperation in education. *School and Society, 6,* 31-35.

Aley, R. J. (1917b). The war and secondary schools. *School and Society, 6,* 751-755.

Aley, R. J. (1918a). The war and secondary schools. *Education, 38,* 628-634.

Aley, R. J. (1918b). The war and secondary schools. *Journal of Education, 87,* 176-178.

All-day school programs for children of working mothers: Services to help states meet needs. (1942, October 15). *Education for Victory (1)* 16, 1-2.

Allen, M. L. (1956). *Education or indoctrination.* Caldwell, ID: Caxton.

Allen, N. B. (1919). Teaching the France of to-day. *Normal Instructor and Primary Plans, 28* (5), 24-25, 69.

Allen, W. H. (1918). Deprussianizing American schools. *Educational Foundations, 29,* 457-462.

Allen, W. H., & Kleiser, C. (1918). *Stories of Americans in the World War.* New York: Institute for Public Service.

Alleviation of wartime weaknesses in mathematics and science. (1943). *School and Society, 56,* 11-12.

Alley, R. J. (1917). Obligations and opportunities of the schools during the war. *Journal of the National Education Association, 2,* 148.

Allyn and Bacon Publishing Company Advertisement. (1946, September). *Journal of the National Education Association, 35* [rear cover].

America and the war. (1917). *Utah Educational Review, 10* (9), 5.

American Association of School Administrators. (1954). *Educating for American citizenship* (32nd Yearbook of the National Education Association). Washington, DC: National Education Association.

American Council Institute of Pacific Relations. (1942). War-time materials for secondary schools—A teachers' guide to far eastern books. *Bulletin of the National Association of Secondary-School Principals, 26* (106), 171-178.

American Council on Education. (1940a). *Education and the national defense.* Washington, DC: Author.

American Council on Education. (1940b). *Educational studies and their use: Vol. 1 (11). Monograph Series.* Washington DC: Author.

American Council on Education. (1941). *Higher education cooperates in national defense: Vol. 1 (15). Studies.* Washington DC: Author.

American Council on Education. (1944). *A design for general education: Vol. 1 (18). Studies.* Washington, DC: Author.

American Council on Education. (1954). *A guide to the evaluation of educational experiences in the Armed Services* (Rev. ed.). Washington, DC: Author.

American education and the war in Europe. (1939). *Journal of the National Education Association, 28*, 225-228.
American notes—Editorial. (1917a). *Education, 37*, 651-655.
American notes—Editorial. (1917b). *Education, 38*, 57-59.
American notes—Editorial. (1917c). *Education, 38*, 183-188.
American Vocational Association Conference: Weighs future responsibilities. (1944, January 20). *Education for Victory, 2* (14), 5-6.
Americanization. (1918). *School Life, 1* (1), 1-2.
Ames, H. V. (1917). How far should the teaching of history and civics be used as a means of encouraging patriotism? *History Teacher's Magazine, 8*, 188-192.
Amidon, B. (1942). Arms and the women. *Survey Graphic, 31*, 244-248, 271.
Amidon, B. (Ed.). (1940). *Democracy's challenge to education*. New York: Farrar & Rinehart.
Anderson, G. L. (1943). *Adapting the high school to wartime and postwar needs: Vol. 1. Modern School Curriculum Series*. Minneapolis: University of Minnesota Press.
Anderson, H. H. (1943). Speed up for the war. *Nation's Schools, 32* (6), 42.
Anderson, H. W. (1943). Mobilizing schools on the home front. *American School Board Journal, 106* (2), 16, 50.
Anderson, K. (1981). *Wartime women: Sex roles, family relations, and the status of women during World War II*. Westport, CT: Greenwood.
Anderson, N., & Rogg, N. H. (1942). Impact of the war on labor and industry. *American Journal of Sociology, 48*, 361-368.
Anderson, R. N. (1943). Counseling youth for wartime jobs. *Teachers College Record, 44*, 319-326.
Anderson, W. A. (1943). School supervision in wartime. *Education, 63*, 327-329.
Anderson, W. A., & Krug, E. A. (1943). The ivory towers fall. *Educational Leadership, 1*, 133-139.
Andrews, F. F. (1916). What the public schools can do toward the maintenance of permanent peace. *Journal of the National Education Association, 1*, 92-94.
Andrews, F. F. (1917). A call to patriotic service. *Utah Educational Review, 10* (9), 9-11.
Andrews, J. N. (1943). The democratic attitudes. *American School Board Journal, 106* (4), 26.
Angell, N. (1915). America and the European war. *Yale Review, 4*, 219-234.
Antonacci, R. J. (1943). Preparing for personal combat training. *Athletic Journal, 24* (1), 26-30, 38.
Appeal to the National Society for the Promotion of Industrial Education and to each state board of education. (1918). *Educational Foundations, 29*, 539-541.
Appy, N. (1942). A westerner looks at schools in wartime. *Educational Method, 22*, 26-29.
Arlin, H. W. (1944). The reconversion of vocational education. *School Shop, 3* (7), 3-5, 30.
Armentrout, W. D. (1939). Educational method in a democracy. *Social Frontier, 5*, 275-277.
Armstrong, O. K. (1940, September). Treason in the textbooks. *American Legion Magazine, 20* (3), 8-9, 51, 70-72.

Army experience and problems of Negro education. (1945, April 20). *Education for Victory, 3* (20), 13–16.
Ashby, L. W. (1942). NEA serves in wartime. *Journal of the National Education Association, 31*, 36–37.
Ashby, L. W. (1943a). Education for the air age. *Journal of the National Education Association, 32*, 73–76.
Ashby, L. W. (1943b). Wartime commencements. *Journal of the National Education Association, 32*, 42.
Ashby, L. W. (1944). The teacher in wartime. *Journal of the National Education Association, 33*, 65–66.
Asquith, H. H. (1918). Introduction. In B. McLaren, *Women of the war* (pp. iii–iv). New York: Doran.
Associated Business Papers. (1942). *Guide to effective wartime advertising*. New York: Author.
Athletics: An aid to national defense. (1941). *Athletic Journal, 22* (3), 32–36.
Austin, A. B. (1942). War and the school board's responsibility. *American School Board Journal, 104* (6), 38.
Avisar, I. (1988). *Screening the Holocaust: Cinema's images of the unimaginable*. Bloomington: Indiana University Press.
Axtelle, G. E. (1940). Social implementation of democracy and education. In G. E. Axtelle & W. W. Wattenberg (Eds.), *Teachers for democracy* (pp. 382–406). New York: Appleton-Century.
Ayling, K. (1943). *Semper fidelis: The U.S. Marines in action*. New York: Literary Classics.
Ayres, L. P. (1917). Military drill in high schools. *School Review, 25*, 157–160.
Azan, P. (1918). *The warfare of to-day* (J. L. Coolidge, Trans.). Boston & New York: Houghton Mifflin.
Babcock, C. D., Jeffery, E., & Troelstrup, A. W. (1942). *Paying for the war: A resource unit for teachers of the social studies* (Bulletin, No. 18). Washington, DC: National Council for the Social Studies.
Babcock, R. (1939). What are schools doing? *Frontiers of Democracy, 6*, 84–86.
Babcock, R. (1941). Educational reconstruction in the post-war world. *Frontiers of Democracy, 8*, 6–7.
Bachrach, E. (1940). Does education influence democracy? *Social Studies, 31*, 195–197.
Bacon, F. L. (1944). Postwar education for teen-age war workers. *Bulletin of the National Association of Secondary-School Principals, 28* (125), 56–59.
Badley, J. H. (1917). *Education after the war*. London: Oxford.
Bagley, W. C. (1918a). Education and our democracy. *Journal of Education, 88*, 367–368.
Bagley, W. C. (1918b). Education and our democracy. *School and Society, 8*, 241–245.
Bahr, L. O. (1943). The effect of war on our life. *Instructor, 52* (10), 37, 67.
Bailey, C. S. (1918). *What to do for Uncle Sam: A first book of citizenship*. Chicago: Flanagan.
Bailey, R. E. (1943a). Camouflage application. *Industrial Arts and Vocational Education, 32*, 264.
Bailey, R. E. (1943b). Camouflage bombardment. *Industrial Arts and Vocational Education, 32*, 181.

Bailey, R. E. (1943c). Camouflage reconnaissance. *Industrial Arts and Vocational Education, 32*, 263.

Bailey, R. E. (1943d). Camouflage shadows. *Industrial Arts and Vocational Education, 32*, 182.

Bailey, R. E. (1943e). Camouflage textures. *Industrial Arts and Vocational Education, 32*, 219-220.

Bailey, R. H. (1977). *The home front: U.S.A.* Arlington, VA: Time-Life.

Baldwin, H. W. (1941). *United we stand! Defense of the western hemisphere.* New York: Whittlesey.

Baldwin, W. A. (1917). Democracy versus efficiency as an aim in education. *Journal of Education, 85*, 621-623.

Balfour, M. (1979). *Propaganda in war 1939-1945: Organizations, policies and publics in Britain and Germany.* London: Routledge & Kegan Paul.

Banay, R. S. (1948). *Youth in despair.* New York: Coward-McCann.

Barker, E. V. (1938). Let's try education for peace. *Social Education, 2*, 117-121.

Barnard, J. L. (1918). A program of civics teaching for war times and after. *History Teacher's Magazine, 9*, 492-502.

Barnes, H. E. (1940). The responsibility of education to society. *Scientific Monthly, 51*, 248-260.

Barnes, R. P. (1927). *Militarizing our youth: The significance of the Reserve Officers' Training Corp in our schools and colleges* (Pamphlet). New York: Committee on Militarism in Education.

Barnum, O. S. (1917). The obligations and opportunities of the schools during the war. *Journal of the National Education Association, 2*, 149-150.

Bartlett. H. (1942). *Social studies for the air age: A text for high school students.* New York: Macmillan.

Baruch, D. W. (1943). *You, your children, and war.* New York: Appleton-Century.

Basinger, J. (1986). *The World War II combat film: Anatomy of a genre.* New York: Columbia University Press.

Battle of the books. (1940, November). *American Legion Magazine, 29*, 68.

Battles, E. E. (1943). Citizenship in athletics. *American School Board Journal, 106* (5), 47.

Bauder, C. F. (1942). The Philadelphia program of vocational education for defense. *Industrial Arts and Vocational Education, 31*, 83-87.

Beale, H. K. (1936). *Are American teachers free?* New York: Scribner's Sons.

Beck, J. B. (1943). Seatwork on war stamps. *Instructor, 52* (3), 9.

Beck, R. (1943). Progressive education in transition. *Progressive Education, 20*, 52-55.

Beck, R. H. (1948). Progressive education faces the future. *Progressive Education, 25* (5), 82-83, 86.

Becker, C. L. (1944). What we didn't know hurt us a lot. *Yale Review, 33*, 385-404.

Bedell, E. L. (1943). Training women for wartime industries. *Industrial Arts and Vocational Education, 32*, 1-4.

Bedell, E. L., & Gleason, W. E. (1943). Detroit public schools in the war effort. *Industrial Arts and Vocational Education, 32*, 85-88.

Beers, H. A. (1918). How American Chicle Co. is nationalizing its "sectional brands." *Printer's Ink, 102* (4), 3-4, 6, 109-110, 112-114, 116-117.

Belgrano, F. N. (1935, February). The Legion way is the American way. *American Legion Magazine*, 18, 16–17, 67.
Bell, B. I. (1949). *Crisis in education: A challenge to American complacency*. New York: McGraw-Hill.
Bell, J. C. (1917). Military training and the school. *Journal of Educational Psychology*, 8, 245–246.
Bell, M. (Ed.). (1944). *Delinquency and the community in wartime. Yearbook of the National Probation Association*. New York: National Probation Association.
Bement, A. (1917). Camouflage. *Teachers College Record*, 18, 458–462.
Benedict, R., & Weltfish, G. (1943). *The races of mankind. No. 85 of Public Affairs Pamphlets*. New York: Public Affairs Committee.
Benne, K. D. (1949). Democratic ethics in social engineering. *Progressive Education*, 26, 201–207.
Bennett, M. E., & Laws, G. (1943). Little girls as women. *Educational Leadership*, 1, 78–81.
Berman, E. (1944). Social studies in the post-war world. *Social Studies*, 35, 347–348.
Bernard, L. L. (1972). *War and its causes*. New York: Garland.
Bernays, E. L. (1940). *Speak up for democracy: What you can do—A practical plan of action for every American citizen*. New York: Viking.
Best kind of high-school training for military service. (1942). *Bulletin of the National Association of Secondary-School Principals*, 26 (107), 5–8.
Bestor, A. E. (1953). *Educational wastelands*. Urbana: University of Illinois Press.
Beveridge, A. J. (1917). The school and the nation. *Journal of the National Education Association*, 1, 906–918.
Bigelow, M. A. (1918). Sex-education and social hygiene in war time. *Educational Foundations*, 29, 263–267.
Bigelow, M. A. (1942). Social hygiene and youth in defense communities. *Journal of Social Hygiene*, 28, 437–447.
Billett, R. O. (1940). *Fundamentals of secondary-school teaching with emphasis on the unit method*. Cambridge: Riverside.
Blackwell, G. W. (1942). War on the home front. *Progressive Education*, 19, 319–322.
Blair, F. G. (1918). A practical program of patriotic instruction. *Journal of the National Education Association*, 2, 829–832.
Blake, K. D. (1917). Opportunities of the war. *Journal of the National Education Association*, 2, 147–148.
Blegen, T. C. (1918). Two standards of national morality. *History Teacher's Magazine*, 9, 457–466.
Bliss, D. C. (1917). Military training in the high school. *School Review*, 25, 161–170.
Bliven, B. (1918a). Has German propaganda died with the War? *Printer's Ink*, 105 (7), 90, 93–94, 96.
Bliven, B. (1918b). Selling the war to the working man. *Printer's Ink*, 102 (5), 8, 10, 12, 89–90.
Bliven, B. (1918c). Selling the war to the working man—Part II. *Printer's Ink*, 102 (7), 69–70, 72, 76, 81–82, 84.

Bliven, B. (1918d). Uncle Sam's megaphone. *Printer's Ink, 105* (4), 3–4, 6, 8, 133–135.
Blum, J. M. (1976). *V was for victory: Politics and American culture during World War II.* New York: Harcourt Brace.
Board of Editors. (1942, December). The mission of education in this war. *Frontiers of Democracy,* 68–70.
Board of Education of the City of New York. (1942). *The war and the curriculum: No. 3. Curriculum Bulletin.* Brooklyn, NY: Author.
Bobbie and the war. (1917). *History Teacher's Magazine, 8,* 177–182.
Bobbitt, F. (1941). *The curriculum of modern education.* New York: McGraw-Hill.
Bode, B. H. (1938a). Dr. Childs and education for democracy. *Social Frontier, 5,* 38–40.
Bode, B. H. (1938b). *Progressive education at the crossroads.* New York: Newson.
Boeckel, F. B. (1935). *Military training vs. public education* (Pamphlet). Washington, DC: National Council for Prevention of War.
Bogen, D. (1944). Juvenile delinquency and economic trend. *American Sociological Review, 9,* 178–184.
Bogen, D. (1945). Trends in juvenile delinquency. *Police Journal, 31* (2), 3–4, 8.
Bond, H. M. (1942). Should the Negro care who wins the war? *Annals of the American Academy of Political and Social Sciences, 223,* 81–84.
Bond, J. E. (1942). Teaching home preparedness. *Instructor, 51* (9), 31, 61.
Bonney, M. E. (1943). Psychological factors in total fitness for war. *Journal of Health and Physical Education, 14,* 254–255, 285–286.
Bonser, F. G. (1920). *The elementary school curriculum.* New York: Macmillan.
Boodin, J. E. (1918). Education and society. *School and Society, 8,* 451–461.
Book burnings. (1940, September 9). *Time, 34,* 64–65.
Boord, K. R. (1944, June). Let's go kids. *American Legion Magazine, 36,* 24, 44–45.
Bossing, N. L. (1955). *Principles of secondary education* (2nd ed.). Englewood Cliffs, NJ: Prentice-Hall.
Boswell, R. (1943). *Leathernecks: Our marines in fact & picture.* New York: Crowell.
Bowen, W. C. (1943). Audio-visual aids: Some suggestions for wartime. *American School Board Journal, 106* (3), 27–28.
Bowers, C. A. (1962). Social reconstructionism: Views from the left and the right, 1932–1942. *History of Education Quarterly, 2,* 22–52.
Bowers, C. A. (1964). The Social Frontier Journal: A historical sketch. *History of Education Quarterly, 4,* 167–180.
Bowman, N. E. (1938). Educating children for peace. *Social Education, 2,* 169–176.
Bradford, M. C. C. (1918). A call to the colors for the teachers of the United States. *Journal of Education, 87,* 153.
Bradford, M. D. (1917). The democratic trend in school administration. *Journal of the National Education Association, 2,* 230–235.
Brameld, T. (1935). Karl Marx and the American teacher. *Social Frontier, 2,* 53–56.
Brameld, T. (1936). American education and the social struggle. *Science and Society, 1,* 1–17.
Brameld, T. (1951). *The battle for free schools.* Boston: Beacon.
Brewster, A. G. (1918). A composition course based on the war. *English Journal, 7,* 207–213.

Briggs, T. H. (1940). The ramparts we defend. *School and Society*, 52, 145-153.
Bringing the sales end through the war: How various houses are finding occupation for their sales forces till return of normal conditions. (1918a). *Printer's Ink*, 102 (1), 3-4, 6, 8, 10, 12.
Bringing the sales end through the war: Part II. (1918b). *Printer's Ink*, 102 (2), 100, 105-106, 108, 113-114, 116.
Bristow, W. H. (1943). Changing curriculum patterns in New York city schools. *Journal of Educational Sociology*, 17, 76-83.
Britain's war posters. (1915). *American Review of Reviews*, 52, 675-680.
Britt, G. (1942). War workers in the making. *Survey Graphic*, 31, 235-240.
Broadhurst, J., & Rhodes, C. L. (Eds.). (1919). *Verse for patriots to encourage good citizenship*. Philadelphia: Lippincott.
Brodinsky, B. P., & Nathan, R. (1944, August). Vocational education: Is it for your class? *Parents' Magazine*, 19 (8), 22-23, 54, 56, 59-60.
Broening, A. M. (1942). English in war and peace. *English Journal*, 31, 676.
Broome, E. C., & Adams, E. W. (1940). *Our democracy*. New York: Macmillan.
Brown, C. H. (1941, November 15). Message from President Brown. *Libraries and the National Defense. American Library Association Circular*, 1 (1), 1.
Brown, F. J. (1941). Organization and activities of defense councils. In American Council on Education (Ed.), *Organizing higher education for national defense: Vol. 1 (13). Studies* (pp. 33-39). Washington DC: American Council on Education.
Brown, F. J. (1942). Editorial. *Journal of Educational Sociology*, 15, 317-319.
Brown, K. I. (1943). Three notes on post-war education. *Journal of Education*, 126, 240-250.
Brown, W. B., Stewart, M. S., & Myer, W. E. (1942). *America in a World at War*. New York: Silver Burdett.
Bruce, W. G., & Bruce. W. C. (1940). Teachers and military service. *American School Board Journal*, 101 (5), 53.
Brueckner, L. J. (1943a). Individualizing pre-induction mathematics courses. *Education*, 63, 559-564.
Brueckner, L. J. (1943b). Mathematics to serve war needs. *Journal of the National Education Association*, 32, 203.
Bryan, A. H. (1942). The highschool in wartime. *Journal of the National Education Association*, 31, 60-61.
Burgess, E. W. (1942). The effect of war on the American family. *American Journal of Sociology*, 48, 343-352.
Burning of the textbooks. (1941). *New Republic*, 105, 296-297.
Burrows, A. H. (1946). The problem of juvenile delinquency. *Journal of Educational Sociology*, 19, 382-390.
Butler, C. E. (1944). P.E.A. news. *Progressive Education*, 21, 139.
Butler, I. (1974). *The war film*. New York: Barnes.
Butler, N. N (1919). Education after the war. *Teachers College Record*, 20, 1-5.
Butts, R. F. (1978). *Public education in the United States: From revolution to reform*. New York: Holt, Rinehart & Winston.

California Elementary School Principals' Association. (1942). *Guiding children in democratic living*. Oakland, CA: Author.
Caliver, A. (1944). *Education of teachers for improving majority-minority relationships* (Bulletin No. 2). Washington, DC: United States Office of Education.
Caliver, A. (1945). *Postwar education of Negroes: Educational implications of Army data and experiences of Negro veterans and war workers*. Washington, DC: United States Office of Education.
Camp, F. S. (1917). Physical education and military drill: What should be our policy? *School Review*, *25*, 537-545.
Campbell, D. A. (1984). *Women at War with America: Private Lives in a Patriotic Era*. Cambridge: Harvard University Press.
Campion, H. A. (1942). A challenge to physical education. *Journal of Health and Physical Education*, *13*, 443-444, 502-503.
Can you learn these planes by name? (1943, January 1). *Education for Victory*, *1* (23), 8-9.
Cardall, A. J. (1943). *A wartime guidance program for your school*. Chicago: Science Research Associates.
Carlson, A. D. (1933). Deflating the schools. *Harper's Magazine*, *167*, 705-714.
Carlson, J. R. (1943). *Under cover: My four years in the Nazi underworld of America—The amazing revelation of how axis agents and our enemies within are now plotting to destroy the United States*. New York: Dutton.
Carpenter, W. W., & Capps, A. G. (1942). A total training program for a total war. *School and Society*, *56*, 197-200.
Carr, E. P. (1917). The war and the school. *Journal of Education*, *86*, 453-454.
Carr, W. G. (1940). This is not treason. *Journal of the National Education Association*, *29*, 237.
Carr, W. G. (1941). Learning the meaning of democracy. *Journal of the National Education Association*, *30*, 179-180.
Carr, W. G. (1942). Learning democratic methods in the classroom. *Journal of the National Education Association*, *31*, 11-12.
Carroll, W. (1948). *Persuade or perish*. Boston: Houghton Mifflin.
Case for advertising. (1940). *Nation's Business*, *28* (3), 33-56.
Case for distribution. (1940). *Nation's Business*, *28* (4), 33-64.
Case, C. B. (1918). *Wartime and patriotic selections: For recitation and reading*. Chicago: Shrewesbury.
Caskey, M. M. (1944). An introduction to the flag salute for a patriotic program. *Journal of the National Education Association*, *33*, 222.
Cassidy, R. (1941). Women's education in a world at war: Ends and means. *Progressive Education*, *18*, 349-358.
Cast, G. C. (1919). Selecting text-books. *Elementary School Journal*, *19*, 468-472.
Castendyck, E., & Robison, S. (1943). Juvenile delinquency among girls. *Social Service Review*, *17*, 253-264.
Caswell, H. L. (1943). How shall a wartime program for schools be developed? *Teachers College Record*, *44*, 275-284.

Caswell, H. L. (1944). Progressive education principles used in the war effort. *Teachers College Record*, 45, 386–397.

CCC's contribution to the war effort and to American education. (1942). *School and Society*, 55, 688.

Central Committee on Civilian Defense and the Schools. (1942). The schools and civilian defense in the war period. *Bulletin of the National Association of Secondary-School Principals*, 26 (103), 9–22.

Chadsey, C. E. (1918). The loyal teacher. *School Life*, 1 (7), 10.

Chakotin, S. (1939). *The rape of the masses: The psychology of totalitarian political propaganda*. London: Routledge.

Chalmers, G. K. (1943). *A new view of the world: A discussion of liberal education after the war*. Denver, CO: University of Denver.

Chamberlain, A. H. (1917). Agricultural preparedness and food conservation: A study in thrift. *Journal of the National Education Association*, 2, 150–160.

Chamberlain, J. (1939). Our jobless youth: A warning. *Survey Graphic*, 28, 579–582.

Chambers, J. W., & Culbert, D. (Eds.). (1996). *World War II, film, and history*. Oxford, UK: Oxford University Press.

Chambers, M. M. (1947). What was good in armed-services training? *School Review*, 55, 285–290.

Chase, L. (1943). *Wartime social studies in the elementary school: Vol. 3. Curriculum Series*. Washington, DC: National Education Association.

Children like real jobs. (1943). *Progressive Education*, 20, 278–279.

Childs, H. L. (Ed.). (1936). *Propaganda and dictatorship: A collection of papers*. Princeton, NJ: Princeton University Press.

Childs, J. F. (1943). *Navy gun crew*. New York: Crowell.

Childs, J. L. (1940). Progressive education and the war. *Frontiers of Democracy*, 7, 69–70.

Childs, J. L. (1942a). Progressive education and the war and the peace. *Progressive Education*, 19, 142–145.

Childs, J. L. (1942b). Teachers and boards of education in a war period. *Frontiers of Democracy*, 8, 166.

Childs, J. L., & Counts, G. S. (1943). *America, Russia, and the Communist Party in the postwar world*. New York: Day.

Churchill, T. W. (1917). Making the high school democratic. *Journal of the National Education Association*, 1, 520–523.

Chute, C. L. (1942). Is juvenile delinquency increasing? *Probation*, 21, 59–60.

Chute, C. L. (1943). Juvenile delinquency in wartime. *Probation*, 21, 129–134; 149–153.

Clapper, R. (1943, January 15). The new advertising. *Printer's Ink*, 16.

Clark, B. H. (1918). Amateur play-producing in war time. *English Journal*, 7, 637–643.

Clark, W. W. (1943). Basic skills in wartime. *Education*, 63, 555–558.

Clayton, F. L. (1945). Let's be allies. *Progressive Education*, 22 (5), 8–10.

Cleveland, F. A. (1918). The war—Its practical lessons to democracy. *History Teacher's Magazine*, 9, 239–244.

Clifton, R. S. (1942a). For liberty: A liberal education—Part I. *Journal of Education*, 125, 113–114.

Clifton, R. S. (1942b). For liberty: A liberal education—Part II. *Journal of Education, 125*, 145–147.
Cocking, W. D. (1943). Education forges a weapon for peace. *School Executive, 63* (3), 28–29, 45.
Cohen, I. D. (1918). Teaching patriotism in the schools. *Education, 39*, 65–72.
Cohen, R. N. (1942). *Flying high: An anthology of aviation literature.* New York: Macmillan.
Cole, C. E. (1939). The war contents of American history textbooks. *Social Studies, 30*, 195–197.
Cole, L. (1946). *The elementary school subjects.* New York: Rinehart & Co.
Coleman, G. W. (1917). National danger. *Journal of Education, 85*, 231–232.
Coleman, N. F. (1917). Social hygiene in relation to national defense. *Journal of the National Education Association, 2*, 86–89.
Collier, J. (1942). The Indian in a wartime nation. *Annals of the American Academy of Political and Social Sciences, 223*, 29–35.
Collier, R. (1989). *Fighting words: The war correspondents of World War Two.* New York: St. Martin's.
Combs, J. E., & Combs, S. T. (1994). *Film propaganda and American politics: An analysis and filmography.* New York: Garland.
Commager, H. S. (1945, March 5). History of federal aid to education. *Senior Scholastic,* 7.
Commission for After-War Educational Reconstruction. (1941). After-War educational reconstruction: A proposal to men of goodwill. *Journal of the National Education Association, 30*, 265–266.
Commission on Children in Wartime. (1942). A children's charter in wartime. *Survey Midmonthly, 78*, 108–110.
Committee on a Democratic Method of Education. (1941). Report of the Committee on a Democratic Method of Education. *Progressive Education, 18*, 323–324.
Committee on Certification of Superintendents of Schools. (1940). *The superintendent of schools and his work.* Washington, DC: National Education Association.
Committee on Educational Reconstruction after the War. (1941). Resolutions. *Progressive Education, 18*, 318–321.
Committee on Military Training Aids and Instructional Materials. (1945). *Use of training aids in the Armed Services: Some implications for civilian education of the use of aids and devices in the training programs of the Armed Services* (Bulletin No. 9). Washington, DC: United States Office of Education.
Committee on Public Information. (1918). *Government war advertising: Report of the Division of Advertising.* Washington, DC: Author.
Committee on Public Information. (1972). *The Creel Report: Complete report of the chairman of the Committee on Public Information 1917; 1918; 1919.* New York: Da Capo. (Original work published in 1927.)
Compton, A. H. (1942). War problems of the physics teacher. *Scientific Monthly, 54*, 370–374.
Compulsory military service. (1915). *American Review of Reviews, 52*, 608–609.

Comstock, A. L. (1942). Women in this war. *Yale Review, 31,* 671–682.
Conant, J. B. (1945). Introduction. In Harvard Committee, *General education in a free society.* Cambridge, MA: Harvard University Press.
Conklin, E. G. (1939). Education for democracy. *Journal of the National Education Association, 28,* 165–167.
Consultative Committee on Secondary Education. (1942). Secondary schools and the war effort. *Bulletin of the National Association of Secondary-School Principals, 26* (104), 13–22.
Cook, D. (1944). *Fighting Americans of today.* New York: Dutton.
Cook, D. E., & Rahbek-Smith, E. (Eds.). (1945). *Educational film guide* (5th ed.). New York: Wilson.
Cooper, E. (1918). The rural school and patriotism. *Educational Foundations, 29,* 286–288.
Cooper, J. H. (1940). Democracy and the classroom teacher. *Journal of the National Education Association, 29,* 78.
Cooperation of the schools and industries in conserving the educational interests of children and youth. (1918). *School Life, 1* (7), 1–2.
Corey, S. M. (1942). Children's questions and the war. *School Review, 50,* 257–263.
Cornebise, A. E. (1984). *War as advertised: The four minute men and America's crusade 1917–1918.* Philadelphia: American Philosophical Society.
Cornell, F. G. (1946). Public-school attendance changes, 1940–44. *School Life, 28* (5), 20–22.
Correspondence study in high-school wartime programs. (1943, July 15). *Education for Victory, 2* (2), 9–11, 22.
Corsi, E. (1942). Italian immigrants and their children. *Annals of the American Academy of Political and Social Sciences, 223,* 100–106.
Cottrell, D. P. (1942). Teacher education in a democracy at war. *Teachers College Record, 44,* 53–55.
Cottrell, D. P. (1943). The educator studies his task in the war situation. *Teachers College Record, 44,* 230–236.
Council of National Defense. (1917). *School and Society, 6,* 296–297.
Counts, G. S. (1938). *The prospects of American democracy.* New York: Day.
Counts, G. S. (1939). Our articles of faith. In C. O. Williams & F. W. Hubbard (Eds.), *Schools for democracy* (pp. 13–25). Chicago: National Congress of Parents and Teachers.
Counts, G. S. (1951). The need for a great education. *Teachers College Record, 53,* 77–88.
Cowles, G. (1943, March). What government wants advertising to do. *Advertising & Selling,* 17–18, 92, 94.
Cowles, V. (1941). *Looking for trouble.* New York: Harper & Brothers.
Craigo, R. T. (1943). The general shop after the war. *Industrial Arts and Vocational Education, 32,* 420–421.
Crasford, W. R. (1942). The Latin American in wartime United States. *Annals of the American Academy of Political and Social Sciences, 223,* 123–131.

Cressy, M. F. (1943). A character alphabet. *Journal of the National Education Association, 32*, 224.
Cromwell, J. H. R. (1941). *Pax Americana: American democracy and world peace.* Chicago: Kroch.
Cronbach, L. J. (1942). Helping pupils adjust to war. *Social Education, 6,* 301–303.
Crowell B., & Wilson, R. F. (1921). *The Giant Hand: Our Mobilization and Control of Industry and Natural Resources 1917–1918.* New Haven: Yale University Press.
Crowther, S. (1916). The nourishment of the pacifists. *Forum, 58,* 8–21.
Crump, I. (1944). *Our marines.* New York: Dodd, Mead.
Culbert, D. H. (Ed.). (1986). *Information control and propaganda: Records of the Office of War Information* (Part II: Office of Policy Coordination. Series A: Propaganda and policy directives for overseas programs, 1942–1945). Frederick, MD: University Publications of America.
Cunningham, E. C. (1959). The wasteland of Professor Bestor. *Journal of Teacher Education, 10,* 158–172.
Curriculum changes evolve from our war experiences. (1944). *Bulletin of the National Association of Secondary-School Principals, 28* (125), 12–23.
Curry, H. B. (1942). Mathematical teaching and national defense. *School Review, 50,* 337–346.
Cushman, C. L. (1942). Shall I continue to teach? *Educational Method, 22,* 9–11.
Daggett, M. P. (1918). *Women wanted: The story written in blood red letters on the horizon of the great World War.* New York: Doran.
Dally, B. W. (1942). Mother Goose helps defense: A patriotic play your children will like. *Grade Teacher, 59* (10), 26, 71.
Dalton, F. W., & Jay, J. (1943). The vocational outlook in wartime and after. *Industrial Arts and Vocational Education, 32,* 148–151.
Danger: The illogical pronouncement of the National Education Association on the question of military training in the public schools. (1915). *Educational Foundations, 27,* 71–75.
Davidson, C. (1944). An integrated curriculum is more functional than the traditional subject-matter curriculum. *Progressive Education, 22* (2), 16, 22–23.
Davidson, P. (1941). *Propaganda and the American Revolution 1763–1783.* Chapel Hill: University of North Carolina Press.
Day, E. E. (1941). *The defense of freedom: Four addresses on the present crisis in American democracy.* Ithaca, NY: Cornell University Press.
De Boer, J. J. (1942). Spring to your places, pioneers! *Educational Method, 22,* 6–8.
De Boer, J. J. (1947). Forward progressives! *Progressive Education, 25,* 225, 251.
De Pauw, L. G. (1998). *Battle cries and lullabies: Women in war from prehistory to the present.* Norman: University of Oklahoma Press.
Dean, A. D. (1918a). Our schools in war time—and after. *Teachers College Record, 19,* 1–14.
Dean, A. D. (1918b). *Our schools in wartime and after.* Boston: Ginn.
DeBauche, L. M. (1997). *Reel patriotism: The movies and World War I.* Madison: University of Wisconsin Press.

Democracy and education in the current crisis: The meaning of democracy. (1940). War speaks out. *Frontiers of Democracy, 7,* 9-10.

Dennis, L. (1935). Education—The tool of the dominant elite. *Social Frontier, 1 (4),* 11-15.

Devane, W. C. (1943). American education after the war. *Yale Review, 33,* 34-46.

Devoe, A. M. (1918). Making an American. *Journal of Education, 87,* 3.

Dewey, J. (1918). Vocational education in the light of the World War. *Journal of Education, 88,* 647-648.

Dewey, J. (1927). Introduction. In R. P. Barnes, *Militarizing our youth: The significance of the Reserve Officers' Training Corp in our schools and colleges* (Pamphlet, pp. 3-4). New York: Committee on Militarism in Education.

Dewey, J. (1940). *Education today.* New York: Greenwood.

Dick, B. F. (1985). *The star-spangled screen: The American World War II film.* Lexington: University Press of Kentucky.

Dickie, P. A. (1918). The status of German. *Journal of Education, 88,* 454.

Distribution of war films. (1943). *School and Society, 57,* 123.

Dobbs, A. A. (1939). *Teaching wholesome living in the elementary school.* New York: Barnes.

Dodd, A. E. (1942). How are we organizing our industrial machine to outproduce the enemy? In *America Organizes to Win the War: A Handbook on the American War Effort* (pp. 161-181). New York: Harcourt, Brace.

Dodds, H. W. (1944). *Out of this nettle, danger . . .* Princeton, NJ: Princeton University Press.

Dodson, S. H. (Ed.). (1918). *Democracy and the war in the addresses of President Wilson and others.* Chicago: Hall & McCreary.

Does this smell of Sovietism? (1940, February 1). *Forbes,* 10.

Doneson, J. E. (1987). *The Holocaust in American film.* Philadelphia: Jewish Publication Society.

Doshay, L. J. (1944). The challenge and solution of juvenile delinquency. *Journal of Clinical Psychopathology & Psychotherapy, 6,* 335-354.

Douglas, H. R. (1942). Two dangerous effects of the War upon the schools. *American School Board Journal, 104 (3),* 32, 76.

Douglass, H. R. (1944). The problems of the post-war period. *Social Studies, 35,* 62-64.

Douglass, H. R. (1949). How can we develop an effective program of education for life adjustment? *National Association of Secondary School Principals, 33,* 157-159.

Dow, A. W. (1917). Art teaching in the nation's service. *Journal of Education, 86,* 151.

Dow, A. W. (1918). Practical fine arts—Emergency art courses for war-time service. *Journal of the National Education Association, 2,* 451-455.

Draft and the schools. (1918). *School Life, 1 (3),* 1-2.

Drummond, R., & Drummond, G. (1969). How reliable is our news? *American Legion Magazine, 86 (6),* 6-11, 51.

Dryer, S. H. (1942). *Radio in wartime.* New York: Greenberg.

Dunigan, L. M. (1918). A lesson plan in patriotism. *Primary Education, 26,* 213-214.

Dunn, L. F. (1942). The powder-mill town. *Journal of Educational Sociology, 15,* 445-446.

DuShane, D. (1940). The schools and the war. *Journal of the National Education Association, 29*, 235–236.
DuShane, D. (1941). The defense of democracy thru education: A challenge to the teaching profession. *Journal of the National Education Association, 30*, 162–163.
Dutcher, G. M. (1917). Summer reading on the war. *History Teacher's Magazine, 8*, 197–198.
Dutcher, G. M. (1918). A selected critical bibliography of publications in English relating to the World War. *History Teacher's Magazine, 9*, 155–183.
Dyer, E. (1943). Let's look at wartime guidance. *Journal of Education, 126*, 83–84, 86.
Dykstra, C. A. (1942). Education and world conflict. *Yale Review, 32*, 128–144.
Earle, E. M. (1941). The threat to American security. *Yale Review, 30*, 454–480.
Earley, C. A. (1989). *One woman's army: A black officer remembers the WAC*. College Station: Texas A & M University Press.
Eastman, M. (1917). What shall we do with patriotism? *Mind and Body, 24*, 9–13.
Eckhardt, C. C. (1917). War and peace in the light of history. *History Teacher's Magazine, 8*, 43–46.
Eckstein, C. G. (1942). War problems in first grade: Methods of overcoming fears. *Instructor, 52* (1), 14.
Edison, C. (1945). The effect of education on democracy. *Journal of the National Education Association, 34*, 17.
Edman, I., & Schneider, R. (1941). *Fountainheads of freedom: The growth of the democratic idea*. New York: Reynal & Hitchcock.
Education after the war. (1917). *Journal of Education, 86*, 294.
Education and citizenship in war time. (1918). *Educational Foundations, 29*, 348–351, 423–426, 485.
Education and the war. (1942). *Journal of the National Education Association, 31*, 191–192.
Education and total war: A statement by the board of editors. (1942). *Frontiers of Democracy, 8*, 228–229.
Education and war conditions. (1917). *School and Society, 6*, 104.
Education for American citizenship. (1944, October 20). *Education for Victory, 3* (8), 13–16, 18.
Education for free men. (1942). *Journal of the National Education Association, 31*, 185.
Education for peace. (1915). *Educational Foundations, 27*, 135–139.
Education for victory. (1943). *Journal of the National Education Association, 32*, 176.
Educational news and editorial comment. (1918). *Elementary School Journal, 18*, 641–642.
Educational Policies Commission. (1937a). *The structure and administration of public education in the United States*. Washington, DC: National Education Association.
Educational Policies Commission. (1937b). *The unique function of education in American democracy*. Washington, DC: National Education Association.
Educational Policies Commission. (1938a). *The purposes of education in American democracy*. Washington, DC: National Education Association.
Educational Policies Commission. (1938b). *The structure and administration of education in American democracy*. Washington, DC: National Education Association.

Educational Policies Commission. (1939a). *American education and the war in Europe.* Washington, DC: National Education Association.

Educational Policies Commission. (1939b). *Federal activities in education.* Washington DC: National Education Association.

Educational Policies Commission. (1940a). *Education and economic well-being in American democracy.* Washington, DC: National Education Association.

Educational Policies Commission. (1940b). *Learning the ways of democracy.* Washington, DC: National Education Association.

Educational Policies Commission. (1941a). Education and civilian morale. *Journal of the National Education Association, 30,* 274.

Educational Policies Commission. (1941b). Strategy of the dictators. *Journal of the National Education Association, 30,* 173–174.

Educational Policies Commission. (1941c). *Suggestions for teaching American history in the present emergency.* Washington, DC: National Education Association.

Educational Policies Commission. (1941d). *The Civilian Conservation Corps, the National Youth Administration, and the public schools.* Washington, DC: National Education Association.

Educational Policies Commission. (1942a). *A war policy for American schools.* Washington, DC: National Education Association.

Educational Policies Commission. (1942b). Education can help to win the war. *Journal of the National Education Association, 31,* 11–12.

Educational Policies Commission. (1943a). A wartime education program. *Journal of the National Education Association, 32,* 13–16.

Educational Policies Commission. (1943b). Education and the people's peace. *Journal of the National Education Association, 32,* 165–168.

Educational Policies Commission. (1943c). *What the schools should teach in wartime.* Washington, DC: National Education Association.

Educational Policies Commission. (1944). *Education for ALL American youth.* Washington, DC: National Education Association.

Educational Policies Commission. (1946). *Policies for education in American democracy.* Washington, DC: National Education Association.

Educational Policies Commission. (1948). *Education for ALL American children.* Washington, DC: National Education Association.

Educational Policies Commission. (1951). *Moral and spiritual values in the public schools.* Washington, DC: National Education Association.

Educational Policies Commission. (1952). *Education for ALL American youth* (Rev. ed.). Washington, DC: National Education Association.

Educational program for the war. (1917). *American School Board Journal, 55* (2), 33.

Educational programs in a world at war. (1943). Children and the war. *Teachers College Record, 44,* 227–229.

Education's part in the war effort. (1946). *The Journal of the National Education Association, 35,* 250.

Educators look beyond the war. (1944). *School Review, 52,* 65–72.

Edwards, J. C. (1991). *Berlin calling: American broadcasters in service to the Third Reich.* New York: Praeger.
18-Year-old. (1942, November 30). *Life*, 103–111.
Eisenhart, L. P. (1949). *The educational process.* Princeton, NJ: Princeton University Press.
Elias, H. (1942). The education of the post-war generation. *School Review, 50*, 504–511.
Elshtain, J. B., & Tobias, S. (Eds.) (1990). *Women, militarism, and war: Essays in history, politics, and social theory.* Savage, MD: Rowman & Littlefield.
Elting, M., & Weaver, R. T. (1943). *Soldiers, sailors, fliers and marines.* Garden City, NY: Doubleday-Doran.
Emergency in education. (1918). *School and Society, 8*, 416–417.
Emergency war courses for schools. (1918). *School Life, 1* (2), 19.
Engelhardt, N. L. (1942). Air age and education. *Education, 63*, 67–79.
English instruction and the war. (1942). *English Journal, 31*, 87–91.
Enrollment of women encouraged by ESMDT. (1942, March 16). *Education for Victory, 1* (2), 8–9.
Essential mathematics for minimum army needs: Excerpt from Committee's report. (1944, January 20). *Education for Victory, 2* (14), 26–28.
Essert, P. L. (1942). Education in a democracy [Review of the book *Education in a democracy*]. *Progressive Education, 19* (3), 180–181.
Ettinger, W. L. (1918). The effect of the war on our elementary schools. *Educational Foundations, 29*, 267–270.
Eurich, A. C. (1942). Wartime consumer education. *Progressive Education, 19*, 384–387.
Evacuation plans. (1942, August 15). *Education for Victory, 1* (12), 3–4.
Everal, A. S. (1917). The girl delinquent. *Journal of the National Education Association, 1*, 841–845.
Everett, R. H. (1943). Some highlights of juvenile delinquency. *Journal of Social Hygiene, 29*, 521–525.
Evjen, V. H. (1942). Delinquency and crime in wartime. *Journal of Criminal Law & Criminology, 33*, 136–146.
Extended school services for children of working mothers: Education's part in child care programs. (1942, November 16). *Education for Victory, 1* (18), 13–15.
Fahey, S. H. (1917a). How the public school can foster the American ideal of patriotism. *Journal of the National Education Association, 2*, 46–55.
Fahey, S. H. (1917b). Moral education: What the school can do. *Journal of the National Education Association, 1*, 634–640.
Fariello, G. (1995). *Red scare: Memories of the American inquisition—An oral history.* New York: Norton.
Farley, B. (1940). By the people, for the people. *Journal of the National Education Association, 29*, 5.
Farmer, P. (1942). English teaching during a wartime emergency. *English Journal, 31*, 230–231.
Faulkner, A. (1943). How tough is American censorship? *Harper's Magazine, 186*, 502–509.

Faunce, W. H. (1918). Education wins wars. *Educational Foundations*, 30, 74-75.
Federal Education War Council. (1943). *Understanding the war.* Washington, DC: U.S. Office of War Information.
Federal Security Agency. (1942). *School and college civilian morale service: How to participate.* Washington, DC: U.S. Office of Education.
Federal Security Agency. (1943). *School services for children of working mothers—Why? What? How? Where? When? Leaflet 1: School Children and the War Series.* Washington, DC: Author.
Federal Security Agency. (1944). *On problems of post-war higher education: Conference workbook.* Washington, DC: U.S. Office of Education.
Fehr, H. F. (1943). Mathematics in pre-induction training. *Teachers College Record*, 45, 161-168.
Fellowship of Reconciliation. (1944). *War, transition and peace.* New York: Author.
Fenn, I. M. (1943). Wartime woodworking industry and vocational training. *Industrial Arts and Vocational Education*, 32, 373-374.
Ferris, F., & Parker, C. (1944). Streamlined radio for wartime needs. *School Shop*, 3 (10), 16-17.
Field, E. (1942). *This freedom: A patriotic pageant drama.* Boston, MA: Baker's Plays.
Field, J. E. (1916). Military training for students. *Colorado School Journal*, 31 (7), 5-6.
Field, S. L. (1994). Scrap drives, stamp sales, and school spirit: Examples of elementary social studies during World War II. *Theory and Research in Social Education*, 22, 441-460.
Finds textbooks tend to "create discontent." (1941, March 5). *Christian Century*, 309-310.
Finegan, T. E. (1918). Training for national service. *School and Society*, 8, 301-305.
Fisher, M. S. (1942). Delinquent behavior in war time. *Frontiers of Democracy* (9) 72, 39-41.
Fisher, M. S. (1943a). Discipline as a skill. *Educational Leadership*, 1, 140-143.
Fisher, M. S. (1943b). If we will—We have the future. *Progressive Education*, 20, 98-102.
Fitzpatrick, E. A. (1942). Educational counseling in wartime. *American School Board Journal*, 105 (3), 19-20.
Fitzpatrick, E. A. (1943). Educational and vocational guidance in wartime. *American School Board Journal*, 106 (4), 15-17.
Fitzpatrick, E. A. (1944). A broad basis of postwar problems. *American School Board Journal*, 109 (3), 19-21.
Fleming, T. (2001). *The New Dealers' war: Franklin D. Roosevelt and the war within World War II.* New York: Basic Books.
Flick, O. S. (1943). A war-time philosophy for schools. *Journal of Education*, 126, 221-222, 224.
Flint, M. (1943). *Dress right, dress: The autobiography of a WAC.* New York: Dodd, Mead.
Forbes, A. W. (1942). Education fails in the crisis. *Journal of Educational Sociology*, 15, 348-351.
Force, A. L. (1917). The public school: The laboratory for citizenship. *Journal of the National Education Association*, 2, 71-74.

Foster, W. T. (1918). Conservation of national ideals in war time. *Journal of the National Education Association, 2,* 375–376.
Fowler, B. P. (1944). A liberal program for secondary schools. *Yale Review, 34,* 306–322.
Fowler, H. E. (1917). American literature for American schools. *English Journal, 6,* 637–644.
Fowler, J. H. (1942). The English teacher in the present emergency. *English Journal, 31,* 730–731.
Fowlkes, J. G. (1942). Planning schools for tomorrow. *Journal of Educational Sociology, 16,* 15–27.
Fox, F. W. (1975). *Madison Avenue goes to war: The strange military career of American advertising, 1941–45.* Provo, UT: Brigham Young University Press.
Foy, P. (2000, December 22). Utah may disband its militia. *Salt Lake Tribune,* C-2, C-8.
Frank, G. (1936). Education and the social welfare. *Journal of the National Education Association, 25,* 103–104.
Frank, L. K. (1940). Children in a world of violence. *Progressive Education, 17,* 393–399.
Frank, R. (1937). The schools and the people's front. *Communist, 26,* 432–445.
Franklin, J. (1942). *Remaking America.* Boston: Houghton Mifflin.
Fraser, H. (1918). *Women and war work.* New York: Shaw.
Fraser, L. (1945). *Germany between two wars: A study of propaganda and war-guilt.* London: Oxford University Press.
Fraser, L. (1957). *Propaganda.* London: Oxford University Press.
Frazier, B. W. (1943). The teacher shortage. *Survey Graphic, 32,* 351–353, 360.
Fredericksen, H. A. (1943). The program for day care of children of employed mothers. *Social Service Review, 17,* 159–169.
Freeman, H. A. (1945). Peacetime conscription. *Journal of the National Education Association, 34,*152.
French, W. M. (1955). *Education for all: An introduction to American education.* New York: Odyssey.
Freud, A., & Burlingham, D. T. (1943). *War and children.* New York: Medical War Books.
Frey, H. (1942). *Victory song book for soldiers, sailors and marines.* New York: Robbins.
Friedrich, C. J. (1934, October). What is academic freedom? *Atlantic Monthly, 154,* 421–426.
Frost, N. (1943). A check list for WAR effort. *American School Board Journal, 106* (2), 47–48, 50.
Function of English in wartime: A symposium. (1942). *English Journal, 31,* 91–109, 227–228.
Galloway, G. B. (1942). *Postwar planning in the United States.* New York: Twentieth Century Fund.
Gambrill, B. L. (1943). Teachers and the war. *Progressive Education, 20,* 208–214.
Gans, R. (1941). Reading: A tool designed to protect democratic living. *Progressive Education, 18,* 419–422.
Gardening a patriotic duty. (1918). *Elementary School Journal, 18,* 643.
Gardner, G. E. (1944). Sex behavior of adolescents in wartime. *Annals of the American Academy of Political and Social Science, 236,* 60–66.

Garlock, M. A. (1916). Military training and the public schools. *Northwest Journal of Education, 27*, 296–299.

Geer, E. W. (1941). A school program for democracy. *Progressive Education, 18*, 104–105.

Geiges, E. (1943). Physical fitness for wartime demands. *Journal of Health and Physical Education, 14*, 11, 53.

Geisinger, J. J. (1918). Damn the torpedoes—Advertise. *Printer's Ink, 102* (9), 54, 57–58.

Gellerman, W. (1938). *The American Legion as educator.* New York: Teachers College Press.

Gellerman, W. (1940). Democracy's Challenge to Education [Review of the book *Democracy's Challenge to Education*]. *Frontiers of Democracy, 6*, 250–251.

Germain, W. M. (1945). Aftermath of World War I. *Police Journal 30* (5), 7–8.

German in schools. (1918). *Journal of Education, 87*, 155.

Gilbert, D. W. (1941a). Un-Americanism in textbooks. *National Republic, 29* (6), 17–18, 29.

Gilbert, D. W. (1941b). Un-Americanism in textbooks. *National Republic, 29* (7), 5–6, 32.

Gilbert, D. W. (1941c). Un-Americanism in textbooks. *National Republic, 29* (8), 3–4, 30–31.

Gilbert, D. W. (1942a). Un-Americanism in textbooks. *National Republic, 29* (9), 7–8, 31.

Gilbert, D. W. (1942b). Un-Americanism in textbooks. *National Republic, 29* (10), 7–8, 32.

Gilbert, D. W. (1942c). Un-Americanism in textbooks. *National Republic, 29* (11), 7–8, 31.

Gilliam, P. B. (1943). Youngsters in trouble. *Educational Leadership, 1*, 98–101.

Ginn Publishing Company Advertisement. (1945, January). *Journal of the National Education Association, 34*, A-9.

Giordano, G. (2000). *Twentieth-century reading education: Understanding practices of today in terms of patterns of the past.* New York: Elsevier.

Giordano, G. (2003). *Twentieth-century textbook wars: A history of advocacy and opposition.* New York: Lang.

Givens, W. E. (1942). Stand where you are and fight. *Journal of the National Education Association, 31*, 155.

Glicksberg, C. I. (1942a). A suggested program of guidance in wartime. *School Review, 50*, 696–702.

Glicksberg, C. I. (1942b). The role of the English teacher in wartime. *English Journal, 31*, 726–729.

Glicksberg, C. I. (1944). Some considerations in postwar educational reconstruction. *School Review, 52*, 299–306.

Glueck, E. T. (1942a). Wartime delinquency. *Journal of Criminal Law & Criminology, 33*, 119–135.

Glueck, E. T. (1942b). Coping with wartime delinquency. *Journal of Educational Sociology, 16*, 86–98.

Goebel, J. E. (1942). Investing for Uncle Sam: A playlet to teach patriotism. *Grade Teacher, 59* (6), 44, 64–65.

Goggio, E. (1918). Why not Italian in the high schools? *Journal of Education, 88,* 47.

Goldenweiser, A. (1940). What can the schools do about war? *Frontiers of Democracy, 6,* 145–147.

Goldman, E. F. (1960). *The crucial decade—And after: America, 1945–1960.* New York: Vintage.

Goldsmith, B., & Morgenstern, S. (1942). *Win-the-war-ballads: Twelve timely songs for children and everybody else.* Radio City, NY: Marks.

Gollomb, J., & Taylor, A. (1943). *Young heroes of the war.* New York: Vanguard.

Gomery, D. G. (1915). *Belgium in war time* (B. Miall, Trans.). New York: Doran.

Good, H. G. (1956). *A history of American education.* New York: Macmillan.

Goodman, N. G. (1935). The crisis in education. *School and Society, 41,* 60–61.

Goodrum, C., & Dalrymple, H. (1990). *Advertising in America: The first 200 years.* New York: Abrams.

Government policies involving the schools in war time. (1918a). *School and Society, 7,* 474–478.

Government policies involving the schools in war time. (1918b). *School Life, 1* (1), 3–4.

Grace, A. G. (1942). Total war and the organization of education. *Education, 63,* 156–161.

Granger, L. B. (1942). Negroes and war production. *Survey Graphic, 31,* 469–471, 543–544.

Great campaign for school attendance. (1917). *Educational Foundations, 29,* 78–80.

Green, A. B. (1989). *One woman's war: Letters home from the Women's Army Corps 1944–1946.* St. Paul: Minnesota Historical Society Press.

Green, L. M. (1915). Military training in the public school. *American Review of Reviews, 52,* 577–583.

Green, R. A. (1943). Wartime acceleration in education. *American School Board Journal, 106* (4), 41.

Greenawalt, L. (1918). Americanism and the public schools. *Educational Foundations, 30,* 69–74.

Gregg. R. T. (1943). The principal and his school in wartime. *Bulletin of the National Association of Secondary-School Principals, 27* (112), 7–18.

Gregory, C. W. (1974). *Women in defense work during World War II: An analysis of the labor problem and women's rights.* New York: Exposition.

Grey, L. (1942). Language, literature, and the war. *English Journal, 31,* 385–391.

Griffing, J. B. (1935). The educational process in the CCC. *Sociology and Social Research, 19,* 376–380.

Griffith, J. L. (1941a). The value of school and college athletics in the present crisis: Athletics in a long drawn-out war. *Athletic Journal, 22* (3), 10–11.

Griffith, J. L. (1941b). The value of school and college athletics in the present crisis: More time needed. *Athletic Journal, 22* (1), 10.

Griffith, J. L. (1941c). The value of school and college athletics in the present crisis. The aftermath. *Athletic Journal, 22* (2), 18–19.

Griffith, J. L. (1941d). The value of school and college athletics in the present crisis: The responsibility of educational administrators. *Athletic Journal, 22* (4), 20.

Griffith, J. L. (1942). War. *Athletic Journal, 22* (5), 18–19.

Grigsby, R. I. (1943). Origin and purpose of the High School Victory Corps. *Education, 64,* 73–75.

Grossman, M. P. (1918). Some of the regrettable effects of the war on children of school age. *Educational Foundations, 29,* 479–482.

Groves, E. R., & Groves, G. H. (1944). The social background of wartime adolescents. *Annals of the American Academy of Political and Social Science, 236,* 26–32.

Groves, L. R. (1945). Preface. In H. D. Smyth, *Atomic energy for military purposes: The official report on the development of the Atomic Bomb under the auspices of the United States government, 1940–1945* (p. v). Princeton, NJ: Princeton University Press.

Grubb, M. B. (1918). War-time posters made by primary pupils. *Primary Education, 26,* 348.

Gruber, C. S. (1975). *Mars and Minerva: World War I and the uses of higher learning in America.* Baton Rouge: Louisiana State University Press.

Gulick, L. H. (1917). Girls enlist. *Journal of Education, 85,* 485–486.

Gwynn, J. M. (1943). *Curriculum principles & social trends.* New York: Macmillan.

Hackett, F. (1941). *What Mein Kampf means to America.* New York: Reynal & Hitchcock.

Hall, G. S. (1916). The war and education. *Journal of the National Education Association, 1,* 85–91.

Hall, G. S. (1918). Some educational values of war. *Journal of Education, 88,* 115–117.

Halsey, E. (1942). The role of college women in war. *Journal of Health and Physical Education, 13,* 283–284, 314.

Hamilton, W. I. (1918). School boys on farms: A wartime experiment. *American School Board Journal, 56* (1), 21–23, 76–78.

Hamlin, C. H. (1973). *Propaganda and myth in time of war: Comprising the war myth in United States History and educators present arms—The use of schools and colleges as agents of war propaganda 1914–1918.* New York: Vanguard. (Original work published in 1927)

Hand, C. H. (1943a). Emerging patterns of communication. In E. O. Melby (Ed.), *Mobilizing educational resources for winning the war and the peace* (pp. 133–145). New York: Harper & Brothers.

Hand, C. H. (1943b). The disorganized teaching profession. In E. O. Melby (Ed.), *Mobilizing educational resources for winning the war and the peace* (pp. 66–81). New York: Harper & Brothers.

Handbook on education and the war. (1943). Washington, DC: National Institute on Education and the War.

Handschin, C. H. (1917). The study of German during the war. *School and Society, 6,* 253–256.

Hanna, P. R. (1942). The classroom—A defense unit. *Journal of Educational Sociology, 15,* 369–376.

Hanna, P. R. (1943). The attack on the three R's. *Educational Leadership, 1,* 173–174.

Hanson, E. H. (1944). Which war-time changes shall we keep? *Nation's Schools, 34* (1), 48–49.

Harding, L. W. (1943). Wartime elementary education. *Journal of the National Education Association, 32*, 47–48.

Harding, S. B. (1918a). Some geographical aspects of the war. *History Teacher's Magazine, 9*, 217.

Harding, S. B. (1918b). Topical outline of the war. *History Teacher's Magazine, 9*, 30–62.

Harris, F. E. (1945). Why juvenile delinquency?—Let's be objective. *Social Studies, 36*, 204–205.

Harris, G. W. (1918). War on the German language. *Journal of Education, 87*, 457–458.

Harris, H. M. (1918). Patriotism and group consciousness. *Education, 39*, 202–208.

Hart, A. B. (1918). The lesson of the obligation of citizenship. *Education, 38*, 740–754.

Hart, F. W. (1942). The education of civilians for national service. *School and Society, 55*, 433–437.

Harting, J. W. (1919). The girl who took a soldier's job. *American Legion Weekly, 1* (14), 18–19, 28.

Hartmann, G. (1940). Has the progressive education movement become militarist?—A letter of protest. *Frontiers of Democracy, 7*, 43–44.

Hartmann, S. M. (1982). *The home front and beyond: American women in the 1940s*. Boston: Twayne.

Harvey, M. T. (1918). Rural schools in the war. *Journal of Education, 88*, 375–376.

Hastie, W. H. (1942). The Negro in the army today. *Annals of the American Academy of Political and Social Sciences, 223*, 55–59.

Hatfield, W. W., & De Boer, J. J. (1942). Teaching English in wartime: An editorial. *English Journal, 31*, 67–69.

Haughton, W. M. (1918). Over the top to victory. *Educational Foundations, 29*, 455–457.

Havighurst, R. J. (1944). The educational problem. In G. B. Huszar (Ed.), *New perspectives on peace* (pp. 162–178). Chicago: University of Chicago Press.

Hawk, H. C. (1940). Democracy and school life. *American School Board Journal, 101* (3), 19.

Headlines and clippings from a newspaper. (1943). *Progressive Education, 20*, 172.

Heaton, K. L. (1943). Schools, teachers, and civilian defense. *Bulletin of the National Association of Secondary-School Principals, 27* (115), 13–19.

Heil, L. M. (1943). The science teacher and the war effort. *Progressive Education, 20*, 70–75.

Heimers, L. (1943). Teaching aids for the wartime program. *Journal of Educational Sociology, 16*, 458–459.

Hendley, C. J. (1939). Unionism in the educational field. *Social Frontier, 5*, 237–240.

Herring, P. (1941). *The impact of war: Our American democracy under arms*. New York: Farrar & Rinehart.

Hewitt, J. E. (1943). Swimming goes to war. *Journal of Health and Physical Education, 14*, 354–356, 398–400.

Hientz, E. (1947). Objectives in the social studies. *Progressive Education, 25* (1), 270–271.

High school teachers and the war. (1942). *Teachers College Record, 42*, 442–467.

High school victory corps. (1942). *Athletic Journal, 23* (2), 5–7.

Higham, A. S. (1942). Women in defense of Britain. *Journal of Educational Sociology*, 15, 293–300.

High-school science and the war. (1942). *School Review*, 50, 613–614.

High-school students and the manpower shortage. (1943, November 1). *Education for Victory*, 2 (9), 20.

Higonnet, M. R., Jenson, J., Michel, S., & Weitz, M. C. (Eds.). (1987). *Behind the lines: Gender and the two world wars*. New Haven, CT: Yale University Press.

Hill, H. C. (1918). Decent literature on civics and other social studies. (1918). *School Review*, 26, 705–708.

Historical light on the league to enforce peace. (1917). *History Teacher's Magazine*, 8, 150.

History Teacher's Magazine [untitled editorial]. (1918a). *History Teacher's Magazine*, 9, 69.

History Teacher's Magazine [untitled editorial]. (1918b). *History Teacher's Magazine*, 9, 203.

Hitchcock, N. D. (1918). The mobilization of women. *Annals of the American Academy of Political and Social Science*, 78, 24–31.

Hobby, O. C. (1943). When girls are soldiers. *Educational Leadership*, 1, 86–89.

Hodson, W. (1943). Layman and social agencies study wartime education. *Teachers College Record*, 44, 237–241.

Hoehler, F. K. (1942). Efforts at community organization. *Journal of Educational Sociology*, 15, 447–459.

Hogan, L. (1918). Home and school war gardens: Increased food production necessary. *Educational Foundations*, 29, 558–559.

Holcombe, A. N. (1941). *Dependent areas in the post-war world*. Boston: World Peace Foundation.

Holland, K., & Hill F. E. (1942). *Youth in the CCC*. Washington, DC: American Council on Education.

Holmes, H. W. (1940). American teachers and the present crisis. *Educational Method*, 20, 7–15.

Holmes, H. W. (1943). The impact of war on secondary education. *Bulletin of the National Association of Secondary-School Principals*, 27 (113), 26–28.

Homan, C. W. (1917). From teacher to trench. *Educational Foundations*, 29, 35–36.

Home economics on a war basis. (1918). *School Life*, 1 (1), 5.

Hoover, H., & Gibson, H. (1943). *The problems of lasting peace*. Garden City, NY: Doubleday, Doran.

Hopkins, L. T. (1941). *Interaction: The democratic process*. Boston: Heath.

Hopkins, L. T. (1943). The war and the curriculum. *Education*, 63, 346–351.

Horn, P. W. (1917). The schools in war times. *Journal of Education*, 86, 270.

Hoskins, J. P. (1918). Modern language instruction after the war. *School and Society*, 8, 601–612.

How can I help win the war? (1917). *Journal of Education*, 86, 19.

How the 100 best war ads came to be written. (1946, January). *Advertising & Selling*, 85–87.

Howe, F. C. (1915). Immigration, industry, and the war. *American Review of Reviews*, 52, 598–602.
Howe, O. H. (1916). War as national discipline. *Education*, 37, 42–48.
Howell, C. E., Ryerson, S. R., & Stullken, E. H. (1942). Schools and the wartime delinquency. *Journal of the National Education Association*, 31, 151–152.
Hoyer, R. A. (1942). The soldier town. *Journal of Educational Sociology*, 15, 486–497.
Hullfish, H. G. (1943). The direct emphasis upon democracy. *Educational Method*, 22, 167–170.
Hulst, C. S. (1918). Patriotism through high-school literature. *English Journal*, 7, 342–343.
Hungerford, H. (1919). Boy leaders in democracy. *Printer's Ink*, 109 (7), 139.
Hunt, C. W. (1918). The child and the book in war times. *English Journal*, 7, 487–496.
Hunt, E. M. (1941). Dr. Robey versus the N.A.M.? *Social Education*, 5, 288–292.
Hunt, M. P., & Metcalf, L. E. (1955). *Teaching high school social studies: Problems in reflective thinking and social understanding*. New York: Harper & Brothers.
Hyams, J. (1984). *War movies*. New York: Gallery.
Illustrations with war-time flavor should be drawn from correct data. (1918). *Printer's Ink*, 102 (2), 49–52.
Impact of war on advertising: Report to advertising and sales management. Part XIX. (1943, June). *Advertising & Selling*, 19–21.
Impact of war on the schools. (1943). *Journal of Educational Sociology*, 16, 424–450.
Indiana Department of Public Instruction. (1943). *Patterns for enriching high school guidance programs* (Pamphlet No. 157). Author.
Information for women interested in war employment and training. (1942, June 15). *Education for Victory*, 1 (8), 23.
Iroquois Publishing Company Advertisement. (1946, May). *Journal of the National Education Association*, 35, A-105.
Is the CCC educational program a success? (1934). *School Executives Magazine*, 53, 340–341, 345.
Jackson, D. (1943). Teachers and teaching in wartime—Conditions teachers face: From Washington. *Progressive Education*, 20, 231–232.
Jacobson, P. B. (1944). General education in the secondary school now and after the war. *Bulletin of the National Association of Secondary-School Principals*, 28 (125), 5–11.
Jeffries, J. W. (1996). *Wartime America: The World War II home front*. Chicago: Dee.
Jersild, A. T. (1942). Children and the war. *Teachers College Record*, 44, 7–20.
Jessen, C. A. (1942). The best kind of high-school training for military service. *Journal of Health and Physical Education*, 13, 390–391, 431–432.
Jessen, C. A. (1944a, February 3). Continuing school attendance while working: Arrangements some schools have made for students. *Education for Victory*, 2 (15), 1–5.
Jessen, C. A. (1944b). Dentist put teeth into the war effort. *School Executive*, 63 (8), 47–48.
Jessen, C. A. (1945). School-work programs for high-school youth. *Education for Victory*, 3 (20), 5–12.
Johnsen, J. E. (1941). *Compulsory military training*. New York: Wilson.

Johnsen, J. E. (Ed.). (1942). *Plans for a post-war world.* New York: Wilson.
Johnsen, J. E. (Ed.). (1943). *World peace plans.* New York: Wilson.
Johnson, C. S. (1942). The Negro minority. *Annals of the American Academy of Political and Social Sciences, 223,* 10–16.
Johnson, E. C. (1947). Shall we have universal military training? *Progressive Education, 24,* 196–198.
Johnson, W. H. (1942). Industrial education in the war program. *School and Society, 55,* 597–600.
Jones, K., & Olivier, R. (1956). *Progressive education is REDucation.* Boston: Meador.
Jones, L. B. (1918). Advertising men as the "cheerleaders" of the nation. *Printer's Ink, 102* (6), 62, 65.
Jones, M. L. (1943). Over here! A schools-at-work program. *School Executive, 63* (1), 32–34.
Jones, V. (1940). A proposed educational plan for national defense. *School and Society, 52,* 473–477.
Jordan, D. S. (1918). *Democracy and world relations.* New York: World.
Josephine. S. (1942). Helping your Uncle Sam: A play about defense stamps. *Grade Teacher, 59* (9), 32, 64–65.
Joyal, A. E. (1941). Another step toward federal control of education. *Frontiers of Democracy, 7,* 142–146.
Joyal, A. E. (1942). The wartime job of administrators. *Frontiers of Democracy, 8,* 208, 212–214.
Joyal, A. E., & Carr, W. G. (1944). Work experience programs in American high schools. *Annals of the American Academy of Political and Social Science, 236,* 110–116.
Joyner, J. Y. (1916). Preparation through education for a democracy. *Journal of the National Education Association, 1,* 78–81.
Judd, C. H. (1919). A national educational system. *Yale Review, 8,* 551–563.
Judd, C. H. (1942). How can young people help? In *America Organizes to Win the War: A Handbook on the American War Effort* (pp. 303–318). New York: Harcourt, Brace.
Juvenile delinquency survey. (1944). *School Executive, 63* (6), 33.
Kagan, N. (1974). *The war film: A pyramid illustrated history of the movies.* New York: Pyramid.
Kahn, O. H. (1918). The poison growth of Prussianism. *Educational Foundations, 29,* 579–585.
Kallen, H. M. (1942a). National solidarity and the Jewish minority. *Annals of the American Academy of Political and Social Sciences, 223,* 17–28.
Kallen, H. M. (1942b). The war and education in the United States. *American Journal of Sociology, 48,* 331–342.
Kandel, I. L. (1941). Subversive or ridiculous? *School and Society, 53,* 82–83.
Kandel, I. L. (1948). *The impact of the war upon American education.* Chapel Hill: University of North Carolina Press.
Kane, K. (1982). *Visions of war: Hollywood combat films of World War II.* Ann Arbor: UMI Research.
Karelsen, F. E. (1942). Do we want military training in the high schools? *Frontiers of Democracy, 8,* 200–202.

Karsch, R. F. (1951). The teaching of American government. *Social Education, 15* (1), 16–20.

Katz, M. B. (1966). American history textbooks and social reform in the 1930's. *Paedagogica Historica, 6,* 143–160.

Kaub, V. P. (1953). *Communist-socialist propaganda in American schools.* Boston: Meador.

Kearney, N. C. (1940). Tomorrow's house in order. *American School Board Journal, 101* (2), 16.

Kefauver, G. N. (1942). Education in a democracy at war. *Frontiers of Democracy, 8,* 115–117.

Keliher, A. V. (1942). Postwar child care and education. *Journal of Educational Sociology, 16,* 28–42.

Keliher, A. V. (1943). Expect this from children . . . when mothers work. *Progressive Education, 20,* 335–337.

Keller, J. O., & Pyle, H. G. (1942). Editorial. *Journal of Educational Sociology, 15,* 352–368.

Keller, K. D. (1915). An American school army. *Harper's Weekly, 61,* 484–486.

Kendall, C. N. (1918). War school message. *Journal of Education, 88,* 368.

Kendall, F. C. (1943, June). Advertising on the home front. *Advertising & Selling,* 62–63.

Kennedy, K. (1999). *Disloyal mothers and scurrilous citizens: Women and subversion during World War I.* Bloomington: Indiana University Press.

Kent, H. W. (1943). The needs students must fill for the War Department. *Education, 64,* 79–80.

Keohane, R. E. (1951). Educating for civic leadership. *The Social Studies, 42,* 99–104.

Kersey, V. (1944). Los Angeles schools at war. *Nation's Schools, 33* (2), 44.

Killian, F. W. (1943). Juvenile delinquency: Wartime trends 1943. *Probation 22,* 138–142.

Kilpatrick, W. H. (1932). *Education and the social crisis: A proposed program.* New York: Liveright.

Kilpatrick, W. H. (1936). The social situation and the curriculum. *Journal of the National Education Association, 25,* 1–2.

Kilpatrick, W. H. (1940). *Group education for a democracy.* New York: Association Press.

Kilpatrick, W. H. (1941a). Teaching democracy in the present crisis. *Frontiers of Democracy, 7,* 134–135.

Kilpatrick, W. H. (1941b). The world today: A positive program for education. *Frontiers of Democracy, 7,* 229–230.

Kilpatrick, W. H. (1942a). Education in wartime: An editorial. *Frontiers of Democracy, 8,* 198–199.

Kilpatrick, W. H. (1942b). Our schools and the war. *Frontiers of Democracy, 8,* 106–107.

Kilpatrick, W. H. (1942c). The war in the Orient and American education. *Frontiers of Democracy, 8,* 103–104.

Kilpatrick, W. H. (1943). The moral obligation of teachers in the war–peace situation. *Journal of the National Education Association, 32,* 127–128.

King, K. (1942). Accelerated clerical typewriting in the war effort. *Journal of Business Education, 18* (3), 15–16.

Kingsley, J. D., & Petegorsky, D. W. (1942). *Strategy for democracy*. New York: Longman, Green.
Kirby, C. V. (1942). Art education to meet present and future needs. *Education, 63*, 229-231.
Kirk, G. (1942). The Filipinos. *Annals of the American Academy of Political and Social Sciences, 223*, 45-48.
Kirk, J. R. (1916). The place of the normal school in a democracy. *Journal of the National Education Association, 1*, 72-76.
Kirk, R. (1954). *A program for conservatives*. Chicago: Regnery.
Kirk, S. A. (1948). Education as national defense. *Progressive Education, 25* (7), 119-120, 144.
Klain, Z. (1942). Education for war and victory. *School and Society, 55*, 532-533.
Klapper, P. (1940). The role of the educator in the present war crisis. *School and Society, 52*, 641-645.
Kliebard, H. M. (1986). *The struggle for the American curriculum 1893-1958*. Boston: Routledge & Kegan Paul.
Kluchesky, J. (1945). Juvenile delinquency. *Police Journal 30* (5), 3-6.
Koerner, J. D. (1959). *The case for basic education: A program of aims for public schools*. Boston: Little, Brown.
Kolbe, P. R. (1918). War work of the United States Bureau of Education. *School and Society, 7*, 606-609.
Koop, T. F. (1946). *Weapon of silence*. Chicago: University of Chicago Press.
Koppes, C. R., & Black, G. D. (1987). *Hollywood goes to war: How politics, profits, and propaganda shaped World War II movies*. New York: Free Press.
Kotschnig, W. M. (1943). *Slaves need no leaders*. New York: Oxford University Press.
Kris, E., & Speier, H. (1944). *German radio propaganda: Report on home broadcasts during the war*. London: Oxford University Press.
Krug, E., & Anderson, G. L. (Eds.). (1944). *Adapting instruction in the social studies to individual differences. 15th Yearbook of the National Council for the Social Studies*. Washington, DC: National Council for the Social Studies.
Krugler, D. F. (2000). *The voice of America and the domestic propaganda battles, 1945-1953*. Columbia: University of Missouri Press.
Kuhn, I. C. (1952, April). Your child is their target. *American Legion Magazine, 44*, 18-19, 54-60.
Kyker, B. F. (1941). Business education and national defense. *National Business Education Quarterly, 10* (1), 21-24, 53.
La Salle, D., & Larrick, N. (1942). Physical fitness and the "Schools at War" program. *Journal of Health and Physical Education, 13*, 475, 459-496.
Lambert, S. C. (1918). War is taking edge off of price as a competitive weapon. *Printer's Ink, 102* (4), 10, 12.
Lamm, L. (1943). Mobilizing a school for war. *Journal of Educational Sociology, 16*, 451-452.
Lammel, R. (1943). Building for new understandings of healthful living in a democracy. *Educational Method, 22*, 210-215.

Lamson, E. E. (1940). Do children who participate in a rich vital school curriculum achieve greater control over school subjects than do children who pursue a formal curriculum? *Journal of Educational Research, 34*, 173-181.

Lane, F. K. (1918a). Address. *School Life, 1* (1), 14-16.

Lane, F. K. (1918b). Demobilization—Industrial and military. *Printer's Ink, 105* (5), 3-4, 6, 104, 107-108, 111, 112.

Lane, F. K. (1918c). The United States volunteer war-garden army. *School and Society, 7*, 350-351.

Lange, A. F. (1917). Our preparedness program. *School and Society, 6*, 361-366.

Langford, H. D. (1936). *Education and the social conflict*. New York: Macmillan.

Langsdorf, W. B. (1943). Teaching issues and the aims of war. *Progressive Education, 20*, 85-87.

Lanigan, J. S. (1940). Education in the CCC: Weapon or feint. *Education, 61*, 91-95.

Lansner, K. (1958). *Second-rate brains*. New York: Doubleday.

LaRocca, J. (1942). Providing community facilities in defense areas. *Journal of Educational Sociology, 15*, 498-503.

Lasswell, H. D. (1951). Political and psychological warfare. In D. Lerner. (Ed.), *Propaganda in war and crisis: Materials for American policy* (pp. 261-266). New York: Stewart.

Lasswell, H. D. (1972). *Propaganda technique in the World War*. New York: Garland.

Latimer, J. F. (1958). *What's happened to our high schools?* Washington DC: Public Affairs Press.

Lavine, H., & Wechsler, J. (1972). *War propaganda and the United States*. New York: Garland. (Original work published in 1940.)

League to enforce peace: The warrant from history. (1917). War and peace in the light of history. *History Teacher's Magazine, 8*, 150-158.

Leake, A. H. (1918). *The vocational education of girls and women*. New York: Macmillan.

Lear, B. (1945). Schools and the army. *Journal of the National Education Association, 34*, 39.

Ledbetter, J. (1943). What is a "V" home? *Instructor, 52* (6), 27.

Leighton, E. V. (1917). Wake up, teachers of America! *Normal Instructor and Primary Plans, 27* (1), 15-16, 74.

Leighton, E. V. (1918a). Our little citizens III. *Primary Education, 26*, 554-555, 606.

Leighton, E. V. (1918b). Teaching civics and making citizens in grades I-IV. *Primary Education, 26*, 88-89.

Lenroot, K. F. (1942). Invaders of the children's world. In F. C. Bingham (Ed.), *Community life in a democracy* (pp. 137-154). Chicago: National Congress of Parents and Teachers.

Lerner, D. (Ed.). (1951). *Propaganda in war and crisis: Materials for American policy*. New York: Stewart.

Lessner, M. (1944). Controlling war-time juvenile delinquency. *Journal of Criminal Law & Criminology, 35*, 242-248.

Lewis, S. (1918). Training women to take men's positions. *Printer's Ink, 104* (1), 3-4, 6, 96, 98-99.

Lindeman, E. C. (1939). The goal of American education. *Survey Graphic, 28*, 570-576.

Lindeman, E. C. (1943). Education in a total war. *Progressive Education, 20*, 4-6.

Lindeman, E. C., & Miller, C. R. (1972). Introduction. In H. Lavine & J. Wechsler. *War propaganda and the United States* (pp. vii–x). New York: Garland. (Original work published in 1940.)

Lindley, M. (1917). War interests at different ages. *Journal of Education, 85*, 175–176.

Linebarger, P. M. (1972). *Psychological warfare*. New York: Arno Press. (Original work published in 1948)

Linglebach, W. E. (1918). European geography and the war. *History Teacher's Magazine, 9*, 218–231.

Literature as a resource in pre-induction training. (1943, December 1). *Education for Victory, 2* (11), 22–24.

Livingston, A. (1939). Introduction. In G. Mosca, *The ruling class* (H. D. Kahn, Trans.) (pp. ix–xii). New York: McGraw-Hill.

Lochner, L. P. (1915). Should there be military training in public schools? *Journal of Proceeding and Addresses of the National Education Association*, 217–222.

Locke, A. (1942). The unfinished business of democracy. *Survey Graphic, 31*, 455–461.

Logan, R. W. (Ed.). (1944). *What the Negro wants*. Chapel Hill: University of North Carolina Press.

Looking for Red tinge in textbooks. (1940, December 25). *Christian Century*, 1604.

Loomis, W. P. (1943). The needs students must fill for industry. *Education, 64*, 82–83.

Lorwin, L. L. (1941). *Economic consequences of the Second World War*. New York: Random House.

Lynd, A. (1950). *Quackery in the public schools*. Boston: Little, Brown.

Lynd, A. (1953, April). Who wants progressive education? *Atlantic Monthly, 191* (4), 29–34.

Lyon, L. S. (1918). The commercial curriculum in secondary schools. *School Review, 26*, 401–415.

MacCracken. H. N. (1918). Foreword. In H. Fraser, *Women and war work* (pp. i–iii). New York: Shaw.

Mackintosh, H. K. (1940). *Elementary education—What is it?* (Bulletin No. 4, Part I). Washington, DC: United States Office of Education.

MacNeil, N. (1944). *An American peace*. New York: Scribner's Sons.

MacVane, J. (1979). *On the air in World War II*. New York: William Morrow & Co.

Magee, E. S. (1944). Impact of the war on child labor. *Annals of the American Academy of Political and Social Science, 236*, 101–109.

Mann, C. (1944). *Lightning in the sky: The story of Jimmy Doolittle* (2nd ed.). New York: McBride.

Mann, E. (1938). *School for barbarians: Education under the Nazis*. New York: Modern Age.

Manufacturers' association abstracts textbooks: Dr. Robey versus the N.A.M.? (1941). *Social Education, 5*, 134–140.

Margolin, L. J. (1946). *Paper bullets: A brief story of psychological warfare in World War II*. New York: Froben.

Marsh, C. S. (1942). *The rural child in the war emergency*. Chicago: Committee on Rural Education.

Marshall, E. E. (1941). Art contributes to national defense. *Educational Method*, 21, 66–70.
Marshall, J. (1938). Education as an instrument of sovereignty. *Social Frontier*, 4, 322–324.
Maskel, A. R. (1943). Democracy in the classroom. *Progressive Education*, 20, 285–287.
Mason, J. F. (1940). Paterson trains for national defense. *American School Board Journal*, 101 (3), 49.
Maxwell, G. L. (1944). Needs which the secondary-school program of tomorrow must satisfy. *School Executive*, 63 (11), 36–37.
Mayer, J. (1943). Your child in war-time. *Educational Method*, 22, 224–229.
McCabe, M. R. (1943). Bibliography on 'war and education.' *Journal of Educational Sociology*, 16, 460–464.
McCarthy, J. (1952). *McCarthyism: The fight for America*. New York: Devin–Adair.
McCartney, L. (1918). School and the war—Protests. *Journal of Education*, 88, 524–525.
McGilvey, L. (1942). To what extent should physical education in the public schools and colleges serve immediate national purposes? *Education*, 63, 145–147.
McGovern, W. M. (1952). In J. McCarthy, *McCarthyism: The fight for America* (pp. vii–viii). New York: Devin–Adair.
McGrath, E. J. (1958). Sputnik and American education. *Teachers College Record*, 59, 379–395.
McLaren, B. (1918). *Women of the war*. New York: Doran.
McLaughlin, A. C. (1917). The Great War: From spectator to participant. *History Teacher's Magazine*, 8, 183–187.
McLaughlin, S. J. (1944). What shall we salvage? *Educational Leadership*, 1, 267–273.
McNaught, M. S. (1917). The elementary school during the war. *Journal of the National Education Association*, 2, 163–166.
McNaught, M. S. (1918). Opportunities of the war. *Journal of the National Education Association*, 2, 635–636.
McNutt, P. V. (1942). School in wartime. *Bulletin of the National Association of Secondary-School Principals*, 26 (108), 7–9.
McSwain, E. T. (1943a). Need supervision be a war casualty? *Education*, 63, 333–339.
McSwain, E. T. (1943b). Our job. *Educational Leadership*, 1, 4–5.
McWilliams, C. (1942). Moving the west-coast Japanese. *Harper's Magazine*, 185, 359–369.
Mead, A. R. (1939). War speaks out. *Frontiers of Democracy*, 6, 6.
Means, J. C. (1943). Wartime education in a small rural high school. *Teachers College Record*, 45, 190–193.
Melby, E. O. (1943). The responsibility of educational leadership in these times. *Education*, 63, 330–332.
Melby, E. O. (1953). Introduction. In E. O. Melby & M. Puner (Eds.), *Freedom and public education* (pp. 1–16). New York: Praeger.
Melby, E. O. (Ed.). (1942). *Mobilizing educational resources for winning the war and the peace*. New York: Harper & Brothers.
Melby, E. O., & Benne, K. (1943). The needed new conception of education control. In E. O. Melby (Ed.), *Mobilizing Educational Resources for Winning the War and the Peace* (pp. 16–35). New York: Harper.

Melchior, W. T. (1942). Schools and the War. *Educational Method, 22,* 102-106.
Melchior, W. T. (1943a). Schools and the War. *Educational Method, 22,* 182-183.
Melchior, W. T. (1943b). Schools and the War. *Educational Method, 22,* 230-233.
Melchior, W. T. (1943c). Schools and the War. *Educational Method, 22,* 284-287.
Melchior, W. T. (1943d). Schools and the War. *Educational Method, 22,* 328-335.
Melchior, W. T. (1943e). Schools and the War. *Educational Method, 22,* 374-379.
Merrill, F. E. (1948). *Social Problems on the home front: A study of war-time influences.* New York: Harper.
Metz, J. J. (1942). Our women mechanics. *Industrial Arts and Vocational Education, 31,* 421.
Meyer, A. E. (1949, February). Are our public schools doing their job? *Atlantic Monthly, 183* (2), 32-36.
Michener, J. A. (1941). What are we fighting for? *Progressive Education, 18,* 342-348.
Michigan Education Association. (1944). *Child growth in an era of conflict.* Lansing, MI: Author.
Miles, F. (1936). The American Legion and the schools. *Journal of the National Education Association, 25,* 177-178.
Militant pacifism. (1915). *Delineator, 86* (2), 1.
Military drill should not take the place of physical education. (1943). *Athletic Journal, 24* (1), 7.
Military training for school boys—(I). (1917a). *Journal of Education, 85,* 147-151, 158-160.
Military training for school boys—(II). (1917b). *Journal of Education, 85,* 185-186.
Military training in public schools. (1917). *Mind and Body, 24,* 470-471.
Military training in the schools. (1915). *School, 27,* 184.
Military training. (1918). *School Review, 26,* 366-367.
Miller, C. G. (1940). Education to save democracy. *Education, 61,* 58-59.
Miller, C. G. (1941). The social science textbook investigation. *Education, 61,* 507-508.
Miller, C. G. (1942). War's corrective influence. *Education, 63,* 189-190.
Miller, D. (1941). *You can't do business with Hitler.* Boston: Little, Brown.
Miller, H. R. (1942). Active reading in wartime. *English Journal, 31,* 486-489.
Miller, J., & Miller, M. (1942). *Parenthood in a World at War.* Harrisburg, PA: Congress of Parents and Teachers.
Millis, W. (1940). *Why Europe fights.* New York: Morrow.
Mills, H. H. (1943). Administering those war activities. *Nation's Schools, 31* (1), 42.
Mitchell, B. (1944). Foreword. In N. Thomas, *Conscription: The test of the peace* (pp. 3-4). New York: Post War World Council.
Mitchell, M. R. (1942). Youth has a part to play. *Progressive Education, 19,* 88-109.
Mitchell, M. R. (1944). Incentives for transition. *Educational Leadership, 1,* 285-287.
Miyamoto, S. F. (1942). Immigrants and citizens of Japanese origin. *Annals of the American Academy of Political and Social Sciences, 223,* 107-113.
Mock, J. R., & Larson, C. (1939). *Worlds that won the war: The story of the Committee on Public Information 1917-1919.* Princeton, NJ: Princeton University Press.
Moen, L. (1941). *Under the iron heel.* New York: Lippincott.

Molinaro, L. A. (1952). A concept of democratic citizenship. *Progressive Education, 29*, 229-232.
Montgomery, L. H. (1932). English teachers, awake. *Education Worker, 2* (3), 3.
Moore, E. C. (1918). Our undertaking and why we undertake it now. *School and Society, 7*, 331-338.
Moore, L., & Zapoleon, M. W. (1943). *Wartime work for girls and women.* (Vocational Division Bulletin No. 227—Occupational Information and Guidance Series No. 11). Washington, DC: U.S. Office of Education.
Morale of high-school youth. (1942). *School Review, 50*, 321-323.
Morden, B. J. (1990). *Army historical series: The Women's Army Corps, 1945-1978.* Washington, DC: Center of Military History United States Army.
Morella, J., Epstein, E. Z., & Griggs, J. (1973). *The films of World War II.* Secaucus, NJ: Citadel.
Morgan, J. E. (1941). The outlook for America. *Journal of the National Education Association, 30*, 65.
Morgan, J. E. (1942a). A war policy for American schools. *Journal of the National Education Association, 31*, 35.
Morgan, J. E. (1942b). The battle for democracy. *Journal of the National Education Association, 31*, 1.
Morgan, J. E. (1943). It is time to act. *Journal of the National Education Association, 32*, 183.
Morgan, J. E. (1946a). Next steps in the victory program. *Journal of the National Education Association, 35*, 279.
Morgan, J. E. (1946b). The outlook for America. *Journal of the National Education Association, 35*, 111.
Morgenthau, H., Jr. (1944). To American teachers and school administrators. *Progressive Education, 22* (1), 27.
Morrison, H. C. (1916, January 27). Schools and defense. *Journal of Education*, 93-94.
Morrison, J. C. (1944). State issues in postwar education. *American School Board Journal, 109* (1), 9-12.
Morse, A. D. (1951, September). Who's trying to ruin our schools? *McCall's, 78*, 26-27, 94, 102, 108-109.
Moulton, G. E. (1943). Physical education in the war and in the peace. *Journal of Health and Physical Education, 14*, 74-75, 126.
Moulton, H. G. (1918). Problems in industrial mobilization. *Annals of the American Academy of Political and Social Science, 78*, 96-106.
Mowrer, L. T. (1941). *Arrest and exile: The true story of an American woman in Poland and Siberia 1940-41.* New York: Morrow.
Mulford, H. B. (1942). War and the school board's responsibilities. *American School Board Journal, 104* (3), 25-27.
Mumford, L. (1942). A long-term view of the war. *Progressive Education, 19*, 358-360.
Murdock, F. F. (1917). School and home gardens. *Journal of Education, 85*, 349, 356.
Murra, W. F. (1943). The social studies mobilize for victory. *Educational Method, 22*, 266-267.

Murrow, E. R. (1959). Foreword. In H. G. Rickover, *Education and freedom* (pp. 5-7). New York: Dutton.

Mursell, J. L. (1946). Progressive Education—Is it through? *Progressive Education*, 23, 248-251, 282.

Myer, D. S. (1971). *Uprooted Americans: The Japanese Americans and the War Relocation Authority during World War II*. Tucson: University of Arizona Press.

Myer, W. E. (1942). *Education for Democratic Survival*. Washington, DC: Civic Education Service.

Myers, A. F. (1940). The attacks on the Rugg books. *Frontiers of Democracy*, 7, 17-22.

Myers, A. F. (1942). The democratic ideal of equality of education and equality of opportunity. *Journal of Educational Sociology*, 16, 3-14.

Nailing down a war-made market. (1918). *Printer's Ink*, 102 (9), 114.

NAM textbook survey arouses storm. (1941, March 1). *Publishers Weekly*, 1023-1024.

NAM to judge school textbooks in the social studies. (1940). The American legion and the alleged teaching of communism. *School and Society*, 52, 651.

Nash, P. C. (1940). Education for peace or for war? *School and Society*, 52, 350-356.

National Biscuit finds its big "family" useful in wartime advertising. (1918). *Printer's Ink*, 102 (8), 20, 25-26.

National Commission for the Defense of Democracy thru Education. (1941). 900,000 teachers clear for action. *Journal of the National Education Association*, 30, 247.

National Commission on Cooperative Curriculum Planning. (1941). *The subject fields in general education*. New York: Appleton-Century.

National Council for the Social Studies. (1944). *The social studies look beyond the war*. Washington, DC: Author.

National Council of Chief State School Officers. (1942). A war-time program in mathematics and physics. *Bulletin of the National Association of Secondary-School Principals*, 26 (108), 41-50.

National Education Association. (1918). Thru the schools in war time. *Educational Foundations*, 30, 54-58.

National Education Association. (1942). *Democracy vs. dictatorship: Teaching American youth to analyze and understand their own and the enemy's ways of life* (Problems in American Life, Unit No. 6). Washington, DC: Author.

National Education Association. (1943a). *My part in this war: Helping on the home front*. Washington, DC: Author.

National Education Association. (1943b). *Bibliography on postwar planning*. Washington, DC: Author.

National Education Association. (1943c). *Wartime handbook for education*. Washington, DC: Author.

National Education Association. (1944a). *Education in the Armed Services*. Washington, DC: Author.

National Education Association. (1944b). *Sources of educational films*. Washington, DC: Author.

National Education Association Library Department. (1918). *School and Society*, 8, 478-480.

National emergency in education. (1918). *School and Society, 7,* 351.

National Resources Planning Board. (1943) Blueprint for postwar education. *Nation's Schools, 32* (5), 19.

National School Service. (1918). Why the war should be studied in schools. *Educational Foundations, 30,* 93–95.

NEA fights for you. (1943). *Journal of the National Education Association, 32,* 264.

Nelson, K. L. (1971). *The impact of war on American life: The twentieth-century experience.* New York: Holt, Rinehart, & Winston.

Nelson, M. R. (1986). Some possible effects of World War II on the social studies curriculum. *Theory and Research in Social Education, 14,* 267–275.

Neumeyer, M. H. (1945). Delinquency trends in wartime. *Sociology and Social Research, 29,* 262–275.

Neumeyer, M. H. (1961). *Juvenile delinquency in modern society* (3rd ed.). Princeton, NJ: Van Nostrand.

Nevins, A. (1942). *American in world affairs.* New York: Oxford University Press.

New patriotism in education. (1917). *Journal of Education, 85,* 658.

New plan for teaching patriotism. (1918). What is Americanization? *School Life, 1* (9), 15.

New policy for new times. (1948). *Progressive Education, 25* (4), 40–41, 46, 58.

New York State Board of Social Welfare. (1943). *The effects of the war on children.* Albany, NY: Author.

Newkirk, L. V. (1943). Industrial-arts education in the war effort. *Industrial Arts and Vocational Education, 32,* 89–91.

Newlon, J. H. (1939). *Education for democracy in our time.* New York: McGraw–Hill.

Newlon, J. H. (1941). Democracy or super-patriotism? *Frontiers of Democracy, 7,* 208–211.

Nickell, V. L. (1949). How can we develop an effective program of education for life adjustment? *National Association of Secondary School Principals, 33,* 153–156.

Nine teachers say "yes": "Progressive Education" interviews teachers about war and education. (1940). *Progressive Education, 17,* 384–386.

Noel, M. (1943). Getting in the scrap. *Instructor, 53* (3), 33, 61.

Noncurriculum war tasks for member of school staffs. (1942, April 15). *Education for Victory, 1* (4), 10.

Norris, G. W. (1943). *Peace without hate: A lecture delivered at the University of Nebraska.* Lincoln: University of Nebraska Press.

Norton, C. (1942a, November 20). Exhibit of wartime advertising. *Printer's Ink,* 18–22.

Norton, C. (1942b, November 27). Exhibit of wartime advertising: Part II. *Printer's Ink,* 17–20, 50.

Norton, C. (1942c, December 4). Exhibit of wartime advertising: Part III. *Printer's Ink,* 21–24.

Norton, J. K. (1941). The Civilian Conservation Corps, the National Youth Administration, and the public schools. *Teachers College Record, 43,* 1–23.

Norton, J. K. (1950). The role of education in a period of mobilization. *Teachers College Record, 52,* 137–144.

Norton, W. H. (1919). A factor in preparedness. *Education, 39,* 299–304.

Noyes, R. M. (1946). The teacher and the atomic bomb. *Journal of the National Education Association, 35*, 296–297.

Nutt, A. S. (1942). Wartime influences on juvenile delinquency. *Child Welfare League of America Bulletin, 21* (9), 1–4, 11–12.

Nutting, H. C. (1918). Democratizing education. *School and Society, 8*, 82–84.

O'Brien, G. E. (1943). What the War has taught me about education. *Educational Method, 22*, 250–253.

Office of Education services to Negroes: Efforts and projects related to the War. (1945, February 20). *Education for Victory, 16* (3), 19–24.

Ogburn, W. F. (1943a). *War, babies, and the future* (Public Affairs Pamphlets, No. 83). New York: Public Affairs Committee.

Ogburn, W. F. (Ed.). (1943b). *American society in wartime*. Chicago: University of Chicago Press.

Ogden, R. M. (1918a). Prospective changes in education standards and ideals. *School and Society, 8*, 661–666.

Ogden, R. M. (1918b). The obligation of intelligence in the present crisis. *School and Society, 8*, 211–215.

Olson, V. H. (1942a). Industrial training in the present emergency. *Industrial Arts and Vocational Education, 31*, 431.

Olson, V. H. (1942b). Wartime industry looks to the schools. *School Shop, 1* (9), 8, 10.

Orton, W. A. (1945). *The liberal tradition: A study of the social and spiritual conditions of freedom*. New Haven, CT: Yale University Press.

Osborne, E. G. (1942). Education's task in a world at war. *Teachers College Record, 43*, 538–547.

Otopalik, H. (1943). What the colleges and high schools can do to help prepare boys for hand-to-hand combat as soldiers. *Athletic Journal, 23* (6), 12–13, 26–27, 35.

Over-the-top war-saving society: Socialized recitation given in Fort Wayne, Indiana. (1918). *Primary Education, 26*, 420–421.

Packets popular on aviation education and post-war planning. (1942, September 1). *Education for Victory, 1* (13), 22.

Parkes, G. H. (1943). A war-training machine shop. *American School Board Journal, 106* (1), 29–30.

Patriotic Service League of Indiana. (1918). *School Review, 26*, 135–136.

Patriotism. (1917). *Journal of Education, 86*, 294.

Pattee, R. (1942). The Puerto Ricans. *Annals of the American Academy of Political and Social Sciences, 223*, 49–54.

Paullin, T. (1943). *Comparative peace plans: Vol. 4.1. World Organization Series*. Philadelphia, PA: Pacifist Research Bureau.

Peace play for playground children. (1915). *Playground, 9*, 17.

Peacetime conscription and national security. (1945). *Journal of the National Education Association, 34*, 87.

Pearse, C. G. (1916). The common school as an instrument of democracy. *Journal of the National Education Association, 1*, 81–85.

Penhale, R. R. (1944). Democracy must be inherent in school organization. *American School Board Journal, 109* (5), 15-16.
Perry, R. B. (1940). *Shall not perish from the earth.* New York: Vanguard Press.
Phillips, J. D. (1918). Teaching patriotism. *Education, 38,* 443-446.
Physical performance levels for high-school girls. (1943, October 15). *Education for Victory, 2* (8), 3-5.
Pitts, L. B. (1943). Creative music and the war. *Music Educators Journal, 29* (3), 7-8.
Planters Peanut Advertisement. (1943, October 21). *Scholastic Coach, 13,* 21.
Pol, H. (1940). *Suicide of a democracy* (H. Norden & R. Norden, Trans.). New York: Reynal & Hitchcock.
Policy on recruitment, training, and employment of women workers: Established by War Manpower Commission. (1943, January 15). *Education for Victory, 1* (22), 15-16.
Porter, H. V. (1943). High school athletics in war time. *Athletic Journal, 23* (10), 13, 34.
Porter, L. (1940). Contemporary political thought and its implications for social studies teachers. *Social Studies, 31,* 154-158.
Postwar planning for young children. (1946). *School Life, 28* (5), 9-12.
Pounds, R. L. (1944). Conflicting theories of secondary education in a time of war. *Bulletin of the National Association of Secondary-School Principals, 28* (120), 55-63.
Powell, L. P., & Powell, G. W. (1918). *The spirit of democracy.* Chicago: Rand McNally.
Preemployment trainees and war production (1943). *Vol. 2. Defense Training Series* (Vocational Division Bulletin No. 224). Washington, DC: U.S. Office of Education.
Preinduction courses in mathematics. (1943, April 1). *Education for Victory, 1* (27), 12-17.
Pre-induction needs in language communication and reading. (1943, December 1). *Education for Victory, 2* (11), 1, 16.
Prescott, D. A. (1942, March). Maintaining the emotional stability of children during wartime. *Handbook of the Elementary Principals Association of California,* 5-16.
Presenting the Cadet Nurse Corps program to high-school girls. (1943, September 1). *Education for Victory, 2* (5), 24-25.
President speaks up for education. (1945). Schools and the army. *Journal of the National Education Association, 34,* 27.
Preston, J. C. (1917). Women and preparedness: Their part in national life, especially in time of war. *Journal of the National Education Association, 2,* 61-65.
Preston, R. C. (1942). Children's reactions to a contemporary war situation. *Teachers College Record, 44,* 57-58.
Price, M. T. (1941). Open letter to NAM regarding their investigation of text-books. *School and Society, 53,* 510.
Problem of the schools. (1918). *School and Society, 8,* 531-533.
Problems of school administrators: In relation to participation of youth in wartime agriculture. (1943, May 1). *Education for Victory, 1* (29), 7-11.
Professors do their bit. (1943, January 1). *Printer's Ink,* 15-16.
Profits of war. (1946). *Progressive Education, 23,* 236.
Program of the NEA for 1943-44. (1943). *Journal of the National Education Association, 32,* 220.

Prosser, C. A. (1939). *Secondary education and life.* Cambridge, MA: Harvard University Press.

Protecting children during war: Plans of all-school emergency committee. (1942, June 1). *Education for Victory, 1* (7), 9.

Protection of children: Evacuation planning consultants appointed. (1942, November 16). *Education for Victory, 1* (18), 3-4.

Protest against war hysteria in high schools. (1943). *School and Society, 57,* 217-219.

Prussianism, democracy, and education. (1917). *Educational Foundations, 29,* 139-140.

Public is not damned. (1939, March). *Fortune,* 83-88, 109-110, 112, 114.

Pulliam, R. (1940). Education, politics, and democracy. *School and Society, 52,* 241-246.

Purcell, H. E. (1918). War-time teaching of Latin American geography. *Journal of Education, 87,* 95-96.

Q & A on wartime training. (1942). *School Shop, 1* (8), 8, 10-12.

Radio and the War. (1942). *Elementary English Review, 19,* 260-261.

Rappleye, C. (1942). Comments on some effects of the war on education. *School and Society, 56,* 538-542.

Ravitch, D. (1985). *The schools we deserve.* New York: Basic.

Ravitch, D. (2000). *Left back: A century of school reforms.* New York: Simon & Schuster.

Rawls, W. H. (1988). *Wake up, America! World War I and the American poster.* New York: Abbeville.

Ray, R. C. (1944). When a school goes to war. *Bulletin of the National Association of Secondary-School Principals, 28* (120), 53-54.

Ream, E. L. (1943). High school bookkeeping and the war effort. *Journal of Business Education, 18* (10), 19-20.

Reckless, W. C. (1942). The impact of the war on crime, delinquency, and prostitution. *American Journal of Sociology, 48,* 378-386.

Reconstruction: Our next job. (1918). *Printer's Ink, 105* (7), 3-4, 6.

Redefer, F. L. (1940). Democratic education. *Progressive Education, 17,* 452-479.

Redefer, F. L. (1942). The school's role in winning the war and peace. *Progressive Education, 19,* 300-318.

Redefer, F. L. (1948). What has happened to progressive education? *School and Society, 67,* 345-349.

Redfield, W. C. (1916). Industrial education. *Journal of the National Education Association, 1,* 119-122.

Reed, C. R. (1943). Our schools and total war. *Journal of Education, 126,* 8-9.

Reeve, W. D. (1943). Essential mathematics for the war effort. *Teachers College Record, 44,* 327-335.

Reichart, R. R. (1942). In the emergency. *English Journal, 31,* 657-660.

Reisner, E. H. (1933). The role of education in a period of mobilization. *Teachers College Record, 35,* 192-201.

Relocating Japanese American students. (1942, September 15). *Education for Victory, 1* (14), 2.

Renov, M. (1988). *Hollywood's wartime woman: Representation and ideology.* Ann Arbor, MI: UMI.

Renzhofer, M. (2002, May 24). The cartoon corps of WWII. *Salt Lake Tribune*, E-1.
Report of the Committee on Military Training in the Public Schools. (1917). *Journal of the National Education Association, 1*, 1006-1018.
Report on the national conference. (1948). *Progressive Education, 25* (3), 9, 29.
Resolutions. (1917). *Journal of Education, 86*, 122.
Responsibilities of vocational education: Cooperation of schools, labor, and employers needed. (1944, February 3). *Education for Victory, 2* (15), 15-17.
Responsibility of education for developing national morale. (1941). *School Review, 49*, 644-645.
Rhodes, A. (1983a). *Propaganda: The art of persuasion: World War II* (Vol. 1). New York: Chelsea House. (Original work published in 1976)
Rhodes, A. (1983b). *Propaganda: The art of persuasion: World War II* (Vol. 2). New York: Chelsea House. (Original work published in 1976)
Rice, E. A. (1918a). The history notebook in the study of war. *History Teacher's Magazine, 9*, 204-205.
Rice, E. A. (1918b). The use of pictures in the study of the war. *History Teacher's Magazine, 9*, 21-22.
Rich, F. M. (1943). Schools geared to war. *Journal of Education, 126*, 39.
Rickover, H. G. (1957a, December 6). A size-up of what's wrong with American schools. *U.S. News and World Report, 43*, 86-91.
Rickover, H. G. (1957b, March 2). Let's stop wasting our greatest resource. *Saturday Evening Post, 229*, 19, 108-109,111.
Rife, M. (1944). What work for children? In *Discipline: An Interpretation* (Bulletin of the Association for Childhood Education) (pp. 30-33). Washington, DC: Association for Childhood Education.
Rippa, S. A. (1958). The textbook controversy and the free enterprise campaign, 1940-1941. *History of Education Journal, 9* (3), 49-58.
Rippa, S. A. (1964). The business community and the public schools on the eve of the great depression. *History of Education Quarterly, 4*, 33-43.
Robinson, D. W. (1943). A war information course. *Social Studies, 34*, 13-14.
Robinson, D. W. (1945). Education for peace. *Social Studies, 36*, 245-248.
Robinson, R. M. (1940). *Toward freedom* (Democracy Readers). New York: Macmillan.
Roeder, G. H. (1993). *The censored war: American visual experience during World War II.* New Haven, CT: Yale University Press.
Rogers, F. R. (1944). The amazing failure of physical education. American *School Board Journal, 109* (6), 17-19.
Rogers, V. M. (1943). Statement by President Rogers. *Frontiers of Democracy, 10* (81), 70.
Rogers, V. M. (1944). Our professional ethics and the war. *Journal of the National Education Association, 33*, 39.
Rogers, V. M., & Tibbetts, V. H. (1943). The directors of the Progressive Education Association vote 12 to 3 to discontinue publication. *Frontiers of Democracy, 10* (81), 70.
Rogerson, S. (1972). *Propaganda in the next war.* New York: Garland. (Original work published in 1938.)

Role of the English teacher in wartime. (1942). *School Review, 50*, 618-619.
Rolo, C. J. (1942). *Radio goes to war: The "Fourth Front."* New York: Putnam's Sons.
Roosevelt, F. D. (1941). Statement by the president of the United States. *Journal of the National Education Association, 30*, 226.
Root, E. M. (1952, December). The propaganda program of our academic hucksters. *American Legion Magazine*, 18-19, 56-58.
Rose is not a rose. (1941). *Frontiers of Democracy, 7* (58), 100.
Rosenberg, A. M. (1942). Women in national defense. *Journal of Educational Sociology, 15*, 287-292.
Rosenstein, D. (1918a). A crucial issue in war-time education—Americanization. *School and Society, 7*, 631-637.
Rosenstein, D. (1918b). Social and educational standards in a democracy at war. *School and Society, 7*, 421-427, 459-465.
Rosenthal, B. (1939). Teaching the recognition of propaganda in the social studies classroom. *Social Studies, 30*, 268-272.
Ross, A. F. (1941). National defense and the schools. *Social Studies, 30*, 243-246.
Ross, S. H. (1996). *Propaganda for war: How the United States was conditioned to fight the Great War of 1914-1918.* Jefferson, NC: McFarland.
Roth, J. J. (Ed.). (1967). *World War I: A turning point in modern history.* New York: Knopf.
Rothenbush, V. F. (1945). Dramatics class: Proving ground for democracy. *Clearing House, 19*, 561-564.
Rowell, E. (1917). The girl problem in the high school. *Journal of the National Education Association, 2*, 254-258.
Roy, V. A. (1942). Preparing the art teacher for wartime service. *Education, 63*, 205-207.
Rudd, A. J. (1942a). Education for a "new social order"—Part One. *National Republic, 30* (1), 5-6, 20, 30.
Rudd, A. J. (1942b). Education for a "new social order"—Part Two. *National Republic, 30* (2), 21-22, 32.
Rudolph, G. A. (1990). *War posters from 1914 through 1918 in the archives of the University of Nebraska-Lincoln.* Lincoln: University of Nebraska.
Rugg, H. (1928). *The child-centered school.* Boston: Ginn.
Rugg, H. (1931). *Culture and education in America.* Boston: Ginn.
Rugg, H. (1933). *The great technology: Social Chaos and the public mind.* Boston: Ginn.
Rugg, H. (1936). *American life and the school curriculum: Next steps towards schools of living.* Boston: Ginn.
Rugg, H. (1941). This has happened before. *Frontiers of Democracy, 7*, 105-108.
Rugg, H. (1943). We accept in principle but reject in practice: Is this leadership? *Frontiers of Democracy, 10* (81), 71-72.
Rugg, H. (1948). Progressive education—Which way? *Progressive Education, 25* (4), 35-37, 45, 52-53.
Rugh, C. E. (1917). Religious education as a means of national preparedness. *Journal of the National Education Association, 2*, 105-109.
Rupp, L. J. (1978). *Mobilizing women for war: German and American propaganda, 1939-1945.* Princeton, NJ: Princeton University Press.

Russell, J. E. (1917). Scouting education. *Teachers College Record, 18*, 1–13.
Russell, J. E. (1918). Education for democracy. *Teachers College Record, 19*, 219–228.
Russell, W. F. (1933). Liberty and learning: A discussion of education and the New Deal. *Teachers College Record, 35*, 89–103.
Russell, W. F. (1942). Post-war education. *Teachers College Record, 43*, 521–531.
Ruutz-Rees, C. (1918). The mobilization of American women. *Yale Review, 7*, 801–818.
Ryan, W. C. (1940). Comments on current happenings of significance for education. *Progressive Education, 17*, 8–11.
Safeguarding war appeals. (1918). *School Review, 26*, 44–45.
Safeguards for wartime recruitment of young workers for wartime agriculture. (1942, March 3). *Education for Victory, 1* (1), 14.
Sanford, C. W., Hand, H. C., & Spalding, W. B. (Eds.). (1951). *Schools and national security*. New York: McGraw-Hill.
Sargent, P. (1942). *Education in wartime*. Boston: Author.
Sargent, P. (1943). *War and education*. Boston: Author.
Sayers, M., & Kahn, A. E. (1942). *Sabotage: The secret war against America*. New York: Harper & Brothers.
Sayers, M., & Kahn, A. E. (1945). *The plot against the peace: A warning to the nation!* New York: Dial.
Schneideman, R. (1945). *Democratic education in practice*. New York: Harper.
Schneider, F. H. (1942). Defense and the woman worker. *Journal of Educational Sociology, 15*, 260–271.
School work improved by working to win the war. (1918). *School Life, 1* (10), 13.
Schools and the defense: Community programs for teachers and other educational specialists. (1941). *Teachers College Record, 43*, 1–23.
Schools and the war. (1917a). *History Teacher's Magazine, 8*, 231–232.
Schools and the war. (1917b). *School Review, 25*, 596–597.
Schools-at-War materials. (1944, September 4). *Education for Victory, 3* (5), 27–28.
Schools called upon to assume larger share in prevention of delinquency: These tragic war casualties can be prevented. (1943, March 15). *Education for Victory, 1* (26), 25–26.
Schools in war: Pupils write about planes, count air mileage, and spell t-o-r-p-e-d-o. (1992). *Ideals, 49* (6), 54–55. (Originally printed in *Newsweek*, September 28, 1942)
Schools in war time. (1918). *Elementary School Journal, 18*, 642–643.
Schottland, C. I. (1942). Working mothers challenge the schools. *Educational Method, 22*, 12–15.
Schuck, F. (1943). The physical education of girls for the war effort. *Journal of Health and Physical Education, 14*, 301, 345.
Scott, C. W., & Hill, C. M. (1954). *Public education under criticism*. New York: Knopf.
Scouting. (1918). *Teachers College Record, 19*, 404–405.
Scrimshaw, S. (1943). Responsibilities of industrial arts in the present crisis. *Industrial Arts and Vocational Education, 32*, 51–52.
Seeley, C. P. (1992). *American women and the U.S. Armed Forces: A guide to the records of military agencies in the National Archives relating to American women*. Washington, DC: National Archives and Records Administration.

Seeley, J. R. (1902). *Introduction to political science: two series of lectures*. New York: Macmillan.

Seerley, H. H. (1917). The obligations and the opportunities of the schools during the war. *Journal of the National Education Association, 2*, 161–163.

Selected war-time bibliography. (1943). *Bulletin of the National Association of Secondary-School Principals, 27* (112), 95–100.

Selections for memorizing. (1943). Wartime commencements. *Journal of the National Education Association, 32*, 143–144.

Selective draft way of compiling a mailing list. (1918). *Printer's Ink, 102* (5), 8.

Shale, R. (1982). *Donald Duck joins up: The Walt Disney Studio during World War II*. Ann Arbor, MI: UMI Research Press.

Shall we have compulsory military training after the war? (1944). *Educational Leadership, 2*, 2–3.

Shallow, J. P, & Young, D. (1942). Foreword. *Annals of the American Academy of Political and Social Sciences, 223*, vii–viii.

Sharpleigh, F. E. (1917). Educational research versus war-time efficiency. *American School Board Journal, 55* (1), 19–20.

Shay, J. F. (1942). Suggestions for defense drawing classes. *Industrial Arts and Vocational Education, 31*, 93–94.

Shea, E. J. (1943). Realistic war training. *Journal of Health and Physical Education, 14*, 200.

Shelburne, J. C., & Groves, K. J. (1965). *Education in the Armed Forces*. New York: Center for Applied Research in Education.

Sheridan, B. M. (1918). *The liberty reader*. Chicago: Sanborn.

Sherrow, V. (1996). *Women and the military: An encyclopedia*. Santa Barbara, CA: ABC-CLIO.

Sheviakov, G. V., & Redl, F. (1956). *Discipline for today's children and youth* (Rev. ed.). Washington, DC: Association for Supervision and Curriculum Development.

Shindler, C. (1979). *Hollywood goes to war: Films and American society 1939–1952*. London: Routledge & Kegan Paul.

Shirer, W. L. (1941). *Berlin diary: The journal of a foreign correspondent 1934–1941*. New York: Knopf.

Shoop, J. D. (1916). Vocational education. *Journal of the National Education Association, 1*, 111–114.

Short, K. R. M. (1983). *Film & radio propaganda in World War II*. Knoxville: University of Tennessee Press.

Should our educational system include activities whose special purpose is preparation for war? (1915). *Journal of Proceedings and Addresses of the National Education Association*, 335–350.

Shuck, L. (1942). World War II and progressive education. *School and Society, 55*, 447–448.

Shulman, H. C. (1990). *The voice of America: Propaganda and democracy 1941–1945*. Madison: University of Wisconsin Press.

Shumaker, R. W. (1941, April). A new order for our schools. *American Legion Magazine, 30*, 5–7, 43–46.

Shumaker, R. W. (1943a, January). Come on, Victory Corps! *American Legion Magazine*, 34, 16-17, 54.
Shumaker, R. W. (1943b, September). Our fighting men are coming back some day—Not to collectivism. *American Legion Magazine*, 35, 22-23, 51.
Shurter, E. D. (Ed.). (1918). *Patriotic selections for reading and speaking*. New York: Lloyd Adams Noble.
Silvia, C. E. (1943). Life-saving in the war-time aquatic program. *Scholastic Coach*, 13 (2), 16, 18, 39.
Silvius, G. H. (1942). Intensive training to provide industrial-arts teachers during the war. *Industrial Arts and Vocational Education*, 31, 321-322.
Simon, C. (1944). Postwar crime problems and their control. *Police Journal*, 30 (2), 7-8, 14.
Simon, J., & Smith, A. E. (1992). *World War II: A selected list of references*. Washington, DC: Library of Congress.
Sinclair, J. A. B. (1918). War is a highly organized science—The soldier and industrial worker both need training in scientific thinking and application. *Journal of the National Education Association*, 2, 540-544.
Sinnott, E. W. (1945). The biological basis of democracy. *Yale Review*, 35, 61-73.
Sisson, E. O. (1917a). Inaugural address of the President of the University of Montana. *School and Society*, 6, 571-576.
Sisson, E. O. (1917b). National education and the world-polity. *Journal of the National Education Association*, 2, 120-126.
60 million circulation for victory: Editorial. (1943, February). *Advertising & Selling*, 122.
Skard, A. G. (1943). Children of conviction. *Educational Leadership*, 1, 106-109.
Slawson, S. J. (1918). Some problems need to be emphasized. *Journal of Education*, 87, 63-64.
Slesinger, Z. (1937). *Education and the Class Struggle: A Critical Examination of the Liberal Educator's Program for Social Reconstruction*. New York: Covici, Friede.
Small, W. S. (1917). Military training in the high school: Why and how? *Journal of the National Education Association*, 1, 566-570.
Smart, T. J. (1918). The policies of state superintendents toward students entering agricultural employment during the war. *School and Society*, 8, 481-487.
Smith, H. J. (1943). Wartime problems in industrial arts. *Education*, 63, 480-485.
Smith, M. (1949). *And madly teach*. Chicago: Regnery.
Smith, M. (1954). *The diminished mind*. Chicago: Regnery.
Smith, M. (1956). *The public schools in crisis: Some critical essays*. Chicago: Regnery.
Smith, P. M. (1945). The prevention of delinquency. *Sociology and Social Research*, 29, 442-448.
Smith, T. C. (1918). The duty of the history teacher in forming public opinion during the war. *History Teacher's Magazine*, 9, 379-380.
Smyth, H. D. (1945). *Atomic energy for military purposes: The official report on the development of the atomic bomb under the auspices of the United States government, 1940-1945*. Princeton, NJ: Princeton University Press.
Snedden, D. (1918a). Liberal education without Latin. *School Review*, 26, 576-599.

Snedden, D. (1918b). The practical arts in general education. *Teachers College Record*, *19*, 15-33.

Snedden, D. (1918c). Vocational education after the war. *School and Society*, *8*, 751-758.

Snowden, P. (1915). Woman and war. *Journal of Proceeding and Addresses of the National Education Association*, 54-56.

Snyder, M. (1917). Dewey's democracy and education. *Educational Foundations*, *28*, 482-483.

Soffner, H. (1943). Hitlerism—A challenge to American education. *Progressive Education*, *20*, 161-165.

Sokolsky, G. E. (1941, March 8). Parents and teachers fight for American schoolbooks. *Liberty*, 39-40.

Soldier opinion on pre-induction training. (1944, March 3). *Education for Victory*, *2* (17), 6-7.

Somervell, B. (1943). Education and the army. *Journal of the National Education Association*, *32*, 185-186.

Sorensen, T. C. (1968). *The word war: The story of American propaganda*. New York: Harper & Row.

Sorenson, R. (1944). Wartime recreation for adolescents. *Annals of the American Academy of Political and Social Science*, *236*, 145-151.

Sorokin, P. A. (1942). *Man and society in calamity*. New York: E. P. Dutton.

Soule, G. (1942, February 2). The lessons of last time. *New Republic*, *106*, 163-184.

Spalding, H. G. (1941). Schools in a world at war. *Social Studies*, *32*, 339-340.

Spalding, W. B. (1951). The responsibilities of the teaching profession for education in world affairs. *Progressive Education*, *29*, 42-50.

Spaulding, F. T. (1943). Education for men and women in military service. *American School Board Journal*, *106* (3), 43-44.

Spears, H. (1943). The curriculum movement helps the high school face total war. *Education*, *63*, 359-376.

Special Committee on Juvenile Delinquency. (1943). *The effects of the war on children*. Albany: New York State Board of Social Welfare.

Special Committee on the Secondary School Curriculum. (1940). *What the high schools ought to teach*. Washington DC: American Council on Education.

Spencer, L. M. (1942). Employment opportunities after the war. *Occupations*, *20*, 572-575.

Sprunk, E. (1943). Primary patriotic seatwork. *Instructor*, *51* (7), 1.

Spykman, N. J. (1942). *America's strategy in world politics: The United States and the balance of power*. New York: Harcourt, Brace.

Staff of Springfield Missouri Public Schools. (1942). Patriotism for our times. *Progressive Education*, *19*, 111-118.

Staley, S. C. (1941). Sports and military preparedness. *Athletic Journal*, *22* (3), 8-9, 57-62.

Stanford University School of Education Faculty. (1943). *Education in wartime and after*. New York: Appleton-Century.

Stanley, G. (1916). America's part in the Great War. *Forum*, *58*, 129-138.

Stanley, W. O. (1948). The sword and the shield. *Progressive Education*, 25 (5), 61-64, 86-87.

Starkey, G. W. (1918). Schools and the war—Protests. *Journal of Education*, 88, 524.

Statement to the U.S. Office of Education Wartime Commission. (1942, September 15). *Education for Victory*, 1 (14), 7-8.

Stead, H. G. (1940). War and the teacher. *Journal of the National Education Association*, 29, 198.

Steele, R. W. (1985). *Propaganda in an open society: The Roosevelt administration and the media, 1933-1941*. Westport, CT: Greenwood Press.

Steele, R. W. (1999). *Free speech in the good war*. London: Macmillan.

Steele, W. S. (1935a). School reds and immorality [Part 1]. *National Republic*, 23 (1), 6-7, 15.

Steele, W. S. (1935b). School reds and immorality [Part 2]. *National Republic*, 23 (2), 14-15.

Steele, W. S. (1935c). School reds and immorality [Part 3]. *National Republic*, 23 (3), 16-17, 24.

Steele, W. S. (1935d). School reds and immorality [Part 4]. *National Republic*, 23 (5), 21-22.

Steele, W. S. (1935e). School reds and immorality [Part 5]. *National Republic*, 23 (6), 21-22, 31.

Steele, W. S. (1936). Education and revolutions. *National Republic*, 23 (12), 15-16, 30-31.

Step toward the new nationalism in education. (1918). *School Review*, 26, 365.

Stephan, A. S., & Wigen, R. A. (1942). Industrial arts and national defense. *School and Society*, 55, 450-452.

Stevens, M. P. (1918). Helps for the arithmetic teacher: War conservation and arithmetic. *Primary Education*, 26, 428-430.

Stever, E. Z. (1917). The Wyoming plan of military training for the schools. *School Review*, 25, 145-150.

Stewart, J. A. (1917). Education's summer work for war. *Journal of Education*, 86, 269.

Stikney, H. O. (1916). Our threatening war problems. *Forum*, 58, 91-102.

Stoddard, A. E. (1942). A program of health and physical education for the larger high schools during our present emergency. *Athletic Journal*, 22 (10), 8, 42.

Stoddard, A. J. (1944). Education and the people's peace. *Journal of the National Education Association*, 33, 135-136.

Stone, G. L. (1917). Geography—A basis for patriotism. *Journal of Education*, 86, 283-285.

Stone, G. L. (1940). Philosophy not enough. *Educational Method*, 19, 292-295.

Stone, H. E. (1918). What is Americanization? *Journal of Education*, 88, 538.

Stowe, L. (1941). *No other road to freedom*. New York: Knopf.

Stowell, E. C. (1915). *The diplomacy of the War of 1914: The beginnings of the War*. New York: Houghton Mifflin.

Stratemeyer, F. B., Forkner, H. L., & McKim, M. G. (1947). *Developing a curriculum for modern living*. New York: Bureau of Publications—Teachers College Columbia University.

Stratemeyer, F. B., McKim, M. G., & Sweet, M. (1952). *Guides to a curriculum for modern living.* New York: Bureau of Publications—Teachers College Columbia University.

Strausz-Hupé, R. (1941). *Axis America: Hitler plans our future.* New York: Putnam's Sons.

Strayer, G. D. (1943). Education in a time of crisis. *Journal of the National Education Association, 32*, 187.

Strickland, V. L. (1918). The war and educational problems. *School and Society, 7*, 394–404.

Stude, O. H. (1943). A value for democracy. *Education, 64*, 55–63.

Studebaker, J. W. (1940). Educating youth to meet national problems. *Journal of the National Education Association, 29*, 173.

Studebaker, J. W. (1941). Our country's training program. *Journal of the National Education Association, 30*, 164.

Studebaker, J. W. (1942a, March 3). Education for victory till victory is won. *Education for Victory, 1* (1), 1.

Studebaker, J. W. (1942b). The United States Office of Education in wartime. *Journal of Educational Sociology, 15*, 320–329.

Students' Army Training Corps. (1918). *Journal of Education, 88*, 261.

Suggestive materials to supplement the girls' programs in physical fitness through physical education. (1944, February 3). *Education for Victory (2)* 15, 7–8.

Survival in combat enhanced by effective pre-induction training. (1943). *Nation's Schools, 32* (1), 26–28.

Susky, J. E. (1959). The logic and weakness of Bestor's position on education. *Journal of Teacher Education, 10*, 173–177.

Sweeney, M. S. (2001). *Secrets of victory: The Office of Censorship and the American Press and radio in World War II.* Chapel Hill: University of North Carolina Press.

Swiggett, G. L. (1918). Why we should study Russian: The nation's need. *School and Society, 7*, 640–644.

Sykes, E. F. (1943). Shall we teach WAR? *Nation's Schools, 32* (2), 29.

Sylvester, C. W. (1942). Training workers for the defense industries. *American School Board Journal, 104* (3), 18–20, 81.

Symposium: Education and citizenship in war time. (1918). *Educational Foundations, 29*, 348–351.

Taft, C. P. (1942a). Editorial. *Journal of Educational Sociology, 15*, 445–446.

Taft, C. P. (1942b). Editorial. *Journal of Educational Sociology, 15*, 460–472.

Taft, C. P. (1943). To attack delinquency: A seven-point program. *Journal of Social Hygiene, 29*, 485–491.

Tappan, P. W. (1949). *Juvenile delinquency.* New York: McGraw-Hill.

Tarbell, R. W. (1942). Civilian defense and the schools. *Industrial Arts and Vocational Education, 31*, 91–93.

Taylor, E. (1940). *The strategy of terror: Europe's inner front.* Boston: Houghton Mifflin.

Taylor, M. F. (1943). Wartime courses of study. *Instructor, 52* (5), 12.

Taylor, P. M. (1983). Propaganda in international politics, 1919–1939. In K. R. M. Short. *Film & radio propaganda in World War II* (pp. 17–47). Knoxville: University of Tennessee Press.

Taylor, R. (1979). *Film propaganda: Soviet Russia and Nazi Germany*. London: Croom Helm.
Teachers as a war necessity. (1918). *Journal of Education*, 88, 322-323.
Teacher-traitors. (1917). *Educational Foundations*, 28, 523.
Teaching arithmetic through defense problems: Can you answer them? (1942, July 15). *Education for Victory*, 1 (10), 6.
Teaching German. (1918). *School Review*, 26, 457-459.
Teaching German in the schools. (1917). *Elementary School Journal*, 18, 92-96.
Teaching war lessons in the schools. (1918). *Journal of Education*, 88, 328
Templeton, P. (1943). Montana Reports. *Progressive Education*, 20, 133-134.
Text of open letter urging limitation of war-time advertising. (1943, January 1). *Printer's Ink*, 16.
Textbook forum. (1917). *Educational Foundations*, 28, 353-355.
Textbook tempest. (1941, February 26). *New York Times*, p. A-20.
Textbooks brought to book. (1941, March 3). *Time*, 39-40.
Thayer, V. T. (1954). *Public education and its critics*. New York: Macmillan.
Thom, D. A. (1944). Sociological changes predisposing toward juvenile delinquency. *American Journal of Psychiatry*, 100, 452-455.
Thomas, M. M. (1987). *Riveting and rationing in Dixie: Alabama women and the Second World War*. Tuscaloosa: University of Alabama Press.
Thomas, N. (1944). *Conscription: The test of the peace*. New York: Post War World Council.
Thompson, A. T. (1917). Preparedness—A veneer or a fundamental—Which will our schools give our children. *Journal of the National Education Association*, 2, 66-71.
Thompson, D. (1953a, February). Do your schools need an SOS? *Ladies' Home Journal*, 11, 14, 86-87.
Thompson, D. (1953b, April). The limits of public-school education. *Ladies' Home Journal*, 11, 14, 124-125.
Thompson, L. A. (1942). Hampton Roads—A boom area. *Journal of Educational Sociology*, 15, 473-485.
Thompson, M. M. (1945). Are young people lazy? *Clearing House*, 19, 467-470.
Threlkeld, C. H. (1943). The war-time program for boys at Columbia High School. *National Association of Secondary-School Principals*, 27 (112), 56-60.
Through the editor's specs. (1941). *Nation's Business*, 29 (7), 7, 12-13.
Thurston, H. W. (1942). *Concerning juvenile delinquency: Progressive changes in our perspectives*. New York: Columbia University Press.
Tibbetts, V. H. (1943). A message from the President of the Progressive Education Association. *Frontiers of Democracy*, 10 (79), 2.
Todd, L.P. (1945). *Wartime relations of the federal government and the public schools 1917-1918*. New York: Columbia University Press.
Todd, T. W. (1918). German in our public schools. *Education*, 38, 531-535.
Tomlinson, H. M. (1940). Propaganda. *Yale Review*, 30, 63-74.
Tope, H. (1943). Harvest for victory. *Instructor*, 52 (9), 8, 43.
Torney, J. A. (1942). Navy pilots must swim. *Journal of Health and Physical Education*, 13, 583, 626-627.

Towle, C. (1943a). Some notes on the war and adolescent delinquency: A case worker's interpretation. *Social Service Review, 17*, 67-73.

Towle, C. (1943b). The effect of the war upon children. *Social Service Review, 17*, 144-158.

Towsend, M. E. (1944). Teaching the war and the peace: Some current resources for teachers. *Teachers College Record, 45*, 519-525.

Training of mechanics for national service. (1918). *School and Society, 7*, 287.

Training schools for juvenile delinquents: Their place and activities in wartime. (1943, September 1). *Education for Victory, 2* (5), 3-4.

Treacherous teaching. (1939, August 15). *Forbes*, 8.

Treadwell, M. E. (1954). *United States Army in World War II: Special studies: The Women's Army Corps*. Washington, DC: Office of the Chief of Military History, Department of the Army.

Trow, C. W. (1918). Women in war times. *Educational Foundations, 29*, 405-409.

Tuell, H. E. (1917). The study of nations—An experiment. *History Teacher's Magazine, 8*, 264-274.

Tuttle, W. M. (1993a). America's home front children in World War II. In G. H. Elder, J. Modell, & R. D. Parke. (Eds.), *Children in time and place: Developmental and historical insights* (pp. 27-46). New York: Cambridge University Press.

Tuttle, W. M. (1993b). *Daddy's gone to war: The Second World War in the lives of America's children*. New York: Oxford University Press.

Tuttle, W. P. (1942, November 13). Total advertising. *Printer's Ink, 15*, 55.

Twentieth Century Fund. (1944). *Postwar planning in the United States: An organization directory*. New York: Author.

Tyler, M. (1939). If America were like Europe. *Journal of the National Education Association, 28*, 269-270.

Tyler, R. W. (1945). Introduction. In N. B. Henry (Ed.), *American education in the postwar period: Part II, structural organization* (44th Yearbook of the National Society for the Study of Education, pp. 1-4). Chicago: University of Chicago Press.

Tyler, R. W. (1949). *Basic principles of curriculum and instruction*. Chicago: University of Chicago Press.

Ugland, R. M. (1979). "Education for Victory": The high school victory cops and curricular adaptation during World War II. *History of Education Quarterly, 19* (4), 435-451.

United States Army Center of Military History. (1993). *The Women's Army Corps: A commemoration of World War II service*. Washington, DC: U.S. Government Printing Office.

United States Bureau of Education. (1917). An educational program for the war. *Educational Foundations, 29*, 36-39.

United States Department of Health, Education, and Welfare. (1956). *Education for national survival: A handbook on civil defense for schools*. Washington, DC: Author.

United States Department of Labor. (1942a). *Children bear the promise of a better world—Are we safeguarding those whose mothers work? Pamphlet No. 2. Defense of Children Series*. Washington, DC: Author.

United States Department of Labor. (1942b). *Children bear the promise of a better world—What are we doing to defend them? Pamphlet No. 1. Defense of Children Series.* Washington, DC: Author.

United States Department of Labor. (1943a). *Controlling juvenile delinquency.* (Publication No. 301). Washington, DC: Author.

United States Department of Labor. (1943b). *Understanding juvenile delinquency.* (Publication No. 300). Washington, DC: Author.

United States Department of the Interior. (1941). *Experiment . . . by schools radio and government.* Washington, DC: Author.

United States Department of the Interior. (1946). *WRA: A story of human conservation.* Washington, DC: Author.

United States Office of Civilian Defense. (1943). *Education in wartime: A manual for education committees of local defense council* (Office of Civilian Defense Publication, No. 3628). Washington, DC: Author.

United States Office of Education. (1938a). *Choosing our way: 15 months of forum demonstrations* (Bulletin Misc. No. 1). Washington, DC: Author.

United States Office of Education. (1938b). *Promote the cause of education: Office of Education* (Bulletin Misc. No. 2). Washington, DC: Author.

United States Office of Education. (1940, September). *March of Education, 21,* 1.

United States Office of Education. (1942a). *Air-conditioning young America.* Washington, DC: Author.

United States Office of Education. (1942b). *Our country's call to service: Pamphlet No. 1. Education and Defense Series.* Washington, DC: Author.

United States Office of Education. (1942c). *Our schools in the post-war world: What shall we make of them?* (Office of Education Leaflet No. 71). Washington, DC: Author.

United States Office of Education. (1942d). *Planning schools for tomorrow: The issues involved* (Office of Education Leaflet No. 64). Washington, DC: Author.

United States Office of Education. (1942e). *Pre-aviation-cadet training in high schools* (Office of Education Leaflet No. 62). Washington, DC: Author.

United States Office of Education. (1942f). *Pre-flight aeronautics in secondary schools* (Office of Education Leaflet No. 63). Washington, DC: Author.

United States Office of Education. (1942g). *Some source materials from government agencies on wartime consumer education* (Office of Education Leaflet No. 67). Washington, DC: Author.

United States Office of Education. (1942h). *Job training for victory* (4th ed.). Washington, DC: Author.

United States Office of Education. (1942i). *Understanding the other American republics: Pamphlet No. 12. Education and National Defense Series.* Washington, DC: Author.

United States Office of Education. (1943a). *Community war services and the High-School Victory Corps: Pamphlet No. 5. Victory Corps Series.* Washington, DC: Author.

United States Office of Education. (1943b). *Guidance manual for the High-School Victory Corps: Pamphlet No. 4. Victory Corps Series.* Washington, DC: Author.

United States Office of Education. (1943c). *High-school Victory Corps.* Washington, DC: Author.

United States Office of Education. (1943d). *Our armed forces: A source book on the Army and Navy for high school students*. Washington, DC: Author.

United States Office of Education. (1943e). *Physical fitness through physical education for the Victory Corps: Pamphlet No. 2. Victory Corps Series*. Washington, DC: Author.

United States Office of Education. (1943f). *Physical fitness through health education for the Victory Corps: Pamphlet No. 3. Victory Corps Series*. Washington, DC: Author.

United States Office of Education. (1943g). *Services in the armed forces Victory Corps: Pamphlet No. 6. Victory Corps Series*. Washington, DC: Author.

United States Office of Education. (1943h). *The communicative arts and the High-School Victory Corps: Pamphlet No. 1. Victory Corps Series*. Washington, DC: Author.

United States Office of Education. (1945). *Open to children: Extended school service*. Washington, DC: Author.

United States Office of the Interior. (1940a). *Civilian Conservation Corps camp life reader and workbook: No. 1. Language usage series*. Washington, DC: Author.

United States Office of the Interior. (1940b). *Civilian Conservation Corps camp life reader and workbook: No. 2. Language usage series*. Washington, DC: Author.

United States Office of War Information. (1943a). *Does our community need to provide day care for the children of working mothers?* (Discussion Guide No. 3). Washington, DC: Author.

United States Office of War Information. (1943b). *Should we have a compulsory National War Service Act?* (Discussion Guide No. 1). Washington, DC: Author.

United States Office of War Information. (1943c). *What is the peace for which we are fighting?* (Discussion Guide No. 9). Washington, DC: Author.

United States school garden army. (1918). *School Life, 1* (5), 2.

United States Treasury Department. (1943). *A handbook of war savings school assembly programs*. Washington, DC: Author.

United States Treasury Department—War Savings Staff. (1942). *Schools at war: A program for action—Handbook of suggestions*. Washington, DC: Author.

Updegraff, R. R. (1918). "Remind them"—The supreme advertising principle. *Printer's Ink, 102* (3), 3-4, 6, 8, 10.

Use of schools in war time. (1918). *School and Society, 7*, 404-405.

Van Fossen, T. W. (1943). Two soldiers look at education: Some things the War has suggested to me. *Educational Method, 22*, 247-250.

Vanderlip, F. A. (1918). War savings and victory. *Educational Foundations, 30*, 95-97.

Vansant, W. K. (1943). A wartime swimming program for high schools. *Journal of Health and Physical Education, 14*, 521-522, 558-559.

Vasché, J. B. (1945). Wartime improvements in school activities. *Clearing House, 19*, 540-542.

Veenker, G. F. (1943). The role of athletes in our military program. *Journal of Health and Physical Education, 14*, 26-27.

Victory Corps, 1943-1944: A basic yet flexible pattern. (1943, October 1). *Education for Victory, 2* (7), 18-31.

Victory Corps. (1942, November 9). *Life, 53*-54, 56.

Victory gardens and the schools in 1945. (1945, January 20). *Education for Victory, 3* (14), 13.

Victory thru education: American education week, 1943. (1943). *Journal of the National Education Association, 32*, 201-202.

Vocational education in rural areas: How the program may function. (1944, September 4). *Education for Victory (3)* 5, 28.

Vocational schools training many "mechanic learners" for Army. (1942, June 1). *Education for Victory, 1* (7), 29-30.

Vocational war production training: Minimum safety regulations for women workers. (1942, July 15). *Education for Victory, 1* (10), 9.

Wachtel, W. W. (1943, March 12). War effort copy outpulls straight product ads. *Printer's Ink*, pp. 16-17, 75.

Wade, J. E. (1943). The wartime curriculum. *Journal of Educational Sociology, 16*, 403-406.

Wakeham, G. (1942). Will high-school mathematics survive the war? *School and Society, 56*, 554-555.

Waller, J., & Vaughn-Rees, M. (1987). *Women in wartime: The role of women's magazines 1939-1945*. London: Macdonald Optima.

Walmsley, L. (1941). *Fishermen at war*. Garden City, NY: Doubleday, Doran.

Walters, R. (1934). The American Legion and the alleged teaching of communism. *School and Society, 40*, 273-274.

Walters, R. (1942). National institute on education and the war. *School and Society, 56*, 197-200.

Walworth, A. (1938). *School histories at war*. Cambridge, MA: Harvard University Press.

War and health. (1917). *Mind and Body, 24*, 189-190.

War and industrial education. (1942). *School Shop, 1* (4), 2.

War and teaching history. (1917). *Elementary School Journal, 18*, 251-252.

War and the schools. (1917). *Elementary School Journal, 18*, 161-162.

War and the schools. (1918a). *American School Board Journal, 56* (1), 65-66, 69.

War and the schools. (1918b). *American School Board Journal, 56* (15), 62-63.

War cabinet in the school. (1918). *School Life, 1* (10), 14.

War creed: The student's pledge. (1917). *Journal of Education, 86*, 437.

War Department Committee on Education and Special Training. (1918). *School and Society, 7*, 358-359.

War facts schools should know: Some questions and answers. (1943, June 15). *Education for Victory, 1* (32), 28-29.

War films for school use. (1942, September 15). *Education for Victory, 1* (14), 12-13.

War message in every ad: Editorial. (1943, July). *Advertising & Selling*, 26.

War modification of education. (1918). *Journal of Education, 88*, 490.

War posters: American artists go all out for victory in big picture campaign. (1942, December 21). *Life*, 54-57.

War problems—1. (1917). The war and the school. *Journal of Education, 86*, 581

War Production Board. (1943). *Your school can salvage for victory: A handbook of suggestions for superintendents, principals and teachers*. Washington, DC: Author.

War production training: Speeding up war production program. (1942, December 15). *Education for Victory, 1* (20), 21-22.
War Relocation Authority. (1942). *Relocation communities for wartime evacuees.* Washington, DC: Author.
War Relocation Authority. (1943a). *Relocation of Japanese-Americans.* Washington, DC: Author.
War Relocation Authority. (1943b). *The relocation program: A guidebook for the residents of relocation centers.* Washington, DC: Author.
War relocation centers: Education program for evacuees of Japanese ancestry. (1942, November 16). *Education for Victory, 1* (18), 7-9.
War relocation centers: Organizing the schools. (1942, December 1). *Education for Victory, 1* (19), 17-18.
War relocation centers: Tule Lake builds for the post-war world. (1943, May 15). *Education for Victory, 1* (30), 25.
War saving stamps. (1918). *Elementary School Journal, 18,* 401-402.
Warburg, J. P. (1941). *Our war and our peace.* New York: Farrar & Rinehart.
Ward, L. W. (1985). *The motion picture goes to war: The U.S. government film effort during World War I.* Ann Arbor: UMI Research.
Ware, C. (1942). *The Consumer Goes to War: A Guide to Victory on the Home Front.* New York: Funk & Wagnalls.
Waring, R. (1943, June). Democracy at war. *American Legion Magazine, 34,* 7.
Warren, G. L. (1942). The refugee and the war. *Annals of the American Academy of Political and Social Sciences, 223,* 92-99.
Wartime acceleration of secondary school pupils. (1942, March 3). *Education for Victory, 1* (1), 6-7.
Wartime adjustments in school attendance and child labor provisions. (1944, February 19). *Education for Victory, 2* (16), 1-4.
Wartime business training programs. (1944, April 20). *Education for Victory, 2* (20), 21.
War-Time Commission. (1942a). Vocational training and the war. *Bulletin of the National Association of Secondary-School Principals, 26* (107), 17.
War-Time Commission. (1942b). War-time acceleration of secondary-school pupils. *Bulletin of the National Association of Secondary-School Principals, 26* (104), 29-32.
Wartime counseling: Some questions and answers. (1943, August 2). *Education for Victory, 2* (3), 20.
War-time graduation program. (1943). *Bulletin of the National Association of Secondary-School Principals, 27* (112), 67-78.
Wartime legislative action relating to the curriculum in public schools. (1944, April 20). *Education for Victory, 2* (20), 5.
Wartime safety education in shops. (1944). *School Shop, 3* (9), 3-5.
Wartime services of the National Education Association: Its departments, committees, and commissions. (1943). *Journal of the National Education Association, 32,* 79.
Wartime teaching aids. (1942). *Journal of the National Education Association, 31,* A-125.
Washburn, P. S. (1986). *A question of sedition: The federal government's investigation of the Black Press during World War II.* New York: Oxford University Press.

Washburne, C. (1942). To all members of the P.E.A. *Progressive Education, 19*, 355.

Watson, G. (1940). What are the effects of a democratic atmosphere on children. *Progressive Education, 17*, 336–342.

Watson, G. (1942). The surprising discovery of morale. *Progressive Education, 19* (3), 33–41.

Weaver, R. C. (1942). Defense industries and the Negro. *Annals of the American Academy of Political and Social Sciences, 223*, 60–66.

Weber, S. E. (1917). The American school in the present war. *Journal of Education, 86*, 429–430.

Wehring, F. W. (1942). Swimming as a factor in winning he war. *Athletic Journal, 22* (9), 44–46.

Weible, W. L. (1943). Fit to fight. *Athletic Journal, 24* (5), 36–37, 39.

Weidman, D. E. (1940). Education to save democracy. *Education, 61*, 95–96.

Wells, G. K. (1943). What shall we teach when the war is over? *Industrial Arts and Vocational Education, 32*, 317–318.

Werner, H. F. (1945). Let's guarantee the children's future. *Clearing House, 19*, 408–410.

West, A. F. (1918). Our educational birthright. *School and Society, 7*, 61–66.

Westerberg, G. G. (1942). Industrial arts in the defense emergency. *Industrial Arts and Vocational Education, 31*, 94.

Wetherill, G. G. (1944). The health of teachers in time of war. *American School Board Journal, 109* (4), 32, 72.

What shall we do about reading today?—A symposium. (1942). *Elementary English Review, 19*, 225–256.

What went wrong with U.S. schools: An interview with Prof. Arthur Bestor, University of Illinois. (1958, January 24). *U.S. News & World Report*, 68–77.

When war shatters market, manufacturer finds new outlet. (1918). *Printer's Ink, 102* (2), 17–20.

White, E. (1918). How are you helping to win the war? *Primary Education, 26*, 422.

White, E. B. (1943). Victory Corps. *Harper's Magazine, 186*, 499–500.

White, W. (1942a). The right to fight for democracy. *Survey Graphic, 31*, 472–474.

White, W. (1942b). What the Negro thinks of the army. *Annals of the American Academy of Political and Social Sciences, 223*, 67–71.

White, W. L. (1940). As I saw it. *Yale Review, 30*, 92–108.

Whitmer, D. P. (1943). Education and post-war planning. *Bulletin of the National Association of Secondary-School Principals, 27* (115), 21–24.

Whitmer, L. (1918). Our flag and their flag. *Primary Education, 26*, 553.

Wiers, P. (1945). Wartime increases in Michigan delinquency. *American Sociological Review, 10*, 515–523.

Wiles, K. (1945). The postwar secondary school: A blueprint for planners. *Clearing House, 19*, 289–292.

Wilkerson, D. A. (1944). Freedom—Through victory in war and peace. In R. W. Logan (Ed.), *What the Negro wants* (pp. 193–216). Chapel Hill: University of North Carolina Press.

Wilkinson, C. S. (1943, March 19). "Help 'em" proves profitable industrial theme. *Printer's Ink*, 17–19.

Williams, C. (1918). Eat honey and help win the war. *Primary Education, 26*, 214.
Williams, C. S. (1941). *Ways of dictatorship*. Evanston, IL: Row, Peterson.
Williams, S. J. (1943). A technique for the war-production training program. *Industrial Arts and Vocational Education, 32*, 111–114.
Williamson, E. M. (1918). War work the schools may do. *Primary Education, 26*, 212–213.
Wilson, C. E. (1941). Total security: A challenge. *Survey Graphic, 30*, 244–246, 263–264.
Wilson, E. (1917). That boy, the problem of the hour, is the hope of the nation. *Journal of Education, 86*, 65–66.
Wilson, J. D. (1942). Winning the war with welders. *School Shop, 1* (9), 3–5.
Wilson, W. (1918). The school's new duties. *Utah Educational Review, 11* (7), 3.
Winkler, A. M. (1978). *The politics of propaganda: The Office of War Information 1942–1945*. New Haven, CT: Yale University Press.
Winkler, A. M. (1986). *Home front USA: America during World War II*. Arlington Heights: Harlan Davidson.
Winning the war in school: The home guards. (1918). *Primary Education, 26*, 283–240.
Winship, A. E. (1917). Patriotic education. *Journal of Education, 86*, 507–508.
Winship, A. E. (1918a). Patriotic instruction. *Journal of Education, 87*, 289–290.
Winship, A. E. (1918b). War modified education in the United States. *Journal of Education, 88*, 649–650.
Winter, C. G. (1939). The teacher and the peace movement. *Social Studies, 30*, 32–33.
Winter, J., & Baggett, B. (1996). *The Great War and the shaping of the 20th century*. New York: Penguin.
Wittke, C. (1942). German immigrants and their children. *Annals of the American Academy of Political and Social Sciences, 223*, 85–91.
Wolf, A. (1942). *Our Children Face War*. Boston: Houghton Mifflin.
Woll, A. L. (1983). *The Hollywood musical goes to war*. Chicago: Nelson-Hall.
Women in Boys School. (1942, April 1). *Education for Victory, 1* (3), 5–6.
Woodring, P. (1953). *Let's talk sense about our schools*. New York: McGraw-Hill.
Woods, E. L. (1942). War and Los Angeles schools. *Educational Method, 22*, 16–21.
Woody. T. (1945). Post-war compulsory military training. *Social Studies, 36*, 191–196.
Woolman, M. S. (1918). Training of girls and women for trade and industry. *Journal of the National Education Association, 2*, 427–429.
Work the schools may do. (1918). *Primary Education, 26*, 16–17.
Worth, C. L. (1943). Scheduling for wartime efficiency. *American School Board Journal, 106* (2), 41, 50.
Year 1943, the schools, and the war. (1943). *American School Board Journal, 106* (1), 15.
Young, A. R. (1943). The arts in wartime. *Teachers College Record, 44*, 583–594.
Young, J. W. (1946, January). What advertising learned from the war. *Advertising & Selling, 34*.

Young, K. (1941). The psychology of war. In J. D. Clarkson, & T. C. Cochran (Eds.), *War as a social institution: The historian's perspective* (pp. 4–20). New York: Columbia University Press.

Zeller, D. (1943). War-time education for girls. *Bulletin of the National Association of Secondary-School Principals*, 27 (114), 57–64.

Zelliott, E. A. (1941). Social business education the post-war period. *National Business Education Quarterly*, 11 (1), 23–26.

Zeman, Z. A. B. (1978). *Selling the war: Art and propaganda in World War II*. London: Orbis.

Ziemer, G. (1941). *Education for death: The making of the Nazi*. London: Oxford University Press.

Zyve, C. T. (1941). Vital school living, the setting for democracy. *Educational Method*, 20, 182–186.

Author Index

Abbot, J. W., 169
Abbott, A., 198
Abbott, J. D., 106, 111
Abbott, W. C., 175, 176
Academic freedom . . . , 205
Academic standards . . . , 182
Acceleration, 142
Ackerman, J. H., 204
Adamic, L., 121
Adams, B., 176
Adams, E. W., 126
Aderhold, O. C., 54
Adler, M. J., 120-121
Advertising as a weapon . . . , 90
Advertising stimulates . . . , 91
Advertising to bridge . . . , 94
Agard, W. R., 138
Agren, R., 147
Ahl, F. N., 213
Ainsworth, D., 157
Air raid protection . . . , 18-19
Air raids and . . . , 14
Alderman, L. R., 175
Aley, R. J., 175, 196, 204
All day school . . . , 60
Allen, M. L., 236
Allen, N. B., 175
Allen, W. H., 196, 198
Alleviation of wartime . . . , 154
Alley, R. J., 173
Allyn and Bacon Publishing Company Advertisement, 222

America and the war, 2
American Association of School Administrators, 231
American Council Institute of Pacific Relations, 35
American Council on Education, 5, 70, 150, 224-225, 229
American education . . . , 131
American notes . . . , 181, 207
American Vocational Association Conference, 148
Americanization, 195
Ames, H. V., 173
Amidon, B., 60, 111
Anderson, G. L., 153, 222
Anderson, H. W., 7
Anderson, K., 60
Anderson, N., 73
Anderson, R. N., 28
Anderson, W. A., 27, 138
Andrews, F. F., 2, 172
Andrews, J. N., 122
Angell, N., 175
Antonacci, R. J., 155
Appeal to the National Society . . . , 175
Appy, N., 26
Arlin, H. W., 148
Armentrout, W. D., 161
Armstrong, O. K., 128, 130
Army experience . . . , 63
Ashby, L. W., 14-16, 34, 69, 70, 74
Asquith, H. H., 188

Associated Business Papers, 96
Athletics: An aid . . . , 154
Austin, A. B., 72
Avisar, I., 87
Axtelle, G. E., 74
Ayling, K., 42
Ayres, L. P., 183
Azan, P., 1-2

Babcock, C. D., 49
Babcock, R., 4, 213
Bachrach, E., 137
Bacon, F. L., 144
Badley, J. H., 30
Baggett, B., 2, 44
Bagley, W. C., 174, 176-177
Bailey, C. S., 191
Bailey, R. E., 147
Bailey, R. H., 8, 13-14, 64, 191
Baldwin, H. W., 31
Baldwin, W. A., 203
Balfour, M., 75
Banay, R. S., 112
Barker, E. V., 131
Barnard, J. L., 182
Barnes, H. E., 136
Barnes, R. P., 186
Barnum, O. S., 174
Bartlett, H., 37
Baruch, D. W., 8-9
Basinger, J., 87
Battle of the books, 128
Bauder, C. F., 147
Beale, H. K., 204
Beck, J. B., 41, 152
Beck, R., 136
Beck, R. H., 224
Becker, C. L., 216
Bedell, E. L., 145-146, 147, 148
Beers, H. A., 91
Belgrano, F. N., 118-119
Bell, B. I., 236
Bell, J. C., 183
Bell, M., 107
Bement, A., 199
Benedict, R., 63
Benne, K., 82, 85
Benne, K. D., 168
Bennett, M. E., 166
Berman, E., 213-214

Bernard, L. L., 77-78
Bernays, E. L., 76
Best kind of high-school . . . , 55
Bestor, A. E., 234
Beveridge, A. J., 173
Bigelow, M. A., 112, 177
Billett, R. O., 137
Black, G. D., 88-89
Blackwell, G. W., 169
Blair, F. G., 181
Blake, K. D., 172
Blegen, T. C., 196
Bliss, D. C., 185, 186
Bliven, B., 91, 93-94
Blum, J. M., 170
Board of Editors, 138
Board of Education of the City of New York, 43
Bobbie and the war . . . , 178
Bobbitt, F., 158-159
Bode, B. H., 161-162
Boeckel, F. B., 227
Bogen, D., 109, 112
Bond, H. M., 61
Bond, J. E., 13
Bonney, M. E., 157
Bonser, F. G., 166
Boodin, J. E., 204
Book burnings, 129
Boord, K. R., 66
Bossing, N. L., 143-144
Boswell, R., 42
Bowen, W. C., 65
Bowers, C. A., 135, 162, 163
Bowman, N. E., 131
Bradford, M. C. C., 179-180
Bradford, M. D., 203
Brameld, T., 135, 237
Brewster, A. G., 199
Briggs, T. H., 134
Bringing the sales end . . . , 91
Bristow, W. H., 141
Britain's war posters, 90
Britt, G., 61
Broadhurst, J., 202
Brodinsky, B. P., 97-98, 145
Broening, A. M., 164
Broome, E. C., 126
Brown, C. H., 36
Brown, F. J., 5
Brown, K. I., 172

Author Index

Brown, W. B., 37
Bruce, W. C., 124
Bruce, W. G., 124
Brueckner, L. J., 153
Bryan, A. H., 150
Burgess, E. W., 113
Burlingham, D. T., 12
Burning of the textbooks, 127
Burrows, A. H., 112
Butler, C. E., 74
Butler, I., 86, 87
Butler, N. N., 208

California Elementary School Principals'
    Association, 121
Caliver, A., 63
Camp, F. S., 208, 209
Campbell, D. A., 59
Campion, H. A., 156
Can you learn . . . , 151
Capps, A. G., 6
Cardall, A. J., 150
Carlson, A. D., 133
Carlson, J. R., 77
Carpenter, W. W., 6
Carr, E. P., 194
Carr, W. G., 67, 121, 134
Carroll, W., 79–81
Case for advertising, 95
Case for distribution, 95
Case, C. B., 198
Caskey, M. M., 125
Cassidy, R., 28
Cast, G. C., 126
Castendyck, E., 109
Caswell, H. L., 138, 169
CCC's contribution . . . , 50
Central Committee on Civilian Defense and
    the Schools, 12
Chadsey, C. E., 205
Chakotin, S., 90
Chalmers, G. K., 27–28
Chamberlain, A. H., 193
Chamberlain, J., 111–112
Chambers, J. W., 88
Chambers, M. M., 151
Chase, L., 47, 138
Children like real jobs, 16, 105
Childs, H. L., 75
Childs, J. F., 42, 213

Childs, J. L., 26, 71–72, 135, 162
Churchill, T. W., 173
Chute, C. L., 106, 109
Clapper, R., 96
Clark, B. H., 204
Clark, W. W., 149
Clayton, F. L., 162
Cleveland, F. A., 175
Clifton, R. S., 144
Cocking, W. D., 124
Cohen, I. D., 199
Cohen, R. N., 37
Cole, C. E., 125
Cole, L., 152
Coleman, G. W., 172
Coleman, N. F., 110, 177
Collier, J., 61
Collier, R., 85–86
Combs, J. E., 89
Combs, S. T., 89
Commager, H. S., 51
Commission for After-War Educational
    Reconstruction, 213
Commission on Children in Wartime, 8
Committee on a Democratic Method of Educa-
    tion, 162
Committee on Certification of Superinten-
    dents of Schools, 164–165
Committee on Educational Reconstruction
    after the War, 212–213
Committee on Military Training Aids and In-
    structional Materials, 43–44
Committee on Public Information, 44, 93, 94
Compton, A. H., 149
Compulsory military service, 186
Conant, J. B., 32
Conklin, E. G., 111
Consultative Committee on Secondary Educa-
    tion, 142
Cook, D., 42–43
Cook, D. E., 45
Cooper, E., 204
Cooper, J. H., 137
Cooperation of the schools . . . , 210
Corey, S. M., 12
Cornebise, A. E., 86
Cornell, F. G., 143
Correspondence study . . . , 54
Corsi, E., 61
Cottrell, D. P., 6, 114, 169

Council of National Defense, 181
Counts, G. S., 73, 131, 133
Cowles, G., 96-97
Cowles, V., 31
Craigo, R. T., 148
Crasford, W. R., 61
Cressy, M. F., 122
Cromwell, J. H. R., 76
Cronbach, L. J., 12
Crowell, B., 4
Crowther, S., 202
Crump, I., 42
Culbert, D., 88
Culbert, D. H., 88
Cunningham, E. C., 234
Curriculum changes . . . , 164
Curry, H. B., 152-153
Cushman, C. L., 34

Daggett, M. P., 188-189
Dally, B. W., 41
Dalrymple, H., 90
Dalton, F. W., 148
Danger: The illogical . . . , 183
Davidson, C., 138
Davidson, P., 79
Day, E. E., 79
De Boer, J. J., 7, 163, 223-224
De Pauw, L. G., 57
Dean, A. D., 2, 3, 203
DeBauche, L. M., 86
Democracy and education . . . , 135
Dennis, L., 135
Devane, W. C., 141
Devoe, A. M., 194
Dewey, J., 161, 186-187, 207
Dick, B. F., 87
Dickie, P. A., 197
Distribution of war films, 44
Dobbs, A. A., 165
Dodd, A. E., 82
Dodds, H. W., 216
Dodson, S. H., 198
Does this smell . . . , 128
Doneson, J. E., 87
Doshay, L. J., 113
Douglas, H. R., 138
Douglass, H. R., 166, 222
Dow, A. W., 177, 206
Draft and the schools, 182

Dryer, S. H., 85
Dunigan, L. M., 182
Dunn, L. F., 113
DuShane, D., 70, 130
Dutcher, G. M., 201
Dyer, E., 123
Dykstra, C. A., 22

Earley, C. A., 61-62
Eastman, M., 172
Eckhardt, C. C., 174
Eckstein, C. G., 9
Edison, C., 122
Edman, I., 134
Education after the war, 174
Education and citizenship . . . , 185
Education and the war, 70-71
Education and total war . . . , 6
Education and war conditions, 209
Education for American citizenship, 222
Education for free men, 22
Education for peace, 186
Education for victory, 74
Educational news . . . , 196
Educational Policies Commission, 7, 14, 22,
   51, 64, 66, 71, 121, 142, 163, 168, 172,
   173, 227, 232
Educational program for . . . , 209
Educational programs in . . . , 213
Education's part . . . , 22-23
Educators look . . . , 228
18-Year-old, 61
Eisenhart, L. P., 149
Elias, H., 213
Elshtain, J. B., 132-133
Elting, M., 43
Emergency in education, 196
Emergency war courses . . . , 177
Engelhardt, N. L., 144
English instruction . . . , 164
Enrollment of women . . . , 28
Epstein, E. Z., 88
Essential mathematics . . . , 154
Essert, P. L., 122
Ettinger, W. L., 209
Eurich, A. C., 169
Evacuation plans, 22
Everal, A. S., 110
Everett, R. H., 109
Evjen, V. H., 106

Author Index 303

Extended school services . . . , 60

Fahey, S. H., 202, 204
Fariello, G., 232
Farley, B., 206
Farmer, P., 163-164
Faulkner, A., 21
Faunce, W. H., 182
Federal Education War Council, 221
Federal Security Agency, 60, 124, 221
Fehr, H. F., 154
Fellowship of Reconciliation, 214
Fenn, I. M., 148
Ferris, F., 147
Field, E., 41-42
Field, J. E., 183
Field, S. L., 168
Finds textbooks . . . , 127
Finegan, T. E., 175
Fisher, M. S., 106, 125, 223
Fitzpatrick, E. A., 28, 29, 65, 140
Fleming, T., 3, 82-83, 88
Flick, O. S., 166
Flint, M., 42
Forbes, A. W., 27, 68
Force, A. L., 202
Forkner, H. L., 167
Foster, W. T., 197
Fowler, B. P., 141
Fowler, H. E., 199
Fowler, J. H., 169
Fowlkes, J. G., 220
Fox, F. W., 83, 104
Foy, P., 7-8
Frank, G., 117-118
Frank, L. K., 137
Frank, R., 110-111, 133
Fraser, H., 92
Fraser, L., 78
Fredericksen, H. A., 59
Freeman, H. A., 214
French, W. M., 211-212
Freud, A., 12
Frey, H., 48
Friedrich, C. J., 145
Frost, N., 140
Function of English . . . , 163

Galloway, G. B., 220
Gambrill, B. L., 166

Gans, R., 26
Gardening a patriotic . . . , 191, 193
Gardner, G. E., 114
Garlock, M. A., 186
Geer, E. W., 134, 137
Geiges, E., 155
Geisinger, J. J., 91, 95
Gellerman, W., 111, 124
Germain, W. M., 110
German in schools, 197
Gibson, H., 2
Gilbert, D. W., 127
Gilliam, P. B., 109, 115
Ginn Publishing . . . , 221
Giordano, G., 126, 130, 135, 141, 161, 205-206
Givens, W. E., 154
Gleason, W. E., 148
Glicksberg, C. I., 14, 169, 225
Glueck, E. T., 108-109
Goebel, J. E., 41
Goggio, E., 195
Goldenweiser, A., 132
Goldman, E. F., 219-220
Goldsmith, B., 48-49
Gollomb, J., 42
Gomery, D. G., 174
Good, H. G., 197
Goodrum, C., 90
Government policies . . . , 208-209
Grace, A. G., 6
Granger, L. B., 61
Great campaign . . . , 181
Green, A. B., 56-57
Green, L. M., 186
Green, R. A., 138
Greenawalt, L., 181
Gregg, R. T., 29
Gregory, C. W., 59
Grey, L., 163
Griffing, J. B., 50
Griffith, J. L., 156-157, 160
Griggs, J., 88
Grigsby, R. I., 53
Grossman, M. P., 174
Groves, E. R., 67
Groves, G. H., 67
Groves, K. J., 230
Groves, L. R., 228
Grubb, M. B., 177
Gruber, C. S., 3

Gulick, L. H., 189
Gwynn, J. M., 66, 225

Hackett, F., 31
Hall, G. S., 173, 186
Halsey, E., 156
Hamilton, W. I., 193
Hamlin, C. H., 86
Hand, C. H., 97, 162
Hand, H. C., 229
Handbook on education . . . , 5, 6, 13, 29, 34, 47, 55, 143, 170
Handschin, C. H., 197
Hanna, P. R., 13, 226
Hanson, E. H., 225
Harding, L. W., 14
Harding, S. B., 199, 201
Harris, F. E., 109
Harris, G. W., 197
Harris, H. M., 197
Hart, A. B., 206
Hart, F. W., 13
Harting, J. W., 190
Hartmann, G., 4-5, 132
Hartmann, S. M., 59
Harvey, M. T., 179-180
Hastie, W. H., 61
Hatfield, W. W., 163
Haughton, W. M., 179-180
Havighurst, R. J., 213
Hawk, H. C., 121
Headlines and clippings . . . , 16
Heaton, K. L., 16
Heimers, L., 35-36
Hendley, C. J., 162
Herring, P., 82
Hewitt, J. E., 155
Hientz, E., 223
High school teachers . . . , 144, 145
High school victory . . . , 155
Higham, A. S., 59
High-school science . . . , 14
High-school students . . . , 61
Higonnet, M. R., 90
Hill, C. M., 236
Hill, F. E., 50
Hill, H. C., 175
Historical light . . . , 203
History Teacher's Magazine, 201
Hitchcock, N. D., 189

Hobby, O. C., 55
Hodson, W., 213
Hoehler, F. K., 113
Hogan, L., 193
Holcombe, A. N., 202
Holland, K., 50
Holmes, H. W., 6, 137
Homan, C. W., 193
Home economics . . . , 208
Hoover, H., 2
Hopkins, L. T., 148-149, 213
Horn, P. W., 173
Hoskins, J. P., 197-198
How can I help . . . , 177
How the 100 best . . . , 95
Howe, F. C., 190
Howe, O. H., 174
Howell, C. E., 111
Hoyer, R. A., 113
Hullfish, H. G., 121
Hulst, C. S., 199
Hungerford, H., 202
Hunt, C. W., 199
Hunt, E. M., 127
Hunt, M. P., 233
Hyams, J., 86-87, 89

Illustrations with war-time . . . , 91
Impact of war on advertising . . . , 97
Impact of war on the schools, 153
Indiana Department of Public Instruction, 54, 68
Information for women . . . , 60
Iroquois Publishing . . . , 221
Is the CCC educational . . . , 50

Jackson, D., 16
Jacobson, P. B., 148
Jay, J., 148
Jeffery, E., 49
Jeffries, J. W., 83
Jenson, J., 90
Jersild, A. T., 8
Jessen, C. A., 53, 67-68, 155
Johnsen, J. E., 130-131, 213, 220
Johnson, C. S., 61
Johnson, E. C., 214-215
Johnson, W. H., 144
Jones, K., 232
Jones, L. B., 91

Jones, M. L., 149
Jones, V., 4
Jordan, D. S., 195
Josephine, S., 41
Joyal, A. E., 26, 51, 67
Joyner, J. Y., 207
Judd, C. H., 50, 207
Juvenile delinquency survey, 107

Kagan, N., 89
Kahn, A. E., 82, 216
Kahn, O. H, 196
Kallen, H. M., 61, 143
Kandel, I. L., 107, 125, 143
Kane, K., 87
Karelsen, F. E., 9, 56
Karsch, R. F., 232-233
Katz, M. B., 126
Kaub, V. P., 232
Kearney, N. C., 166
Kefauver, G. N., 135
Keliher, A. V., 16, 213
Keller, J. O., 27
Keller, K. D., 186
Kendall, C. N., 176
Kendall, F. C., 95
Kennedy, K., 133, 187
Kent, H. W., 45
Keohane, R. E., 233
Kersey, V., 149
Killian, F. W., 109
Kilpatrick, W. H., 12, 73-74, 111, 133, 135, 136-137
King, K., 142
Kingsley, J. D., 5
Kirby, C. V., 170
Kirk, G., 61
Kirk, J. R., 203
Kirk, R., 236-237
Kirk, S. A., 216
Klain, Z., 13
Klapper, P., 123
Kleiser, C., 198
Kliebard, H. M., 141, 167
Kluchesky, J., 114
Koerner, J. D., 237
Kolbe, P. R., 193
Koop, T. F., 86
Koppes, C. R., 88-89
Kotschnig, W. M., 5-6

Kris, E., 77
Krug, E. A., 138
Krugler, D. F., 78
Kuhn, I. C., 232
Kyker, B. F., 29, 144

La Salle, D., 1, 7
Lambert, S. C., 91
Lamm, L., 6-7
Lammel, R., 121
Lamson, E. E., 162
Lane, F. K., 94, 174, 191
Lange, A. F., 203
Langford, H. D., 133
Langsdorf, W. B., 5
Lanigan, J. S., 50
Lansner, K., 234
LaRocca, J., 113
Larrick, N., 1, 7
Larson, C., 78
Lasswell, H. D., 75, 84
Latimer, J. F., 143, 153-154
Lavine, H., 79
Laws, G., 166
League to enforce peace . . . , 202-203
Leake, A. H., 208
Lear, B., 34
Ledbetter, J., 152
Leighton, E. V., 174, 181, 182
Lenroot, K. F., 47, 66
Lerner, D., 75
Lessner, M., 113
Lewis, S., 190-191
Lindeman, E. C., 79, 123, 165
Lindley, M., 182
Linebarger, P. M., 74-75
Linglebach, W. E., 199
Literature as a resource . . . , 164
Livingston, A., 27
Lochner, L. P., 205
Locke, A., 5
Logan, R. W., 62
Looking for Red tinge . . . , 126-127
Loomis, W. P., 53
Lorwin, L. L., 215
Lynd, A., 235
Lyon, L. S., 208

MacCracken, H. N., 187
Mackintosh, H. K., 140

MacNeil, N., 224
MacVane, J., 85
Magee, E. S., 66
Mann, C., 43
Mann, E., 120
Manufacturers' association . . . , 127
Margolin, L. J., 75
Marsh, C. S., 66, 150
Marshall, E. E., 47
Marshall, J., 135
Maskel, A. R., 122
Mason, J. F., 27
Massey, E. L., 147
Mayer, J., 125
McCabe, M. R., 35
McCarthy, J., 232
McCartney, L., 179-180
McGilvey, L., 155
McGovern, W. M., 232
McGrath, E. J., 233
McKim, M. G., 167
McLaren, B., 188
McLaughlin, A. C., 195-196
McLaughlin, S. J., 228
McNaught, M. S., 190, 194
McNutt, P. V., 142
McSwain, E. T., 26-27, 138
McWilliams, C., 21
Mead, A. R., 132
Means, J. C., 148
Melby, E. O., 27, 82, 85, 134-135, 237
Melchior, W. T., 26, 143
Merrill, F. E., 107, 225
Metcalf, L. E., 233
Metz, J. J., 147
Meyer, A. E., 229
Michel, S., 90
Michener, J. A., 121
Michigan Education Association, 111
Miles, F., 119-120
Militant pacifism, 183
Military drill should not . . . , 155, 160
Military training for . . . , 183
Military training in public . . . , 185-186
Military training in the schools, 186
Military training, 183
Miller, C. G., 4, 116, 127
Miller, C. R., 79
Miller, D., 31
Miller, H. R., 164

Miller, J., 113
Miller, M., 113
Millis, W., 31
Mills, H. H., 123
Mitchell, B., 222-223
Mitchell, M. R., 141, 214
Miyamoto, S. F., 61
Mock, J. R., 78
Moen, L., 31
Molinaro, L. A., 237
Montgomery, L. H., 133
Moore, E. C., 177
Moore, L., 58
Morale of high-school youth, 106
Morden, B. J., 56
Morella, J., 88
Morgan, J. E., 69, 71, 73, 74
Morgenthau, H., Jr., 23-24
Morgenstern, S., 48-49
Morrison, H. C., 183
Morrison, J. C., 227
Morse, A. D., 237
Moulton, G. E., 157
Moulton, H. G., 207
Mowrer, L. T., 31
Mulford, H. B., 143
Mumford, L., 139
Murdock, F. F., 193
Murra, W. F., 213
Murrow, E. R., 233
Mursell, J. L., 165-166
Myer, D. S., 19
Myer, W. E., 36, 37
Myers, A. F., 129, 213

Nailing down . . . , 91
NAM *textbook survey* . . . , 127
NAM *to judge* . . . , 126
Nash, P. C., 212
Nathan, R., 97-98, 145
National Biscuit . . . , 91
National Commission for the Defense of Democracy thru Education, 70
National Commission on Cooperative Curriculum Planning, 166-167
National Council for the Social Studies, 43
National Council of Chief State School Officers, 154
National Education Association, 14, 36, 45, 51-52, 57, 59, 60, 64, 65, 68, 72-73, 112,

140, 142, 149–150, 174, 220–221
National Education Association Library Department, 198
National emergency . . . , 207
National Resources Planning Board, 215–216, 222
National School Service, 174
NEA fights for you, 74
Nelson, K. L., 226
Nelson, M. R., 168
Neumeyer, M. H., 109–110
Nevins, A., 3
New patriotism . . . , 203
New plan for teaching . . . , 195
New policy for new times, 224
New York State Board of Social Welfare, 106–107
Newkirk, L. V., 148
Newlon, J. H., 31–32, 134, 136
Nickell, V. L., 167
Nine teachers . . . , 137
Noel, M., 41
Noncurriculum war tasks . . . , 22
Norris, G. W., 214
Norton, C., 97, 99, 100, 102, 104
Norton, J. K., 51, 228–229
Norton, W. H., 172
Nutt, A. S., 113
Nutting, H. C., 208

O'Brien, G. E., 34
Office of Education services . . . , 63
Ogburn, W. F., 6, 56
Ogden, R. M., 204, 208
Olivier, R., 232
Olson, V. H., 147
Orton, W. A., 226
Osborne, E. G., 9–12, 143
Otopalik, H., 155
Over-the-top . . . , 181

Packets popular on . . . , 150–151
Parker, C., 147
Parkes, G. H., 147
Patriotic Service League of Indiana, 198–199, 209
Patriotism, 172
Pattee, R., 61
Paullin, T., 213
Peace play . . . , 202

Peacetime conscription . . . , 214
Pearse, C. G., 203
Penhale, R. R., 122
Perry, R. B., 31
Petegorsky, D. W., 5
Phillips, J. D., 181
Physical performance . . . , 156
Pitts, L. B., 49
Planters Peanut Advertisement, 104
Pol, H., 31
Policy on recruitment . . . , 59
Porter, H. V., 159
Porter, L., 136
Postwar planning . . . , 59
Pounds, R. L., 165, 179
Powell, G. W., 199
Powell, L. P., 199
Preemployment trainees . . . , 148
Preinduction courses . . . , 153, 154
Pre-induction needs . . . , 164
Prescott, D. A., 8
Presenting the Cadet Nurse Corps . . . , 27
President speaks up . . . , 216
Preston, J. C., 189
Preston, R. C., 8
Price, M. T., 127
Problem of the schools, 182
Problems of school . . . , 68
Professors do their bit, 96
Profits of war, 222
Program of the NEA . . . , 107
Protecting children . . . , 13
Protection of children . . . , 21–22
Protest against war hysteria . . . , 12
Prussianism, democracy, and education, 175
Public is not damned, 95
Pulliam, R., 136
Purcell, H. E., 172
Pyle, H. G., 27

Q & A on wartime training, 147

Radio and the War, 85
Rahbek-Smith, E., 45
Rappleye, C., 6, 142
Ravitch, D., 165, 197, 204
Rawls, W. H., 7, 44, 90
Ray, R. C., 144
Ream, E. L., 125
Reckless, W. C., 113

Reconstruction . . . , 94
Redefer, F. L., 6, 134, 227
Redfield, W. C., 207
Redl, F., 211
Reed, C. R., 6
Reeve, W. D., 154
Reichart, R. R., 163
Reisner, E. H., 133
Relocating Japanese American students, 19, 21
Renov, M., 90
Renzhofer, M., 89
Report of the Committee . . . , 185
Report on the national conference, 224
Resolutions, 210
Responsibilities of vocational . . . , 148
Responsibility of education . . . , 123
Rhodes, A., 83–84, 87, 89
Rhodes, C. L., 202
Rice, E. A., 201
Rich, F. M., 123
Rickover, H. G., 233–234
Rife, M., 66
Rippa, S. A., 126, 144
Robinson, D. W., 55, 223
Robinson, R. M., 116
Robison, S., 109
Roeder, G. H., 98
Rogers, F. R., 158
Rogers, V. M., 135–136, 165
Rogerson, S., 82, 84
Rogg, N. H., 73
Role of the English teacher . . . , 32
Rolo, C. J., 85
Roosevelt, F. D., 122–123
Root, E. M., 232
Rose is not . . . , 162–163
Rosenberg, A. M., 59
Rosenstein, D., 194
Rosenthal, B., 136
Ross, A. F., 116, 126
Ross, S. H., 90
Roth, J. J., 3, 172, 224
Rothenbush, V. F., 170
Rowell, E., 190
Roy, V. A., 170
Rudd, A. J., 217–218
Rudolph, G. A., 90
Rugg, H., 127–128, 136, 162, 223, 226
Rugh, C. E., 202

Rupp, L. J., 59
Russell, J. E., 177–178, 204
Russell, W. F., 133, 138
Ruutz-Rees, C., 187
Ryan, W. C., 131–132
Ryerson, S. R., 111

Safeguarding war appeals, 180
Safeguards for wartime . . . , 66–67
Sanford, C. W., 229
Sargent, P., 112, 113
Sayers, M., 82, 216
Schneideman, R., 138
Schneider, F. H., 60
Schneider, R., 134
School work improved . . . , 193
Schools and the defense . . . , 5
Schools and the war, 193, 201
Schools-at-War . . . , 63
Schools called upon . . . , 112, 114–115
Schools in war time, 209
Schools in war . . . , 152
Schottland, C. I., 22
Schuck, F., 156
Scott, C. W., 236
Scouting, 189
Seeley, C. P., 57
Seeley, J. R., xix
Seerley, H. H., 2, 174
Selected war-time . . . , 35
Selections for memorizing, 122
Selective draft way . . . , 91
Shale, R., 89
Shall we have . . . , 227–228
Shallow, J. P., 61
Sharpleigh, F. E., 210
Shay, J. F., 147
Shea, E. J., 155
Shelburne, J. C., 230
Sheridan, B. M., 198
Sherrow, V., 57, 59
Sheviakov, G. V., 211
Shindler, C., 87
Shirer, W. L., 31
Shoop, J. D., 206–207
Short, K. R. M., 78
Should our educational . . . , 183
Shuck, L., 138
Shulman, H. C., 78

Shumaker, R. W., 54–55, 124, 128
Shurter, E. D., 198
Silvia, C. E., 155
Silvius, G. H., 146
Simon, C., 112
Simon, J., 31
Sinclair, J. A. B., 210
Sinnott, E. W., 216
Sisson, E. O., 2, 3, 172
60 million circulation . . . , 97
Skard, A. G., 138
Slawson, S. J., 206
Slesinger, Z., 133
Small, W. S., 49, 183
Smart, T. J., 210
Smith, A. E., 31
Smith, H. J., 144
Smith, M., 235–236
Smith, P. M., 114
Smith, T. C., 177
Smyth, H. D., 228
Snedden, D., 207, 208, 209–210
Snowden, P., 202
Snyder, M., 206
Soffner, H., 139
Sokolsky, G. E., 129
Soldier opinion . . . , 154
Somervell, B., 34
Sorensen, T. C., 78
Sorenson, R., 114
Sorokin, P. A., 226
Soule, G., 2–3
Spalding, H. G., 121
Spalding, W. B., 229
Spaulding, F. T., 34
Spears, H., 168
Special Committee on Juvenile Delinquency, 106
Special Committee on the Secondary School Curriculum, 143
Speier, H., 77
Spencer, L. M., 220
Sprunk, E., 41
Spykman, N. J., 78
Staff of Springfield Missouri Public Schools, 123
Staley, S. C., 155
Stanford University School of Education Faculty, 6, 30, 142–143, 170, 222

Stanley, G., 203
Stanley, W. O., 223
Starkey, G. W., 179–180
Statement to the U.S. Office . . . , 152
Stead, H. G., 162
Steele, R. W., 83, 88
Steele, W. S., 116–117
Step toward . . . , 172
Stephan, A. S., 144
Stevens, M. P., 199
Stever, E. Z., 182–183
Stewart, J. A., 182
Stewart, M. S., 37
Stikney, H. O., 203
Stoddard, A. E., 155
Stoddard, A. J., 221
Stone, G. L., 4, 137, 173
Stone, H. E., 173
Stowe, L., 31
Stowell, E. C., 171–172
Stratemeyer, F. B., 167
Strausz-Hupe, R., 76, 84
Strayer, G. D., 72
Strickland, V. L., 181
Stude, O. H., 122
Studebaker, J. W., 32–33, 35, 57, 141
Students' Army Training Corps, 182
Stullken, E. H., 111
Suggestive materials to . . . , 156
Survival in combat . . . , 28, 29
Susky, J. E., 234
Sweeney, M. S., 85
Sweet, M., 167
Swiggett, G. L., 195
Sykes, E. F., 56
Sylvester, C. W., 27
Symposium: Education and . . . , 196

Taft, C. P., 105, 113
Tappan, P. W., 109
Tarbell, R. W., 147
Taylor, A., 42
Taylor, E., 31
Taylor, M. F., 168
Taylor, P. M., 78, 84
Taylor, R., 88
Teachers as a war . . . , 175
Teacher-traitors, 204
Teaching arithmetic . . . , 153

Teaching German, 196-197
Teaching German in the . . . , 197
Teaching war lessons . . . , 175
Text of open letter . . . , 96
Textbook forum, 197
Textbook tempest, 129-130
Textbooks brought . . . , 126
Thayer, V. T., 231
Thom, D. A., 115
Thomas, M. M., 57-58, 228
Thomas, N., 223
Thompson, A. T., 205
Thompson, D., 236
Thompson, L. A., 113
Thompson, M. M., 144
Threlkeld, C. H., 146-147
Through the editor's specs, 128-129
Thurston, H. W., 112
Tibbetts, V. H., 135-136, 165
Tobias, S., 132-133
Todd, L. P., 214
Todd, T. W., 197
Tomlinson, H. M., 76, 90
Torney, J. A., 155-156
Towle, C., 12, 124-125
Towsend, M. E., 36
Training of mechanics . . . , 207-208
Training schools . . . , 68, 115
Treacherous teaching, 129
Treadwell, M. E., 56
Troelstrup, A. W., 49
Trow, C. W., 189-190, 191
Tuell, H. E., 198, 199, 201
Tuttle, W. M., 12-13, 13-14, 47, 122
Tuttle, W. P., 97
Twentieth Century Fund, 221
Tyler, M., 131
Tyler, R. W., 167, 238

Ugland, R. M., 55
United States Army Center of Military History, 190
United States Bureau of Education, 193, 209
United States Department of Health, Education, and Welfare, 230-231
United States Department of Labor, 33, 107, 110
United States Department of the Interior, 19-20
United States Office of Civilian Defense, 65

United States Office of Education, 28-29, 32, 33, 53, 59-60
United States Office of the Interior, 50
United States Office of War Information, 35
United States school . . . , 191, 192, 193
United States Treasury Department, 33, 35
United State Treasury Department-War Savings Staff, 49
Updegraff, R. R., 91, 94
Use of schools . . . , 181

Van Fossen, T. W., 34
Vanderlip, F. A., 179-180
Vansant, W. K., 155
Vasché, J. B., 144
Vaughn-Rees, M., 95-96
Veenker, G. F., 160
Victory Corps, 1943 . . . , 35
Victory Corps, 52-53
Victory gardens . . . , 191
Victory thru education . . . , 220
Vocational education . . . , 67
Vocational schools training . . . , 145
Vocational war production . . . , 145

Wachtel, W. W., 98
Wade, J. E., 168
Wakeham, G., 138
Waller, J., 95-96
Walmsley, L., 31
Walters, R., 34, 126
Walworth, A., 171, 195
War and health, 177
War and industrial . . . , 148
War and teaching . . . , 195
War and the schools, 177, 194, 208
War cabinet . . . , 177
War creed . . . , 177
War Department Committee on Education and Special Training, 209
War facts schools . . . , 55
War films for . . . , 44-45
War message . . . , 97
War modification . . . , 210
War posters . . . , 9
War problems . . . , 181
War Production Board, 33-34
War production training . . . , 59
War Relocation Authority, 19, 20-21
War relocation centers: Education . . . , 19, 21

War relocation centers: Organizing . . . , 19
War relocation centers; Tule Lake . . . , 19, 21
War saving stamps, 179–180
Warburg, J., 31
Ward, L. W., 202
Ware, C., 36
Waring, R., 124
Warren, G. L., 61
Wartime acceleration . . . , 141–142
Wartime adjustments . . . , 67, 112
Wartime business . . . , 27
War-Time Commission, 13, 141, 142
Wartime counseling . . . , 67
War-time graduation . . . , 16
Wartime legislative . . . , 168
Wartime safety education . . . , 147
Wartime services . . . , 71
Wartime teaching aids, 71
Washburn, P. S., 83
Washburne, C., 71
Watson, G., 137, 138
Weaver, R. C., 61
Weaver, R. T., 43
Weber, S. E., 195
Wechsler, J., 79
Wehring, F. W., 156
Weible, W. L., 155
Weidman, D. E., 50
Weitz, M. C., 90
Wells, G. K., 148
Weltfish, G., 63
Werner, H. F., 109, 115
West, A. F., 175
Westerberg, G. G., 147–148
Wetherill, G. G., 17–18
What shall we do . . . , 164
What went wrong . . . , 234
When war shatters . . . , 91
White, E., 177
White, E. B., 53–54
White, W., 61, 62
White, W. L., 76
Whitmer, D. P., 65

Whitmer, L., 181
Wiers, P., 107
Wigen, R. A., 144
Wiles, K., 169
Wilkerson, D. A., 62–63
Wilkinson, C. S., 98
Williams, C. S., 31, 76–77, 79, 84
Williams, S. J., 147
Williamson, E. M., 178
Wilson, C. E., 124
Wilson, E., 177
Wilson, J. D., 147
Wilson, R. F., 4
Wilson, W., 177
Winkler, A. M., 59, 83
Winning the war . . . , 181
Winship, A. E., 172, 195, 196, 199
Winter, C. G., 132
Winter, J., 2, 44
Wittke, C., 61
Wolf, A., 36
Woll, A. L., 89
Women in Boys School, 28
Woodring, P., 236
Woods, E. L., 152
Woody, T., 214
Woolman, M. S., 190
Work the schools . . . , 177
Worth, C. L., 142

Year 1943 . . . , 213
Young, A. R., 170
Young, D., 61
Young J. W., 95
Young, K., 225–226

Zapoleon, M. W., 58
Zeller, D., 112
Zelliott, E. A., 147
Zeman, Z. A. B., 9, 85, 90
Ziemer, G., 31
Zyve, C. T., 137

Subject Index

Academic freedom, 204–205
Accelerated curriculum (*see* Curriculum)
Advantages of war (*see* Benefits of war)
Advertising, 90–104
African Americans, 61–63
Alarmist warnings
    Educators, 7–18
    Government, 18–22
American Federation of Teachers, 61
Anti-Americanism (*see* Patriotic education)
Anti-German initiatives, 195–198
Anti-German language (*see* Anti-German initiatives)
Arousing support for war, 175–177
Atomic age, 228–231

Benefits of war, 174–175

Careers, 27–29
CCC (*see* Civilian Conservation Corps)
Cinema (*see* Materials, Films)
Civil Air Patrol Cadets, 52
Civilian Conservation Corps, 50–52
Communism, 117, 118, 215–220, 231–234
Communist threats (*see* Communism)
Conservatives, xxi, 116–125, 211–242
Crime (*see* Juvenile delinquency)
Curriculum
    Accelerated, 141–143
    Definition, 140–141
    English, 163–164

Life adjustment, 164–168
Mathematics, 152–154
Models for vocational curricula, 147–148
Physical education, 148–161
Pragmatic, 168–170
Progressive, 161–168
Science, 152–154
Skills-Based, 148–161
Sports, 156–161
Vocational, 143–148, 206–209
Women's, 156
World War I, 205–210

Day care, 59–60
Democratic education, 120–122
Department of Labor, 66–67
Depression, xx

Education for Victory, 156
English curriculum (*see* Curriculum)
Extraordinary responsibilities
    Schools, 22–26
    Source of stress, 26–27

Films (*see* Materials)

Garden army, 191–195
Gardening (*see* Garden army)
German language (*see* Anti-German initiatives)
Great depression (*see* Depression)

High School Victory Corps, 52–55
Hollywood (*see* Film)
Home gardening (*see* Garden Army)

Junior Salvage Army, 51–52
Juvenile delinquency, 105–116

Liberal journals (*see* Social Frontier)
Liberals, xx–xxiii, 130–132, 136–139, 202–205, 211–242
Life adjustment curriculum (*see* Curriculum)

Materials
   Advice from military personnel, 30–34
   Alternative resources, 46–49
   Commercial publishers, 36–43
   Directories, 34–36
   Distinctive resources, 30–34
   Films, 43–45, 46, 86–90
   Post World War II, 220–222
   World War I, 198–202
Mathematics curriculum (*see* Curriculum)

National Education Association, 69–74
Nationalistic education, 123–125
NEA (*see* National Education Association)
National Association for the Advancement of Colored People, 62
National Urban League, 61
National Youth Administration, 51

Pacifists, 130–135
Patriotic education, 116–123
Patriotism (*see* Patriotic education)
Peace movement (*see* Pacifists)
Persons with disabilities, 63–66
Physical education curriculum (*see* Curriculum)
Post–World War II, xxiii–xxiv, 211–237
Pragmatic curriculum (*see* Curriculum)
Pre-induction training, 55–56, 182–187
Professional educational organizations, 69–74
Programs for women (*see* Women's Programs)
Progressive curriculum (*see* Curriculum)
Progressive Education Association, 136–139, 161–170, 211–242
Propaganda, 10, 11, 15, 25, 37, 40, 74–89

Radio, 83–86
Resources (*see* Materials)
Rural youths (*see* Workers, Rural youths)

Scholastic nationalism, 1–18, 173–174, 177–182
School responsibilities (*see* Extraordinary responsibilities)
Science curriculum (*see* Curriculum)
Seditious textbooks, 125–130
Skills-based curriculum (*see* Curriculum)
Social Frontier, 135–136
SPAR, 57
Special wartime programs (*see* Wartime programs)
Success of vocational curricula, 148

Textbooks (*see* Seditious textbooks)
Theories of war and education, 224–228
Total war, 1–7
Truancy (*see* Juvenile delinquency)

Un-Americanism (*see* Patriotic education)
United States Department of Labor (*see* Department of Labor)

Vocational curriculum (*see* Curriculum)

WAC, 56–57, 60
WAFS, 57
Wartime programs, 177–182
WASP, 57
WAVES, 57
Women marines, 57
Women's programs, 187–191
Workers
   Rural youths, 66–67
   Student, 67–68, 209–210
   Women, 56–63
World War I curriculum (*see* Curriculum)
World War I, xix–xx, 90–94, 171–210

THIS SERIES EXPLORES THE HISTORY OF SCHOOLS AND SCHOOLING in the United States and other countries. Books in this series examine the historical development of schools and educational processes, with special emphasis on issues of educational policy, curriculum and pedagogy, as well as issues relating to race, class, gender, and ethnicity. Special emphasis will be placed on the lessons to be learned from the past for contemporary educational reform and policy. Although the series will publish books related to education in the broadest societal and cultural context, it especially seeks books on the history of specific schools and on the lives of educational leaders and school founders.

For additional information about this series or for the submission of manuscripts, please contact the general editors:

>	Alan R. Sadovnik	Susan F. Semel
>	Rutgers University-Newark	The City College of New York, CUNY
>	Education Dept.	138th Street and Convent Avenue
>	155 Conklin Hall	NAC 5/208
>	175 University Avenue	New York, NY 10031
>	Newark, NJ 07102

To order other books in this series, please contact our Customer Service Department:

> 800-770-LANG (within the U.S.)
> 212-647-7706 (outside the U.S.)
> 212-647-7707 FAX

Or browse online by series at:

> www.peterlangusa.com